HTML FOR DUMMIES™

Ed Tittel

and

Steve James

IDG BOOKS

IDG Books Worldwide, Inc.
An International Data Group Company

Foster City, CA • Chicago, IL • Indianapolis, IN • Braintree, MA • Dallas, TX

HTML For Dummies

Published by
IDG Books Worldwide, Inc.
An International Data Group Company
919 East Hillsdale Boulevard, Suite 400
Foster City, CA 94404

Library of Congress Catalog Card No.: 95-79568

ISBN 1-56884-330-5

Printed in the United States of America

10 9 8 7 6 5 4 3 2

Distributed in the United States by IDG Books Worldwide, Inc.

 is a registered trademark of IDG Books Worldwide, Inc.

For More Information...

For general information on IDG Books in the U.S., including information on discounts and premiums, contact IDG Books at 800-434-3422.

For information on where to purchase IDG's books outside the U.S., contact Christina Turner at 415-655-3022.

For information on translations, contact Marc Jeffrey Mikulich, Foreign Rights Manager, at IDG Books Worldwide; fax number: 415-655-3295.

For sales inquiries and special prices for bulk quantities, contact Tony Real at 800-434-3422 or 415-655-3048.

For information on using IDG's books in the classroom and ordering examination copies, contact Jim Kelly at 800-434-2086.

The ...*For Dummies* book series is distributed in Canada by Macmillan of Canada, a Division of Canada Publishing Corporation; by Computer and Technical Books in Miami, Florida, for South America and the Caribbean; by Longman Singapore in Singapore, Malaysia, Thailand, and Korea; by Toppan Co. Ltd. in Japan; by Asia Computerworld in Hong Kong; by Woodslane Pty. Ltd. in Australia and New Zealand; and by Transword Publishers Ltd. in the U.K. and Europe.

Welcome to the world of IDG Books Worldwide.

IDG Books Worldwide, Inc. is a subsidiary of International Data Group, the world's largest publisher of computer-related information and the leading global provider of information services on information technology. IDG was founded more than 25 years ago and now employs more than 7,200 people worldwide. IDG publishes more than 233 computer publications in 65 countries (see listing below). More than fifty million people read one or more IDG publications each month.

Launched in 1990, IDG Books Worldwide is today the #1 publisher of best-selling computer books in the United States. We are proud to have received 3 awards from the Computer Press Association in recognition of editorial excellence, and our best-selling ...*For Dummies*™ series has more than 17 million copies in print with translations in 24 languages. IDG Books, through a recent joint venture with IDG's Hi-Tech Beijing, became the first U.S. publisher to publish a computer book in the People's Republic of China. In record time, IDG Books has become the first choice for millions of readers around the world who want to learn how to better manage their businesses.

Our mission is simple: Every IDG book is designed to bring extra value and skill-building instructions to the reader. Our books are written by experts who understand and care about our readers. The knowledge base of our editorial staff comes from years of experience in publishing, education, and journalism — experience which we use to produce books for the '90s. In short, we care about books, so we attract the best people. We devote special attention to details such as audience, interior design, use of icons, and illustrations. And because we use an efficient process of authoring, editing, and desktop publishing our books electronically, we can spend more time ensuring superior content and spend less time on the technicalities of making books.

You can count on our commitment to deliver high-quality books at competitive prices on topics consumers want to read about. At IDG, we value quality, and we have been delivering quality for more than 25 years. You'll find no better book on a subject than an IDG book.

John J. Kilcullen

John Kilcullen
President and CEO
IDG Books Worldwide, Inc.

About the Authors

Ed Tittel is the author of numerous books about computing and a contributing editor to WindowsUser magazine. He's the co-author (with Bob LeVitus) of three best-selling books: *Stupid DOS Tricks*, *Stupid Windows Tricks*, and *Stupid Beyond Belief DOS Tricks*. He's also a co-author (with Deni Connor and Earl Follis) of the best-selling NetWare for Dummies, now in its second edition. These days, he's turning his focus to Internet-related topics and activities, both as a writer and as a member of the NetWorld + Interop program committee.

Ed's last "real job" was as the director of technical marketing for Novell, Inc. In this position, he tried his best to control technical content for Novell's corporate trade shows, marketing communications, and presentations. He has been a frequent speaker on LAN-related topics at industry events, and was even a course developer for Novell in San Jose, where he designed and maintained several introductory LAN training classes.

Ed has been a regular contributor to the computer trade press since 1987, and he has written more than 100 articles for a variety of publications, with a decided emphasis on networking technology. These publications include Computerworld, InfoWorld, LAN Times, LAN Magazine, BYTE, Macworld, MacUser, NetGuide, and IWAY. He is also a regular columnist and contributing editor for MAXIMIZE! magazine.

You can contact him at:

CompuServe ID: 76376,606/Internet e-mail: etittel@zilker.net

Steve James is a long-time computer-industry writer who's covered the documentation needs of organizations as diverse as the U.S. Army Corps of Engineers and The Psychological Corporation. A former biological researcher, Steve has concentrated his efforts in one computer-related operation or another for the past fifteen years. Along the way, he's fathered more than 50-odd manuals and other lengthy works of technical prose, and has made some excellent friends along the way.

Currently, Steve divides his time between the keyboard, his family, and the great outdoors, where the thrill of competitive bicycling continues to lure him, despite his accelerating decrepitude.

You can reach Steve on the Internet at snjames@wetlands.com

Credits

Vice President and Publisher
Christopher J. Williams

Publishing Director
Amorette Pedersen

Editorial Director
Anne Marie Walker

Technical Reviewer
Mark Gaither

Director of Production
Beth Roberts

Indexer
Liz Cunningham

Composition and Layout
Ronnie Bucci

Proofreader
C^2 Editorial Services

Book Design
University Graphics

Cover Design
Kavish & Kavish

Acknowledgments

We have way too many people to thank for this book to get it all right in a short space, so we would like to start out by thanking everybody who helped us that we don't mention by name. Actually, we couldn't have done it without you, even if we can't recall who you are! Thanks, anyway.

Ed Tittel: I want to share my thanks with a large crowd. First off, there's my family: Suzy, Austin, Chelsea, and Dusty — you were there for me when it counted. Thanks! Second, a talented crew of technical people helped me over a variety of humps, large and small. I would like to specifically mention Mark Gaither, Carl de Cordova, Sebastian Hassinger, and Mike Irwin. You guys are the greatest! Third, there's a whole crowd of other folks whose information has helped me over the years, especially the originators of the Web — most notably, Tim Berners-Lee and the rest of the CERN team. I'd also like to thank the geniuses, sung and unsung, at NCSA, MIT, Netscape Communications, Stanford, HaL, and anyplace else whose Web collections I visited, for helping pull the many strands of this book together. I'd also like to thank Steve James for stepping in at the eleventh hour to help keep me on schedule! Finally, I'd like to thank my lucky stars, for making it possible for me to work at home, and make writing a part of my daily routine.

Steve James: First and foremost I have to thank Ed Tittel for asking me to co-author this book with him. He has been my inspiration and mentor in this, my first venture into the world of book publishing. My eternal gratitude to my understanding family, Trisha, Kelly, Chris, and Randle-Ann (cattus extraordinarius) for putting up with my writer's quirks and schedule, especially during late-night work sessions. My appreciation to Mark Gaither for his excellent technical editing and UNIX HTML tools screen shots, and Jeff Evans for providing Macintosh HTML tools screen shots and advice.

Many thanks to Michael Stewart our WebMeister and research assistant extraordinaire.

And last, but certainly not least, out thanks to all of the HTML tool developers and HTML Web page authors on the Net for selflessly providing fantastic tools, information, and Web pages for the WWW community to enjoy.

Together, we want to thank the editorial staff at IDG books, especially Anne Marie Walker, one of the best project editors we've ever had the chance to work with; Amy Pedersen, the lady who made it all happen; the production folks, including Beth Roberts and Ronnie Bucci, and of course, David Solomon, the man with the golden touch!

Please feel free to contact either of us, care of IDG books, IDG Books Worldwide, 919 East Hillsdale Blvd, Suite 400, Foster City, CA 94404.

The publisher would like to give special thanks to Patrick J. McGovern, without whom this book would not have been possible.

Contents at a Glance

Cartoons at a Glance

by Rich Tennant

page 1

page xxvii

page 45

page 77

page 189

page 257

page 285

page 305

page 397

page 337

Table of Contents

Introduction

*W*elcome to the wild, wacky, and wonderful possibilities inherent in the World Wide Web. In this book, we'll introduce you to the mysteries of the HyperText Markup Language used to build Web pages and initiate you into the select, but growing community of Web authors.

If you've tried to build your own Web pages before, but found it too forbidding, now you can relax. If you can dial a telephone or find your keys in the morning, you too can become an HTML author. (No kidding!)

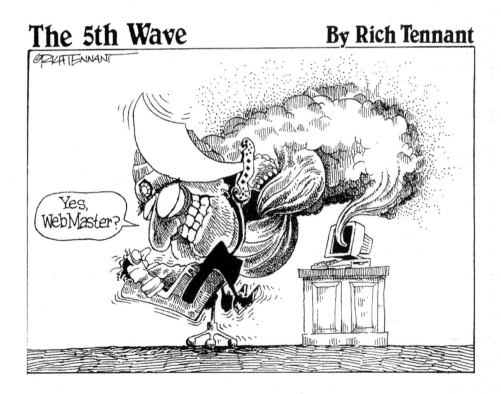

The 5th Wave   By Rich Tennant

Yes, WebMaster?

When we wrote this book, we took a straightforward approach to telling you about authoring documents for the World Wide Web. We've tried to keep the amount of technobabble to a minimum, and stick with plain English as much as possible. Besides plain talk about hypertext, HTML, and the Web, we've included lots of sample programs and tag-by-tag instructions for building your very own Web pages.

We've also included a peachy diskette with this book, that contains each and every HTML example in usable form, and a number of other interesting widgets for your own documents. In addition, this diskette also includes the magnificent and bedazzling source materials for the *HTML For Dummies* Web pages, which you might find to be a source of inspiration and raw material for your own uses!

About This Book

Think of this book as a friendly, approachable guide to HTML, and to building readable, attractive pages for the World Wide Web. Although HTML isn't hard to learn, it can be hard to remember all the details needed to write interesting Web pages. Some sample topics you'll find in this book include the following:

- ✔ the origins and history of the World Wide Web
- ✔ designing and building Web pages
- ✔ creating interesting page layouts
- ✔ testing and debugging your Web pages
- ✔ mastering the many aspects of Web publication

Although you might think that building Web pages requires years of training and advanced aesthetic capabilities, we hasten to point out that this just ain't so. If you can tell somebody how to drive from their house to yours, you can certainly build a Web document that does what you want it to. The purpose of this book isn't to turn you into a rocket scientist; it's to show you all the design and technical elements you need to build a good-looking readable Web page, and give you the know-how and confidence to go out and do it!

How to Use This Book

This book tells you what the World Wide Web is all about and how it works. Then, it tells you what's involved in designing and building effective Web documents to bring your important ideas and information to the whole wide world, if that's what you want to do.

All HTML code appears in monospaced type like this:

```
<HEAD><TITLE>What's in a Title?</TITLE></HEAD>...
```

When you type in HTML tags or other related information, be sure to copy the information exactly as you see it between the angle brackets (< and >) because that's part of the magic that makes HTML work. Other than that, you'll learn how to marshal and manage the content that makes your pages special, and we'll tell you exactly what you need to do to mix the elements of HTML with your own work.

Due to the margins in this book, some long lines of HTML markup, or designations of World Wide Web sites (called URLs, for Uniform Resource Locators), may wrap to the next line. On your computer though, these wrapped lines will appear as a single line of HTML, or as a single URL, so don't insert a hard return when you see one of these wrapped lines. Each instance of wrapped code is noted as follows:

```
http://www.infomagic.austin.com/nexus/plexus/lexus/sexus/this_is_a_
                 deliberately_long.html
```

HTML doesn't care if you type tag text in uppercase, lowercase, or both (except for character entities, which must be typed exactly as indicated in Chapter 8 of this book). In order for your own work to look like ours as much as possible, you should enter all HTML tag text in uppercase only. ▪

*Assume = Makes an A** Out of U & Me*

They say that making assumptions makes a fool out of the person who's making them, and the person who's the subject of those assumptions. Nevertheless, we're going to make a few assumptions about you, our gentle reader:

- ✔ You can turn your computer on and off.
- ✔ You know how to use a mouse and a keyboard.
- ✔ You want to build your own Web pages for fun, profit, or because it's part of your job.

In addition, we assume you already have a working connection to the Internet and one of the many fine Web browsers available by hook, by crook, or by download from that selfsame Internet. You don't need to be a master logician, or a wizard in the arcane arts of programming, nor do you need a Ph.D in computer science. You don't even need a detailed sense of what's going on in the innards of your computer to deal with the material in this book.

If you can write a sentence and know the difference between a heading and a paragraph, you will be able to build and deploy your own documents on the World Wide Web. If you have an imagination and the ability to communicate what's important to you, you've already mastered the key ingredients necessary to build useful, attractive Web pages. The rest is details, and we'll help you with those!

How This Book Is Organized

This book contains nine major parts. Each part contains two or more chapters, and each chapter contains several modular sections. Any time you need help or information, just pick up the book and start anywhere you feel like it, or use the Table of Contents and Index to look up specific topics or key words.

Here is a breakdown of the nine parts and what you'll find in each one:

Part I: Welcome to the World Wide Web

This part sets the stage and includes an overview of and introduction to the World Wide Web, its history, and the software that people use to mine its treasures. It also explains how the Web works, including the HyperText Markup Language to which this book is devoted, and the server-side software and services that deliver information to end-users.

Part II: Building Better Web Pages

HTML documents, also called Web pages, are the fundamental units of information organization and delivery on the Web. In Part II you'll learn what HTML is about, and how hypertext can enrich ordinary text. You'll also work through a primer on basic Web page layout and design, to help you begin the process of building your own HTML documents.

Part III: A Tour of HTML Basics

HTML mixes ordinary text with special strings of characters, called markup, that instruct browsers how to display HTML documents. In this part of the book, you'll learn about markup in general, and HTML in particular. This includes logical groupings for HTML tags, a complete dictionary of HTML tags, and an equally detailed discussion of HTML character entities. By the time you're finished with Part III, you'll have a good overall idea of what HTML is and what it can do.

Part IV: Advanced HTML

Part IV takes all the elements covered in Part III and puts them together to help you learn how to build commercial-grade HTML documents. This includes building complex pages, developing on-screen forms to solicit information and feedback, and creating clickable image maps to let graphics guide your user's on-screen navigation. Finally, you'll have a chance to examine the work being done to extend HTML beyond its standard definitions.

Part V: Beyond HTML? (CGI Scripting and "Real" Applications)

Much of the real power of the World Wide Web lies in its ability to support user interaction and to link all kinds of server-based programs into attractive, visually-appealing documents that are easy to understand and control. In this part of the book, you'll go behind the scenes on your Web server to understand how the Web can absorb and handle input from users and interact with them. By the time you've finished this section, you should understand how open-ended and powerful your Web documents can be.

Part VI: Call the Exterminator: Debugging Web Pages

Once you've built your HTML documents, the real fun begins, as your work meets the ultimate test: what users like or don't like about it. As you're getting ready to release your Web site to a possibly indifferent world, you'll be prepared to catch and kill potential bugs yourself. You'll also be armed with strategies to enlist user feedback, to help you effectively communicate online, and to avoid having to deal with too many problems once you've taken your work public.

Part VII: Going Public: Serving Up Your Web Pages

After you've tested and debugged your work, it's time to publish your documents. In this part of the book, you'll learn how to blow your own horn, and let the world know not just where your pages are, but why they're worth a visit. You'll also be prepared to deal with the potential onslaught of users, and to decide whether you'll put your pages on somebody else's Web server, or build your own.

Part VIII: It's Tool-time: HTML Development Tools and Environments

When it comes to building HTML, you can do it alone, with only your trusty text editor. But it doesn't have to be that way. In Part VIII you'll be exposed to the many different tools available to help you build the Web pages of your dreams, and to manage those pages once they're built. Along the way, you'll have a chance to see what's available for UNIX, Macintosh, Windows, and other computing platforms by way of HTML editors and related tools, and Web servers and related services.

Part IX: The Part of Tens

In the concluding part of the book we sum up and distill the very essence of what you've learned. Here, you'll have a chance to review the top do's and don'ts for HTML markup, to rethink your views on document design, and to catch and kill any potential bugs and errors in your pages before anybody else sees them. Finally, you'll end your adventure by revisiting your Web server situation, as you reconsider whether your pages should reside on an Internet provider's Web server, or whether you should be building a Web server of your very own.

Icons Used in This Book

This icon signals technical details that are informative and interesting, but not critical to writing HTML. Skip these if you want (but please, come back and read them later).

This icon flags useful information that makes HTML markup, Web page design, or other important stuff even less complicated than you feared it might be.

This icon points out information you shouldn't pass by — don't overlook these gentle reminders (the life you save could be your own).

Be cautious when you see this icon. It warns you of things you shouldn't do; the bomb is meant to emphasize that the consequences of ignoring these bits of wisdom can be severe.

When you see this spiderweb symbol, it flags the presence of Web-based resources that you can go out and investigate further. You can also find all these references from the Table of Contents page on the diskette that comes with this book!

Where to Go from Here

This is the part where you pick a direction and hit the road! *HTML For Dummies* is a lot like the parable of the seven blind men and the elephant. It almost doesn't matter where you start out, you'll be looking at lots of different stuff as you prepare yourself to build your own Web pages. Who cares if anybody else thinks you're just goofing around — we know you're getting ready to have the time of your life.

Enjoy!

About the Disk

In this section of the book, we explain what you'll find on the *HTML For Dummies* disk. In a nutshell, it contains the following goodies:

- A collection of Web documents built just to help you find your way around the book's materials.
- A hotlist of all the URLs mentioned in the book, to make it easy for you to access any of the Web resources we've mentioned.
- An online version of the book's glossary, to help you look up all the strange and bizarre terminology Webheads are prone to use from time to time.
- Copies of all the HTML examples, easily accessible by chapter and heading, along with any graphics they use.
- A hyperlinked table of contents for the book, to help you find your way around its many topics and treasures.
- A specially-compressed archive of Common Gateway Interface (CGI) programs, built especially for you, to help add functionality to your own Web server (and to provide what we hope are sterling examples of the art of CGI programming).

All of this and more will be available on your own hard disk, if you simply follow the installation instructions in the next section.

Installing the Disk

Installing the *HTML For Dummies* disk is a completely straightforward process. If you have a PC running Windows 3.1 (or later like Windows for Workgroups 3.11 or the Windows 3.11 update), you can install in two easy steps:

1. Insert the disk into the floppy drive on your PC; double-click that drive's icon in File Manager (or some reasonable facsimile, like Norton Desktop for Windows).

2. Double-click on the program named WINSTALL.EXE and follow the instructions it gives you.

That's all there is to it!

Doing the default thing

We strongly recommend that you allow the installation program, WINSTALL.EXE, to install the files into the program's default drive and directory — namely, **C:\DUMMIES**. This will allow the HTML files to function correctly without requiring additional modification, and will make it much easier to access the material in those files.

During the installation process, you will be prompted for a drive on which to install the files (the default is **C:**). You will also be prompted for a directory to install the files and subdirectories that unpack from the compressed files (the default is **\DUMMIES**).

The disk's inside story

If you look at the contents of the *HTML For Dummies* disk, here's what you'll see:

```
DISKID              includes WINSTALL information
HTML4DUM.001        compressed HTML For Dummies files
INSTALL.DAT         WINSTALL installation script
LICENSE.TXT         WINSTALL license information
README.TXT          description of disk's contents,
                    installation, etc.
WINSTALL.EXE        the Windows program that drives the
                    installation process
```

When you execute the WINSTALL.EXE program, the contents of HTML4DUM.001 will be unpacked; only then will you be able to see what is on the disk — except it'll now be on your hard disk, too!

The HTML For Dummies Files

Once unpacked, you'll find that the installation program has created four directories, in the following arrangement:

```
Directory Tree          Full Directory Specification
--------------          ----------------------------
C:
 |-other directories
 |-\DUMMIES             C:\DUMMIES
    |-CGI               C:\DUMMIES\CGI
    |-HTML4DUM          C:\DUMMIES\HTML4DUM
       |-GRAPHICS       C:\DUMMIES\HTML4DUM\GRAPHICS
```

By describing the contents of each of these directories and naming the important files in each one, we can provide an excellent road map to what's on the disk.

You probably won't need to interact with too many of the individual files in these directories because most of them are linked together as HTML documents that you can explore using almost any Web browser. Since this includes most of the major players in this field — like Netscape, WinWeb, Mosaic, WebSurfer, etc. — you shouldn't have too much difficulty using your browser to help you look around. To give you an idea of what's there, we'll cover the files according to their home directory (assuming, of course, that you've accepted the installation defaults and the files actually live where we say they do).

C:\ DUMMIES

There are only three files in this directory, which acts as the root directory for the rest of the *HTML For Dummies* files. Here's a listing of the files, with an explanation of their contents:

- ✔ **LICENSE.TXT:** the WINSTALL license information, which proves that we used the program legally (we're required to include this file on the disk, but you can delete it if you want to).

- ✔ **README.TXT:** a detailed description of the *HTML For Dummies* files including an installation overview, information on changing the install program's defaults, using the *HTML For Dummies* Web pages, and unpacking the CGI programs in the CGI directory.

- ✔ **REGISTER.TXT:** an electronic version of the *HTML For Dummies* registration page (which you can find in hard copy at the back of the book); we've decided to let you fill it out electronically and e-mail it to us if you'd care to. Registration is purely voluntary.

That's all there is to the files at the top-level directory: just a little acknowledgment, information, and a registration form.

C:\ DUMMIES\CGI

This directory contains a single file named **CGIS.TAR**. It has been compressed using the UNIX *t*ape *ar*chival (*tar*) program. While you could unpack it on your PC, using any of a number of excellent programs available for DOS or Windows (e.g., WinZIP, WinCode, etc.), we'd recommend that you leave it until you find a UNIX or Macintosh machine to unpack it on (or some other kind of system, like Windows NT, that can handle filenames not hampered by the DOS 8x3 filenaming limitations).

Because the CGI (Common Gateway Interface) programs included in this archive are intended to be used on either a Macintosh- or UNIX-based Web server, you should think of them simply as a black box of latent Web capability while they're on your Windows machine. Once you put them in the right place, though, you'll be able to put them to good use as well. See the **README.TXT** file in the **C:\DUMMIES** directory for further details on installing and using these programs.

C:\DUMMIES\HTML4DUM

This directory contains the majority of the *HTML For Dummies* files, both in terms of importance and capturing key components of the book. Nearly every file in this directory ends with the extension **.HTM**, indicating that it is an HTML document.

The files in this directory fall into two categories:

1. Those that begin with **CHnn**, where **n** is a digit between 0 and 9, are keyed to chapters in the book. Thus, **CH07** indicates that the file in question is related to Chapter 7 of the book (the HTML Markup Reference chapter, in fact). These filenames continue on with the notation -Enn, where again, **n** is a digit between 0 and 9. This keys the file to a specific figure number for the chapter. Thus, the file named **CH07-E14.HTM** keys to figure 7-14, which illustrates the capabilities of the HTML paragraph tag (<P>). For other chapters, like 13, **CH13CERN.MAP** indicates the clickable map file supplied for the CERN *httpd* implementation, while **CH13NCSA.MAP** represents its NCSA counterpart.

2. Those files that begin with something other than CHnn are HTML documents that belong to a collection of *HTML For Dummies* sample pages that we've constructed as a teaching aid and as a navigational tool, to help you find your way around the materials we've assembled for the book. Here's an alphabetical listing of what's what:

```
COMMENT.HTM      To comment on Web pages, the book, or
                 to ask questions(not functional on
                 disk; must be installed on server)
CONTACT.HTM      Author contact information
CONTENT2.HTM     Table of Contents [2/4]
CONTENT3.HTM     Table of Contents [3/4]
CONTENT4.HTM     Table of Contents [4/4]
CONTENTS.HTM     Table of Contents [1/4]
DEFAULT.HTM      Default HTML page for servers
EDTITTEL.HTM     Ed Tittel's bio page
EXCERPT2.HTM     Book excerpts [2/2]
```

```
EXCERPTS.HTM      Book excerpts [2/2]
FTPSTUFF.HTM      FTP page: not functional on disk
GLOSSAR2.HTM      Glossary [2/4]
GLOSSAR3.HTM      Glossary [3/4]
GLOSSAR4.HTM      Glossary [4/4]
GLOSSARY.HTM      Glossary [1/4]
HELPINFO.HTM      Information to optimize viewing of
                  HTML For Dummies Web pages
HOTLISTS.HTM      Short collection of good hot lists
HTML4DUM.HTM      The HTML For Dummies home page
INDEX.HTM         Another default HTML page for servers
JCKTBLRB.HTM      Text from book cover
JMSTEWRT.HTM      Michael Stewart's bio page
MARKGTHR.HTM      Mark Gaither's bio page
SEARCH4D.HTM      Menu and search page: search function
                  not present on disk
SEBASTIN.HTM      Sebastian Hassinger's bio page
STEVEJMS.HTM      Steve James' bio page
URLINBK.HTM       URLs in book [1/3]
URLINBK2.HTM      URLs in book [2/3]
URLINBK3.HTM      URLs in book [3/3]
```

All in all, the best way to explore the *HTML For Dummies* Web pages is to fire up your browser, and point it at the file named *C:\DUMMIES\HTML4DUM\ HTML4DUM.HTM*, the home page for the whole collection. As an initial run-through, if you simply select the "NEXT" link at the bottom of each page, you'll end up taking a guided tour of the whole shebang, and get a pretty good idea of what's available and how you might use it.

We're especially proud of the online glossary, and your ability to use our "Web-ified" Table of Contents pages to locate the HTML documents for all the examples that appear in the book. But you'll probably find some other things to like in here as well...

If you see anything you don't like or don't understand, please send us e-mail: as our book recommends, we believe in asking for, listening to, and reacting to our users' feedback — this means you! (Thanks in advance, by the way.)

C:\DUMMIES\HTML4DUM\GRAPHICS

The only remaining holdout in the directory collection is the graphics subdirectory. As its name implies, this is where all the .GIF (Graphics Information Files) files for images in our sample HTML documents reside. If we used it in an example (or on the *HTML For Dummies* Web pages), you'll find it in here. All we can say further is "Help yourself!"

For the incurably curious, here are the details:

```
DUMMYGUY.GIF    Dummy Guy (the series mascot!)
IND1.GIF        Blank spacer 1
IND2.GIF        Blank spacer 2
IND3.GIF        Blank spacer 3
IND4.GIF        Blank spacer 4
IND5.GIF        Blank spacer 5
MBOX.GIF        Mailbox icon
README.GIF      Newspaper
LANGBAR.GIF     The "Language Bar" from Chapter 13
LANWL-SM.GIF    LANWrights logo
IMPACTSM.GIF    IMPACT Online logo
LINE.GIF        Colored line
DUMGUYSM.GIF    Small Dummy Guy (a miniature mascot)
SWIRL1.GIF      Swirl icon
BOGUSB.GIF      Sample button bar
RAINBOLG.GIF    Rainbow line
DOTRED.GIF      Red dot
DOTWHITE.GIF    White dot
DOTBLUE.GIF     Blue dot
OPENDOOR.GIF    Open Door icon
PHONE.GIF       Telephone icon
HTMLFDUM.GIF    Book cover logo
```

At the very least this small collection of graphical items should give you some interesting raw material to draw on for your own Web creations!

Non Windows Users

You may request a non-Windows version of the files that can be used on any platform which supports text .html files and .gif graphic files. E-mail the Web-Master, Michael Stewart at mcintrye@io.com or Ed Tittel at etittel@zilker.net. The files are available in the following formats: gunzip, tar, .sit, .hqx, .Z, and .zip

Where to Go from Here

We really can't make you go anywhere from this point in your reading, but we hope you decide to install the *HTML For Dummies* disk, and experience its contents first-hand. We also hope that you might read this book while you're at it, too! Enjoy!

Part I

Welcome to the World Wide Web

The 5th Wave   **By Rich Tennant**

In This Part...

HTML stands for HyperText Markup Language. It's a driving force behind the myriads of colorful interactive screens of text, graphics, and multimedia — called Web pages — popping up all over the place today on the World Wide Web (known as WWW or W3). Before you can understand the ins and outs of building Web pages, you'll need to learn a little about the World Wide Web, and the Internet universe in which it lives.

Part I is your introduction to W3, and includes a quick review of Internet basics, along with a history of the Web and how it works. This coverage will be old hat for seasoned Internauts, but should provide plenty of background for those less well-traveled in Cyberspace. By the time you make it through the first three chapters, you should have a good understanding of what the Web is about, why it's important, and what it can (and can't) do.

Along the way, you should also gain an appreciation of the vast skeins of knowledge, wit, folklore, esoterica, and information already strung through W3. It's humbling to think that your own work with HTML may someday result in stringing that web just a bit further!

Chapter 1

Welcome to the World Wide Web

● ●

In This Chapter

▶ Defining the World Wide Web

▶ Encountering cheerful chaos on the Internet

▶ Examining other Internet search tools

▶ Explaining why the Web is important

▶ Making the most of the Web: Browsers and search tools

● ●

*I*n order to understand HTML, you first have to understand the environment that it serves, and the world in which that environment operates. HTML is a text-based markup language that provides the underpinnings for one of the most exciting information search and navigation environments ever developed: This environment is called the World Wide Web (WWW or W3, for short), and represents a major step forward in making all kinds of information accessible to average folks like you and me.

From Small Things, Big Things Sometimes Come

The first version of the Web was introduced by a group of developers at the European Laboratory for Particle Physics (CERN) in Geneva, Switzerland in 1991. Their mission was to build an online system for ordinary users to easily share and disseminate text and graphics, without having to master arcane commands or esoteric interfaces. From its small and humble beginnings, use of the Web has exploded across the Internet, primarily because its developers succeeded in realizing their mission.

You'd have to figure that an information access and retrieval system origi-nally built for high-energy physicists would use rocket science to the max. If you did, though, you'd be dead wrong: the W3 environment, and the tools that make it available, are easy to use and understand.

In fact, even brief exposure to any of the many W3 interfaces quickly creates ardent Web aficionados, even out of diehard technophobes. Today, you can easily find graphical Web interfaces — called browsers — for the Macintosh, Microsoft Windows, and the various UNIX GUI environments, like X Windows and Motif. (Later on we'll also look at a popular non-graphics, text-based browser, called Lynx.)

All graphical Web browsers share a common "point and click" approach to interacting with information. Even character-based browsers, like Lynx, still make it easy to pick and follow links by selecting the appropriate highlighted text. All it takes to get started is Internet access, a Web browser, and informa-tion about where to enter the Web. After that, you scan the information that shows up on your screen; to navigate within the Web, select any highlighted item with your mouse (or your cursor, for character-mode tools), and you can follow chains of information for the rest of your life, without ever again having to come up for air.

But wait a minute! Before you get lost in the infinite strands of the World Wide Web, you may want to consider a few more details about its workings and its use. (But don't let us stop you — just check back in right here when you come back!)

What Is the Web, and Where Is It Strung?

By now, you should have a vague idea that the World Wide Web is a vast amorphous blob of text, images, audio, and video data scattered across net-works and computers world-wide. Hence the name, World Wide Web.

You should also be aware that HTML is the markup language that Web authors use to describe the structure and behavior of a Web page.

And now, a word from our sponsor...

To add a little more structure, let's examine a more formal definition of the Web. According to Tim Berners-Lee, one of the Web's chief architects (and a founding father for the original development at CERN), the World Wide Web is "the universe of network-accessible information, an embodiment of human knowledge.... It has a body of software, and a set of protocols and conventions. W3 uses hypertext and multimedia techniques to make the Web easy for anyone to roam, browse, and contribute to." (This quotation is taken from a Web page written by Berners-Lee entitled "The World Wide Web" that explains the ongoing project that resulted in the Web's existence and continued maintenance.)

Welcome to the center of the universe!

Let's pick the Berners-Lee statement apart, to help illustrate where the Web exists. As "the universe of network-accessible information" it represents any and all information accessible throughout the Internet, wherever that may be.

Consider for a moment that today, the Internet spans most of the globe — Internet domain names include country codes for virtually every country represented in the United Nations, and then some — and that over three million networks are interconnected in some way to this universe.

Practically speaking, this definition encompasses only all publicly accessible information, because many organizations choose to share only a subset of what's on their networks rather than everything they've got. Even so, this is a huge collection of material, which is why it's also referred to as an "embodiment of human knowledge." Much of what people know and care about is already available today in some form through the Internet!

This equips us to answer the question about where the Web is strung. The answer is: Everywhere there is publicly accessible information on the Internet, there is potential access to that information using a Web browser, or a related tool. The short version of this answer is, more simply: Everywhere.

"What it is," is what it is!

As for what the Web is, we can turn to some particular terminology in the B-L definition to explain further, with more of the relevant details. Here are the important parts:

- W3 is "a body of software" — that is, W3 is the marriage of a growing number of servers which are large, fast machines distributing information, a small number of clients also known as browsers or navigators which allow users to investigate and retrieve information, and suites of applications programs that interact among servers, clients, and databases.

✔ W3 also uses "a set of protocols and conventions" — that is, W3 is built around a set of shared rules for communicating data requests across a network, and for responding to those requests. Since this is what constitutes any protocol, it includes the http (hypertext transfer protocol) used to move Web page information from servers to clients, and the other network protocols used to access associated Internet information (more on this later on). The shared conventions refer to ways of representing and linking pages supplied by HTML, the markup language that underlies W3. This is what you'll be learning most about as you work through this book.

✔ Hypertext is a particularly important concept for W3. It is a way of representing non-structured information, with built-in references to related information. These references are commonly called "links." If the non-structured information includes images, audio, video, as well as text, it is called hypermedia which is a direct descendent of hypertext.

✔ Multimedia support allows W3 to deliver many different kinds of information, including text and two-dimensional graphics, and also sound, animation, video, and combinations of these things. Multimedia adds great depth and impact to your Web site.

✔ But perhaps the most essential ingredient that explains the Web's appeal and popularity is the stipulation that it be "easy to roam, browse, and contribute to." This helps to account for its incredible growth, and for its contribution to overall Internet activity and traffic (and traffic jams!).

By learning HTML, you too, will be able, not only to roam and browse, but to contribute to the Web as well!

The Cheerful Anarchy of the Internet

In order to appreciate the magnitude of the playing field across which the World Wide Web is strung, it's necessary to wrestle with some mind-numbing statistics. In 1991, at the end of its first year of existence, there were already more than 500 W3 sites up and running. Every full year since then, the number of sites has increased approximately tenfold. Here is what the mathematics of this proposition dictates:

✔ 1992: 5,000

✔ 1993: 50,000

✔ 1994: 500,000

In February of 1995, as we're writing this book, it seems likely that the number of Web sites might actually beat the 5,000,000 predicted by the growth curve.

Flagrant proliferation is clearly the trend for Web sites and activity. As more and more organizations hang out their "virtual signposts" in Cyberspace, a Web site has become the method of choice for establishing an electronic presence on the Internet.

Before the Web: Other Internet Navigation Tools

To help understand the extraordinary impact W3 has had, it might help to examine the state of the art for other Internet navigation tools, such as they are. In the following subsections, you'll meet some of the other cast of characters that experienced Internauts already know too well.

The point, however, is that all of these tools require considerably more user expertise than do the browsers used in the W3 environment. So sit back, and ponder, while you take a lightning tour.

While you're taking this trip down memory lane, please keep this in mind: Although Web browsers can supplant a lot of this functionality, they can co-opt these tools as well. In fact, part of the Web's unique charm is its ability to turn these tools to its own use, by allowing HTML links to call on these other services to locate and retrieve files, messages, and other goodies from the vast storehouse of riches that comprises the Internet.

FTP (no, it's not about delivering flowers — that's FTD!)

FTP (File Transfer Protocol) is a cross-platform tool for transferring files to and from computers anywhere on the Internet. Cross-platform means you don't have to be using the same kind of computer operating system in order to access files on the remote system.

For good use or bad, most of this incredible assemblage of material — which ranges from electronic books, to catalogs, to "free software" (shareware or freeware), to recipes, to graphical images, to whatever else you might desire — exists in one file or another, somewhere out there on the Internet.

FTP is the right Internet tool to use when you know that the information you're after is in some kind of file format, and when you know exactly where that file resides (and what name it takes). FTP lets you reach out across the Internet, attach to a remote computer, root around in its file system, and grab just the file you need for your own inscrutable purposes.

A special variety of FTP acts as a pillar in the foundation for the free flow of information across the Internet. It's called Anonymous FTP because it makes files available to anyone without having an account on the host computer. All that's required is to log into the FTP server using the account name *anonymous* (it's customary to supply your e-mail address as the password, but anything will do, in most cases). After that, you'll be free to browse the FTP server's collection of available files, and grab anything that takes your fancy.

Therein lies the rub: To use FTP effectively, you need to know how to navigate within the file system of the FTP server you're accessing. In most cases, this means knowing how to use *cd*, *ls -la*, and other UNIX file system commands; in other cases, it might mean knowing how to navigate a VAX/VMS, MVS, or Chronos file system. If you're lucky enough to have a graphical FTP implementation, you'll be able to use graphical controls on your side of the connection and avoid most of this arcane syntax. Unfortunately, many users are not that lucky.

The point is: to navigate on the remote system using FTP directly, you have to know what you're doing. With the proper use of HTML, you can make all these shenanigans unnecessary for people following your page links.

Figure 1-1 shows a graphical FTP menu; notice that the PC file system is displayed on the left (what's on your machine) and the remote file system on the right (what's on the FTP server). By navigating the directories on the two systems, you can copy from one to the other, as your access rights allow.

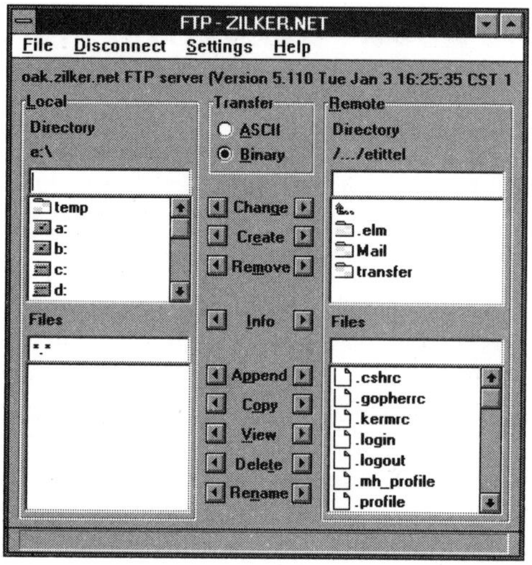

Figure 1-1:
A graphical
view of FTP.

Burrowing around in Gopherspace

Where FTP lets you transfer files to and from computers anywhere on the Internet (and Anonymous FTP lets you grab stuff from any anonymous FTP server), Gopher attempts to impose a little structure on the plethora of files that FTP makes available.

Gopher is the creation of a team of dedicated programmers at the University of Minnesota, home of "The Golden Gophers." More than just a totemic animal, Gopher is a good tool to use when browsing for files on the Internet. Unlike FTP, which is subject to the dictates of the file system of whatever machine the FTP server occupies, Gopher uses the same set of commands no matter what kind of machine it's running on.

In addition, Gopher servers are extensively interlinked: Much like the Web, all Gophers are inextricably intertwined so that, with sufficient burrowing, you can eventually find your way to the right Gopher hole. In addition, all Gopher interaction occurs through a consistent menu interface, so that all systems look the same. You can search by keyword, or by filename, so you have more flexibility in finding your way around. You can also rely on Gopher to deliver files to you directly, without having to know where the file is coming from, or what format it originated in.

For Gopher, the downside isn't as obvious as for FTP, but it's still necessary to navigate explicitly. By looking at Figure 1-2, you can also see that Gopher doesn't actually let you examine information in a meaningful way: You have to guess from an index listing whether you're interested in a particular item. Ultimately, you'll have to download a text file, or grab some kind of binary file (and switch to another application) to examine things in detail. W3 lets you examine items as you navigate, and provides a single consistent interface for reading text, viewing graphics, or dealing with multimedia. What's the difference? In a word: Convenience!

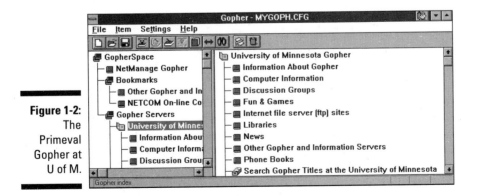

Figure 1-2:
The
Primeval
Gopher at
U of M.

The beauty of mailing lists & electronic mail

It's a little-known bit of trivia that much of the information on the Internet is available through e-mail, as well as through tools like FTP and Gopher. By stating the proper requests to the right e-mail servers and accessing mail service programs like *listserv* and *majordomo*, users with sufficient savvy can get to just about anything on the Internet through e-mail that they could get at with more interactive tools.

The benefit of this approach is that any dial-up, character-mode Internet user can grab a much broader variety of things than one might initially think. The downsides are legion, though: a clunky, character-mode interface, long turn-around time between asking for something and getting it delivered by e-mail, and the requirement that users master the syntax of the e-mail server and know precisely what they're after.

Nevertheless, this capability extends Internet access to a broad pool of users who might otherwise be unable to do much on the Internet. For W3 users, e-mail provides a workaround for browsers that can't handle interactive forms for feedback, orders, or information requests. E-mail also provides a great mechanism for users to deliver feedback, be it to request new features and functions for Web pages, or to suggest new topics for coverage. Although it's often slow and sometimes cumbersome, proper use of e-mail in Web applications can open the door for the public to contribute to, as well as consume, the contents of Web pages.

Usenet

It's hard to cover the Internet without some mention of Usenet. While Usenet is not strictly part of the Internet, for many people Usenet newsgroups are the main reason they have Internet access. If you described Usenet as a giant meeting hall crossed with a neighborhood bar, you wouldn't be far from the truth. Actually, Usenet is a gathering place for ongoing electronic discussions of everything from motorcycles to the Grateful Dead to arcane computer standards of every conceivable stripe and color. Through Usenet, you can make friends, flame enemies, cuss and discuss topics that interest you, and uncover answers to most conceivable questions.

Usenet is organized into named groups, organized by topic and focus, with varying degrees of organization (from strict moderation to free-form conversation). In some cases, you could approach Usenet with a specific question and come away immediately with an answer, while other queries might go unanswered for weeks on end. Persistence, coupled with an appreciation for Usenet's workings and "netiquette" are your keys to success.

One of the best things about most Usenet newsgroups is their lists of fre-quently asked questions (known by their acronyms as FAQs — pronounced "fax" for the plural, "fack" for the singular). The upside for Usenet is its tremendous variety and coverage, which leads to its inevitable downside — namely, volume. Many sites that comprehensively cover Usenet dedicate gigabytes of disk space just to maintain a two- or three-day deep collection of Usenet messages.

HTML gives Web users transparent access to Usenet newsgroups, which can be particularly useful for linking to the most current FAQ on any given topic. Linking to particular areas also saves users from sifting through swine to get to the pearls. Figure 1-3 shows a small fraction of a listing of Usenet messages on the topic of "ISDN" (Integrated Services Digital Network, a higher-bandwidth digital replacement for modem-based network access, among other services).

Figure 1-3:
Usenet
messages
from
comp.dcom.
isdn.

NEWTNews - ed [comp.dcom.isdn]	
File Disconnect Groups Messages Settings Help	
Flags From	**Subject**
<aaleona@pacbell.com>	Re: ISDN Test Equipment: What & How Much?
<bob@larribeau.com>	PPPML Interoperability Workshop
<bob@larribeau.com>	PPPML Interoperability Workshop
<cicat@cais.com>	Re: Has anybody done 128K to Internet over BRI?
<claytonn@onramp.net>	Re: Primary Rate and Basic Rate - do they work tog
<claytonn@onramp.net>	Re: Understanding SWB Tarriff
<crf@digex.net>	US West ISDN Contact info?
<jrg@galloway.sj.ca.us>	Small table sizes on Ascend Pipeline50[HX] :-(
<jrg@galloway.sj.ca.us>	Solaris-Sparc intercom app wanted [voice over IP or
<jrg@galloway.sj.ca.us>	Ascend P50 system loggin under Solaris 2.3, whats
<jrg@galloway.sj.ca.us>	automated/batch parameter change on Ascend P50,
<nickl@ngc.com>	PPP Multilink
<Simpson@WorldLinx.Com>	Eicon PC/ISDN Boards Reputation
<vhalkka@cc.Helsinki.FI>	Re: ISDN and the Mac
<yra@acl.nyit.edu>	ISDN bridge
Dave	Re: Please, entertain me...
Adakcom	ADAK 220/221 upgrade

Wide-Area Information Service (WAIS)

WAIS (pronounced "ways" or "wase") is one of a limited handful of Internet search tools that can spread itself across the network, to scour multiple archives and handle multiple data formats. It searches tirelessly throughout the entire Internet for the information you request. WAIS can help you find things, especially when you're not sure of precise filenames, menu entries, or other name-specific information.

WAIS differs from many other Internet search tools in that it does more than examine filenames or index listings: It's actually capable of investigating the contents of stored items as well as their names. This means that WAIS exam-ines a stupefyingly large amount of information as it performs your search.

WAIS differs from other Internet tools in another dimension as well: It was developed as a commercial database search application by Thinking Machines

Corporation, in tandem with Apple Computer, Dow Jones' News Retrieval Division, and KMPG Peat Marwick.

Although WAIS remains a highly useful tool by itself, you can also use special links into HTML to take advantage of the program's exhaustive searching capabilities. With proper programming, you can help users limit their searches to take even better advantage of WAIS than they might be able to do on their own.

Other tools

The Internet also sports a wide variety of other tools. Some, like Archie and Veronica, help to organize and search the vast resources of Anonymous FTP servers, by providing keyword and string-matching searches of comprehensive databases of directory listings around the Internet. Others, like telnet and *rsh*, offer direct access to remote computers with specialized applications and databases such as library card catalogs. While there is no dearth of tools available, it remains true that none of them beats a good Web browser, and none has the breadth and scope of the Web behind it!

 To learn more about the Internet, take a trip to your local bookstore. You'll find no shortage of Internet-related titles there. (We counted over 100 on our last visit!) You should pay particular attention to John R. Levine and Carol Baroudi's *The Internet for Dummies*, 2nd Edition (1994) and *More Internet for Dummies* (1994), both from IDG books. ▪

Why is the Web a "Big Deal"?

Hopefully you can come up with some of the answers to this question on your own by now. But let's run this one down just to be completely sure: W3 is a major development in information access on the Internet. It's a big deal because it covers an astonishing amount of ground, because it makes it easy and intuitive for users to find their way around huge collections of data, and because it hides most of the ugly details of how to grab and use information on the Internet.

Any one or two of these things would make the Web important and useful; all of them taken together make it a genuine step forward in the way we use and share information as a part of our daily lives. Even though some people believe that the Information Superhighway (or Infobahn, for the folks in the know) requires 500 channels of interactive television and bandwidth to burn, a lot of people believe that the Infobahn is here and now, and that W3 is its primary manifestation!

Of Browsers and Search Tools

For most end users, their Web access software — called a browser, or a Web client — is the most important piece of Internet software they use. Today, there are lots of options available for PCs running Windows (more limited ones for DOS-only machines), and also for the Macintosh, UNIX machines, and other platforms. We'll conclude our introductory overview of W3 with a cursory look at some of these browsers.

Lynx

Lynx is a primitive, text-only shareware Web browser. It cannot display or deliver graphical or multimedia elements (although it can be configured to display graphics using an external file viewer on appropriate systems). Even so, Lynx provides useful Web functionality for users on so-called "dumb terminals" because it supports keyboard navigation and boldface display of hypertext links (which is where we think the program got its name: lynx = links, get it?).

Navigating around the Web, Lynx displays innumerable lists of text items featuring hyptertext links. It also makes creative use of bullet characters — including the asterisk (*), plus sign (+), and lowercase o, as shown in Figure 1-4 to indicate heading levels in its Web page displays. Despite its limitations, Lynx remains a useful Web access tool, especially for terminal- or DOS-based users. Or for users with a slow Internet connection who don't want to wait for graphics to download.

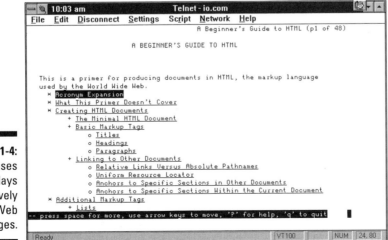

Figure 1-4:
Lynx uses
text displays
effectively
for Web
pages.

Mosaic

Mosaic is a graphical Web browser developed at the National Center for Super-computing Applications (NCSA). Many flavors of this program are available today, including one for X Windows (primarily for UNIX systems), Microsoft Windows, and the Macintosh.

Mosaic takes advantage of a powerful, interactive, graphical user interface to show off the W3 environment to its full advantage. Mosaic is capable of showing inline graphics, as shown in Figure 1-5, which features the NCSA Mosaic for Microsoft Windows home page. To follow links to other Web pages, users select graphics or highlighted words in the text.

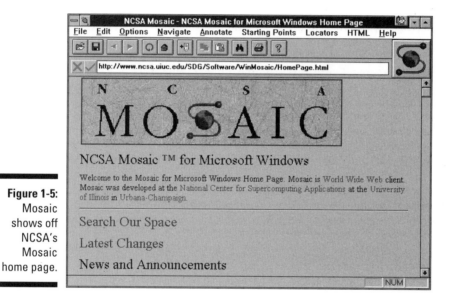

Figure 1-5:
Mosaic
shows off
NCSA's
Mosaic
home page.

In this kind of display, bit-mapped fonts can be used to clearly differentiate and emphasize various header levels. Color is used to highlight text links, and other elements of the display include on-screen buttons and navigational aids.

Developed at NCSA by Marc Andreesen and a team of other programmers, Mosaic has become the model for graphical Web browsers. Because NCSA has made shareware versions of Mosaic widely available on the Internet, and has begun licensing Mosaic code to a number of Internet utilities vendors — including companies like Spry, NetManage, Quarterdeck, and Frontier Technologies — to build Mosaic-derived Web browsers, Mosaic is the most popular Web browser in use today.

WinWeb (and MacWeb)

Today, a second generation of graphical Web browsers has become available, expanding the capabilities introduced by Mosaic. WinWeb, and its Macintosh sibling, MacWeb, were developed by programmers at the Microelectronics and Computer Consortium (MCC) in Austin, Texas.

WinWeb introduced useful innovations overlooked in Mosaic, including the ability to download multiple images in parallel, along with the use of sophisticated cursors and status displays to indicate progress on individual downloads. This shows users how their navigation is progressing, and provides better program feedback.

Figure 1-6 shows the Enterprise Integration Galaxy, a project begun at MCC in 1991 to provide complex system integration services to member companies and paying customers, based on research and development work undertaken at MCC. This home page also includes access to a WAIS-based search engine (not depicted) that can locate Web pages related to a number of topics. The EINet pages also feature a common toolbar that offers immediate access to previous page links (Up, Home), to on-screen Help, and to the search engine (Search) at any time.

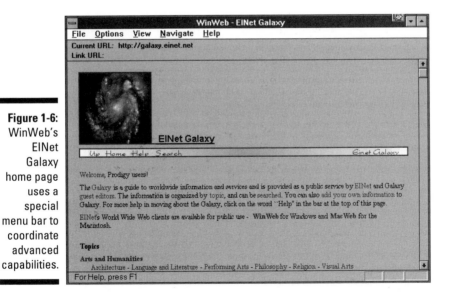

Figure 1-6: WinWeb's EINet Galaxy home page uses a special menu bar to coordinate advanced capabilities.

Both WinWeb and MacWeb are available as shareware, and have proved popular in the user community.

Netscape

Netscape represents Marc Andreesen's second effort at a graphical Web browser, under the aegis of a private company, Netscape Communications, Inc. It offers clear evidence of its developer's wisdom and experience, and includes some advanced features not found in other Web browsers. These include the ability to begin navigating within a Web page even before its contents are completely downloaded to the client. (Mosaic, and earlier Web browsers, required users to wait for the download to be fully complete before allowing navigation.)

Netscape also includes a secure implementation of the hypertext transfer protocol (https), active status information, and excellent file capture and navigation tools. Available both as shareware and in a commercial release, Netscape provides one of the best Web interfaces we've encountered anywhere.

Figure 1-7 depicts the home page for CERN, where all this W3 activity started. It also shows a row of navigation buttons on the upper third of the screen. These allow users to take a guided tour of the program, to inquire about new Netscape developments and activities, to examine a list of FAQs, to access a search engine, a directory of resources, or a collection of Usenet newsgroups. This represents easy access to lots of the capabilities and services that the Web has to offer.

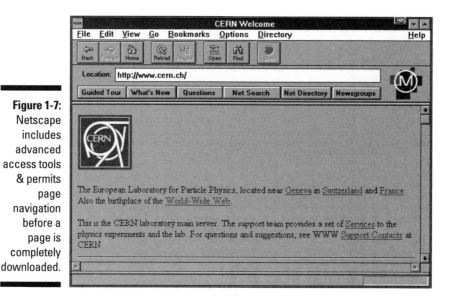

Figure 1-7: Netscape includes advanced access tools & permits page navigation before a page is completely downloaded.

Hopefully, you now have a better appreciation of the Web and can hardly wait to publish your own home page. But wait! Before you can become a Web aficionado, you have to pass Web History 101 — a.k.a. Chapter Two.

Chapter 2

Back to the First Strands: A Brief History of the Web

*T*im Berners-Lee and his colleagues at CERN had no idea what they were starting when they first began hacking together their ideas for the Web. Nevertheless, they succeeded in starting something strange and wonderful that has taken the whole Internet community by storm. In this chapter, you'll learn more about the Web's origin and history, as you probe its original motivation, and the factors that have shaped its form and capabilities.

Particle Physicists Are Like Rocket Scientists

You'd think that a group of high-energy particle physicists wouldn't shrink from an arcane and demanding software tool. But even a rarefied group of researchers and academics wanted an information access tool that would make their lives easier.

Although CERN is located in Geneva, Switzerland, researchers working for and with CERN were likely to be scattered anywhere around Europe, or for that matter, anywhere else in the world.

The nature of working groups at CERN — with members likely to be widely dispersed, and only loosely affiliated — played a powerful role in designing the Web. The Web was designed to solve the task of sharing information all over the world, and of making that information easy to access.

Before the Web, CERN researchers had to share data the old-fashioned way — by physically moving it around. This meant going through the same tedious, time-consuming set of motions for each item of interest to any group:

- ✔ searching for (and hopefully, locating) the required item on a computer somewhere on the Internet;

- ✔ making a remote connection to the computer where the item resided;

- ✔ retrieving the item to a local machine, including handling necessary copying and reformatting activities along the way.

Each step in this process might have required a separate application, and broad access to a wide range of dissimilar computer systems.

The researchers at CERN were looking for something much simpler and more elegant. What they wanted was a system that would support uniform access to a broad range of information through a single, common interface. Furthermore, they wanted ready access to that information, without performing the multi-step contortions required to get information from "there" to "here" described in the preceding paragraph.

The formulation of this goal kicked off the design activity in 1989 that ultimately led to the World Wide Web's introduction in 1991. In the meantime, the proposal for the project was fully developed and refined, and coding got underway. By the end of 1990, the researchers at CERN had built a text-mode browser similar to Lynx (depicted in Figure 1-4 on page 13), and had prototyped a graphical browser for the NeXT computer (today available as part of NeXTStep) that helped to fuel considerable interest in the project throughout the scientific community.

Throughout 1991, access to the Web and its browsers was heavily promoted within CERN. The initial implementation let users access normal hypertext Web pages and the contents of several Usenet newsgroups. As enthusiasm for this environment became apparent, the appetite for additional sources of information through the Web spurred the development of interfaces to WAIS, FTP, Telnet, and Gopher. By the end of 1991, most publicly-available information resources on the Internet were also accessible by those lucky enough to have access to the Web.

In 1992, CERN began promoting the Web outside the confines of its sister institutions, and outside the research and academic communities. The same impetus that made the Web an ideal tool for researchers and academicians also gave it tremendous appeal to Internauts of all persuasions. Clearly, it was an idea that appealed to more than the "rocket scientist" crowd!

With the publication of source code for W3 servers and browsers, 1992 witnessed two parallel thrusts in furthering the Web's increased presence on the Internet:

1. Users and organizations alike began producing Web pages and making them available through Web servers all over the Internet. These pages covered a complete spectrum of interests and subjects (occasioning the "embodiment of human knowledge" remark included in the Berners-Lee Web description).

2. Developers — notably, the Mosaic team at NCSA and the WinWeb, MacWeb teams at MCC — began creating powerful, graphical browsers for a broad range of desktop computers and workstations.

By the end of 1993, you could find browsers for many flavors of UNIX workstations running X Windows, the Macintosh, and PCs running Microsoft Windows.

Within the next six months, the Web emerged as the most popular tool for Internet surfing. You'll get a look at some of the related statistics on this phenomenon later in this chapter (see the section entitled "Danger! Explosive Growth" for some truly impressive stats). At this point, it's vital to understand only that what made the Web attractive to CERN researchers also made it attractive to the general run of Internet users, no matter what they did for a living.

UNIX and the Web

But to really understand the whys and wherefores, as well as the workings, of the Web, you'll have to take a detour back to the origins of the Internet itself. Nobody disputes that the Internet's original implementation was clearly the result of funding and support from the (Defense) Advanced Research Projects Administration (ARPA, later known as DARPA to acknowledge the role of the Department of Defense (DoD) in supplying funding).

However, most Internet historians agree that the real launching platform for the Internet as we know it today was the inclusion of TCP/IP-based networking protocols and services in the release of the 4.2BSD (Berkeley Software Distribution) version of the UNIX operating system in 1983. The DoD had already adopted TCP/IP as its "official standard" networking protocol in 1982, following its initial development and deployment on the ARPANET in the early 1980s. But TCP/IP's biggest boost came from its widespread dissemination in the research and academic community, fomented by its inclusion into BSD UNIX.

BSD UNIX was a repackaged release of AT&T's core UNIX technology (with permission and licensing from AT&T) enhanced by add-ins and add-ons collected from around the world . This flavor of UNIX was widely employed as a teaching and research tool, used in thousands of colleges, universities, and research institutions around the world throughout the 1980s. Access to this technology was ubiquitous and so inexpensive as to be nearly "free." Adding TCP/IP to this environment put Internet access in reach of nearly anyone who wanted to take the trouble to establish and maintain a connection. This capability is what really made the Internet grow to its current dimensions, and established the foundation for an information access environment that cried out for the technology afforded by the Web and its browsers.

The burden of Internet history

Assuming that your Web-spinning platform isn't UNIX, why should you care about UNIX in any way, shape, or form? This is where "the burden of history" comes into play: Because of its origins, there's a strong UNIX flavor to much of what you'll encounter on the Internet.

This affects HTML and the Web in several ways:

- **resource names:** It conditions the kinds of filenames and directory paths you'll see in references to Web resources. For instance, it means that protocols or devices are followed by a colon, that domain names are embedded into Web resource names, and that forward slashes (/) separate directory path elements. This is the way UNIX does it, so it'll seem quite familiar to UNIX-heads; for PC or Macintosh users, it takes a little getting used to.

- **commands and syntax:** UNIX is an operating system built by computer scientists for use by an array of scientists; so it can sometimes appear mysterious and intimidating. How else can you explain a system where "grep" makes perfect sense because it's an acronym for general regular expression parser, and everybody knows what that means, right?

  HTML itself doesn't suffer from this — it's got a different ancestry — but if you ever have to work with setting up and managing a Web server, you'll learn UNIX syntax and command names which may seem strange to you at first, but you'll soon come to appreciate the power of UNIX.

Of domain names and filenames

When it comes to locating resources on the Internet, nothing is more important than knowing where they live. For files, it's almost as important to know what they're called, but if you know how to root around in a UNIX file system, you can often find your way to what you need, file-wise.

On the Internet, everything's an eminent domain!

The key to knowing where things live on the Internet is to know their domain names. If you've got an Internet account, you're linked to a domain name, too. Ed's and Steve's Internet names look like this for e-mail purposes:

```
Ed Tittel <etittel@zilker.net>
Steve James <snjames@wetlands.com>
```

The only part the Internet cares about is the part inside the angle brackets (< >). The information on the left-hand side of the at-sign (@) identifies them uniquely as Ed and Steve, but the information to the right-hand side identifies where their accounts reside. The at-sign indicates where Ed and Steve can be located; in other words, it identifies their assigned Internet domain name.

The structure of the Internet is most visible in the domain name, because this is where the number of levels in an organization might show up: Larger, more hierarchical organizations will have more names separated by periods than will flatter, less hierarchical ones. In general, the more to the right a name occurs in the domain name part of an address, the more significant that name will be.

Ed's domain name ends with the extension ".net" and Steve's with the extension ".com". Meaningful identifiers for domain names within the United States include the following possibilities:

.com   commercial institution or service provider

.edu   educational institution (school, college, etc.)

.gov   government institution or agency

.mil   U.S. military

.net   network service provider

.org   nonprofit organization

Outside the United States, Internet domain names end with a two-letter country code, and are preceded by the remainder of the domain name. For instance "info.cern.ch" is the name of an important source for Web information at CERN. The "info" part indicates it's an information source, the "cern" indicates that it's at CERN, and the "ch" stands for Cantons de Helvetia, known to most English speakers as Switzerland.

For files, the name's the thing, but the path gets you there

Because of the preponderance of UNIX systems on the Internet, the UNIX file system has lent its character to many aspects of Internet navigation. This applies as much to filenames, which identify individual files, as it does to directory specifications, which locate collections of files in a file system.

In UNIX, filenames are much richer than DOS or Macintosh filenames. Rather than the restrictive 8x3 file naming for DOS (up to eight characters for a filename, and three for an extension, separated by a period), UNIX file specifications can be up to 127 characters long, and can include a great many more special characters than are permitted for either DOS or Macintosh filenames. Don't be surprised to see long names, multiple periods, and other apparent oddities when accessing Web resources. Just make sure you type in exactly what's specified, or you may never gain access to what it is you seek.

The same richness applies to UNIX directory names as well. They, too, can be much longer than names you might be accustomed to. Directory levels will also be separated by a forward slash (/), rather than the backward slash (\) common on DOS file systems. Old DOS heads will experience a moment of euphoria when they're told that the cd command works similarly for UNIX as in DOS (the DOS version is actually a UNIX copycat, somewhat stripped down).

Uniform resources on the Web

Web resources are identified with special names, called Uniform Resource Identifiers (URIs), that identify objects accessible through the Web. Whenever you navigate to a Web page, you do so through its Uniform Resource Locator (URL), which describes the protocol needed to access it, and points to its Internet location and home directory. Another category of URI is the Uniform Resource Name (URN), which is still in draft status right now, but may some day be used to name additional resources and services that are more persistent than URLs.

URLs hold the keys to the Web

As you examine a URL for a specific HTML file, it will look something like this:

```
http://info.cern.ch:80/hypertext/WWW/Addressing/Addressing.html#spot
|--1--|------2-----|-3-|----------4-----------|------5--------|-6-|
```

This URL is composed of six parts, that work as follows:

(1) *protocol/data source*: for network resources, this will usually be the name of the protocol used to access the data that resides on the other end of the link. The syntax for this part of the name is as follows:

- ✔ ftp:// points to a file accessible through the File Transfer Protocol.
- ✔ gopher:// points to a file system index accessible through the gopher protocol.
- ✔ http:// points to a hypertext document (typically, an HTML file) accessible through the hypertext transfer protocol.
- ✔ mailto:// links to an application that allows you to compose a message to be sent to a predefined address using e-mail.
- ✔ news:// points to a USENET newsgroup, and uses the network news transfer protocol (NNTP) to access the information.
- ✔ telnet:// links to a remote login on another Internet computer, typically to select from a predefined menu of choices or options.
- ✔ WAIS:// points to a Wide Area Information Server on the Internet, and provides access to a system of indexed databases.

    For local data (typically, reading HTML files from one of your desktop machine's hard disks or other drives), the syntax varies from browser to browser, but usually starts with:

- ✔ file:// which indicates that it's a local file, rather than a public Web page (that is, not available outside your directory or local network).

(2) *domain name*: This is the domain name for the Web server where the desired Web page or other resource resides.

URL Syntax and Punctuation

Strictly speaking, the syntax requirements of a URL are such that a colon (:) is only allowed between the protocol or data source identifier and the rest of the name, followed by two forward slash characters. But with access to local files, we'd recommend that you first look for a menu selection in your browser that will let you search your local file system for an HTML file to open (look for choices like "Open File" or "Open Local File"). If that doesn't work, we've had pretty good results with the following approach:

```
file:///<drive ID>|<directory spec>
        <filename>
```

Notice the three forward slashes after the colon. After the drive ID (which would be a letter for DOS, or the volume name for Macintosh, NetWare, etc.), use a vertical bar character (|) in place of a colon. Then when specifying the directory path, use forward slashes to separate directory levels. Follow this with the exact name of the file, and you should be able to access it with your browser, too!

3. *port address*: In most cases, the default port address for http is ":80" (and can be omitted), but you may see URLs with other numbers in use; this number identifies which process address a Web session needs to connect with. In general, if a number appears in the URL, it's a good idea to include it (even if it is ":80").

4. *directory path*: This is the location of the Web page in the Web server's file system.

5. *object name*: This is the actual name of the HTML file for the desired Web page or the name of whatever other resource is required.

6. *spot*: Sometimes, getting users to the HTML file isn't enough: You'll want to drop them at a particular location within the file. By preceding the name of an HTML anchor with a pound sign (#) and tacking it onto the HTML filename, you can direct a browser to jump right to a specific location. This is especially handy for larger documents, where quite a bit of scrolling might otherwise be required for readers to get to the desired information.

All in all, the most important thing about URLs is to enter them exactly as they're written because they won't work if they're not exactly correct. When building Web pages, therefore, this means it's absolutely critical to test each and every embedded URL reference to make sure the syntax is right and to make sure the site is still up — Web sites come and go. When using a Web browser, this also means it's better to cut and paste URLs into a HotList, Bookmark, or a text file than to write them out by hand, and introduce the possibility of a transcription error.

Many servers have a default name so you don't have to know an exact HTML file. When in doubt about a URL, try the following syntax first:

```
http://www.companyname.com/
```

This will often default to a file called index.html or default.html that represents the company's home page.

What else is there, besides HTML files?

For some applications — for example, FTP — the name of the directory containing the files ends the URL. For example, in this URL — ftp://ftp.nevada.edu/pub/music/guitar — the directory "guitar" contains files we want to look at and when we navigate there we get a listing of files in the directory and can then select the ones we want. If you only want to make one particular file available through a link you can provide a specific pointer to only that file. So, for example, you'd have: ftp://ftp.nevada.edu/pub/music/guitar/LeoKottke.html.

For more information on URLs, consult this URL:

```
http://info.cern.ch/hypertext/WWW/Addressing/Addressing.html
```

It describes the details for URL syntax and supported protocols, and points to specifications and other documents on this subject. A word to the wise: the CERN site gets a lot of traffic so you may get timed out trying to connect. I've had good luck getting there at off-hours like 3AM EST. ▦

Early Web Tools and Unnatural Appetites

In their earliest implementations, Web browsers started out as pretty primitive beasts. They were generally character-oriented, rather than graphical, and didn't include the bells and whistles for displaying pictures, icons, and multimedia that make more up-to-date implementations so appealing.

When building your Web pages, though, remember that some users still use these first-generation tools; for them, it's very often a character-mode browser or no Web access at all. So, when you're designing three-dimensional pages with complicated graphics and animated displays, remember that some users won't be able to see your work.

Don't let a lack of sophisticated displays keep low-end users from reading your information. Since content is at least as important as form, this should be doable in most cases. For those of you trying to build interactive museum tours or other Web pages where graphics are crucial to your content, we apologize, because this really doesn't apply to you. Even then, you might want to think about ways for those readers to see what you can't show them, be it ways to order a copy of the museum catalog, or reference or art books that include some of the images you want them to see.

Always be aware that any Web pages you publish on the Internet will be viewed by a broad range of browsers, from character-mode displays on dumb terminals, to bleeding edge, experimental implementations of as-yet-incomplete HTML specifications. Among many other things — which we'll try to cover in this book — this means that you must include at least one character-mode browser in your test suite, as you check your own HTML coding work before inflicting it on others!

An additional tip could be **do not** rely on specific features of a browser when publishing Web information. For example, many browsers do not support the <CENTER> HTML behavior tag, and relying on this additional feature, will break other browsers and make your information unusable. This will be covered in the Parts of Ten: HTML Do's & Don'ts. ▦

Danger! Explosive Growth

While the image of an exploding Web conjures up something that isn't safe to crawl onto, that's just what the Web is doing in terms of its growth. Even though its introduction in 1991 makes it one of the newest Internet applications around, it has already become the most popular Internet application of all time.

According to the work of one Web aficionado, MIT student Michael Gray, the Internet carries more Web data in a six-hour period today, than it did for the entire year of 1992! If you assume little or no Internet Web traffic in 1991 (when it was pretty much restricted to CERN and a "small circle of friends"), this translates into annual growth of over 200,000% (or 2,000 times more, year over year, if you like smaller numbers)!

Other sources estimate that today, 10% of all Internet traffic is Web-related, up from 1% at the beginning of 1994, and an infinitesimal fraction the year before that. This fits Mr. Gray's numbers nicely, but from a different perspective.

Another amazing statistic comes from Network Wizards, an Internet and networking consultancy in Menlo Park, California. According to their January, 1995, Internet Domain Survey, "www has risen to the top of the most popular host [domain] name list." In other words, there are more domain names on the Internet that include the string "www" than any other single host name in use. This argues very strongly that the Web occupies a major place in today's Internet culture!

Wherever you get your data about the Web, it's unanimous that its usage is growing dramatically, and the ranks of users are swelling robustly. The only real question then becomes: How can I possibly manage to find what I really need out there on the Web? For Web publishers this translates into: How can I let the people know where my pages are?

Here are the URLs for the references we mentioned:

Michael Gray's "Growth of the Web":

    http://www.netgen.com/info/growth.html

The Internet Domain Survey by NetWizards:

    http://www.nw.com:80/zone/WWW/top.html

A good general source for Web and Internet statistics is:

    http://WWW.Stars.com:80/Vlib/Misc/Statistics.html

This last URL includes links to most of the other Web and Internet surveys and statistics worth mentioning, including "official" and personal efforts in that direction. ■

A Scintillating Survey of the Web, World Wide

To conclude this chapter, you'll get a tour of some of the treasures that the World Wide Web can offer. At this point, you should have some idea about the Web's origins and its design goals; now it's time to take a quick look at some of the many treasures it offers.

Jumping-off points galore

Every browser comes with a predefined home page; many of these offer excellent starting points for your Web travels. Three browsers in particular: NCSA Mosaic, Netscape, and WinWeb/MacWeb offer outstanding home pages that provide orientation tools (often called "Starting Points"), topic indexes, and search capabilities to help you locate items of interest using keyword searches across a large population of Web servers on the Net. However, the Web is a kind of mystical thing — whose circumference is nowhere, and its center everywhere — so there really is no "perfect starting point" in reality.

Search pages, anyone?

There are a variety of so-called search pages on the Web, providing a link to background applications that can examine loads of data repositories on the Internet, based on the keyword(s) you supply, and return URLs matching the topics you want.

All of the major search pages are nicely represented in a number of places, including the Netscape home page. For variety, we'd recommend checking out the page that describes search engines at a regional access provider's Web site in the Baltimore, Maryland area. (See Figure 2.1.) The URL for this page is:

```
http://www.charm.net/info.search.html
```

Try it on for size; pick a search engine, and try it out with a term of particular interest (for best results, pick something specific, like "coriander," rather than something general like "spices"). ▨

The "Whole Internet Catalog" page

Taken from the resource guide in Ed Krol's outstanding book, *The Whole Internet User's Guide & Catalog*, 2nd edition (O'Reilly & Associates, 1994), this online version is regularly updated and maintained by the folks at O'Reilly as part of their Global Network Navigator (GNN) Web site. The URL is:

```
http://nearnet.gnn.com/wic/newrescat.toc.html
```

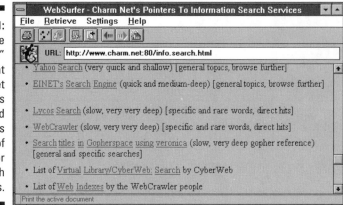

Figure 2-1:
The "Delve and Plumb" page at charm.net includes good descriptions of most of the major Web search engines.

As shown in Figure 2-2, the Whole Internet Catalog page starts with a jump table for especially hot topics, called a hotlist. Beneath the hotlist, this page includes an index of topics that ranges from "Arts & Entertainment" to "Travel," in alphabetical order, each with numerous subtopics.

Figure 2-2:
The Whole Internet Catalog page is a good place to start surfing the Net.

There are lots of other interesting places to start your Web investigations, but we'll save some more good ones for later on. This should be plenty to get you started. As you travel around the Web, pay attention to how pages are laid out, and how indexes, graphics, and hotlists are used. You can learn a lot from these examples, both good and bad. You can also select View Source from your browser's menu to see the HTML code that represents each of these pages.

Chapter 3

Under the Hood:
How the Web Works

• •

In This Chapter

▶ Understanding browsers and servers

▶ Communicating across the Web

▶ Interpreting Web pages

▶ Accessing the Web

• •

*N*ow that you know what the Web is, where it came from, and just what a big deal it has turned into, it's time to start grappling with how it actually works. Despite the volume of information it connects, and the many different ways of presenting and delivering that information, there's a basic set of mechanisms that make the Web work. In this chapter you'll learn about the communications that underlie the Web, the roles that clients and servers play, and how you can use the Web to share information around the corner, or around the world!

Of Clients & Servers, Responses & Requests

Understanding how information flows over most networks requires that you understand the "client/server" approach to computing. This is based on some pretty interesting assumptions. Walking through them will help you understand how the Internet — and other networks — really work, and why they work the way they do.

On the Web, front and back ends play different roles

By now, you're familiar with the idea that there are all kinds of resources available through the Web, somewhere "out there" on the Internet. You also know that in order to navigate the Web, you need an Internet connection and a browser installed on your desktop.

In reality, what's going on is a division of labor in handling Web information, and a separation of roles that is entirely appropriate to hooking individual users up to collections of shared data. The division of labor splits the task of handling Web information between storage and retrieval, and display of that information on your computer screen.

The storage and retrieval part is typically handled by the Web server, away from human observation elsewhere on a network — that's why it's called the "back end" of the client/server model. The display of information (and recognition of input, when appropriate) is handled by the browser on a user's workstation, right in front of its audience — which is why it's called the "front end" of the client/server model.

In other words, the role of the front end, or desktop computer in accessing the Web is to handle requests for resources on demand, and then to display the information that is returned.

While this is an important job — so important that you couldn't use the Web without it — the back end role is every bit as important, and is what makes handling the multitudes of Web users possible. Each Web site is handled by a machine (server) that is ready to accommodate requests for Web information (identified by the domain name in a URL or other uniform name). Because it simply returns Web pages or other resources in response to Web requests from users on the network, the server doesn't do displays, or interact with users; it simply returns the items being requested, or an error message if a resource cannot be provided.

Here's an example: consider the communciation process involved at your local bank. A bank teller (the server), Biff, sits and waits for customers at his window. The customer (the client), Carmela, enters the bank and approaches her favorite teller, Biff. Carmela and Biff negotiate a check cashing transaction according to bank rules. Carmela walks away with her money as Brian approaches Biff to negoiate his bank transaction. This is the same for a client and server transaction. Clients ask for things, and if they can follow the rules, the server will give them what they ask for.

Web clientology

Because not all Web users necessarily have desktop computers — some may be using "dumb terminals" that provide a screen and keyboard, but get their smarts from a computer somewhere else on the network — it makes more sense to distinguish between front and back end roles by calling them clients and servers.

The front end role is that of a client — owned and operated by a user who makes a request for certain information from a known source, and who deals with the responses to that request.

Lest the client's role be underrated, it's also important to know what's involved in being a good client. It's more than just asking for things, and then displaying them when they're delivered. Clients must also handle:

✔ supporting a network connection addressing whatever servers might be available over the network. This includes handling the set-up, mainte-nance, and orderly tear-down of network connections as users enter, use, and then leave the network;

✔ managing network communications, that is, talking to servers. This includes making a connection to a Web site, translating user requests into formal computer communications, and handling communication and delivery errors that occur from time to time;

✔ displaying responses which often means a great deal more than just flashing characters onto a screen. Particularly for the Web, the client's job is to interpret and convert character-based information into graphi-cal form, and to properly combine the many sources of information — sound, graphics, text, and multimedia — into the hypertext documents that the Web supports.

There's a lot going on under a Web browser's hood, and all of those comput-ing chores must be supplied by the computer running the client software that makes it work. This book is going to explain much of what's involved in turn-ing the information delivered by Web servers into specific on-screen displays, and how best to structure that information to handle the broadest possible audience in the best way.

Serving up Web resources

On the back end, though, there's an awful lot of work to do as well. When clients supply URLs to a Web site, they're really asking the server to deliver back to them some specific data across the Internet.

This kind of back end role is called a server, speaking generically; clients that ask for Web resources typically interact with a server whose role is specialized to handle such requests. That's why we call them "Web servers."

A simple explanation of a Web server relies on the idea that a particular machine on the network is running the software necessary to recognize and accommodate Web requests. If a client sends a request to an address where the right software is running, that software will attempt to satisfy the request, or at least respond with an error message that says why it can't.

A Web server's job consists of three basic activities:

1. listening for specific requests for Web resources that arrive from the network;

2. interpreting valid requests as they arrive, and attempting to locate the requested resources while logging clients' requests;

3. providing those resources over the network, or providing an error message explaining why a request cannot be honored (connection not available, item not found, invalid request format, etc.).

This general sequence of activities — listening for requests, interpreting and logging requests, and providing responses — describes the way most network servers do their jobs (and also explains how other Internet services like Telnet, FTP, Gopher, etc. work as well).

The benefits of client/server revealed

In the grand scheme of things, this approach to handling information delivery is called "client/server computing." Client/Server has become an industry buzzword; nevertheless, this approach does confer some appreciable benefits:

✔ Because the processing load is divided, clients can concentrate on providing the best possible interface to users; this makes it easier to offer cool graphical displays and powerful visual controls.

✔ Likewise, servers can concentrate on maximizing their ability to service lots of requests; the division of labor is what makes it possible for Web servers to handle tens of thousands of resource requests per day (which is an average load for a modestly popular site on the Web today). Splitting applications between clients and servers allows multiple types of clients to coexist peacefully. Much of the power of the Web derives from its ability to service PCs, Macintoshes, UNIX machines, and dumb terminals with more or less equal facility. This is possible because the split between client and server was designed to let a single server service many types of clients.

✔ Another benefit from the client/server split derives from where it leaves the information that clients use: residence on a server makes information ideal for sharing, permits better controls over that data, and lets information providers decide how much power and capability they want their servers to provide.

✔ By allowing dollars and data to concentrate in one place — namely, at the server — client/server helps to maximize performance on the server, where it's going to do the most users the greatest amount of good. This also ensures that information is located where it can be protected through backups, where access to the data can be more rigorously controlled, and request statistics (known as "hits") can be logged.

For client/server the dynamics keep coming back to the division of labor: By dividing the world into clients and servers, this approach lets clients handle the job of user interaction, and servers to tackle the rapid retrieval and delivery of information. This capability has been well-realized in the Web, which features powerful graphical clients (browsers) and fast, powerful servers, both of which contribute to its burgeoning popularity.

Networking Takes Protocols

In diplomatic circles, a protocol is a set of rules that keeps professionals, friends and enemies alike, from making fools of each other (or themselves). For networks, methods of bulletproof communication are equally necessary and appreciated. Thus, it shouldn't surprise you to learn that the rules and formats that govern the methods by which computers communicate over a network are also called protocols.

How Webs talk: the HyperText Transfer Protocol (HTTP)

Because HTTP is an Internet protocol for a specific application — the World Wide Web — it rides at the top of the stack of protocols that make up the Internet. It provides a way for Web clients and servers to communicate with one another, primarily through the exchange of messages from clients (like, "give me this" or "get me that") and servers (like "here's the page you asked for" or "huh? I can't find what you're looking for").

In order to fully understand HTTP, you'd need to fully understand TCP/IP. A longish sort of acronym, TCP/IP stands for Transmission Control Protocol/Internet Protocol, the name given to the full set of protocols used on the Internet. To make things more confusing, TCP and IP are really the names of two separate but widely used protocols themselves, that give the forty-odd other protocols in the collection their collective name.

WARNING!

Acronymophobes, Beware!

One thing you've got to realize, if you're going to become a real WebMaster, is that when you climb onto the Web, you're joining the Internet community. If there's ever been an unabashed bastion for acronyms — those multi-letter combinations nerds use to refer to things like personal computers (PCs), a disk operating system (DOS), random access memory (RAM), or compact disk, read-only-memory (CD-ROM) — it's the Internet crowd.

While you're learning about Web lore, the term WebMaster is a ubiquitous name for a person who holds the Web protocols on high, is a vet-

ern of the Web trenches, and lives, eats, and breathes the Web. You might be lucky and good enough to be called a WebMaster yourself— some day!

So, if your most fiendish nightmare is of drowning in a bowl of alphabet soup, maybe you'd better rethink your Web-oriented efforts! That's because networking in general, and the Internet in particular, is a field that seems to revel in acronyms. When it comes to discussing Internet protocols, there's no better gathering spot for bizarre alphanumeric combinations.

Even more confusing, this collection of protocols — called a "protocol suite" — is often referred to simply as IP. Pronounced "eye pea," this double acronym is probably used just because the full acronym is too long to pronounce quickly. (TCP/IP is pronounced "tea see pea eye pea," and is a real mouthful; IP's a lot quicker!) However, TCP/IP is an umbrella standard; it is an abstraction of the other underlying protocols and makes it easier to talk about them as a group.

TECHNICAL STUFF

Welcome to the Nebulous Zone...

It's a place where different kinds of computers can freely exchange information with one another, where mere implementations bow to the demands of an all-encompassing standard. TCP/IP is a world unto itself: more bits use TCP/IP in a day on today's Internet than all the bits required to store every piece of printed material known to mankind before 1950.

When it comes to TCP/IP, there's a lot to learn, and a lot to know. Covering TCP/IP in any depth at all is way beyond the scope of this book. Therefore, we'd like to give you some choice references:

✔ The Internet is the subject of two books by the same authors, John R. Levine and Carol Baroudi: *The Internet for Dummies*, 2nd edition (IDG Books, 1994) and *More Internet for Dummies* (IDG Books, 1994). Both of these books are a good place for beginners to start investigating the basics of TCP/IP.

✔ John Quarterman and Smoot Carl-Mitchell are the authors of *Practical Internetworking with TCP/IP and UNIX* (Addison-Wesley, 1993). This book is aimed at the system or network administrator who

(continued)

works on a TCP/IP network, and wants to understand how things work, and why.

✔ *TCP/IP for Dummies* by Marshall Wilensky and Candace Leiden (IDG Books 1995) is a great place to continue your TCP/IP investigations. In addition to covering the topic in wonderfully amusing detail, it provides a gentle introduction to TCP/IP that is hard to beat.

✔ Matthew Flint Arnett is the first in a series of 14 co-authors for *Inside TCP/IP* (New Riders Press, 1994), another book aimed at helping those who must run a TCP/IP network or internetwork, or those who must oversee an Internet connection.

✔ O'Reilly & Associates covers TCP/IP with a Nutshell Handbook for UNIX system administrators, *TCP/IP Network Administration*, by Craig Hunt.

✔ A truly definitive look at TCP/IP comes from Douglas E. Comer, author of *Internetworking with TCP/IP*, a 3-volume set (Prentice-Hall, 1991, 1991, 1993; Volumes 2 and 3 were authored with David L. Stevens). Comer's books are widely regarded as the best general references on the subject.

✔ Another comprehensive two-volume treatise on TCP/IP is available from W.

Richard Stevens (assisted by Gary R. Wright on the second volume, Addison Wesley, 1994). These books are more up-to-date than Comer's, and offer detailed "war stories" taken straight from life on the Internet. For a reference that brings many salient TCP/IP details together in one place, this is a good choice.

✔ The ultimate authority on TCP/IP comes from a standards body called the Internet Architecture Board (IAB). Within the IAB, the Internet Engineering Task Force (IETF) is responsible for drafting and maintaining Internet standards of all kinds, including those for protocols, in the form of numbered documents called "Requests for Comment" (RFCs).

For a listing of all the current protocol-related RFCs, consult RFC 1720 "Internet Official Protocol Standards," which is available in at least three ways (if 1720 isn't current any more, it'll tell you it's been obsoleted by a new document, and you can follow a link to the new reigning standard).

If you take the time to poke around in the RFC collection, you'll be going straight to the horse's mouth, where TCP/IP and related matters are concerned!

Table 3-1: Three methods for examining RFCs

Service	Method
e-mail	send e-mail to mailserv@ds.internic.net with "file /ftp/rfc/rfc1720.txt" in the message body
FTP	anonymous FTP to DS.INTERNET.NET (password = your e-mail address);
	look in directory rfc/ for the file named rfc1720.txt
Web	<URL: http://www.cis.ohio-state.edu/htbin/rfc/rfc1720.html> for the contents of RFC 1720
	<URL: http://www.cis.ohio-state.edu/hypertext/information/rfc.html> has general RFC info

The straight dope on HTTP

As the client/server discussion should illustrate, protocols that link clients and servers together will have to address the issues related to handling requests and responses. Consequently, it should come as no surprise that information exchanges on the Web come in four parts, all classed as specific message types for HTTP:

1. **Connection:** this type of message occurs as a client tries to connect to a specific Web server (your browser may display a status message like "Connecting to HTTP Server"). If the client can't make the connection, the attempt will usually time out and the browser displays a "Connection timed out" message.

2. **Request:** this is where the client asks for the Web resource it's looking for. This includes the protocol to be used (which indicates the type of resource), the name of the object to be provided, and information about how the server should respond to the client.

3. **Response:** now it's the server's turn. If the server can deliver the requested object, it responds in the manner requested by the client to deliver the necessary data. If it can't deliver, it sends an error message explaining why not.

4. **Close:** after the information has been transferred in response to the request, the connection between client and server will be closed. It can easily be re-opened with another request — for example, by clicking on a link in the current object — but that jumps you back to step 1, where a connection must once again be established.

Once a requested object has been completely transferred, HTTP has done its job. Now it's up to the browser to interpret and display what the server has delivered, and another strand in the Web unfurls. From a distance, HTTP's job is to move requests from clients to servers, and responses from servers to clients. From a closer vantage point, HTTP actually takes advantage of a technique for aggregating message components into a single file that was developed to extend the capability of Internet e-mail.

This technique is called MIME (Multipurpose Internet Mail Extensions) which defines a way to bundle one or more attachments within a single message file. For instance, if you wanted to attach a document to an e-mail message, you'd simply enclose a copy of it as a MIME attachment. This allows a single network information transfer to move multiple items within a single package.

Because Web pages can include text, graphics, sound, and more, the ability to lump all these things together for a single network transfer makes an ideal fit between HTTP and MIME. Moving messages thus serves multiple masters on the Internet, including e-mail programs and Web responses and requests.

Since MIME is a well-understood and widely used extension to the Internet Simple Mail Transfer Protocol (SMTP) it is a service available to most Internet servers. For Web servers, it's a must!

HTML: HyperText Markup Language

Once the response to a Web request is returned by a Web server, it's the work of the browser to interpret and display the information.

What is HTML?

HTML is a markup language that describes the structure of a Web document's content plus some behavioral characteristics. It is a standard language that all Web browsers are able to understand and interpret. And now it's time to introduce another buzzword — HTML is a subset of a larger markup language, SGML, called Standard Generalized Markup Language. (That's as much as you need to know about SGML in order to write Web documents.)

HTML is a way of representing text, and linking that text to other kinds of resources — including sound files, graphics files, multimedia files, etc. — that allows these different kinds of data to be displayed together, to let them augment and reinforce one another.

As delivered by a Web server, HTML is nothing more than a plain text file that includes two kinds of text:

1. **the content:** text or information to be displayed or played back on the client's screen, speakers, etc.
2. **the markup:** text or information to control the display, or to point to other information items in need of display or playback.

The browser must also be prepared to convert a third kind of data — encoded files — and to hand them off to the right kind of facility. This might involve a graphics program for an icon or image, a sound player program to handle audio, a video player program to play back a video file, or whatever else is needed to reproduce a particular kind of information.

A usual cast of characters

By itself, though, HTML is simply a string of characters. Some of these characters represent content, which has to be displayed for the client in some form or fashion. Others represent format, placement, or handling controls that control where the content is placed, and how it is handled within the browser, or which point to other nontext sources of information.

In its most formal sense, HTML is a descriptive markup language that defines the structure and behavior of a document and allows the client to render each document's element in a particular way

In reality, however, HTML files include both control information and content, which together describe the appearance and contents of Web pages, the basic unit for how Web information is displayed and handled by clients. This book will teach you how to organize and situate content, but it will primarily focus on how to take advantage of the controls that HTML provides.

Text for content, tags for control

From another perspective, HTML consists of a collection of special text tags and symbols, used by browsers to render the content information supplied for Web pages.

Thus, HTML is a way to describe the structure, layout, and behavior of a Web document, and it is the basic mechanism for distributing information on the WWW.

Finally, HTML provides the mechanisms for tying in the other Internet protocols and services available through the Web — like FTP, Gopher, USENET, e-mail, WAIS, Telnet, and HTTP — so that Web pages can deliver many kinds of resources.

Accessing the Web

The crucial ingredient in gaining access to the Web — the one that makes it live up to two of the three W's in its name (World Wide, that is) — is an attachment to the Internet. As you'll learn in this book, it's possible to set up private Webs that are either restricted to your own machine, or to a purely local network. But that's not where the Web as we know it gets its reach, or its incredible range and depth. That's what makes Internet access crucial.

In fact, the biggest constraint on your enjoyment of the Web is likely to be the size of the "pipe" that connects you to it, and it to you. The term "pipe" refers to how much data the connection between you and the Web server can accommodate; like a water pipe, the more capacious the connection between you and your server, the faster things can move. Since waiting for screens to complete is the biggest drag there is, the faster the data goes, the better you'll like it!

When it comes to Internet link-ups, there are basically two ways to go:

1. Over the telephone system, and into another computer or network that's connected to the Internet.

2. Over a network, and onto the Internet (or onto another computer that's properly connected).

In virtually every case, the size of the pipe provided by option 1 is going to be considerably smaller than option 2. Even so, if you're trying to get connected from home, or don't have access to a direct network link, that option can still be made workable, if you take the right approach.

The Web by phone, and more...

For many dedicated Web-heads, the Plain Old Telephone Systems (POTS) is the only way to get to other computers. The phone system is their link to the world, whether on or off the Internet, or for online information services like CompuServe, America Online, GEnie, Prodigy, or whathaveyou.

The Web's client/server nature requires a different kind of connection than more ordinary Internet links (or the kinds of links used for most other online services). Because the browser acts as an independent front end, it must be able to "join up" to the network, and use TCP/IP protocols directly. This in turn, normally requires a dial-up IP connection to the network, which in turn requires that the low-level protocol used over the phone lines be one of the following protocols:

- ✔ **SLIP (Serial Line Interface Protocol):** this is the original implementation of TCP/IP communications over phone lines; as such, it's a bit slower and clunkier than the others we'll mention. It's OK to use it, but only if one of the others isn't available or appropriate (or if the others cost too much).

- ✔ **PPP (Point-to-Point Protocol):** this is a more modern communications protocol for normal telephone or synchronous lines. It has lower overhead, offers better performance, and handles connections more robustly than SLIP.

- ✔ **Multilink PPP (MPPP):** this is a method for combining multiple PPP connections to aggregate bandwidth, which is a complicated way of informing you that MPPP lets you add multiple smaller pipes to create a single bigger one. Unless you plan on adding multiple phone lines together, or are using ISDN (Integrated Services Digital Network), MPPP is probably not an option for you today.

These options are listed in order of speed, bandwidth, and expense. In order to use them, you must make prior arrangements with your Internet service provider (or the company on the other end of the call, if you dial into a private network to access the Internet). Where you might expect to pay from ten to twenty dollars a month for a vanilla dial-up connection to the Internet, expect to pay upwards of twenty dollars a month for these types of connections, depending on the level of service you need.

For a current list of Internet access providers, take a look at the following URL:

```
http://www.digital.com/gnn/helpdesk/access/index.html
```

The Web via ISDN

For years now, tongue-in-cheek pundits have claimed that ISDN stands for "I Still Don't Know" rather than the more official translation (Integrated Services Digital Network). However, ISDN is starting to find toeholds all over the United States (and in other pockets around the globe), especially in the areas served by Pacific Bell, Southwestern Bell, and Nynex (all are Regional Bell Operating Companies, or RBOCs).

To make things far simpler than they deserve to be, ISDN lets your computer take advantage of a pure digital network that the phone company can bring to your door. Most ISDN interfaces provide one or two 64 Kbps channels between you and your Internet provider. ISDN offers more bandwidth than normal telephone lines to start with. Because it's digital (not analog like POTS lines), ISDN also offers a more direct type of computer-to-computer link-up, without the digital-to-analog and reverse conversions required when using POTS.

Of bandwidth and throughput...

When it comes to measuring data pipes, computer jocks like to talk about something called "bandwidth." What they're talking about is the maximum amount of data that the pipe can carry at any given moment. That's why you'll see terms like "usable bandwidth" in some technical materials — this refers to the amount of capacity that the data can actually occupy.

A helpful techno-synonym for usable bandwidth is "throughput," which refers to the amount of data that can be *put through* a connection (or pipe, as we're calling it here) in a given amount of time. Don't let these terms lead you too far astray, though — they're really just trying to tell you how fast information can move!

TECHNICAL STUFF

For modem Web access, more is clearly better

No matter what kind of connection you obtain, you'll want to buy the fastest modem that your provider can support. Today, most providers offer 14.4 Kbps connections for V.32/V.42 modems, and some providers are starting to offer 28.8 Kbps connections for V.34/V.42 modems.

Even though faster connections cost more, it's best to get as much bandwidth as you can afford for Web access, because of the volume of data that's so often involved. Table 3-2 outlines the kind of performance you can expect at typical dial-up speeds when transferring a 1 megabyte file.

It should be obvious that faster is better, in terms of raw performance. The fastest modems provide response times that are much more acceptable than the slowest ones, particularly for Web use. There's another conclusion to draw from this table — namely, that 4-to-1 compression provided by V.42bis protocols are well worthwhile, and can bring response times for even a relatively sizable Web graphic down to a tolerable level.

That's why we say that when it comes to modems, more is clearly better. Most cost-benefit studies for systems that charge by the hour of connect time — and this applies squarely to most Internet providers — show that for heavy users a faster modem can pay for itself in as little as two months, and for more occasional users, in six months. This may propel your interest and use of the Web, but it will also make your time online more productive!

Table 3-2: Times to transfer a 1 MB file (assuming 10% overhead on actual data transferred, except for ISDN)

Modem Speed	Transfer Rate	Achieved Compression	Transfer Rate After Compression
2.4 Kbps	469.3 sec	9.6 Kbps	117.3 sec
4.8 Kbps	234.7 sec	19.2 Kbps	58.7 sec
9.6 Kbps	117.3 sec	38.4 Kbps	29.3 sec
14.4 Kbps	78.2 sec	57.6 Kbps	19.55 sec
19.6 Kbps	57.5 sec	78.4 Kbps	14.4 sec
23.8 Kbps	47.3 sec	95.2 Kbps	11.8 sec
28.8 Kbps	39.1 sec	115.2 Kbps	9.8 sec
ISDN (64 Kbps)	16 sec	256 Kbps	4 sec

The upshot, as Table 3-2 shows, is that ISDN runs quite a bit faster than modem connections, assuming equivalent compression across the two technologies. If you can get ISDN in your neighborhood, and can afford the installation and monthly fees, it may be your ticket to the fast lane on the Infobahn. It certainly takes the sting out of Web use. However, ISDN is a "bridge" technology; bridging the POTS of the past and present, and ATM technologies of the future. It has an anticipated short life span and the hardware needed to implement ISDN is still pricey.

For more information on ISDN, check out these URLs:

```
http://www.pacbell.com/isdn/isdn_home.html
http://www.bellcore.com/ISDN/ISDN.html
```

The Web by network

Most network technologies today run at least 64 times faster than ISDN (4 Megabit Token-ring, for instance). Table 3-3 outlines the speeds of most common networking technologies, compared to ISDN. It should be pretty clear from the numbers that even though there's no compression over the network, that lack doesn't amount to much!

Table 3-3: Times to transfer a 1 MB file for ISDN and common networking technologies

Connection	Transfer
2.5 Mbps ARCnet	0.40 sec
4 Mbps Token ring	0.25 sec
10 Mbps Ethernet (56%)	0.18 sec
16 Mbps Token ring	0.06 sec
100 Mbps technologies	0.01 sec
ISDN (256 Kbps compressed)	4.00 sec

Upon profound reflection, we'd have to say that network access to the Web is definitely the way to go, if the option's open to you!

The only way to get network access to the Web is to have access to an existing network — usually at your workplace; they're not too popular for the home market yet. That network must also be connected to the Internet in some form or fashion, usually at fractional T-1 speeds of 56 Kbps or faster.

The reason why the network is preferable is purely because it's the fastest way for you and your favorite Web servers to get together!

When Web access happens

So you've got the right software — a browser and the underlying TCP/IP support — and an Internet connection, all primed and ready to go. What actually happens when you supply a URL to your browser?

With all the right ingredients, it's nothing more than the request-response messages that HTTP provides. Suppose, for example, you're requesting a Web page:

1. The browser sends a message to the server specified in the URL to try to establish a connection, which the server either accepts or denies. (If the domain name part of the URL is invalid, the browser waits a certain period of time to inform the user that the server could not be found.)

2. The browser sends a request for a Web page.

3. The server responds with the page (and appropriate actions follow).

4. When the transfer is complete, the connection is broken, ready to be reactivated, or reused by someone else.

5. The browser begins the job of interpreting the information delivered from the Web server to drive its corresponding display.

The only difference between methods of access — be they telephone, ISDN, or network-based — is the speed with which the steps get completed. In case you haven't already figured it out, most of the communications time is spent in doing Step 3. In the next chapter, you'll finally get to more of the details of Step 5, which is the true focus of this book.

Part II
Building Better
Web Pages

In This Part...

There's more to establishing a presence on the Web than mastering the ins and outs of hypertext. Nevertheless, the foundation for Web pages is built atop HTML, the HyperText Markup Language used to define and describe Web Pages.

Part II is your introduction to HTML, and starts with an overview of HTML basics and capabilities, along with an analysis of a typical Web page layout. For the first time you'll learn what makes HTML tick, what it can do on its own, and where it needs help in dealing with the many forms that Web information can take.

As you step through the analysis of a Web page, you should begin to appreciate how simple and straightforward HTML can be. You should also understand clearly how important it is to remember that any Web page is just a means to an end — the real goal is to communicate clearly, effectively, and as entertainingly as possible. As you learn some of the elements of effective page style and design, this goal should become your ultimate goal as well.

As the pyramids of Egypt so eloquently demonstrate, simple tools and technologies do not have to produce bland, simple results. They can also produce monumental creations that speak to everyone who visits them.

Chapter 4

Getting Hyper

● ●

In This Chapter

▶ Understanding basic HTML concepts

▶ Linking up the strands in the Web

▶ Looking for hypertext examples

▶ Getting past hypertext, to hypermedia

▶ Going for the graphics

▶ Dealing with multimedia display/playback

▶ Bringing multiple media together on the Web

● ●

*T*he real secret behind the HyperText Markup Language is that there is no secret: Everything's out in the open in an HTML document, just waiting for the right interpretation. The beauty of HTML is that it is just a stream of plain characters, which makes any half-witted text editor a potential HTML generator. The challenge of HTML is that it is very sensitive to the order in which those characters occur, and the way that they get used, to produce the right results.

Even though HTML can be very forgiving if certain elements are omitted or misstated, the best way to work within HTML is to understand and work within its structure. Because there are so many different browsers for Web pages, you'll want to get consistent appearance and behavior for everyone who reads your HTML document. The only way to make this happen is to know the rules and use them to your readers' best advantage!

In this chapter, you'll learn about the fundamental ideas behind HTML, and about the concepts and operation of hypertext. Along the way, you should also begin to appreciate some of the basics behind building well-structured, readable Web pages.

HTML Basics

HTML stands for HyperText Markup Language. Its name reflects the two key concepts that make it work, and that make the World Wide Web such an incredible phenomenon:

1. **HyperText:** A way of creating multimedia documents. Also, a method for providing links, within (or across) documents.
2. **Markup Language:** A method for embedding special tags that describe the structure as well as the behavior of a document (not a way of discussing the younger generation's efforts with crayons on the wall!).

The simplicity and power of HTML markup makes it easy for anyone to create Web documents, for private or public use. The power of hypertext, with its built-in support for multimedia and document links, creates the threads that compose the incredible breadth and reach of the Web. It's so easy and straight-forward, anyone can do it — as long as you can play the game by its rules.

Of Links and Sausages

HTML supports links within the same document and to completely different data somewhere else on the Web. Both types of links work the same way: you simply put the correct HTML tags around text or graphics to create an active (linked) area. Then when someone visits your Web site and clicks on the active area, they're transported either within the same file or off to another place on the Net. Figure 4-1 shows a block of text from Carl de Cordova's Web Developer's HotList that includes links to several resources on HTML (they're the underlined items beneath the heading "HTML Development" that read "Creating a Web site," "A Beginner's Guide to HTML," etc.). Each of these links can carry you off to a valuable source of HTML information.

The method of indicating a link varies from one browser to the next but all browsers give some kind of visual clue that you're selecting an active area of the screen. You may see text underlined in a bright color, font changed to bold, or a graphic outlined in a contrasting color.

Jumping around inside documents

One variety of link connects points inside the same document. WebMasters often use this kind of link from a table of contents at the top of an HTML file, to the related sections throughout the document.

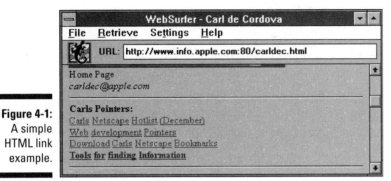

Figure 4-1:
A simple
HTML link
example.

This points to a key advantage of hypertext — namely, the ability to circumvent the linear nature of paper documents by providing rapid, obvious ways to navigate within (or among) documents. Sure, you could do the same thing with the table of contents or the index for a paper book, but you'd have to do more work yourself, and spend some time flipping pages. Hypertext automates this for you, making it effortless to jump inside and between documents by creating links that are easy to use.

Jumping across documents (and services)

By using a combination of links and Uniform Resource Locators (URLs), HTML can also provide links that point to other Web pages. Because URLs can reference a variety of protocols and services on the Internet (not just other HTML files), you can link through Telnet, WAIS, Gopher, FTP, USENET newsgroups, and to e-mail responses to queries or forms.

The same hypertext technology that lets you jump around inside a document also provides a way of reaching any other resource available through the Web, so long as you know its exact address. This simple text tagging technique provides any Web document with the potential of reaching any other Internet resource. It erases the difference between "here" and "there" with a single click of the mouse (or selection of the right text field).

Not all of these resources would be germane to any particular topic or focus, so universal access is kind of silly. But the work of individual authors to include links to other documents that they believe are relevant is what has led to the construction of the Web as we know it today. That is, it's not only the documents that make up the Web, it's the links between them that constitute its many evanescent threads.

Whenever you reference a URL in an HTML document, try to cut and paste the URL from a browser if at all possible. You'll save time on typing — some URLs can get pretty long — and even better, you'll be sure to get the reference right, especially if you test the URL with a browser before copying it, to make sure it's still valid. ▪

In the most literal way, the Web is made of the links that all the many Web authors have included in their Web pages. These links can span the world or point to another document on the same Web server. Either way, jumping across them is as easy as selecting a link, and waiting for it to download on your screen. The strands in the Web are made of those links among documents that tie people, ideas, and arbitrary locations together.

You've Used Hypertext, Without Even Knowing It

At this point, you may be saying something like, "What is this Hypertext stuff?" While it may seem strange and exotic, you're probably much more familiar with hypertext than you think. Your own desktop, in fact, may be home to several hypertext applications that you use regularly.

For example, if you're a Microsoft Windows user, every time you run the Windows Help utility, you're using a hypertext application. Figure 4-2, for instance, shows a screen that covers some of Microsoft's technical support options. The four buttons on the upper portion of the screen shot are labeled: "Contents," "Search," "Back," and "History." These work very much like the navigation tools for a Web browser, in that they can let you see and return to where you've been (Back and History), or examine the range of available links within a document (Contents and Search).

Macintosh users should be able to identify HyperCard or SuperCard as forms of hypertext; others will have to take our word for it, and not assume these are games of chance! Here again, there are common concepts with the Web: some kind of home page, various navigation tools (shaped arrows and specific commands), multimedia data, and plenty of links to select.

Likewise, UNIX users familiar with FrameMaker or other multimedia authoring tools should also be able to find some common ground with the Web's hypertext capabilities. Once again, the concepts of a home page, document navigation and linkage, and integrated multimedia, help to realize the notion of hypertext and how it operates.

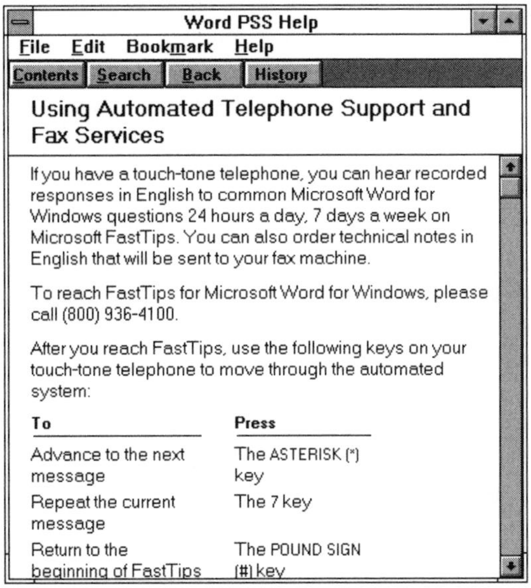

Figure 4-2:
Microsoft's
Windows
Help engine
is a well-
known
example of
hypertext.

The differences among all these examples and the Web is the kinds of links that are supported: Only the Web offers the ability to jump across the Internet to follow links to other Web documents and servers. This is what gives HTML its unique value and, of course, what's made the Web possible.

Beyond Text, There's Multimedia

When it comes to including non-text files (like sound, graphics, and video) in Web pages, there's a certain amount of alchemy involved. In Chapter 3, you learned how shipping Web information in MIME format makes it possible for a Web server to deliver multiple forms of information to your browser in a single information transfer. Here, you'll learn a little more about how this works.

When a MIME file with attachments shows up at your workstation, additional processing begins to occur immediately. The text portion of the message file arrives first. This part contains the text-only HTML page description, which means the browser can get right to work building and displaying the text portions of the page. This is why you'll see placeholders or icons for graphics when Web pages are first displayed. The placeholders get replaced with graphics or other forms of data once the relevant attachments have been received.

As the page is being displayed, the browser is receiving attachments in the background. As they're received, they're identified by a file type, or description information in the attachment tag, as specified by the MIME format. Once a file has been identified, it can then be handled for playback or display. Table 4-1 provides a list of common file types, including expansions for the inevitable acronyms such files can often entail.

Table 4-1: Common sound, graphics, and motion-video formats

Extension	Format	Explanation
Sound Formats		
SBI	Sound Blaster Instrument	Used for a single instrument with Sound Blaster cards (multi-instrument: .IBK).
SND, AU	8khz mulaw	Voice-grade sound format used on work-stations (e.g., Sun, NeXT, HP9000, etc.).
WAV	Microsoft Waveform	Sound format used in Windows for event notification.
Still-Video (Graphics) Formats		
BMP	Windows Bitmap	Native Windows display format, similar format used for OS/2. Uncompressed, large file sizes common.
EPS	Encapsulated PostScript	Form of PostScript intended for use within other files (embedded use).
GIF	Graphics Interchange Format	Compressed graphics format commonly used on CompuServe, easy to render multi-platform. Can be interleaved or not, depending on how image is created.
JPEG, JPG	Joint Photographic Experts Group	Highly compressed format for still images, widely used for multi-platform graphics.
PCD	Kodak Photo CD	Kodak's proprietary CD-ROM photograph format.
PCX	Zsoft Image	Format developed by Zsoft for PC Paint-brush, used in many graphics and desktop publishing programs.

Extension	Format	Explanation
PDF	Portable Document Format	Adobe's format for multiplatform document access through its Acrobat software.
PS	PostScript	Adobe's type description language, used to deliver complex documents that include layout, font descriptions, and graphics over the Internet.
RLE	Run-Length Encoding	Technique for compressing Windows BMP files.
TGA,VDA, ICB, VST	Targa formats	Formats created by Truevision for use with their 24-bit high-resolution graphics hardware ("Targa boards"); now used by several high-resolution graphics vendors.
TIFF,TIF	Tagged Image File Format	Supports up to 24-bit color images across a variety of formats, files may be compressed or uncompressed, not all TIFF implementations work with all viewers.
WPG	WordPerfect Graphic	WordPerfect's format for graphics information.
XBM	X-Window Bitmap	Image bitmap used by X-Windows, primarily on UNIX workstations.

Motion-Video Formats

Extension	Format	Explanation
AVI	Audio Video Interleaved	Microsoft's Video for Windows standard format; found on many CD-ROMs.
DVI	Digital Video Interactive	Another motion-video format, also found on CD-ROMs.
FLI	Flick	Autodesk Animator motion-video format.
MOV	QuickTime	Apple's motion video and audio format; originated on the Macintosh, but also available for Windows.
MPEG, MPG	Motion Picture Experts Group	Full-motion video standard using frame format similar to JPEG with variable compression capabilities.

Hyperhelpers: useful "helper" applications

When referenced by a Web page, non-text data shows up as attachments to the HTML file. Sometimes the browser itself will handle playback or display: this is very often the case for simple, two-dimensional graphics, including .GIF and .JPEG files. Even so, these may be handled by other applications (especially when using character-mode Web browsers like Lynx).

But when other kinds of files show up and are identified, they require specialized capabilities beyond the scope of most browsers. In that case, such files will be handed off to other applications for playback or display, where those applications have the built-in smarts to handle the formats and processing necessary to deliver the contents of those files on demand. It normally works something like this:

✔ The browser builds a page display that includes an active region (underlined or outlined in some way) to indicate that sound, video, or animation playback is attached.

✔ If the user selects the active region (the link), the browser calls on another application to handle playback or display.

✔ The other application takes over and either plays back or displays the file.

✔ When the display or playback is complete, the browser reasserts control, and the user can continue on (or select the active region again, and get another playback or display).

The applications that provide this kind of assistance to a Web browser are called "helper applications," because they augment its functionality. It's becoming a standard part of browser configuration to supply the names and locations of helper programs to assist the browser when such data arrives. If no helper application is available, the browser will simply not respond to an attempt to display or play back the requested information.

For instance, WPlany and Wham are two common shareware sound player applications for PCs running Windows. Most browsers supply a method for linking particular file types (like the .SBI and .WAV file extensions common on the PC) with a helper application, as part of their configuration or setup.

By establishing an association between the sound playback application WPlany or Wham, and the related audio file extensions, the browser will automatically launch whichever application you designate whenever it encounters files with those extensions. This will cause the sounds to play (which we assume is a good thing!).

You can find Wplany and Wham at:

```
ftp://ftp.ncsa.uiuc.edu/Web/Mosaic/Windows/viewers/wplny09b.zip
ftp://ftp.law.cornell.edu/pub/LII/Cello/wham131.zip
```

Other useful helper applications for Windows include:

- **for still graphics:** Lview is a good, small graphics viewer that can handle .GIF, .PCX, and .JPEG files. It also supports interesting image editing capabilities (see Chapter 9 for more details). You can find Lview at the following URL:

  ```
  ftp://ftp.ncsa.uiuc.edu/Web/Mosaic/Windows/viewers/lviewp1a.zip
  ```

- **for video:** You'll want to use either QuickTime for Windows (for Quick-Time movies) or MPEGplay for .MPEG video files. You can find these applications at:

  ```
  ftp://ftp.ncsa.uiuc.edu/Web/Mosaic/Windows/viewers/mpegw32h.zip
  ftp://ftp.ncsa.uiuc.edu/Web/Mosaic/Windows/viewers/qtw11.zip
  ```

- **for PostScript viewing:** Ghostview for Windows works with a companion program called Ghostscript that allows users to view or print PostScript files from any source, including the Web. Since so many documents on the Internet are published in this format, we've found this to be a useful program. You can find it at:

  ```
  ftp://ftp.law.cornell.edu/pub/LII/Cello/gswin.zip
  ```

All in all, a good set of helper applications can make your browser even more effective at bringing the wonders of the Web to your desktop. With the right help, it should be able to play back or render just about anything you'll run into!

The value of visuals

There's no doubt that graphics add a lot of impact and interest to Web pages, but there's a price to pay for the extra punch that they provide. It's easy to get carried away by the appeal of pictures, and to overdo their use on Web pages. This applies as much to the small images used as buttons and visual on-screen controls as it does to large images that help to dress up or expand the content of any particular page.

When using graphics, it's important to remember two things:

1. Not everybody reading your page can see the graphics. This may be because they're using a character-mode browser that can't display them, or because they've decided to switch graphics display off (a common option for most Web browsers) to conserve bandwidth and improve response time.

2. Graphics files — even compressed ones — can sometimes be quite large, often ten or more times greater in size than the HTML file that they're attached to. Moving graphics across the network takes time, and consumes bandwidth. It also penalizes users attached to narrower pipes far more than those attached directly to the Internet.

There will be times when graphics are essential — for example when using a diagram or illustration to explain your material. There are also situations where impact is important — for example on a home page where you'll be making a first impression. In these circumstances, it's perfectly appropriate to use graphics, but be sensitive to the different capabilities and bandwidths of your readers.

Here are some rules of thumb for using graphics effectively in your Web pages (as you examine the work of others, see what happens to your attitude when some or all of these rules are violated):

✔ Keep your graphics small and uncomplicated whenever possible. This reduces file sizes and keeps transfer times down.

✔ Use compressed formats whenever possible (like .GIF and .JPEG) to keep file sizes smaller.

✔ If you must use larger, more complex graphics, create a small version (called a thumbnail) for inclusion in your page, and make the thumbnail a link to the full-size version. This will spare casual readers the impact of downloading the larger version every time they access the page (and will keep Internet usage under better control, making you a better netizen!).

✔ Keep the number of graphic elements on a page to a minimum. Practically speaking, this means two or three graphic items at most per page, where one or two of them would contain compact, icon-like navigation controls, and the other would be a content-specific graphic. Here again, the idea is to limit page complexity and to speed up transfer times. ■

Sometimes, the temptation to violate these rules of thumb will be nearly overwhelming. If you must break the rules, be sure to run your results past some disinterested third parties (you'll learn more about testing techniques in Part VI of this book). Watch them read your pages if you can, but listen carefully to their feedback to see if you've merely bent these rules, or broken them to smithereens!

Also, remembering that not everybody who accesses the Web can see your graphics should help to keep you humble. For readers who don't have access to graphical browsers, try to think of ways to enhance their reading experience even without graphics.

Mavens of multimedia

Everything that goes for graphics, goes double for other forms of multimedia. If graphics files are large compared to HTML text files, sound and video files are huge. Although they're appealing and certainly do add considerable interest to some topics, they're not germane to every topic on the Web.

Here again, the trick is to make large files available through links, rather than including them on pages that everyone will probably try to download. It's also a good idea to label the active regions with the file size so people know what they're in for if they choose to download it. (Warning! This points to a 40K sound byte of a barking seal.) ∎

Bringing It All Together with the Web

The key to building good Web pages is in their content. If the content is well-organized, engaging, and contains links to interesting places, the Web can be a potent tool for education and communication. If not, it can be an exercise in sheer frustration (and humiliation for the WebMaster!).

Because the capabilities of individual browsers are so different, the content remains the major component that all readers will have in common. Therefore, if you put your energy into providing high-quality content, and link your readers to other important and valuable pages, your Web site will be a howling success. If you don't, your site will be the electronic equivalent of a ghost town!

In the next chapter, you'll have a chance to understand what's involved in using — and building — documents for use on the Web, as you fly into our parlor for a look at what's in (and on) a Web page.

Chapter 5

What's in a Page?

* * *

* * *

*T*he trick to understanding HTML lies in knowing how to separate the content from the controls. Content can be presented in a plain ASCII file with no tagging whatsoever. If you look at an HTML source file, you'll see some markup in the file that doesn't show up when your browser displays the page. While it may not show up on the screen, it is crucial to controlling how the Web page looks and acts.

The really interesting parts of HTML are the combinations of form and content, like the commands used to entitle pages, or that control textual guideposts like headers, graphics, lists of elements, and more. Learning how to read and understand HTML depends on being able to separate the structure from the controls.

Learning how to build good Web pages requires that you not only understand this distinction, but that you be able to use it to its best effect. In this chapter, you'll begin to appreciate the components of a Web page, and how these pieces can be brought together to create readable Web documents.

It's All in the Layout

The human eye is a marvelous instrument — it's capable of distinguishing incredible amounts of information, and of scanning large amounts of material to zero in on the most important things.

When it comes to building Web pages, your job as a designer is to aid the eye in recognizing salient features or elements, and in locating the items of interest quickly and efficiently. Nothing communicates this concern — or its lack — more quickly than a document's layout.

The layout is nothing more than the way the visual elements of a document are arranged, from a fairly gross perspective. Layout doesn't usually concern itself with the placement of individual text elements on a page. Rather, layout is a way of designing and describing what a page looks like as a whole — namely, the number of elements it contains, how they are arranged, and how much white space is around them.

This means the layout of a document — be it a Web page, a letter to your sister, or an advertisement in a magazine — is a crucial part of communicating with a reader. For materials where interest is mandatory, layout may not appear to be important at all (this may explain why tax forms are so boring to look at). For content where interest has to be generated, layout is at least as important as the information a document delivers, if not more so!

Think of all the textbooks you've slogged through where the text was all crammed together, and the graphics and text ran right into each other. Perhaps it was more important to save money by squeezing as much information as possible onto a page, than it was to make the information intelligible and understandable. Even though layout may not have been a concern here, it helps to explain why some reading materials are so much easier to fall asleep over than others. (And you're all still awake, RIGHT?)

By comparison, think of some print or television advertising you've seen lately. The people who designed them assume they have to hook their readers or viewers, and they do this by creating eye-catching images, using appealing language, and by combining the elements of their communications to be as arresting as possible.

When it comes to building Web pages, you may assume that your job is not as challenging as the one faced by advertising designers. By the same token, you shouldn't assume that because your material is of such great interest to the world at large, that your Web pages can stress content at the expense of layout. Fortunately you can do a lot with HTML to make your pages easy to read and navigate.

Because attention to layout adds to the accessibility of any document, you'll be doing your readers a service by building a good layout. At the same time that you're making it more pleasant for them to read, you'll deliver the content more quickly and effectively. There are lots of opinions as to what constitutes a good layout, and there's plenty of room for variation within the bounds of effective document design. Throughout the rest of this chapter you'll be learning ways to design documents not just to get your ideas across, but to communicate them readily and effectively.

What Are You Trying to Say?

As markup languages go, HTML is fairly simple and easy to learn. Unfortunately, this creates a nearly overwhelming temptation to rush right out and start building pages, as soon as the need for Web-based publishing asserts itself.

Whether you're an individual trying to share information with others, or an organization trying to advertise its products and services, the impetus is powerful to publish online as quickly as possible. Nevertheless, we'd advise you to step back and do a little analysis and design work before trying to build "killer Web pages" on the fly.

Who's listening?

Knowing your audience is a hypercritical requirement for building quality Web pages. If you don't know who is likely to visit your Web site, and why they're passing through, you won't be able to tell them what they're trying to find out.

It's important to start any document design based on certain assumptions about the audience. While this is as true for advertisements as it is for encyclopedias, the focus is a little more intense and urgent for the former than the latter. You could do worse than to create the interest and impact of an advertisement, but you'll want to do more than most ads can do—namely, to deliver the content that your audience is most likely to want.

How can you get to know your audience? Think of it as a form of hunting: identify your target group, and then start hanging around their haunts, whether in cyberspace or in the real world. Once you understand their interests, you'll be able to meet their needs and give due consideration to the other factors that can hook them into your content. While you're at it, it's a really good idea to deliver solid, usable information for your target group, because that's what will keep them coming back for more (and will make them spread the word about what you have to offer).

Design springs from content — and intent

The more complex the idea or concept you're presenting, the more difficult effective design becomes. Likewise, the more material you're covering, the more critical are to the organization and navigation tools and to the document's structure and design. In other words, long or complicated documents take more forethought than short, simple ones.

Creating an outline before you start writing (or programming in HTML, for that matter) will usually be sufficient to help you figure out how to organize your information. The outline should also help you to decide the order of topics and coverage, and to determine the need for graphics, sound, or other multimedia information sources.

Knowing the various topics and identifying elements of a document will also help you to understand the relationships between those components (and possibly other information on the Web). This will play a key role in establishing links, and presenting visual clues to your readers on how to read and navigate the information your document contains.

The intent behind a document — whether to inform, educate, persuade, or question — must also play a role in its design.

- ✔ If your goal is to inform, you'll be less inclined to include eye-catching displays, and more inclined to direct readers right to the information your document contains.
- ✔ If your goal is to persuade or sell, you'll try to hook readers with compelling visuals and riveting testimonials as a way to provoke their interest, and then follow through with the important details.
- ✔ If your goal is to question something, you'll raise the issues to be queried early on, and provide pointers to additional discussion and related information afterward.

In each case, the goal behind the document strongly conditions its execution and delivery. That's why understanding your intent is so important to building the right kind of document.

Establish your key messages

At the beginning of your document design, you need to answer the question at the head of this section — namely, "What are you trying to say?" One way to approach this is to write down the key ideas or messages that you want to convey. Then, follow them up with supporting points or other relevant information to make your case, prove your point, or otherwise substantiate what you're saying.

If you follow this exercise carefully, you'll find much of the content emerging gracefully from your outline. You'll also find that the important relationships among the various elements of your document (and other documents) will more or less establish themselves as you work your way through the outlining process.

Think about superstructure and information flow

Superstructure refers to the formal mechanics of how you communicate a document's organization and navigation. This includes things like:

- ✔ a table of contents
- ✔ a set of common controls
- ✔ an index
- ✔ a glossary of technical terms

In short, the superstructure is the wrapping that you build around your content to help readers find their way to the information they want, and to help them understand what it is they're reading or viewing. For any given document, you might not need every possible element of superstructure, but for most documents — especially longer ones — some elements of superstructure will be helpful, others downright essential.

The TOC (Table of Contents)

From a lifetime of exposure to printed materials, we've come to expect to find a table of contents at the head of most documents, to lay out their topics and coverage. The beauty of hypertext is that you can build links that will take readers from any entry in the TOC to the corresponding information in the document. Thus, the TOC becomes not just an organizational map for your document, but also a navigation tool.

There are some dangers in this approach, though. The idea of a hyperlinked TOC is that you are invited to follow interesting links from it. You arrive at the target information and follow another interesting, related link. This can be repeated numerous times until your curiosity is quenched and you realize that you're "lost in space!" It's quite possible to navigate many links away from the original TOC, so that finding it again can prove exhausting or downright aggravating. That's why consistent navigation controls are so important to document design — i.e., a link to the TOC on every page or at least links to every section header. (You don't want your Web site nicknamed "No Exit.")

Common controls for all screens

To promote readability and familiarity within your Web site, it's a good idea to include common controls for each individual document. This might consist of a set of clickable icons to go backward or forward a page, to jump back to the TOC, or to return to the Home Page for your document. If you've included a search tool for keywords in the document, make it accessible from any point in any of your documents. Whatever you do, establish a common look and feel for your pages and your readers will find it much easier to navigate. Consistency may be "the last refuge for the unimaginative," but it does promote familiarity and ease of use!

For more information on these controls, and some common page designs for longer, more complex documents, please consult Chapters 22 and 27. ▪

An index, or a search engine...

Helping readers locate keywords or individual topics can often help them get the best use out of your content. One of the best things about hypertext is that an old-fashioned index may not be necessary: because all of your content is online and accessible to the computer, you can often replace the functionality of an index with a built-in search engine for your information space.

Chapter 16 includes a discussion of search engines, including tools you can use to provide index capabilites for your documents. ▪

A glossary helps manage specialized terms and language

If you're covering an area that's full of jargon, technical terms, or other forms of arcane gibberish beloved by experts and feared by newcomers, you may find it useful to include a glossary with your Web pages. Fortunately, HTML includes a text style specifically built for defining terms, making it easy to construct a glossary whenever you need one. Alas, you'll still have to come up with the definitions yourself!

Making superstructure provide structure that's super

Given a choice between a large, complex page, and a collection of simpler, interrelated pages, you probably realize by now that breaking big chunks of information into smaller ones is a good thing to do when designing a document. This lets readers grab the information in small doses that impose less waiting and frustration between bites, and doesn't require them to download more information than they may ultimately be interested in reading.

For short, simple documents superstructure may seem like overkill, but it can have a role even in a one-screen layout, like a personal home page. When it comes to organizing and delivering more complex collections of information, careful use of superstructure guarantees your readers a more positive visit to your site.

The audience is listening...

If you've ever had the pleasure of viewing a movie at a THX-equipped theater, the phrase at the head of this section is a dead giveaway to its topic. If not, the phrase comes up at the conclusion of the THX demonstration, which usually happens after the trailers, just prior to the screening of today's feature presentation.

The THX demonstration consists of a simple "THX" graphic that fills the entire screen. It's accompanied by a loud, sustained orchestral chord, overlaid with a powerful pipe organ, that goes on for about 90 seconds. At first, the note builds to an almost painful level, and then fades away slowly, leaving on a low pedal-tone from the organ (about 30 Hz, Ed's trained ear tells him). Having raised the audience nearly out of its seats, the demonstration concludes with the words "the audience is listening."

If you've never seen it, you'll just have to believe that the audience is indeed listening — if not cowering — after an incredible roar of sound. While this effect isn't recommended for Web pages, we hope you get the idea that you want to grab your readers' attention when they first glimpse your page.

Nothing will do this as effectively as a tasteful image, coupled with a brief, compelling introduction to your page. Include information that tells what the page is for, what it contains, and how to get around. Get your readers interested, get them oriented, and then they'll be hooked!

They're after the goods... don't get in the way!

Once you've got their attention, make it easy for them to get to the real content that your Web site contains. While your superstructure should be visible, it shouldn't get in the way. Any pointers that you include to direct them to more detailed content should be obvious and easy to separate from the rest of the page. An overly complicated design, layout, or information flow will prevent easy access to the information. Make sure you work with other people — friends, coworkers, and associates — to review and critique your work, to make sure it makes as much sense to them as you think it should.

This translates into some important rules of thumb, particularly for introductory materials. Use short, direct sentences. Keep your focus on the topic(s) at hand. If you've built some document superstructure, you might want to include a link to an "About this document" area, for those who want to understand its structure and function.

Whatever you do with your initial, welcoming page, keep it as simple and elegant as possible. Too much information is just as bad as not enough, so try to walk the line between pointing your readers at the content, and equipping them to understand what that content is all about. In the examples that follow in this and other chapters, you will see these principles at work.

What should they remember?

It's a well-known educational principle that people exposed to new materials will generally remember 10% of the content, at best. When designing your Web documents, keep asking yourself "What 10% do I want my readers to remember?" This will help you focus on the really important ideas, both to direct the audience to them, and to reinforce those ideas throughout your Web pages.

It's also true, if somewhat sad, that the volume of material that most readers will remember is limited as well. Remembering 10% of the concepts in a document doesn't translate into 10% of its overall content: Would you remember ten out of a hundred pages in a document you'd never seen before?

Therefore, don't be too ambitious in your document's coverage: strongly related concepts will linger far better than loosely linked or unrelated ones. As with so much else in life, sticking to your focus is a key ingredient for successful communication.

Within the required structure and elements of a Web page, you must somehow manage to meet your audience head-on. The real challenge is not in mastering the form and design of your pages, even though they are important. The real work stays where it always has been: knowing your material well enough to understand completely, so you can put yourself in your readers' shoes. That way, you can take them through the steps necessary to comprehending and appreciating your document's content. This is the same challenge that all writers face, whether they're building Web pages, or writing for print publication.

Meet the Elements of Page Design

OK, you've been exposed to some important design concepts for building Web pages. At this point, you should be ready to meet the elements that make up an HTML document. Many of these elements will sound familiar, because they're integral parts of any well-written document. Others may be less familiar, perhaps because of the terminology used or because the concepts — like hypertext links — don't correspond to normal printed materials.

Nevertheless, these are the building blocks that make up Web pages. Following a tour of these basic elements, we'll conclude the overview with a discussion of information flows for Web documents, and the creation and use of design elements within Web pages.

Tagging text

Including tags along with text is what separates HTML from any ordinary ASCII file. In HTML, tags are enclosed within angle brackets: for instance, a document head is indicated with a <HEAD> tag. Most HTML tags travel in pairs, so that the <HEAD> tag actually marks the beginning of a document head and a corresponding </HEAD> marks its end.

Some tags include particular values, called attributes, that help describe a pointer or a reference to an external data element. Other attributes help to label information to be communicated back to a Web server, while still others may add to the physical description of a display object (like the alignment or dimensions of a graphical element, for instance).

Attributes provide the source and destination information for links within and across documents: These link attributes describe the relationship between two named locations (usually called link anchors or anchors for short) in the Web, whether or not they're in the same document.

That "location" is indicated by a document reference (for access to other documents), a location reference (for a point inside the same document), or a combination of the two (for a point inside another document). For more information on such links, please read about <BASE>, <A> (anchor), and <LINK> tags in Chapter 7. ▨

Many HTML tags require certain attributes to be specified, some others can take on optional attributes and values, and still others never acquire attributes. You'll learn how to tell the difference as you learn the elements of document design throughout this book.

Titles and labels

Every HTML document should have a title, to identify itself to its readers. There are three other important aspects of a title:

1. The title is saved in hotlists so it becomes a navigation tool for readers who use hotlists.

2. Titles allow Web Walkers to decipher what HTML documents are about which makes their corresponding entries into search databases accurate and useful.

3. Titles make it easier for you to manage your documents, especially when they're complex and voluminous.

Typically, the title shows up in the window's title bar when the document is displayed. Figure 5-1 shows the window for an HTML Style Guide with the title, "Style Guide for Online Hypertext," prominently displayed.

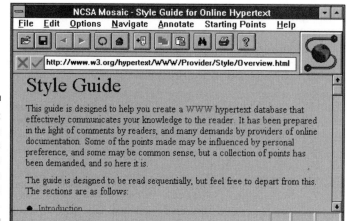

Figure 5-1:
The document's title shows up on the window's title bar.

Note the URL for the document in Figure 5-1; it's a worthwhile read for more page and document design tips. Like so many other well-designed Web documents, it also leads to other interesting URLs:

```
http://www.w3.org/hypertext/WWW/Provider/Style/Overview.html
```

Labels aren't required but they're a good document organizing tool. Labels help to identify sections or topic areas in a document and provide better navigation for readers, especially when used for links. As you'll see in Parts III and IV of this book, using the NAME attribute inside an anchor, you can direct an HTML link to a named section in a document, as well as to the head of that document. Anchors also signal to other browsers that "Hey, if you want to point to me, reference me by my anchor's NAME attribute":

```
<A NAME="Mexican Dove">Linda Paloma</A>
```

If some author, or even the original author, wants to link to the Linda Paloma area of the current document, all they need to do is create an HTML link definition using the anchor's name, (in this case "Mexican Dove").

Text and hypertext links

There is only one kind of link available to anyone writing HTML — a uni-directional association between a source and a target. There are four purposes for links in HTML files:

1. Intra-document linking provides a way to move from one location inside a document to another location inside the same document.

2. Inter-document linking provides a way to move from one document to another.

3. Linking to an agent program that acts on behalf of the server provides a way for a document to handle a query or provide a service like information gathering.

4. Linking to a nontext object provides a way to access a graphic, sound, video, or other multimedia file.

Interestingly enough, the associations from inside HTML files to other types of data — like sound, graphics, motion video, etc. — are what make the hypertext aspects of HTML possible. In addition to these external associations, the inter- and intra-document links that HTML supports create the connections that compose the Web. Remember, no matter how they're used, links contribute to the Web's appealing look and feel.

Using graphics effectively

In our earlier discussion of THX, we tried to indicate the impact that an attention-grabbing display can have on an audience. The idea behind using graphics on Web pages isn't entirely dissimilar, but it is subject to the limitations of the network over which so many users access the Web.

First impressions are critically important, so you'll want to use your most potent, eye-catching images on the initial page that your readers will see. Even then, remember that bigger images mean longer download times — especially for dial-in users. You'll have to trade the positive impact of a big, complex image against the negative impact of wait time (while also realizing that some readers will have no graphics capabilities at all).

What does this mean for effective use of graphics? Here are some tips for using graphics in Web documents:

✔ Use graphics only when they add to the impact, intelligibility, or value of a page. A picture can be worth a thousand words — providing a flow chart of a complex process, for instance. But if those words are irrelevant or only tangential to the content, an image may end up detracting from a document's ability to communicate with its readers. In general, try to avoid "chart junk" a phrase coined by Edward R. Tufte, author of *The Visual Display of Quantitative Information* and other seminal books about effective use of graphics.

✔ Keep your graphics as small as possible, both in terms of image space and file size. The two are related, but you can reduce file sizes by using .JPEG with heavier amounts of compression to render large images from a relatively small amount of data. Be sure to check the image on a lower-resolution display, and turn the compression almost to the point where resolution begins to suffer.

✔ If you must use large graphics, insert a thumbnail version of the graphic and make it a link to the full-size version. Also indicate the file size of the full version so users can decide how badly they really want to see it (translation: how long they want to wait).

✔ Keep the number of graphical elements per page to a minimum. Each graphic adds to the time it takes to build a page. If you must use numerous graphical elements on a page, keep them small to minimize transfer time. In other words, multiple icon-sized elements on a page are fine; more than one or two large graphical elements typically is not. ◼

The temptation to add multimedia can be very strong. Nevertheless, each time temptation strikes, you have to ask yourself the question: "What does this add to my document?" Then, you have to genuinely like the answer before giving way to that temptation. Finally, if you don't get positive comments from your page testers, don't inflict these fetching but time-consuming elements on the general public!

Overcoming two-dimensional thinking

Although hypertext is new and exciting, the legacy of thousands of years of linear text is hard to overcome. In other words, even though document designers can do incredibly nifty and creative things with linking and hypermedia, they have to fight the nearly overwhelming tendency to make their documents read like books. Even though hypertext can make lots of interesting displays and links available, a hypertext document won't live up to its potential unless you exploit these capabilities in the most appealing and useful ways.

In the sections that follow, you'll have a chance to examine some common organizational techniques for building documents for the World Wide Web. You'll also encounter some documents that could only exist on the Web.

Stringing pages together the old-fashioned way

Even so, some pages demand to be read in sequence, like narrative for example, that builds on each previous element. In this case, it's a good idea to string pages together, as outlined in Figure 5-2. A document of five pages or more — if you believe Tim Berners-Lee in his *Hypertext Online Style Guide* referenced earlier — should be chained together in this manner anyway.

Figure 5-2: Chain pages together to read them in sequence.

The nice thing about hypertext is that you can chain pages together forward and backward, making it easy to "turn" pages in each direction. Don't be afraid to also include other appropriate links in this basic structure (e.g., to other HTML documents, a glossary, or other points inside your document).

Hierarchies are easy to model in HTML

If you're used to constructing a document from an outline, a hierarchical approach to document links should immediately make sense. Most outlines start with major ideas and divisions, which get refined and elaborated, ultimately winding up with all the details of a formal document. Figure 5-3 shows a four-level hierarchical document structure that organizes the entire work.

HTML itself has no limits on the kinds of hierarchies that you can build; the only limit is your and your audience's ability to handle complexity. For both your sakes, we'd suggest keeping the hierarchy from getting too big or too deep.

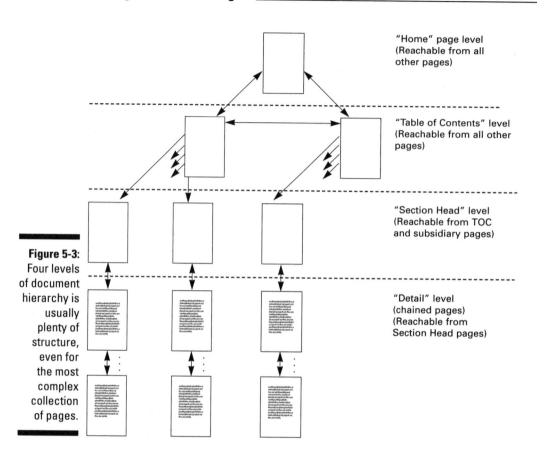

"Home" page level
(Reachable from all
other pages)

"Table of Contents" level
(Reachable from all other
pages)

"Section Head" level
(Reachable from TOC
and subsidiary pages)

Figure 5-3:
Four levels
of document
hierarchy is
usually
plenty of
structure,
even for
the most
complex
collection
of pages.

"Detail" level
(chained pages)
(Reachable from
Section Head pages)

Multiple tracks for multiple audiences

It isn't unusual to build a document that includes different levels of information to meet the needs of different audiences. HTML makes it easy to interlink
basic introductory documents (like a tutorial or technical overview) with
more pointed, in-depth reference materials. That way, you can design a home
page that points beginners to a tutorial, then leads them through an overview,
before assaulting them with the down and dirty details of your "real" content.

This kind of organization, depicted in Figure 5-4, lets you notify experienced
readers how to access your in-depth content directly, bypassing the introductory and explanatory materials. Such an approach lets you design for
multiple audiences, without doing a lot of extra work.

The organization in Figure 5-4 differs somewhat from what's depicted in Figures
5-2 and 5-3. It emphasizes the links between related documents more than the
flow of pages within those documents. In fact, the kind of document pictured in
Figure 5-4 would probably combine elements from both a linear and a hierarchi-

cal structure in its actual page flows. A tutorial is typically meant to be read from front to back, or at least a chapter at a time, while reference materials will usually be consulted by topic and only rarely read all the way through.

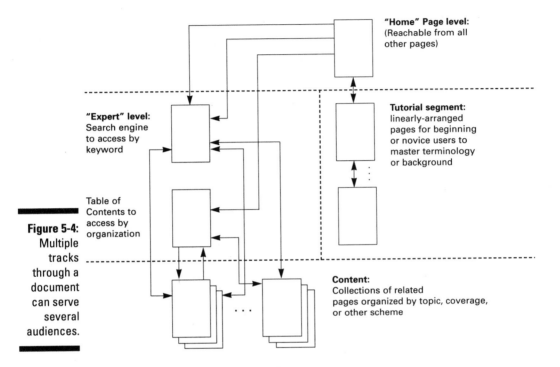

"Home" Page level: (Reachable from all other pages)

"Expert" level: Search engine to access by keyword

Tutorial segment: linearly-arranged pages for beginning or novice users to master terminology or background

Table of Contents to access by organization

Figure 5-4: Multiple tracks through a document can serve several audiences.

Content: Collections of related pages organized by topic, coverage, or other scheme

A bona-fide Web wonder: the "hotlist" or "jump page"

Some of the best resources we've located on the Web consist of nothing more than a list of annotated references to other documents, usually related to one or more specific topics. This kind of document structure is illustrated in Figure 5-5, which shows a single page pointing off to multiple pages in various locations. This is a case where the picture fails to do complete justice to the concept. For better illustrations, there's no substitute for real Web pages. Consequently, we'd also advise you to check out one or two of the URLs listed below the figure — they should be quite convincing as examples of what a good hotlist can do!

There are more good hotlists on the Web than you can shake a stick at. Here are some of our particular favorites:

```
http://akebono.stanford.edu/yahoo.html
http://atlantis.austin.apple.com/people.pages/carldec/
        Carls.Bookmarks.html
http://www.ncsa.uiuc.edu/SDG/Software/WinMosaic/HomePage.html
http://home.mcom.com/home/welcome.html ▪
```

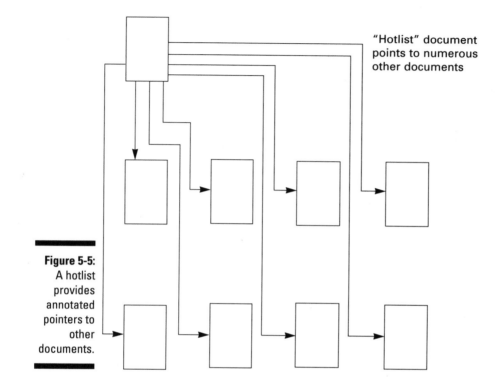

"Hotlist" document
points to numerous
other documents

Figure 5-5:
A hotlist
provides
annotated
pointers to
other
documents.

Extending the Web, a piece at a time

Another kind of Web page solicits input from readers who help create an open-ended document. Readers contribute comments, additional text and hyperme-dia, or add to an ongoing narrative. The structure of such a document is hard to predict, and therefore hard to depict. Suffice it to say that this kind of Web document can grow like a colony of coral, more by accretion than by prior organization or design.

For an example of this kind of living, ongoing document, consult the following URL:

```
http://bug.village.virginia.edu/
```

WAXweb is a hypermedia implementation of a feature-length independent film, "WAX or the discovery of television among the bees" (David Blair, 85:00, 1991). WAXweb is a large hypermedia database available over the Internet with an authoring interface that lets users collaborate in building onto the story. It includes thousands of individual elements, ranging from text, to music, motion videos, and video transcriptions of motion picture clips. ∎

The only limitations on how you structure documents are those imposed by your need to communicate effectively with your audience. Once you realize that, you will be able to use the various page flows and organizational techniques we've outlined here to their best effects.

Now that you know the first building block of Web page design — layout and organization — it's time to initiate you into the world of markup languages. In Chapter 6 we look at what HTML looks like and how it's used to structure a document. Here comes the good stuff!!

Part III
A Tour of HTML Basics

The 5th Wave   By Rich Tennant

IN THE AFTERMATH OF ANOTHER FAILED BID TO CAPTURE THE HOME PC MARKET, "KLEIN'S DEPARTMENT STORE" ATTEMPTS TO UNLOAD ITS INVENTORY OF CHIA-PET PCs.

CHIA-PETS
JUST ADD WATER
AND WATCH THEM
GROW

MicroWave
SlowCooker
COOKS ALL DAY—
IN AN INSTANT!
BY POPULAR DEMAND!

FINALLY!

SALE

THE
Chia-Pet
PC

In This Part...

Ok, this is where things really start to get interesting. In this part of the book, you'll get to know — and hopefully, love — the syntax and capabilities of the HyperText Markup Language. You'll begin with a general look at what markup languages are all about to help you better understand what's behind the strange sequences of characters that make HTML do its thing.

Then you'll get a look at the whole set of markup tags that make up HTML, from A to V. Sorry, there's no markup these days that starts with any of the remaining letters of the alphabet — W, X, Y, or Z — except for some codes that are now obsolete. While you're learning about each tag, you'll get a chance to examine its syntax, attributes, and how it relates to all the other tags. You'll also see examples for most tags, including the occasional screen shot that shows how they display.

After you've worked your way through the tags, you'll learn how HTML represents special characters, including the symbols that ordinarily indicate to browsers that they're part of the markup language itself. You'll conclude your tour with a table of character codes that covers everything from A to Z, and ~ to |, and way beyond, as we take you through the ISO-Latin-1 character set for HTML. By the time you're through, you'll have seen most of what there is to see under the HTML umbrella!

Chapter 6

What's a Markup Language?

*I*n this chapter, you'll finally see what HTML looks like. You'll begin to appreciate what's involved in a markup language, and start to understand how to use HTML to create your own Web pages. Because this chapter is an overview, you won't be able to run right out and start building pages after you've read it, but you should have a pretty good idea of the pieces and parts that make HTML do its thing.

A Markup Language Is Not a Form of Graffiti

HTML represents a way to take ordinary text and turn it into hypertext, just by adding special elements that instruct Web browsers how to display its contents. These special elements are called markup tags.

The purpose of a markup language is to give either machines or humans clues about the structure, content, and behavior of a document. There are two types of markup: descriptive and procedural. HTML is a descriptive markup language. A descriptive markup language describes the structure and behavior of a document. This allows an author to concentrate on content and structure and less on formatting and presentation. Here's an example:

```
<H1>Cooking for One</H1> — display  level one header
<OL> — begin ordered (numbered) list
<LI>Take Lean Cuisine out of fridge.
<LI>Place in microwave.
<LI>Set timer for 5 min.
</OL> — end ordered list
```

The tags H1, OL, and LI describe an object and its components. It's up to a browser to render these properly on your screen. In fact, from browser to browser, each of these objects would be rendered differently. But the important thing is that each browser has a meaningful way to display a first level header (H1) and a numbered list (OL and LI). From a portability standpoint, this is a good thing.

The other kind of markup language, procedural, describes formatting rather than structure. An example is troff, the dinosaur UNIX markup language, which looks like this:

```
.center .12 .Helvetica .bold Table of Contents
```

These troff tags tell the output device to render an object as "centered, 12 point Helvetica bold":

Table of Contents

As you can imagine, this is not very portable and is difficult to maintain.

HTML tags not only govern how a browser will display the contents of an HTML document, but also control how the browser can draw in graphics, video, sound, etc., to create a multimedia experience.

In the same vein, still other HTML tags instruct browsers how to handle and display hypertext links, either within the same HTML file, or to other documents or Web-accessible services. The key to building attractive, readable Web pages depends on knowing how to use HTML markup to highlight and organize your content.

A syntax is not a levy on cigarettes!

When it comes to any kind of formal, computer-readable language, there's invariably a set of rules governing its terms and their order of placement. This set of rules is called the syntax of the language. In HTML the syntax describes how a Web browser can recognize and interpret the instructions contained in the markup tags.

What makes HTML particularly interesting is that it's all pure text — in fact, HTML can work completely within the confines of the ASCII 7-bit character set (ISO 646), which contains only 128 distinct viewable characters. Nevertheless, HTML can handle display of so-called higher-order ASCII characters, which normally require 8 bits to represent directly, sometimes called 8-bit ASCII or the Latin-1 character set (ISO 8859/1).

This lets HTML display things like accents, umlauts, and other diacritical marks often associated with non-English languages (or loan words, like resumé, from those languages), by including instructions on what characters to represent as a part of the markup. In other words, HTML can provide instructions to a browser even if you can't always see things in the same format when you're writing the HTML. For example, <OL> and <LI> don't look like a numbered list inside your text file, but they do when the browser interprets them.

Elements of HTML syntax

The special control characters that separate HTML markup from ordinary text are the left and right angle brackets: < (left bracket) and > (right bracket). These characters indicate that the browser should pay special attention to what they enclose. And here's your big chance to learn another buzzword: *parser.* Inside the browser software there's a parser that does the work of reading and constructing the display information. A parser reads information in the HTML file, and decides which elements are markup and which ones aren't, permitting the browser to take appropriate action.

In HTML, left and right angle brackets can enclose all kinds of special instructions, called tags. The next eight chapters of this book are devoted to introducing, explaining, and demonstrating HTML tags. ■

In the meantime, here's a general introduction to the way HTML tags look and behave: a tag takes a generic form that looks something like this:

```
<TAG-NAME {ATTRIBUTE{="VALUE"}...}>Text{</TAG-NAME>}
```

(By the way, text within the tags is case insensitive but for readability we're using all caps.)

Let's look at the pieces of this generic form:

✔ **<TAG-NAME>:** All HTML tags have names. For example, H1 is a level one header; OL is an ordered list. Tags are surrounded by angle brackets that mark their contents for special attention from the parser software.

✔ **{ATTRIBUTE{="VALUE"}...}:** Some HTML tags require or permit certain named attributes to be associated with them. Here the notation using curly braces — for example, {ATTRIBUTE} — indicates that attributes may be present for some tags, but not for others. In the same vein, some attributes require that values be associated to them, as when supplying the name of an HTML document for a hypertext link; other attributes may not require associated values at all, which is why {="VALUE"} is also in curly braces. For example, in an <IMG> tag used to point to a graphics file, a required attribute is SRC (source), to provide a pointer to the file where the graphic resides, as in <IMG SRC="../gifs/redball.gif." This proves yet again how important it is to stay close to your source!

Finally the ellipsis (...) indicates that some HTML tags may even include multiple attributes, each of which may take a value or not, depending on the circumstances.

✔ **Text:** This is the content that's modified by a tag. For instance, if the tag were a document title, the HTML string:

```
<TITLE>HTML for Dummies Home Page</TITLE>
```

would display the words "HTML for Dummies Home Page" in the title bar at the top of a graphical browser's window. Enclosing this text within <TITLE> and </TITLE> tags marks it as the title for the document. (Whew! I bet you got what TITLE is now, right?)

✔ **{</TAG-NAME>}:** The closing tag-name is denoted by the left angle bracket (<), followed by a right-hand slash (/), then the tag-name, and finally a closing right angle bracket (>). The curly braces indicate that this element does not always occur. However, over 70% of the HTML tags require a closing tag as well as an opening tag, so the omission of a closing tag should be considered the exception, rather than the rule. Don't worry, most if not all browsers will simply ignore closing tags if they're not necessary.

The majority of HTML tags don't require the assignment of attributes, so don't be too overwhelmed by their full-blown formal syntax. By and large, most of them will resemble the <TAG-NAME>Text</TAG-NAME> layout like <TITLE>HTML for Dummies Home Page</TITLE>.

The ampersand (&) is another special HTML control character. It's used to denote a special character for HTML content that might not belong to the 7-bit ASCII character set (like an accent grave or an umlaut), or that might otherwise be interpreted as a markup character (like a left or right angle bracket). Such tagged items are called character entities, and can be expressed in a number of ways. For instance the string "è" produces a lowercase "E" with a grave accent mark (è), while the string "<" produces a left angle bracket (<).

Warning: Entering the Acronym Zone

Nearly any writing, speech, or documentation that has to do with computers will be rife with technical jargon and gibberish, no matter what the specific subject might be. To make matters even more confusing, the cognoscenti would much rather abbreviate frequently-used technical terms like HyperText Markup Language as HTML or Standard Generalized Markup Language as SGML, instead of having to say all the words for the concept each time it's mentioned.

The use of strings of first letters for technical terms — like ROM for Read-Only Memory, RAM for Random-Access Memory, CPU for Central Processing Unit, etc. — happens across the board in the computer world, so you might as well get used to it! Because this kind of shorthand is called an acronym (which literally means "from the point or head of the name" in Greek), we've got to warn you that you've entered a world where acronyms are commonplace. To make your lives a little easier, dear readers, we've tried to include all of the acronyms we use in this book in the Glossary at the end. That way, if you forget what a particular string of letters means, you'll at least be able to look it up!

Chapter 8 supplies the complete set of HTML character entities. If you work in a language other than English, you might want to consider building macros to replace familiar higher-order ASCII characters in your HTML files. Such macros would let you automate this kind of search-and-replace maneuver as a post-processing step. Then, you could avoid keying seven or eight characters of HTML to produce one output character (this is what computer science nerds like to call "an unfavorable input-output ratio")! Even better, check out some of the HTML authoring tools in Part VIII: most of them will automate this kind of thing for you. ▪

In the next section, we'll uncover the roots of HTML, namely SGML, Standard Generalized Markup Language.

Standard Generalized Markup Language (SGML)

Technically speaking, HTML is not a programming language, nor can an HTML document be called a program. Normally, a program is defined as a set of instructions and operations to be applied to external data (usually called the input).

HTML combines instructions within the data to tell a display program, called a browser, how to render the data that the document contains. Even though it's not a programming language *per se*, HTML provides plenty of structuring and layout controls to manage a document's appearance, and the linkage mechanisms necessary to provide hypertext capabilities.

Actually, HTML is defined by a particular type of document — called a Document Type Definition, or DTD — within the context of SGML. Thus, any HTML document is also an SGML document, representing a specific subset of SGML capability.

Generalized markup covers many sins

SGML originated with work begun at IBM in the 1960s to overcome the problems inherent in moving documents across multiple hardware platforms and operating systems. IBM's efforts were called GML, for General Markup Language. GML was originally targeted for local use at IBM, rather than as a generic way of representing documents. This was the first publish-once, multiplatform strategy for document preparation — a concept that's become extremely popular today.

GML's originators — Charles Goldfarb, Ed Mosher, and Ray Lorie (the original "GML") — realized by the 1970s that a more general version of markup would make documents portable from one system to another. Their work led ultimately to the definition and birth of SGML in the 1980s, which is today covered by the ISO 8879 standard.

SGML is a powerful and complex tool for representing documents of all kinds. It offers the ability to create document specifications of all kinds, that can then be used to define and build individual documents that conform to those specifications.

Some commercial and government institutions, like the Department of Defense (DoD), have adopted SGML. The DoD mandates that contractors and subcontractors now submit all documentation to the government in SGML. The DoD even mandates the DTDs to which the contractors' documents must conform.

Several quotes from the SGML standard, ISO 8879, should help to illustrate its aims, while underscoring a strong relationship to HTML. First, there's the notion of the markup process:

> *Text processing and word processing systems typically require additional information to be interspersed among the natural text of the document being processed. This added information, called "markup" serves two purposes:*

a) Separating the logical elements of the document; and

b) Specifying the processing functions to be performed on those elements.

> — Charles F. Goldfarb, *The SGML Handbook*, (Clarendon Press, Oxford, 1990) p. 5.

In stature and in scope, SGML far outstrips HTML; it is used to define complex document types like those used for military standard (Milspec) documents, or aircraft maintenance manuals, whose specifications alone can run into thousands of pages.

The notion of "generalized markup" is what makes SGML's document definition system so all-encompassing and powerful. Goldfarb has this to say on that subject:

..."generalized markup" [...] does not restrict documents to a single application, formatting style, or processing system. Generalized markup is based on two novel postulates:

a) Markup should describe a document's structure and other attributes rather than specify processing to be performed on it, as descriptive markup need be done only once and will suffice for all future processing.

b) Markup should be rigorous so that the techniques available for processing rigorously-defined objects like programs and data bases can be used for processing documents as well.

> — Charles F. Goldfarb, *The SGML Handbook*, (Clarendon Press, Oxford, 1990) pp. 7-8.

Even though SGML, like HTML, is still oriented toward producing documents, the goal is to make them behave more like programs, to behave predictably in a computer-oriented world.

Building better pieces and parts

The whole idea behind SGML is to create a formal method for describing the sections, headings, styles, and other components that make up a document, so that references to individual items or entries in a document will be described by such definitions. This lets a document be rendered in a consistent way, no matter what platform it gets displayed on. In simplistic terms, SGML is a general-purpose tool for describing documents of just about any conceivable kind.

In its most generic form, an SGML document comes in three parts:

1. a description of the legal character set and the characters used to distinguish plain text from markup tags.

2. a declaration of the document type, including a listing of the legal markup tags it may contain.

3. the document itself, which includes actual references to markup tags, mixed with the content for the document.

Where HTML fits under the SGML umbrella

All three of these parts do not have to be included in the same physical file. In fact, HTML works from the same set of definitions for items 1 and 2, so that only the contents and tags that make up an HTML document need to be included with the document itself, as described in item 3.

For HTML, item 1 is covered by the ISO Latin-1 character set, which defines character entities for higher-order ASCII characters, along with the angle brackets and right-hand slash used to indicate markup tags. Given a standard DTD for HTML, item 2 is also covered.

Therefore, HTML can be conveyed by pure ASCII text files that conform to the definitions and requirements covered in items 1 and 2 to create instances of item 3. In other words, all that HTML consists of is content text, character entities, and markup tags.

Welcome to HTML

Despite its more limited nature, HTML shares several important characteristics with its SGML "parent" — namely:

✔ a character-based method for describing and expressing content.

✔ a desire to deliver that content equally to multiple platforms.

✔ a method for linking document components (and documents) together to compose compound documents.

While HTML may be less generalized than SGML, it still leaves plenty of room for unique and powerful expressions, as any quick perusal of Web pages will illustrate. Though it may be less than completely generalized, HTML's tags and entities can still do justice to a broad range of content!

Delivering content to a variety of platforms

HTML's tremendous power and appeal come from its ability to service character-mode and graphical browsers with identical content. The "look and feel" of any document's content remains the same, subject only to the display limitations of whatever browser you're using.

When you add the ability to group multiple related sources of information together — text, graphics, sound, and video — and the ability to link documents together, the result is hypertext. HTML's combination of a simple concise form, powerful controls, and hypertext linkages helps to explain the overwhelming popularity of the Web as an information retrieval and investigation tool.

The four-plus faces of HTML

In a manner of speaking, all there is to HTML besides content is a collection of character entities and markup tags. Some purists insist on remaining within the confines of the SGML DTD for HTML, but the number and kinds of tags and entities used in various Web environments (especially in some of the more advanced browsers) continues to expand with each passing day, and each new version of browser software.

While some browsers may recognize tags and entities unknown to other browsers, HTML includes the convention that all unrecognized markup is ignored. You may lose some of the finer formatting controls with some browsers (like the <BLINK> tag, currently recognized only by Netscape) but the content should still be quite accessible.

Today, there are also several standardization levels for HTML, numbered zero through three:

0 was the original text-only markup language developed for prototype browsers at CERN prior to HTML's release to the general public. You shouldn't see any tools that remain at this level, except for "historical curiosities."

1 is the initial public implementation of HTML markup, which included the ability to reference graphical elements, in addition to text controls. Many browsers — for example, Lynx and Cello — still operate at level 1 HTML.

2 is the current implementation of HTML markup, which includes all of the markup elements for level 1, plus tags for interactive forms. Most graphical browsers — like Mosaic, Netscape, and WinWeb or MacWeb — support level 2 HTML.

3 is the level currently under development. Sometimes called HTML+ ("HTML plus"), level 3 will add support for on-screen table formatting and complex mathematical notation. As this book is being written, HTML 3 is still under debate, and is expected to be completed some time in the second half of 1995.

To find out what's current for HTML, you can always go trolling on the Web itself. You should be able to find the current specification, in the form of the HTML DTD, along with online documentation on HTML markup and usage, as well as current information on SGML.

HTML Elements

Well-structured HTML documents come in 3 parts, consisting of:

1. a head, that identifies the document as HTML and establishes its title.

2. a body, that contains the content for a Web page. This is where all displayed text on a page comes from (except for the title), as well as all links to graphics, multimedia information, and to locations inside this HTML file or to other Web documents.

3. a footer, that labels the page by identifying its author, date of creation, and version number (if applicable).

In reality, HTML is very forgiving so you can sometimes get away with skipping some of these elements. As a matter of good style and practice, however, we strongly recommend that any pages you design begin with the information necessary for all three elements.

Go to the head of the document

An entire HTML document should be bracketed by the identification tags <HTML> to open the document and </HTML> to close it. These identify the DTD for the document to an SGML-sensitive program, to allow it to interpret its contents properly. You can get away with omitting this tag for most browsers, but with the increasing convergence of HTML and SGML this may limit the shelf-life of your Web pages.

An optional line may sometimes precede your document head. It is called a document type prolog. This describes, in SGML, that the following HTML document complies to the indicated level of the HTML DTD. Here is an example:

```
<!DOCTYPE HTML PUBLIC "-//IETF//DTD HTML 2.0//EN">
```

By deciphering this line, you can tell that the HTML document conforms to the HTML 2.0 DTD distributed by the Internet Engineering Task Force (IETF). You can also tell that the DTD is PUBLIC and is not system dependent. Finally, you can tell that the HTML tag set is defined by the ENGLISH language (the "EN" in the DOCTYPE statement above). This DOCTYPE statement can also be used by local SGML parsers to validate the HTML document; that is, to check the document's syntax for conformance and correctness. This will become increasingly important in the future.

A document title is flagged by the HTML tags <TITLE>, to open the heading section, and </TITLE> to close it. Within this section, you'll commonly find the actual title, and possibly some other document heading tags, which we'll cover in more detail in Chapters 7 and 9, among others. The important thing about an HTML document heading is that it identify itself in an informative and catchy way. ■

HTML also includes a pair of tags, <HEAD> and </HEAD> to physically identify the head of a document. As with the <HTML> and </HTML> tags, many browsers will happily let you skip this tag, but for readability and structure, we recommend including it anyway.

The bulk's in the document body

The real content for any HTML document occurs in the body section, which is enclosed within <BODY> and </BODY> tags. Here's where you'll describe your document's layout and structure, by using a variety of tags for text headings, embedded graphics, text paragraphs, lists, and other elements. Not surprisingly, the majority of HTML tags occur within a document's body, simply because that's where all the beef is!

Chapter 7 covers all of the HTML tags in brief form, and Parts III, IV, and V of this book provide lots of examples. Remember, this is just the overview. ■

The good stuff's in the graphics and links

You'll also find all of the hypertext content within the document's body section. This could take the form of references to graphics or other files, as indicated by the appropriate use of text tags like <IMG> for in-line graphics. Or, you could have links to other points within the same document or to outside documents by using the anchor tags (<A>, </A>) with the appropriate attributes. In fact, because anchors point to generalized URLs (not just other HTML documents), you can also use them to invoke services like FTP to transfer multimedia files from within your Web pages.

Chapters 10, 13, 14, and 16 offer lots of details about using graphics within HTML documents, including good sources for material, appropriate usage, and other sorts of graphical information goodies. By the time you're through with this book, you'll be slinging HTML graphics around with the best WebMasters! ▪

A footer may be optional, but it's a good idea

Technically speaking, HTML doesn't include a separate tag to denote a page footer — that is, there's no <FOOT> and </FOOT> pair to label the information that would typically appear in a footer. Nevertheless, we strongly recommend that you include a footer on every Web page that you create, just for the record.

What's in a footer, you ask? Well, it should contain information to describe the page and its author(s). A good footer will also help identify a document's vintage and contents, and let interested readers contact the owners of the page if they spot errors or want to provide feedback.

For your own sake, it's also smart to include date and version information in each of your HTML files. This will enable you to recognize what you're dealing with whenever you look at a page, plus it provides a great reminder of how stale your pages are getting. As any real Web-head knows, the older the information, the more likely it is to be out-of-date!

Chapter 10 provides lots of details about page footers and includes a particularly fine example of what a good footer should look like. Be sure not to miss it. ▪

Ladies and Gentlemen, Start Your Engines!

OK, so now you've seen the basic elements of HTML. In the chapters that follow, you'll get introduced to the details, including more tags than at a "Red Tag" sale at your local department store. As you come to know and love what HTML can do, you'll be able to apply what you're learning to building great Web pages.

Chapter 7

Pigeonholing Page Contents: HTML Categories

● ●

In This Chapter

▶ Defining HTML's tag syntax in detail

▶ Categorizing HTML tags

▶ Stepping through HTML, tag-by-tag

● ●

*A*t last you've arrived at your first real in-depth look at HTML in this book. In this chapter we'll talk some more turkey about HTML syntax, to make sure you can keep up with all the gory details. We'll also establish some categories for what HTML can do and group the markup tags in meaningful categories to make them easier to learn and use. The remainder of the chapter is a reference tool, where we describe all the HTML tags in alphabetical order for easy access.

HTML Syntax Redux

In the preceding chapter, you learned about a general syntax for HTML tags. At this point, here's what you know:

✔ Tags are enclosed in left and right angle brackets; for example, <HEAD> marks the beginning of the head of an HTML document.

✔ By convention only — there's no requirement for upper or lowercase in HTML itself — for readability we present all tags in uppercase. That's why you'll see <HEAD> but not <Head> or <head> in the rest of this book, even though all three are perfectly legal — and equivalent — HTML tags. We recommmend you follow this practice yourself, because it'll help you separate the tags from the real text.

✔ Tags usually come in pairs, so <HEAD> marks the beginning of a document heading block and </HEAD> marks the end. All the text that occurs between the opening and closing tags is considered to be the focus of that tag and will be appropriately handled. The majority of HTML tags work this way, so we'll be sure to flag all of the possible exceptions as we introduce them.

✔ Tags can sometimes take on one or more attributes to define data sources or destinations, to specify URLs, or to further specify the characteristics of the text to which a tag will be applied. For instance, the <IMG> tag for placing graphics can use the following attributes to help specify the source and placement of an image on a page:

SRC = source for image, same as URL

ALT = alternate text to display inline if browser isn't graphics-capable, or graphics are turned off

ALIGN = (TOP | MIDDLE | BOTTOM) and (\[WIDTH=number] &r [HEIGHT=number]\) controls placement of a graphic. We'll explain this in more detail later, when we tell you what you don't already know!

ISMAP: if this attribute is present, it indicates that the graphic is a clickable image map, with one or more links to other locations built onto the image. If it's absent, it means the image is not a map.

Some attributes take on values — in this case, SRC, ALT, and ALIGN all require at least one value — while others, like ISMAP, do not. Attributes that do not require values are usually true ("turned on") if present and false ("turned off") when omitted. Tags will also have default values for required attributes that are omitted, so make sure you check the HTML specification if you are unsure.

At this point, you already know quite a bit about HTML syntax and layout. But there is quite a bit of additional stuff you'll need to know, some of which we had to use in our discussion in the preceding bullet item. This will explain some of the goofy characters you see that aren't part of HTML itself, but are necessary to explain it formally.

In the sections that follow, we'll begin with some formal syntax conventions, and then move on to some of the more interesting properties of HTML itself.

Syntax conventions are no party!

While we're providing formal definitions of the various HTML commands we'll use typographical notation in an equally formal way. What this means in English is that you'd better pay attention to how some things get written down because the notation is intended to describe how terms should be combined, constructed, and used.

Metacharacters, anyone?

Describing a formal syntax means using certain characters in a special way, to talk about how to treat elements that appear in conjunction with these characters. This is nearly identical to these HTML notions:

✔ that angle brackets surround a tag (e.g., <HEAD>)

✔ that a forward slash following the left angle bracket denotes a closing tag (e.g., </HEAD>)

✔ that an ampersand leads off a character entity and a semicolon closes it (e.g., è)

These are special characters that clue us (and our browser software) into the need for special handling.

The characters we're going to use for our HTML syntax are derived from conventions developed for a formal syntax developed for programming languages, called a Backus-Naur Form (or BNF grammar, for short). Because we're forced to deviate somewhat from BNF, we'll lay out all of the special characters we'll use to describe syntax — which are called metacharacters, by the way — with their definitions, and an example for each one, in Table 7-1.

Table 7-1: The HTML syntax metacharacter set

Char(s)	Name(s)	Definition	Example
|	vertical bar	separates legal choices	ITEM1|ITEM2|ITEM3
( )	parentheses	defines a set of items to treat as a unit	(ITEM1|ITEM2) or (ITEM3|ITEM4)
\ \	backslash	one or more items can be selected	\ITEM1|ITEM2|ITEM3\
and	logical and	both items must be selected	(ITEM1|ITEM2) and (ITEM3|ITEM4)
or	logical or	one or the other item must be selected	ITEM1 or ITEM2
&r	and/or	one or both items must be selected	ITEM1 &r ITEM2
[ ]	square brackets	nonstandard items, not supported by all browsers	[WIDTH=number]
integer	integer	whole numbers only	1, 2944, -40
...	ellipsis	repeat elements as needed	ITEM1|ITEM2|...
{ }	curly braces	contain optional elements, not required	{ITEM1|ITEM2}

Decoding a complex metacharacter example: ALIGN = ?

Nothing beats an example for making sense out of this potential gibberish. Recall our definition of the ALIGN attribute for the <IMG> tag:

```
ALIGN = (TOP|MIDDLE|BOTTOM) and (\[WIDTH=number] &r [HEIGHT=number]\)
```

This can be restated as follows, to make sure you understand what this formalism means:

ALIGN can take one of the three values: TOP, MIDDLE, or BOTTOM. This is what ALIGN = TOP|MIDDLE|BOTTOM means. Basically, it's a way to say whether you want an image at the top, middle, or bottom of a display area on-screen.

ALIGN can also take a member of the set (TOP|MIDDLE|BOTTOM), and it can sometimes take one or both members of the set (\[WIDTH=number]| [HEIGHT=number]\).

Sometimes, ALIGN can take either or both of a WIDTH and HEIGHT setting. That's indicated by the backslashes around the WIDTH and HEIGHT entries, and the logical and/or (shown as &r). Each of those two entries must be assigned some integer value corresponding to a position relative to the current display area, as indicated by the "number" part. WIDTH and HEIGHT are also supported only on certain browsers, as indicated by the square brackets.

As you can see, what we were able to describe in a single complex line of type took three paragraphs of details to explain completely. The brevity and compactness of formal syntax makes it appealing to computer nerds; hopefully you'll be able to work your way through this syntax to fully grasp what HTML can do as you work through the various tags. If not, never fear — we'll provide plenty of examples for each and every tag throughout the remainder of the book, so that you should be able to absorb by osmosis what you can't grasp through formalism! Ouch!

Interesting HTML properties

In addition to the formal syntax for HTML which we'll use throughout the remainder of the book, the markup language itself has some interesting general properties that are worth covering before you encounter the tags directly.

No embedded blanks, please!

All HTML tags require that the characters in a name be contiguous. No extra blanks can be inserted within a tag or its surrounding markup without causing that tag to be ignored (which is what browsers do with tags they can't recognize).

This means that </HEAD> is a valid closing tag for a document heading, but that none of the following is legal:

```
< /HEAD>
</ HEAD>
</H EAD>
</HE AD>
</HEA D>
</HEAD >
```

Hopefully you get the idea: no blanks inside tags, except where you're using a blank deliberately to separate a tag name from an attribute name (this is why <IMG SRC="sample.gif"> is legal, but <IMGSRC="sample.gif"> is not).

When assigning values to attributes, however, spaces are OK. This means that all four possible variants for this SRC assignment are legal:

```
<IMG SRC="sample.gif">
<!- Previous line: no spaces before or after = sign ->
<IMG SRC = "sample.gif">
<!- Previous line: spaces before and after = sign ->
<IMG SRC= "sample.gif">
<!- Previous line: no space before, one after = sign ->
<IMG SRC ="sample.gif">
<!- Previous line: one space before, none after = sign ->
```

Where one space is legal, multiple spaces are legal. Don't get carried away with what's legal or not, though — try to leave your HTML documents as readable as possible and everything else will flow naturally.

We sneaked some more HTML markup into the preceding example. After each <IMG> tag line, we inserted readable HTML comments to describe what occurred on the preceding line. This lets you infer that the HTML markup to open a comment is the string <!— and to close a comment the string —>. As you go through the markup section later on, we'll cover some style guidelines for using comments effectively and correctly. ∎

What's the default?

If a tag can support an attribute, what does it mean when the attribute isn't present? For ISMAP on the <IMG> tag, for instance, you already know that when the ISMAP attribute is present, it means that "the image is a clickable map." If ISMAP is absent, this means "the image is not a clickable map."

This is a way of introducing the concept of a *default*, which is not a way of assigning blame, but rather a way of deciding what to assume when an attribute is not supplied for a particular tag. For ISMAP, the default is absent, which means that an image is only assumed to be a clickable map when the ISMAP attribute is explicitly supplied.

But how do images get displayed if the ALIGN attribute isn't defined? As a quick bit of experimentation will show you, the default for most graphical browsers is to insert the graphic at the left-hand margin. These kinds of defaults are important, too, and we'll try to tell you what to expect from them as well.

The nesting instinct

Sometimes it's necessary to insert one set of markup tags within another. You might decide that one word within a heading needs to have special emphasis to make it stand out. For example, it might be more dramatic to have the word "Emergency" stand out in the heading "Emergency Phone Numbers" for a list of numbers you've put together.

When you start enclosing one set of markup within another, it's called "nesting." When the nesting instinct strikes you, the best rule of thumb is to close first what you've opened most recently. For instance, the text tags <STRONG> ... </STRONG> provide a way of bracketing text requiring strong emphasis. If this were to occur within a level two heading, <H2> ... </H2>, the proper way to handle the emphasis is like this:

```
<H2><STRONG>Emergency</STRONG> Phone Numbers</H2>
```

That way, you close the nested <STRONG> tag with its mate, before you close out the <H2> heading. Some browsers may let you violate this rule, but others may behave unpredictably if you don't open and close tags in the right order. Figure 7-1 shows what this looks like. (Notice that the word "Emergency" appears in heavier type than the rest of the heading.)

There are also some tags where nesting just doesn't make sense. For instance, within <TITLE> ... </TITLE>, you're dealing with information that will show up only on a window title, rather than on a particular Web page. Text and layout controls clearly do not apply here (and will be cheerfully ignored by some browsers, while making others curl up and die).

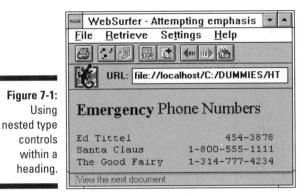

Figure 7-1:
Using
nested type
controls
within a
heading.

Always look back to the left as you start closing tags you've already opened. Close the closest one first, the next one next, and so on. Check the tag details later on in this chapter to find out what tags are OK to nest within your outer-most open tag. If the tag you want to use isn't on the OK list, then don't try to nest that tag inside the current open ones. Close out what you've got open and then open the tag you need.

Keeping your tags in the right nests will keep your readers' browsers from getting confused! It'll also make sure that you hatch only good-looking Web pages... ■

A matter of context

As you learn which tags can appear inside other tags, you'll begin to develop an appreciation for the controls and capabilities offered by HTML. We'll cover this under the heading of the context in which a tag can appear to indicate what's OK (and by exclusion, what's not OK).

HTML Categories

Before we take you through the HTML tags in alphabetical order, we'd like to introduce them to you grouped by category. These categories will help to explain how and when the tags are used, and what functions they provide.

Hopefully, the categories presented in Table 7-2 will also help you to organize and understand HTML's numerous tags. (For a complete listing of the HTML character entities, please consult Chapter 8.) Since so many tags come in pairs, we'll use an ellipsis between opening and closing tags to indicate where text and other elements can appear.

Table 7-2: HTML categories and their respective tags

Category Tags	Tag Names	Category Description Brief Explanation
Comments		To document HTML design, techniques, etc.
<!— ... —>	Comment	Supports author comments; ignored by browser but digestable by SGML parsers or document management systems
Document Structure		Basic document layout and linkage structures
<HTML> ... </HTML>	HTML	Blocks out an entire HTML document
<HEAD> ... </HEAD>	Head	Blocks out a document's head
<BODY> ... </BODY>	Body	Blocks out a document's body
<BASE>	Base	Indicates complete document URL, establishes location context for other URLs referenced
<ISINDEX>	Isindex	Indicates that document supports CGI script for searches
<LINK>	Link type	Sets relationship between current document and other documents
<NEXTID>	Next document	Indicates the "next" document that follows current, to permit HTML documents to be chained together
Document Headings		Supply document title and heading levels, provide important organization & layout elements
<TITLE> ... </TITLE>	Title	Supplies title that labels entire document
<H1> ... </H1>	Level 1 head	First-level heading
<H2> ... </H2>	Level 2 head	Second-level heading
<H3> ... </H3>	Level 3 head	Third-level heading
<H4> ... </H4>	Level 4 head	Fourth-level heading
<H5> ... </H5>	Level 5 head	Fifth-level heading
<H6> ... </H6>	Level 6 head	Sixth-level heading

Category Tags	Tag Names	Category Description / Brief Explanation
✳ **Links**		Create links to anchor or another document, or create anchor point for another link
<A> ... </A>	Anchor or link	Provides fundamental hypertext link capabilities
✳ **Layout Elements**		Control document appearance, add elements
<ADDRESS> ... </ADDRESS>		Author contact information for document
<BLOCKQUOTE> ... </BLOCKQUOTE>		Use to set off long quotes or citations
 	Line break	Forces a line break into on-screen text flow
<HR>	Horizontal rule	Draws a horizontal line across the page
✳ **Graphics**		References to inline images for documents
<IMG>	Image	Inserts a referenced image into a document with alternate text, clickable map, & placement controls
✳ **Forms**		Forms-related markup tags
<FORM> ... </FORM>	Form block	Marks beginning & end of form block
<INPUT>	Input widget	Defines type & appearance for input widgets
<TEXTAREA> ... </TEXTAREA>		Multiline text entry widget
<SELECT> ... </SELECT>	Input pick list	Creates a menu or scrolling list of input items
<OPTION> [... </OPTION>]	Selectable item	A way of assigning a value or default to an input item
✳ **Paragraphs**		Break up running text into readable chunks
<P>	Paragraph	Breaks up text into spaced regions

Category Tags	Tag Names	Category Description Brief Explanation
✳ **Lists**		Provide methods to lay out item or element sequences in document content
<DIR> ... </DIR>	Directory list	Unbulleted list of short elements (less than 20 characters in length)
<LI>	List item	Within a list of any type <LI> marks a member item
<OL> ... </OL>	Ordered list	Numbered list of elements
<UL> ... </UL>	Unordered list	Bulleted list of elements
<MENU> ... </MENU>	Menu list	A pickable list of elements
<DL> ... </DL>	Glossary list	A special format for terms and their definitions
<DT>	Definition term	The term being defined in a glossary list
<DD>	Definition datum	The definition for a term in a glossary list
✳ **Text Controls**		Character formatting tags
<B> ... </B>	Boldface	Produces bolded text
<CITE> ... </CITE>	Short citation	Distinctive text for citations
<CODE> ... </CODE>	Code font	Used for code samples
<DFN> ... </DFN>	Defined term	Used to emphasize a term about to be defined in the following text
<EM> ... </EM>	Emphasis	Adds emphasis to enclosed text
<I> ... </I>	Italic	Produces italicized text
<KBD> ... </KBD>	Keyboard text	Text to be typed at keyboard
<SAMP> ... </SAMP>	Sample text	Sample in-line text
<STRONG> ... </STRONG>	Strong emphasis	Maximum emphasis to enclosed text
<TT> ... </TT>	Typewriter text	Produces a typewriter font
<VAR> ... </VAR>	Variable	Variable or substitution for some other value

Now, let's review the HTML categories just introduced, before providing detailed syntax for each tag:

- **Comments:** Comments give HTML authors a way to annotate their documents and browsers will not ordinarily display them. Any assumptions, special conditions, or nonstandard elements should be enclosed in comments, to help other readers understand what the document is trying to accomplish, and to assist with the testing process.

- **Document Structure:** There are numerous tags defined to provide structure to HTML documents. They provide an overall HTML label and break up documents into head and body sections. They also provide markup to establish links to other documents and to indicate support for electronic indexing capabilities. While this markup produces little in the way of visible display, it is important to the construction of well-designed Web pages.

- **Document Headings:** Headings provide structure for a document's content, starting with its title, all the way down to sixth-level headings. They provide meaningful clues for document navigation, and when used in conjunction with a hypertext table of contents, can permit readers to quickly jump to other sections.

- **Links:** Links provide the controls to anchor points within a document or to link one document to another. They are the fundamental foundation for the Web's hypertext capabilities.

- **Layout Elements:** Layout elements introduce specific items within the text of a document, including line breaks, lengthy quotes, and horizontal rules to divide up distinct text areas. They also include a format for building author information on a page, which is something we recommend for all good Web pages.

- **Graphics:** Graphics enter an HTML file through the <IMG> command, which we've already covered in some detail. Suffice it to say that <IMG> points to the graphics source, provides a text alternative for nongraphical browsing, and indicates whether the graphic is a clickable map.

- **Forms:** Forms provide the essential mechanism for soliciting reader feedback and input on the Web. Forms tags cover how forms are set up, provide a variety of graphical and text widgets for soliciting input, and supply methods to let readers select options from various types of pick lists.

- **Paragraphs:** The paragraph is the fundamental unit of text for HTML documents, as well as ordinary text. The <P> tag lets authors break their content up into easily digestible chunks.

- **Lists:** HTML includes numerous styles for building lists, ranging from numbered to bulleted lists, glossary entries complete with definitions, and selectable menu entries. All of these provide useful tools for organizing lists of items or elements to improve readability.

Text Controls HTML also offers numerous inline controls for adding emphasis or special appearance to text. It provides tools for describing user input and for including samples of computer code, computer output, variables, and sample text. The idea is to be able to represent different kinds of online text for building materials for online use.

From managing document structure to controlling the look and feel of text on a page, HTML includes tags to make these things happen. In the next section we'll examine the nitty-gritty details of all the various HTML tags.

HTML Tags

The remainder of this chapter is devoted to an alphabetical listing of a broad range of HTML tags, taken from the HTML 2.0 DTD.

Because so many browser builders are adding extensions to HTML for their own use, and because HTML 3.0 will be introducing significant changes and enhancements to HTML, this list can be considered neither exhaustive nor complete. We do hope it is informative and useful, however, and we encourage you to skim it over, just to see all the possibilities that HTML offers.

The run-down on attributes

In HTML, attributes typically take one of two forms within a tag:

1. Sometimes they take the form ATTRIBUTE="value", where value is typically enclosed in quotes, and might be one of the following kinds of elements:

URL	a uniform resource locator
name	a user-supplied name, probably for an input field
number	a user-supplied numeric value
text	user-supplied text
server	server-dependent name (e.g., page name defaults)
(X|Y|Z)	one member of a set of fixed values

2. ATTRIBUTE where the name itself provides information about how the tag should behave (e.g., ISMAP in <IMG> indicates that the graphic is a clickable map).

As we discuss attributes for individual tags, you'll see them in a section under the tag name. For each one we'll provide a definition. We'll also indicate choices for predefined sets of values or provide an example for open-ended value assignments.

Tag information layout

Before we provide our alphabetical list of tags, you need to understand what information we'll be presenting and how it will be presented. Using the by-now familiar image tag (<IMG>) here's what a typical listing will look like:

<IMG>

Definition:

Supplies image source, placement, and behavior information. Used to place in-line graphics on a page.

Attributes:

SRC="URL"

URL is a standard uniform resource locator and specifies the location for image file, which will usually be .gif or .jpeg format.

ALT="text"

Supplies an alternate string of text to display (and possibly make clickable) if the browser has no graphics capability or if graphics are turned off.

ALIGN=("TOP"|"MIDDLE"|"BOTTOM") and [WIDTH="number"] &r [HEIGHT="number"]

Standard use calls for ALIGN to be set to one of the following values: TOP, MIDDLE, or BOTTOM to define placement.

Optional values also permit more precise placement using a pixel-level height and width specification.

ISMAP

Indicates by its presence that the image (or its text replacement) should be a clickable map. This often invokes special map-handling software through the CGI interface on the Web server handling the request.

Context:

<IMG> is legal within the following markup tags:

<ADDRESS> <B> <CITE> <CODE> <DD> <DT> <EM> <H*> <I> <KBD> <LI> <PRE> <SAMP> <STRONG> <TT> <VAR>

Note: When referring to heading tags <H1> through <H6> we'll abbreviate the whole series as <H*> as we did above.

Suggested style/usage:

Keep images small and use them judiciously; graphics should add impact and interest to pages without adding too much bulk (or wait time).

Examples:

```
<IMG SRC="images/redball.gif" ALIGN="TOP" WIDTH="50" HEIGHT="50"
ALT="Menu Items">
<IMG SRC="http://www.noplace.com/show-me/pictures/fun.gif" ALIGN="TOP"
ISMAP ALT="Fun places to visit">
```

Tag layout commentary

Notice the use of our HTML syntax notation in the Attributes section; this is where you'll be seeing it most often. Because <IMG> is a stand-alone tag (i.e., there's no </IMG>) we don't show a pair of tags here but tags will be shown in pairs whenever appropriate.

The last item for discussion is the Context section. This shows where it's legal to put <IMG> tags inside other markup, meaning between <PRE> ... </PRE> tags for example. Just because it's possible to use this tag in such a way doesn't mean you have to do so; as always, use markup judiciously to add impact or value to information. Complex compositions seldom delight anyone other than their makers, so try to keep things simple whenever possible.

The HTML tag team

This section is built around an alphabetical listing of the most common and widely used HTML tags, taken from the HTML 1.0 and 2.0 DTDs. Where applicable, we will also include information on widely used extensions to standard tags. See Chapter 14 for an in-depth look at nonstandard tags and other browser-specific extensions to HTML.

<A> ... </A> Anchor

Definition:

An anchor marks either the source or the destination of a document link. If it's the destination, it will use the NAME attribute; if it's the source, the HREF attribute.

Attributes:

HREF="URL"

URL is a standard uniform resource locator specifying the location of another network resource, usually the URL for another HTML file, but it can also be a pointer to services provided by FTP, Telnet, WAIS, e-mail, or Gopher.

NAME="text"

Supplies a marked location point within the document to act as a destination for a hypertext link; the text supplied for this attribute acts just like an anchor "to hold a place" for a link to attach to.

REL=("next" | "previous" | "parent" | "made")

The REL attribute specifies the relationship between the current anchor and the destination.

"next" indicates that the URL points to the next page in a sequence, "previous" that it points to the prior page, while "parent" indicates that the current page is the parent of the destination page. "made" indicates that the destination page contains information about the current anchor page's maker or owner. (Note: this attribute is proposed and not yet supported in an "official" HTML DTD.)

REV=("next" | "previous" | "parent" | "made")

REV is the reverse of the REL attribute and indicates the destination and the current anchor. All of the attribute values are the same but apply to the page that the URL points to. Here, "made" indicates that this document contains information about the maker or owner of the destination page. (Note: this attribute is proposed and not yet supported in an "official" HTML DTD.)

TITLE="text"

Provides advisory information about the title of the destination document (usually, the same text as enclosed by the <TITLE> ... </TITLE> tags in that document).

Context:

<A> ... </A> is legal within the following markup tags:

<ADDRESS> <B> <BLOCKQUOTE> <BODY> <CITE> <CODE> <DD> <DT> <EM> <FORM> <H*> <I> <KBD> <LI> <P> <PRE> <SAMP> <STRONG> <TT> <VAR>

The following markup can be used within <A> ... </A>:

<B>
 <CITE> <CODE> <EM> <H*> <I> <IMG> <KBD> <SAMP> <STRONG> <TT> <VAR>

Suggested style/usage:

Anchors should be innermost when used within nested markup, except when using embedded character controls, font styles, or line breaks. Relative URLs make for more compact references but require more maintenance.

Examples:

```
<A HREF="../../MailRobot/Overview.html">Mail Robot</A>
<A HREF="http://www.w3.org/hypertext/WWW/Archive/
www-announce">archive</A>
```

<ADDRESS> ... </ADDRESS> Attribution info

Definition:

<ADDRESS> ... </ADDRESS> tags enclose attribution information about an HTML document, which should usually include things like the author's name and address, signature files, contact information, etc. For more details, please see Chapter 10.

Attributes:

None.

Context:

<ADDRESS> ... </ADDRESS> is legal within the following markup tags:

<BLOCKQUOTE> <BODY> <FORM>

The following markup can be used within <ADDRESS> ... <ADDRESS>:

<A> <B>
 <CITE> <CODE> <EM> <I> <IMG> <KBD> <P> <SAMP> <STRONG> <TT> <VAR>

Suggested style/usage:

Recommended for inclusion at the end of any document, to supply author contact information for questions or feedback.

Example:

```
<ADDRESS>Ed Tittel 5810 Lookout Mountain Drive <BR>
Austin, TX 78731-3618<BR>
E-mail: etittel@zilker.net</ADDRESS>
```

<B> ... </B> Bold style

Definition:

Encloses text to be boldfaced.

Attributes:

None.

Context:

<B> ... </B> is legal within the following markup tags:

> <A> <ADDRESS> <B> <BLOCKQUOTE> <BODY> <CITE> <CODE> <DD>
> <DT> <EM> <FORM> <H*> <I> <KBD> <LI> <P> <PRE> <SAMP>
> <STRONG> <TT> <VAR>

The following markup can be used within <B> ... </B>:

> <A>
 <CITE> <CODE> <EM> <I> <IMG> <KBD> <SAMP>
> <STRONG> <TT> <VAR>

Suggested style/usage:

To provide special focus on specific words or phrases in text. For more discussion on effective use of character tags, please consult the following URL:

```
  http://www.hal.com/products/sw/olias/Build-html01994-10-17/
              GDgs0XBMCmF84aK.html
```

Examples:

```
<P>The only reason for the trouble, to our way of thinking, is <B>the
complete lack of respect</B> for the older generation.
```

<BASE> Basis for relative addressing

Definition:

<BASE> normally occurs within <HEAD> ... </HEAD> and provides the URL basis for subsequent URL references in <LINK> or anchor statements within the body of the document. This makes URLs quicker and more compact to write, if the <BASE> represents a good starting point for other references (ideally, they should all be within one directory level of this reference).

Attributes:

HREF="URL"

The fully qualified URL for the current document is required here.

Context:

<BASE> is legal within the following markup tag:

   <HEAD>

No additional markup can be used within <BASE>.

Suggested style/usage:

Whenever you build complex, multipage collections, it's a good idea to use the <BASE> tag in each page, and to build a directory structure that's easy to use and navigate.

Example:

```
<HEAD>
  <TITLE>Sample Document</TITLE>
  <BASE HREF="http://www.w3.org/hypertext/WWW/">
</HEAD>
```

<BLOCKQUOTE> ... </BLOCKQUOTE> *Quote style*

Definition:

<BLOCKQUOTE> ... </BLOCKQUOTE> is used to set off material quoted from external sources, publications, or other materials.

Attributes:

None.

Context:

<BLOCKQUOTE> ... </ BLOCKQUOTE > is legal within the following markup tags:

   <BLOCKQUOTE> <BODY> <DD> <FORM> <LI>

The following markup can be used within <BLOCKQUOTE> ... </BLOCKQUOTE>:

   <A> <ADDRESS> <B> <BLOCKQUOTE>
 <CITE> <CODE> <DIR>
   <DL> <EM> <FORM> <H*> <HR> <I> <IMG> <ISINDEX> <KBD> <MENU>
   <OL> <P> <PRE> <SAMP> <STRONG> <TT> <UL> <VAR>

Suggested style/usage:

Whenever you use a quote more than one line long from an external source, it's a good idea to use <BLOCKQUOTE>. Don't forget to attribute your sources (remember to use <CITE> to highlight the actual publication, if applicable).

Example:

```
<BLOCKQUOTE>A man who knows not how to write may think this no great
feat. But only try to do it yourself and you shall learn how arduous is
the writer's task. It dims your eyes, makes your back ache, knits your
chest and belly together. It is a terrible ordeal for the whole
body.</BLOCKQUOTE>
```

(Anonymous quote taken from Goldfarb's *SGML Handbook*; as true today as it was in the 12th century!)

< BODY> ... </ BODY> Mark off HTML document body

Definition:

The <BODY> ... </BODY> tags delimit the body of an HTML document, and should completely enclose its content.

Attributes:

None.

Context:

<BODY> ... </BODY> is legal within the following markup tag:

   <HTML>

The following markup can be used within <BODY> ... </BODY>:

   <A> <ADDRESS> <B> <BLOCKQUOTE> <CITE> <CODE> <DIR> <DL>
   <EM> <FORM> <H*> <HR> <I> <IMG> <ISINDEX> <KBD> <MENU> <OL>
   <P> <PRE> <SAMP> <STRONG> <TT> <UL> <VAR>

Suggested style/usage:

<BODY> ... </BODY> has only one use: to set off the body of an HTML document. It is an explicit structure tag that is required for strictly interpreted HTML.

Example:

```
<HTML>
<HEAD><TITLE>Sample Document</TITLE></HEAD>
<BODY>This document ain't got much body.</BODY>
</HTML>
```


 Force line break

Definition:

 forces a line break in HTML text flow.

Attributes:

None.

Context:

 is legal within the following markup tags:

> <A> <ADDRESS> <B> <BODY> <CITE> <CODE> <DD> <DT> <EM> <FORM>
> <H*> <I> <KBD> <LI> <P> <PRE> <SAMP> <STRONG> <TT> <VAR>

No markup can be used within
 (it's a singleton markup element).

Suggested style/usage:

 can force line breaks in text whenever desired. It comes in handy for creating short lines of text.

Examples:

```
There was an old woman<BR>
Who lived in a shoe<BR>
```

<CITE> ... </CITE> Citation markup

Definition:

Use <CITE> ... </CITE> to highlight document, publication, or other external resource citations.

Attributes:

None

Context:

<CITE> ... </CITE> is legal within the following markup tags:

> <A> <ADDRESS> <B> <BLOCKQUOTE> <BODY> <CITE> <CODE> <DD>
> <DT> <EM> <FORM> <H*> <I> <KBD> <LI> <P> <PRE> <SAMP>
> <STRONG> <TT> <VAR>

The following markup can be used within <CITE> ... </CITE>:

> <A> <ADDRESS> <B> <BLOCKQUOTE>
 <CITE> <CODE> <EM>
> <DD> <DT> <FORM> <H*> <I> <KBD> <LI> <P> <PRE> <SAMP>
> <STRONG> <TT> <VAR>

Suggested style/usage:

Use to highlight citations or other references to external data sources.

Example:

```
<CITE>The Iliad</CITE> is arguably Homer's greatest epic.
```

<CODE> ... </CODE> Program code text

Definition:

<CODE> ... </CODE> is meant to enclose programs or samples of program code to make it easier to read. (See Figure 7-2.)

Attributes:

None.

Context:

<CODE> ... </CODE> is legal within the following markup tags:

<A> <ADDRESS> <B> <BLOCKQUOTE> <BODY> <CITE> <CODE> <DD> <DT> <EM> <FORM> <H*> <I> <KBD> <LI> <P> <PRE> <SAMP> <STRONG> <TT> <VAR>

The following markup can be used within <CODE> ... </CODE>:

<A> <B>
 <CITE> <CODE> <EM> <I> <IMG> <KBD> <SAMP> <STRONG> <TT> <VAR>

Suggested style/usage:

To set off samples of program code or other computer-based information within a document body.

Example:

```
<CODE>
void main &#40;&#41; &#123;<BR>
crispy rice1, rice2, rice3, rice4;<BR>
&#47;&#47; rice4 gets the value of rice3 &#40;with i =2&#41;;<BR>
rice4 = &#40;rice1, rice2, rice3, rice3&#41;;;<BR>
&#125;
</CODE>
```

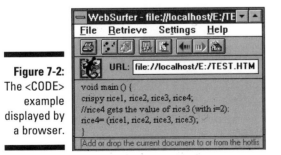

Figure 7-2:
The <CODE> example displayed by a browser.

<DD> Definition description

Definition:

The descriptive part of a definition list element.

Attributes:

None.

Context:

<DD> is legal within the following markup tag:

<DL>

The following markup can be used within <DD>:

<A> <B> <BLOCKQUOTE>
 <CITE> <CODE> <DIR> <DL> <EM>
<FORM> <I> <IMG> <ISINDEX> <KBD> <MENU> <OL> <P> <PRE>
<SAMP> <STRONG> <TT> <UL> <VAR>

Suggested style/usage:

For glossaries or other kinds of lists where a single term or line needs to be associated with a block of indented text. (See Figure 7-3.)

Example:

```
<DL>
<DT>atlotl
<DD>a curved throwing stick used in hunting, esp. in Mesoamerican cultures
<DT>atman
<DD>the innermost essence of each individual
</DL>
```

Figure 7-3:
The browser view of the "atlotl/atman" definition list.

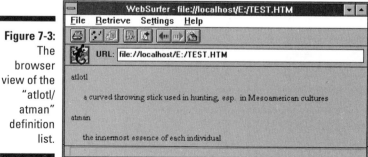

<DIR> ... </DIR> Directory list

Definition:

List style typically used for lists composed of short elements, like filenames. (See Figure 7-4.)

Attributes:

COMPACT

Renders the directory style list more compactly than usual. Warning: this attribute is currently not supported by all browsers.

Context:

<DIR> ... </DIR> is legal within the following markup tags:

<BLOCKQUOTE> <BODY> <DD> <FORM> <LI>

The following markup can be used within <DIR> ... </DIR>:

<LI>

Suggested style/usage:

Use <DIR> ... </DIR> to build lists of short elements (usually, shorter than 20 characters long).

Example:

Here are some files you'll commonly find in a top-level DOS directory:

```
<DIR>
<LI>AUTOEXEC.BAT
<LI>COMMAND.COM
<LI>CONFIG.SYS
<LI>IMAGE.DAT
</DIR>
```

Figure 7-4:
A sample
<DIR> ...
</DIR>
listing.

<DL> ... </DL> Definition List

Definition:

<DL>... </DL> encloses a collection of definition items <DD> in a definition list, usually used for glossaries or other situations where short, left-justified terms are followed by longer blocks of indented text. Definition lists are usually rendered with the term (<DT>) in the left margin and the definition (<DD>) on one or more lines indented slightly from the term.

Attributes:

COMPACT

Indicates that line leading (white space between lines) should be reduced (see example). Warning: this attribute is currently not supported by all browsers.

Context:

<DL> ... </DL> is legal within the following markup tags:

<BLOCKQUOTE> <BODY> <DD> <FORM> <LI>

The following markup can be used within <DL> ... </DL>:

<DT> <DD>

Suggested style/usage:

For lists of terms and definitions, like glossaries or a dictionary or other situations where left-justified elements are followed by longer indented blocks of text. (See Figure 7-5.)

Example:

```
<DL COMPACT>
<DT>atlotl
<DD>a curved throwing stick used in hunting, esp. in Mesoamerican cultures
<DT>atman
<DD>the innermost essence of each individual
</DL>
```

Figure 7-5:
Compact version of definition listing from Figure 7-3.

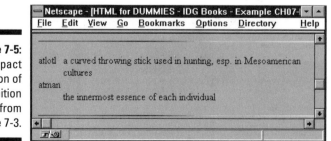

<DT> Definition term

Definition:

The descriptive part of a definition entry.

Attributes:

None.

Context:

<DT> is legal within the following markup tag:

   <DL>

The following markup can be used within <DT>:

   <A> <B>
 <CITE> <CODE> <EM> <I> <IMG> <KBD> <SAMP>
   <STRONG> <TT> <VAR>

Suggested style/usage:

For glossaries, definition lists, or other situations where left-justified short entries pair up with longer blocks of indented text.

Example:

See definitions for <DL> and <DD>.

<EM> ... </EM> Emphasis

Definition:

The <EM> tag provides typographic emphasis, usually rendered as italics. While <EM> and <I> often give the same effect, use <EM> except when referring to formatting in the text, as in "The italic parts are mandatory." This improves consistency between documents from various sources if, for example, a reader prefers to use color instead of italics for emphasis. (See Figure 7-6.)

Attributes:

None.

Context:

<EM> ... </EM> is legal within the following markup tags:

   <A> <ADDRESS> <B> <BLOCKQUOTE> <BODY> <CITE> <CODE> <DD>
   <DT> <EM> <FORM> <H*> <I> <KBD> <LI> <P> <PRE> <SAMP>
   <STRONG> <TT> <VAR>

The following markup can be used within <EM> ... </EM>:

<A> <B>
 <CITE> <CODE> <EM> <I> <IMG> <KBD> <SAMP> <STRONG> <TT> <VAR>

Suggested style/usage:

Wherever mild emphasis in text is needed, but be sure to keep usage to a minimum, both in terms of the number of words emphasized and how often text emphasis occurs.

Example:

```
"What we have here," said the Warden, "is a <EM>failure</EM> to communicate."
```

Figure 7-6:
Use of
simple text
emphasis
in-line.

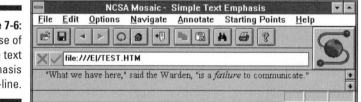

<FORM> ... </FORM> User input form

Definition:

For defining an area that contains objects to solicit user input, ranging from selecting buttons or checkboxes, to areas for text input.

Attributes:

ACTION="URL"

URL is a standard uniform resource locator. ACTION specifies the name of a resource for the browser to execute as an action in response to clicking on an on-screen Submit or Reset button.

The URL will typically point to a CGI script or other executable service on a Web server that performs an action in response to being accessed. (Note: CGI stands for Common Gateway Interface, and defines how browsers can communicate with servers on the Web; for more details on CGI, please consult Chapter 12.)

METHOD=("GET" | "POST")

The METHOD attribute tells the browser how to interact with the service designated by the ACTION's URL. If no method is specified, GET is the default.

If GET is selected, the browser constructs a query URL that consists of the URL of the current page that contains the form, followed by a question mark, followed by the values of the form's input areas and other objects. The browser sends this query URL to the target URL specified by ACTION. The WWW server in the specified target URL uses the information supplied in the incoming URL to perform a search, process a query, or provide whatever services it has been programmed to deliver.

If POST is selected, the browser sends a copy of the form's contents to the recipient URL as a data block to the standard input service (stdio( ) or STDIN in the UNIX world). This makes it easy to grab and process form data. POST is the preferred method for most HTML programmers because with POST you can pass much more information in a cleaner fashion to the server than with the GET method.

Anything the recipient program writes to output will be returned as a new HTML document to the sender for further display or interaction. The recipient program can also save form data to a file on the local WWW server.

ENCTYPE="MIME type"

This attribute specifies the format of the submitted data in case the protocol does not impose a format itself. With the POST method, this attribute is a MIME type specifying the format of the posted data. The default value is "application/x-www-form-urlencoded" (for a discussion of URL encoding, see Chapter 16).

Context:

<FORM> ... </FORM> is legal within the following markup tags:

<BLOCKQUOTE> <BODY> <DD> <LI>

The following markup can be used within <FORM> ... </FORM>:

<A> <ADDRESS> <B> <BLOCKQUOTE> <CITE> <CODE> <DIR> <DL> <EM> <H*> <HR> <I> <IMG> <INPUT> <ISINDEX> <KBD> <MENU> <OL> <P> <PRE> <SAMP> <SELECT> <STRONG> <TEXTAREA> <TT> <UL> <VAR>

Suggested style/usage:

Use <FORM> ... </FORM> whenever you want to solicit input from your readers, or to provide additional back-end services through your Web pages.

Not all browsers are equally adept with forms, so it's often a good idea to include an FTP URL that includes plain text for the form, with instructions about how to submit the information via e-mail. This will not be as convenient or straightforward as processing the form within the browser, but it enables readers with nonadept browsers to submit their input or queries anyway. ■

Example:

Because forms are so complex, we'll refer you to the examples in Chapter 12 instead of providing one here. ▪

<H*> ... </H*> Header levels 1 through 6

Definition:

Headers come in different styles and weights to help you organize your content for better readability.

Attributes:

None.

Context:

<H*> ... </H*> is legal within the following markup tags:

   <A> <BLOCKQUOTE> <BODY> <FORM>

The following markup can be used within <H*> ... </H*>:

   <A> <B>
 <CITE> <CODE> <EM> <I> <IMG> <KBD> <SAMP>
   <STRONG> <TT> <VAR>

Suggested style/usage:

Use headings regularly and consistently to help add structure and provide guideposts to your documents. Some experts don't recommend using a sub-header level unless you plan on using at least two of them beneath a parent level. In other words, they recommend that you don't use a single <H3> ... </H3> beneath an <H2> ... </H2> pair. This follows the old principle of out-lining, where you don't indent unless you have at least two sub-topics to put beneath a topic. We think that the occasional exception is OK, but this remains a pretty good guideline.

Notes:

1. One of our examples below violates this guideline, to better squeeze all 6 levels into a single screen shot. (See Figure 7-7.)

2. Heading levels should be used in increments or decrements of one (when transitioning up or down in document hierarchy).

Examples:

Good Style:

```
<H1>Level One First</H1>
<H2>Level Two A</H2>
<H2>Level Two B</H2>
```

```
<H3>Level Three AA</H3>
<H3>Level Three BB</H3>
<H1>Level One Second</H1>
```

Bad Style:

```
<H1>Level One First</H1>
<H4>Level Four A</H4>
<H3>Level Three B</H3>
<H6>Level Six AA</H6>
<H3>Level Three BB</H3>
<H1>Level One Second</H1>
```

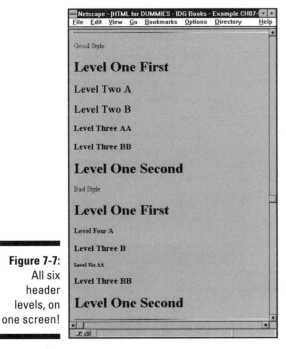

Figure 7-7:
All six
header
levels, on
one screen!

<HEAD> ... </HEAD> Document head block

Definition:

Defines page-level information about an HTML document, including its title, Base URL, index information, next page pointer, and possible links to other HTML documents.

Attributes:

None.

Context:

<HEAD> ... </HEAD> is legal within the following markup tag:

<HTML>

The following markup can be used within <HEAD> ... </HEAD>:

<BASE> <ISINDEX> <LINK> <META> <NEXTID> <TITLE>

Suggested style/usage:

For strictly interpreted HTML <HEAD> ... </HEAD> is required at the head of an HTML document. Even though many browsers will render documents that lack a <HEAD> ... </HEAD> block at the beginning, it's still good practice to include one, especially if you want to establish a BASE URL when you have numerous graphics or local document links in your page.

Note: although the <HEAD> ... </HEAD> block produces no browser output other than a document title, it remains an important component of proper HTML page design.

Example:

```
<HTML>
<HEAD>
<TITLE>A Nearly Pointless HTML Page</TITLE>
<BASE HREF="http://www.bigcorp.com/index.html">
</HEAD>
<BODY>
...
</BODY>
</HTML>
```

<HR> Horizonal rule

Definition:

Draws a horizontal rule across the page, usually one or two pixels wide.

Attributes:

None standard. Netscape offers attributes to control the width, length, thickness, and shading of horizontal rules (see Chapter 14 for more information on current extensions). ▓

Context:

<HR> is legal within the following markup tags:

<BLOCKQUOTE> <BODY> <FORM> <PRE>

No markup can be used within <HR> because it is a singleton tag that takes no attributes.

Suggested style/usage:

Wherever good design will benefit from placement of a horizontal rule — typically to emphasize natural divisions between text items or topics, or to separate a page header and footer from the body — the <HR> tag can add a lot to page design. (See Figure 7-8.)

Examples:

```
<HTML>
<HEAD>
<TITLE> The Horizontal Rule Rule </TITLE>
</HEAD>
<BODY>

<IMG SRC="bogusb.gif" ALIGN="MIDDLE">
```

<!— This image is a bogus button bar plucked from another application —>

```
<HR>

It's a good idea to start your page with a &lt;HR&gt; to separate header
graphics from the body of the page.
It's a good idea to end your page with another &lt;HR&gt; to separate
your body from the page footer, too.
<HR>
<ADDRESS>
Anonymous HTML, Inc. 1015 No Street Anytown, USA
URL: http://www.hmi.com/bogus.html e-mail: info@hmi.com
</ADDRESS>

</BODY>
</HTML>
```

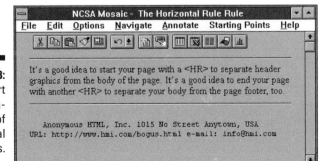

Figure 7-8:
A short demonstration of horizontal rules.

<HTML> ... </HTML> Main document head

Definition:

These tags should enclose an entire HTML document, as the outermost layer of document structure. For most browsers in use today, this tag is optional, but movements toward more rigorous interpretation of SGML DTDs for HTML indicate that this may not remain true for much longer.

Attributes:

VERSION="version information"

This reports the DTD version to an application. To date, the default value is "-//IETF//DTD HTML//EN//2.0".

Context:

<HTML> ... </HTML> is not legal within any other markup tags.

The following markup can be used within <HTML> ... </HTML>:

<BODY> <HEAD>

Suggested style/usage:

Use <HTML> ... </HTML> to enclose all HTML documents.

<I> ... </I> Italicize text

Definition:

Italicizes all enclosed text.

Attributes:

None.

Context:

<I> ... </I> is legal within the following markup tags:

<A> <ADDRESS> <B> <BLOCKQUOTE> <BODY> <CITE> <CODE> <DD>
<DT> <EM> <FORM> <H*> <I> <KBD> <LI> <P> <PRE> <SAMP>
<STRONG> <TT> <VAR>

The following markup can be used within <I> ... </I>:

<A> <B>
 <CITE> <CODE> <EM> <IMG> <KBD> <SAMP>
<STRONG> <TT> <VAR>

Suggested style/usage:

Use italics sparingly for emphasis or effect, remembering that its distinctiveness fades quickly with overuse. (See Figure 7-9.)

Examples:

```
In the arena of TCP&#47;IP-based electronic mail, <I>MIME</I> is an
abbreviation for <I>M</I>ulti-purpose <I>I</I>nternet <I>M</I>ail
<I>E</I>xtensions.
```

Figure 7-9:
Use italics
sparingly for
emphasis.

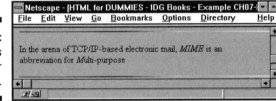

<IMG>

Definition:

Supplies image source, placement, and behavior information. Used to place in-line graphics on a page.

Attributes:

SRC="URL"

URL is a standard uniform resource locator specifying the location of the image file which will usually be .gif or .jpeg format.

ALT="text"

Supplies an alternate string of text to display (and possibly make clickable) if the browser has no graphics capability, or graphics are turned off.

ALIGN=("TOP"|"MIDDLE"|"BOTTOM") and \WIDTH="number" &r
HEIGHT="number"\

Standard use calls for ALIGN to be set to one of the following values: TOP, MIDDLE, or BOTTOM to define placement of graphic.

Optional values for HEIGHT and/or WIDTH also permit more precise placement using a pixel-level height and width specification.

ISMAP

Indicates by its presence that the image (or its text replacement) should be a clickable map. This often invokes special map-handling software through the CGI interface on the Web server handling the request.

Context:

<IMG> is legal within the following markup tags:

<A> <ADDRESS> <B> <BLOCKQUOTE> <CITE> <CODE> <DD> <DT> <EM> <FORM> <H*> <I> <KBD> <LI> <P> <PRE> <SAMP> <STRONG> <TT> <VAR>

Suggested style/usage:

Keep images small and use them judiciously; graphics should add impact and interest to pages without adding too much bulk (or wait time).

Examples:

```
<IMG SRC="images/redball.gif" ALIGN="TOP" ALT="Menu Items">
<IMG SRC="http://www.noplace.com/show-me/pictures/fun.gif"
ALIGN="TOP" ISMAP ALT="Fun places to visit">
```

<INPUT> Input object

Definition:

<INPUT> defines an input object within an HTML form; these objects come in several different types, and also include several different ways to name and specify the data they contain.

Attributes:

TYPE = ("TEXT" | "PASSWORD" | "CHECKBOX" | "HIDDEN" |

"RADIO" | "SUBMIT" | "RESET")

Defines the type of input object being described. TEXT, CHECKBOX, and RADIO define how data entry areas will appear on-screen; PASSWORD is used to prompt for a password; HIDDEN allows the form to pass data to the Web server that users can't see; SUBMIT and RESET provide methods to ship the information on a form to the server, or to clear the data from the form.

NAME = "text"

The name of the input item, as passed to the CGI script for the form as part of a name, value pair (this is how the script identifies values with their corresponding form fields).

VALUE = "text"

The value for the input item, as passed to the CGI script for the form as part of a name,value pair.

SIZE = "number"

The size of a TEXT type input item, as measured by the number of characters it contains.

MAXLENGTH = "number"

The maximum number of characters allowed in a TEXT type input item.

CHECKED

For checkboxes or radio buttons, inclusion of this attribute indicates that the box was checked or the button selected, usually as a default.

ALIGN=("TOP" | "MIDDLE" | "BOTTOM")

Determines how text and images in a form will align, for forms that contain images. Otherwise, these settings behave the same as for <IMG>.

Context:

<INPUT> is legal within the following markup tag:

   <FORM>

As a singleton tag, <INPUT> will not permit other markup to be used within its operation.

Suggested style/usage:

<INPUT> is an essential ingredient for HTML forms of all kinds, since it provides the mechanism to solicit input from readers, and deliver it to the underlying forms-handling services supplied by the related CGI script or other forms-handling program.

Example:

Since HTML forms are pretty complex, we'll refer you to Chapter 12 for a number of informative and interesting examples. ▪

<ISINDEX> Document is indexed

Definition:

<ISINDEX> indicates that a searchable index for the document is available on the server, typically in the form of a CGI script that allows searches (normally supplied by a "SEARCH" button somewhere in the document).

Attributes:

None.

Context:

<ISINDEX> is legal within the following markup tags:

    <BLOCKQUOTE> <BODY> <DD> <FORM> <HEAD> <LI>

No markup can be used within <ISINDEX>.

Suggested style/usage:

Long, complex documents typically benefit from being searchable, but any kind of document with large numbers of terms or details (for example the HTML specifications or the IETF's RFCs) can benefit from <ISINDEX> support. With <ISINDEX> documents can be queried with a keyword search mechanism by adding a question mark to the end of the URL followed by a list of keywords separated by a plus sign (which, not coincidentally, happens to be called "URL encoding"). For example:

```
http://www.biggus.com/rome/gov/index.html?empire+fall+europe
```

Example:

Please consult Chapter 16 for a detailed discussion of search engines, for more information on URL encoding, and for how to use <ISINDEX> in your documents. ■

<KBD> ... </KBD> Keyboard text style

Definition:

Indicates that text should be typed in at a computer keyboard. <KBD> ... </KBD> changes the type style for all the text it contains (typically, into a Courier font, or some other font like those typically used in character-mode computer terminal displays). (See Figure 7-10.)

Attributes:

None.

Context:

<KBD> ... </KBD> is legal within the following markup tags:

    <A> <ADDRESS> <B> <BLOCKQUOTE> <BODY> <CITE> <CODE> <DD>
    <DT> <EM> <FORM> <H*> <I> <LI> <P> <PRE> <SAMP> <STRONG>
    <TT> <VAR>

The following markup can be used within <KBD> ... </KBD>:

<A> <B>
 <CITE> <CODE> <EM> <I> <IMG> <SAMP> <STRONG>
<TT> <VAR>

Suggested style/usage:

Whenever you want to illustrate text to be typed in on a computer, please use
<KBD> ... </KBD> to set it off from the body text.

Example:

```
When you want to copy all the files from a DOS floppy onto your hard
disk, and you want to preserve the underlying directory structures from
the floppy, try the <TT>XCOPY</TT> command. For example<BR>
<BR>
<KBD>XCOPY A:*.* C:\TEST</KBD><BR>
<BR>
will place all the files and directories from the floppy in the
<TT>A:</TT> drive underneath the <TT>C:\TEST</TT> directory.
```

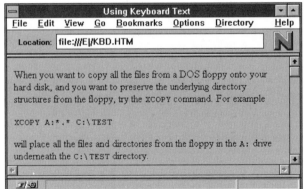

Figure 7-10:
Using
keyboard
text style.

<LI> List item

Definition:

An element belonging to one of the various HTML list styles.

Attributes:

None.

Context:

<LI> is legal within the following markup tags:

   <DIR> <MENU> <OL> <UL>

As a singleton tag, no markup can be used within <LI>.

Suggested style/usage:

Use to set off elements within lists. (See Figure 7-11.)

Example:

```
Dear Santa Claus:
<P>Here's what I want for Christmas:
<UL>
<LI>a plain-paper fax machine
<LI>a 28.8 modem
<LI>World Peace
</UL>
```

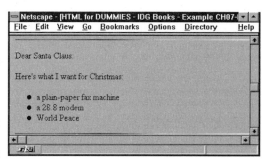

Figure 7-11:
A seasonal
sample
of list
elements.

<LINK>

Definition:

Provides information that links the current document to other documents or URL resources.

Attributes:

   HREF = "URL"

   The address of the current link destination, accessible through normal Web linkage mechanisms. Works the same as the anchor tag <A>...</A>.

URN="permanent name"

   A Uniform Resource Name provides a permanent address for a Web-based resource; unlike a URL, which can move or disappear over time, a URN is meant to be a permanent fixture on the Web landscape. This may be a text field with an FTP address, or provide contact information requiring human (not browser) action to follow.

REL=("next"|"previous"|"parent"|"made")

The REL attribute specifies the relationship between the current anchor and the destination (also known as a "forward relationship type"). "next" indicates that the URL points to the next page in a sequence, "previous" that it points to the prior page, while "parent" indicates that the current page is the parent of the destination page. "made" indicates that the destination page contains information about the maker or owner of the current anchor page.

REV=("next"|"previous"|"parent"|"made")

REV is the reverse of the REL attribute, and indicates the destination and the current anchor. All of the attribute values are the same, but apply to the page that the URL points to. Here, "made" indicates that this document contains information about the maker or owner of the destination page.

TITLE="text"

Provides advisory information about the title of the destination document (usually the same text as enclosed by the <TITLE> ... </TITLE> tags in that document).

METHODS="method1,method2,method3,..."

Provides a comma-separated list of HTTP methods for accessing the object or objects on the other side of the link (e.g., http, FTP, GOPHER, WAIS, news, etc.). This helps to instruct the browser as to the best methods to access the information from the destination (that is, like the TITLE attribute, METHODS supplies advisory information to guide the browser's action).

Context:

<LINK> is legal only within the <HEAD> ... </HEAD> tags.

As a singleton tag, <LINK> permits no enclosed markup.

Suggested style/usage:

Typical uses include authorship attributions, access to glossaries or tutorials, and information about prior (outdated) or newer (more current) versions of the document in which the <LINK> occurs.

Example:

See Chapter 11 for an example of this tag in use. ▪

<MENU> ... </MENU>

Definition:

Encloses a menu list, where each element is typically a word or a short phrase that fits on a single line, rendered more compactly than most other list types.

Attributes:

COMPACT

   Renders the list as compactly as possible (not currently supported by all browsers).

Context:

<MENU> ... </MENU> is legal within the following markup tags:

   <BLOCKQUOTE> <BODY> <DD> <FORM> <LI>

The following markup can be used within <MENU> ... </MENU>:

   <LI>

Suggested style/usage:

For short, simple lists the <MENU> list style provides the most compact way to display such information. Use the COMPACT attribute to really squeeze things down, if you must.

Example:

```
<H3>Common Sea Shells</H3>
<MENU COMPACT>
<LI>Abalone
<LI>Barnacle
<LI>Clam
<LI>Dog Whelk
<LI>Fan Star
<LI>...
</MENU>
```

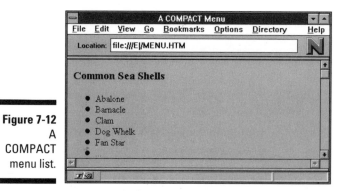

Figure 7-12
A
COMPACT
menu list.

<OL> ... </OL> Ordered list

Definition:

An ordered list numbers the elements by order of occurrence. (See Figure 7-12.)

Attributes:

COMPACT

Renders the list as compactly as possible (not currently supported by all browsers).

Context:

<OL> ... </OL> is legal within the following markup tags:

<BLOCKQUOTE> <BODY> <DD> <FORM> <LI>

The following markup can be used within <OL> ... </OL>:

<LI>

Suggested style/usage:

Ordered lists work well for step-by-step instructions or other information where the order of presentation is important. (See Figure 7-13.)

Example:

```
<H3>3 Steps to Successful Communication</H3>
<OL COMPACT>
<LI>Tell them what you're gonna tell them.
<LI>Tell them.
<LI>Tell them what you told them.
</OL>
```

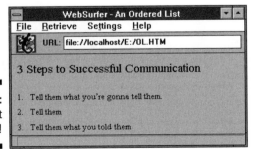

Figure 7-13:
A short
ordered list!

<OPTION>

Definition:

Defines the various options available within a <SELECT> ... </SELECT> tag pair for a forms definition, where users must select a value from a predefined list of options. Also provides a mechanism for selecting a default value, if the user chooses no value explicitly.

Attributes:

VALUE="text"

Defines the value for a specific <SELECT> option, which equals the text string assigned to VALUE.

SELECTED

Defines a default value for a <SELECT> field within a form, should the user choose no value explicitly.

Context:

<OPTION> is legal only within the <SELECT> ... </SELECT> tag pair.

As a singleton tag <OPTION> cannot include any markup inside it.

Suggested style/usage:

For defining a set of scalar values for a <SELECT> field, and for supplying a default for such sets where appropriate.

Example:

Because forms are so complex, we can't fit a good example here; please examine the contents of Chapter 12 to find all the information you'll need. ▪

<P>

Definition:

<P> defines paragraph boundaries for normal HTML text, where the break occurs immediately before the text that follows the tag.

Attributes:

None.

Context:

<P> is legal within the following markup tags:

   <ADDRESS> <BLOCKQUOTE> <BODY> <DD> <FORM> <LI>

As a singleton tag, no markup is valid within <P>.

Suggested style/usage:

Paragraphs are a fundamental unit of text, used to break the flow of ideas or information into related chunks. Good writing style calls for regular use of paragraphs, and for treating each idea or concept separately in its own paragraph. (See Figure 7-14.)

Example:

```
<P>When drinking cabernets sauvignon, we strongly advise using a glass
with an enclosing bowl shape. This helps to retain the marvelous bouquet
so typical of such wines.
<P>It's also a good idea to drink cabernets at a temperature of
65-70&#176;, because this qualifies as "room temperature" in Europe.
Normal American households will typically be at 70&#176; or warmer, meaning
that a light chill is the best way to prepare the wine for drinking.
```

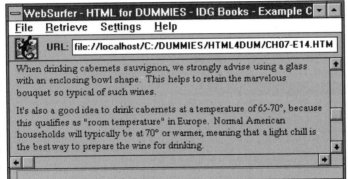

Figure 7-14:
Using the
<P> tag to
break up
text.

<PRE> ... </PRE> Preformatted style

Definition:

<PRE> ... </PRE> provides a way of inserting preformatted text into HTML files. This can be valuable for reproducing formatted tables or other text where you want to preserve its original layout, like code listings where you want to be able to preserve exact formatting, indentation, etc. (See Figure 7-15.)

Attributes:

WIDTH="number"

This specifies the maximum number of characters for a line and allows the browser to select an appropriate font and indentation setting.

Context:

<PRE> ... </PRE> is legal within the following markup tags:

<BLOCKQUOTE> <BODY> <DD> <FORM> <LI>

The following markup can be used within <PRE> ... </PRE>:

<A> <B>
 <CITE> <CODE> <EM> <HR> <I> <KBD> <SAMP>
<STRONG> <TT> <VAR>

Suggested style/usage:

When assembling text to use within a <PRE> ... </PRE> block, it's OK to use
link tags and text controls. You can obtain line breaks just by using the
return key, but because <PRE> text is typically set in a monospaced font (like
Courier), try to keep line lengths at 80 columns or less. This tag is great for
presenting text-only information, like .sig files or other e-mail information, or
USENET news articles.

Example:

```
<H2>The XYZ Company Phone List</H2>
<PRE>
Name                Phone                   E-mail
Adam Smith          513-544-5125            asmith@cc.xyz.com
Bob Jones           512-339-7711            bjones@au.xyz.com
Cindy Campion       512-339-7689            ccampion@au.xyz.com
Nestor LeBarta      513-544-5006            nlebarta@cc.xyz.com
Lembat Pikkat       212-466-5117            lpikkat@ny.xyz.com
</PRE>
```

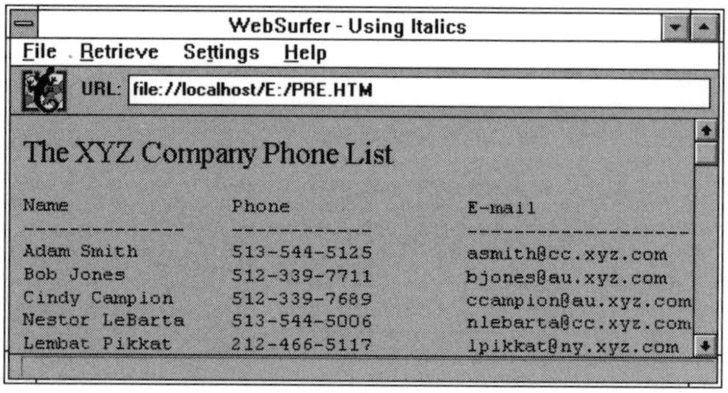

Figure 7-15:
<PRE>
makes it
easy to
enclose
prefor-
matted text.

<SAMP> ... </SAMP> Sample text

Definition:

<SAMP ... </SAMP> should be used for sequences of literal characters, or to
represent output from a program or other data source. (See Figure 7-16.)

Attributes:

None.

Context:

<SAMP> ... </SAMP> is legal within the following markup tags:

> <A> <ADDRESS> <B> <BLOCKQUOTE> <BODY> <CITE> <CODE> <DD>
> <DT> <EM> <FORM> <H*> <I> <KBD> <LI> <P> <PRE> <SAMP>
> <STRONG> <TT> <VAR>

The following markup can be used within <SAMP> ... </SAMP>:

> <A> <B>
 <CITE> <CODE> <EM> <I> <IMG> <KBD> <SAMP>
> <STRONG> <TT> <VAR>

Suggested style/usage:

Whenever you want to reproduce output from a program, script, or other
data source, use <SAMP> ... </SAMP>.

Example:

```
After using the <CODE>SORT</CODE> command, the list of adjectives for
the major global land masses returned by the program looks like this:
<SAMP>
African<BR>
Antartican<BR>
Asian<BR>
Australian<BR>
European<BR>
Indian<BR>
North American<BR>
South American<BR>
</SAMP>
```

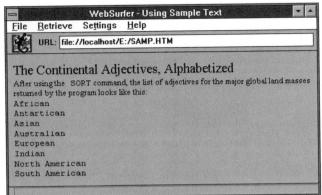

Figure 7-16:
A listing of
sample
SORT
output.

<SELECT> ... </SELECT> Select input object

Definition:

The SELECT tags allow users to pick one or more options out of a list of possible values supplied in an input form, where each alternative is represented by an <OPTION> element.

Attributes:

MULTIPLE

This attribute appears when users are allowed to select more than one element from the set of <OPTION> values supplied within a <SELECT> ... </SELECT> tag pair.

Context:

<SELECT> ... </SELECT> is legal only within the <FORM> tag.

The following markup can be used within <SELECT> ... </SELECT>:

<OPTION>

Suggested style/usage:

Use to provide pickable lists of scalar values within HTML forms whenever users can pick only from a predetermined set of possible values.

Example:

Because HTML forms are so complex, please refer to Chapter 12, which covers them in considerable detail.

<STRONG> ... </STRONG> Strong emphasis

Definition:

A text control for providing strong emphasis on key words or phrases within normal body text, lists, etc. (See Figure 7-17.)

Attributes:

None.

Context:

<STRONG> ... </STRONG> is legal within the following markup tags:

<A> <ADDRESS> <B> <BLOCKQUOTE> <BODY> <CITE> <CODE> <DD> <DT> <EM> <FORM> <H*> <I> <KBD> <LI> <P> <PRE> <SAMP> <STRONG> <TT> <VAR>

The following markup can be used within <STRONG> ... </STRONG>:

<A> <B>
 <CITE> <CODE> <EM> <I> <IMG> <KBD> <SAMP> <STRONG> <TT> <VAR>

Suggested style/usage:

Use within running text to provide the strongest degree of in-line emphasis available in HTML. Remember, overuse blunts the effect, so use emphatic text controls only sparingly in your documents.

Example:

```
<H2>The Art of Emphasis, Strong Form</H2>
<BLOCKQUOTE>"After spending the last ten years
locked in a cell, there was <STRONG>no way
</STRONG> that Mr. Peabody could conceive of
not taking advantage of the sudden earthquake
that opened a passage to the outside world, and
freedom."
</BLOCKQUOTE>
<P>
From <CITE>My Life as a Convict</CITE> by James T. Peabody, Esq.
```

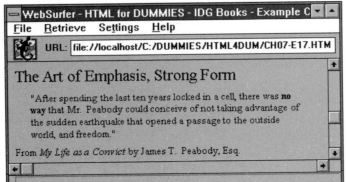

Figure 7-17:
Using
strong
emphasis
for high
impact.

<TEXTAREA> ... </TEXTAREA> Text input area

Definition:

Used to define a text input area for an HTML input form, typically for multiple lines of text.

Attributes:

NAME="text"

Supplies a name for the form field, which will be paired with the value that's ultimately entered for submission to the underlying CGI script or other service program that processes the form. This is a required attribute for which no reasonable default is possible.

ROWS="number"

"number" defines the number of lines of text that the field can accommodate. Typical values for nonnarrative forms range from 2 to 6, but HTML will allow large text areas if needed. (Prudence dictates that page-long input would be better handled by allowing users to upload text files from the editor of their choice, rather than typing into a text field on a form.) This is a required attribute, but takes a default of 1.

COLS="number"

"number" defines the number of columns for any given line of text in the TEXTAREA field. Common practice is to limit the number of columns to 72 or less, that being a common limitation for the number of characters a line can hold within the outside page frame of a browser program on-screen (80 is the typical maximum for normal character-mode displays). This is a required attribute but takes a default of 80.

Context:

<TEXTAREA> ... </TEXTAREA> is legal within the following markup tag:

<FORM>

No markup is allowed in the <TEXTAREA> tag.

Suggested style/usage:

The end tag marks the end of the string used to initialize the field (which can include a default string supplied by the form's author). Thus, even if the field is empty — meaning that <TEXTAREA> and </TEXTAREA> are adjacent to one another — the end tag is essential to indicate a null value for the field.

Use TEXTAREA whenever you have a multiline input field in a form.

Example:

Forms are fairly complex HTML structures that require nearly all of the possible forms-related tags to create a working example. We therefore refer you to Chapter 12, which covers forms in great detail and includes several useful examples. ■

<TITLE> ... </TITLE> Document title

Definition:

Encloses the title for an HTML document, which commonly appears in the title bar in the browser's window. If a title is not supplied, the default title is the HTML filename.

Attributes:

None.

Context:

<TITLE> ... </TITLE> is legal only with <HEAD> ... </HEAD>.

No markup can be used within <TITLE> ... </TITLE> since it does not normally display within an HTML document, but rather on the title bar of the window in which the document appears.

Suggested style/usage:

We strongly recommend that you define a useful title for each and every HTML document you write. Because many Webcrawlers and other automated search tools use titles to help locate information for users, an accurate, descriptive title will help them find your content.

Example:

See any of the figures in this section: we've tried to entitle all of them to be informative about the example at hand. A title about titles is a bit much, even for us!

<TT> ... </TT> Teletype text

Definition:

Encloses text to be displayed in a monospaced (teletype) font (typically, some variety of Courier is used in most browsers). (See Figure 7-18.)

Attributes:

None.

Context:

<TT> ... </TT> is legal within the following markup tags:

  <A> <ADDRESS> <B> <BLOCKQUOTE> <BODY> <CITE> <CODE> <DD>
  <DT> <EM> <FORM> <H*> <I> <KBD> <LI> <P> <PRE> <SAMP>
  <STRONG> <TT> <VAR>

The following markup can be used within <TT> ... </TT>:

  <A> <B>
 <CITE> <CODE> <EM> <I> <IMG> <KBD> <SAMP>
  <STRONG> <TT> <VAR>

Suggested style/usage:

Use for monospaced text, where character position is important, or when trying to imitate the look of line-printer or typewriter output.

Example:

```
<H2>The Typical Typewriter Keyboard Exercise</H2>
In typing class in eighth grade, we all had to type the
same line repeatedly, to measure our much-heralded WPM:
<BR><TT>
The quick red fox jumped over the lazy brown dog.<BR>
The quick red fox jumped over the lazy brown dog.<BR>
The quick red fox jumped over the lazy brown dog.<BR>
</TT>
```

Figure 7-18:
The archetypal <TT> example.

```
WebSurfer - Using Typewriter Text
File   Retrieve   Settings   Help
URL: file://localhost/E:/TT.HTM
```

The Typical Typewriter Keyboard Exercise

In typing class in eighth grade, we all had to type the same line repeatedly, measure our much-heralded WPM:

```
The quick red fox jumped over the lazy brown dog.
The quick red fox jumped over the lazy brown dog.
The quick red fox jumped over the lazy brown dog.
```

<UL> ... </UL> Unordered list style

Definition:

An HTML list style that produces bulleted lists of items. (See Figure 7-19.)

Attributes:

COMPACT:

If present, COMPACT instructs the browser to render this list with only a minimal amount of leading between the lines (this reduces the amount of white space, and makes the listing more compact).

Context:

<UL> ... </UL> is legal within the following markup tags:

   <BLOCKQUOTE> <BODY> <DD> <FORM> <LI>

The only markup that can be used within <UL> ... </UL> is <LI>.

Suggested style/usage:

To create bulleted lists of items where their order is not important, or where sequence does not apply.

Example:

```
<HTML>
<HEAD>
<TITLE>Unordered List</TITLE>
```

```
</HEAD>
<BODY>
<H2>Unordered lists have their uses</H2>
Even though order may not be an issue when listing some collections of
elements, we think the following capabilities make unordered lists simply
peachy:
<UL>
<LI> You can add as many elements as you need.
<LI> You can enter those elements as they occur to you.
<LI> Some elements might be short.
<LI> Other elements might grow long enough to get tiresome, especially if
you insist on reading every single wonderful word that issues from the
list-writer's fertile imagination.
<LI> ...and, you can keep adding elements as the spirit moves you.
</UL>
</BODY>
</HTML>
```

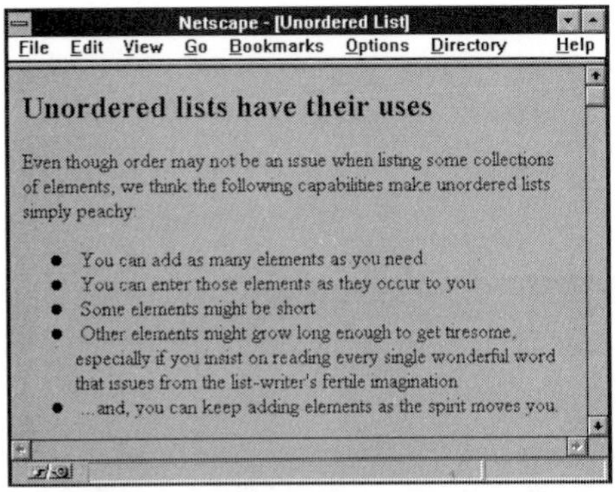

Figure 7-19:
A typical
unordered
list.

<VAR> ... </VAR> Variable text style

Definition:

This text control tag pair is used to highlight variable names in HTML text, to indicate to users that they will be supplying this information when they input text at the keyboard. (See Figure 7-20.)

Attributes:

None.

Context:

<VAR> ... </VAR> is legal within the following markup tags:

<A> <ADDRESS> <B> <BLOCKQUOTE> <BODY> <CITE> <CODE> <DD>
<DT> <EM> <FORM> <H*> <I> <KBD> <LI> <P> <PRE> <SAMP>
<STRONG> <TT> <VAR>

The following markup can be used within <VAR> ... </VAR>:

<A> <B>
 <CITE> <CODE> <EM> <I> <IMG> <KBD> <SAMP> <STRONG> <TT> <VAR>

Suggested style/usage:

Use to indicate a placeholder for a value that the user will supply when entering text at the keyboard (see example).

Example:

```
<H2>Variable text means "user-supplied"</H2>
Sometimes, you need a way to set off text that's generic when you explain
it, but will be particular when a user actually substitutes a real value:

<P>
When you use the DOS <CODE>COPY</CODE> command the syntax is <BR>
<CODE>COPY</CODE> <VAR>filename</VAR><BR>
<P>

Thus, if you wanted to copy the file named <CODE>"FOO.BAR"</CODE> you
would enter the string:<BR>
<CODE>COPY FOO.BAR</CODE>
```

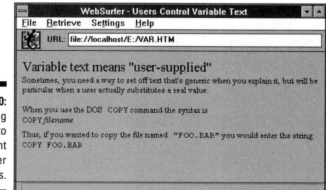

Figure 7-20:
Using
<VAR> to
highlight
user
variables.

Whew! That's the facts, Jack. Time for a break or a deep breath and then take another giant step forward in your budding WebMaster career. Join us in Chapter 8 where you get the rest of the HTML puzzle pieces with an in-depth discussion of entities.

Chapter 8

Introducing the Unrepresentable: HTML Entities

In This Chapter

▶ Coloring outside the character boundaries

▶ Producing special characters

▶ Inspecting the ISO-Latin-1 character set

*N*ow you've seen the panoply of HTML tags, and gone through a number of examples in Chapter 7 that included strange notations like "<" or "°". These odd locutions aren't as cryptic as they first appear — they're simply a way to instruct the browser to look up these symbols as it renders a document, and replace them with equivalent characters. The symbol < produces the less-than sign "<" on your computer screen, while the symbol ° produces the degree symbol "°".

Entities Don't Have to Be an Alien Concept

Why are these contortions necessary? There are three important reasons:

1. To let browsers represent characters that might otherwise be interpreted as markup.

2. To let browsers represent higher-order ASCII characters (those with codes over 127) without having to fully support higher-order ASCII or non-ASCII character types. Also, these codes support some characters that are even outside the ASCII character set altogether (as is the case with non-Roman

alphabet character sets, and some widely-used diacritical marks for non-English languages).

3. To increase portability of SGML documents. They are placeholders in the SGML document instance and can be rendered on the fly according to the specifications of the particular site's requirements. An example is the &COMPANY; entity. One subcontractor would define this entity to be rendered as "ACME Software" while another would define it as "Alternative Software Solutions."

OK, so now you know what character and numeric entities are for. They let browsers display symbols and not interpret them as markup tags. They also let browsers represent a larger range of characters than might otherwise be possible, while keeping the actual character set as minimal as possible.

As you travel into the land of HTML character and numeric entities, you'll encounter strange characters and symbols that you may never use. On the other hand, if your native language isn't English, you'll probably find lots of diacritical marks, accents, and other kinds of character modifications that will let you express yourself much more effectively!

Producing Special Characters

There are three characters that act as special signals to the browser to let it know that it should look up a string in a character table, rather than just display the string on-screen:

1. If a string starts with an ampersand (&), this flags the browser that what follows is a character code, rather than an ordinary string of characters.

2. If the next character is a pound sign (#), this tells the browser that what follows next is a string of numbers that corresponds to the character code for the symbol to be produced on-screen. This kind of code is called a "numeric entity."

   If the next character is anything other than the pound sign, this tells the browser that the string that follows is a symbol's name, which must be looked up in a built-in table of equivalent character symbols. This kind of code is called a "character entity."

3. When the browser sees a semicolon (;), this signals the end of the string that represents a character code. The browser then uses whatever characters or numbers follow either the ampersand or the pound sign to perform the right kind of lookup operation and display the requested character symbol. If it doesn't recognize the information supplied, most browsers will display a question mark (?) instead.

There are also a couple of things about character and numeric entities that might differ from your expectations, based on what you've learned about HTML tags so far, and on what you might know about computer character sets:

1. When reproducing the string of characters for an entity, HTML is case-sensitive. Because this means that < is different from < you need to reproduce character entities exactly as they're stated in Table 8-1. That's one reason why we prefer using numeric entities — it's less easy to make a mistake. The following code sample and browser display in Figure 8-1 make this point rather nicely:

```
<HTML>
<HEAD>
<TITLE>Checking character codes</TITLE>
</HEAD>
<BODY>
<H2>Copy character entities exactly...or else!</H2>
<P>
<TT>
<!- semicolon has a numeric code of 59       ->
<!- space has a numeric code of 32           ->
<!- ampersand has a character code of &amp; ->
<!- less-than has a character code of &lt;   ->
Less-than lowercase:&#32; &amp; lt &#59; &#32; = &lt;<BR>
Less-than uppercase:&#32; &amp; LT &#59; &#32; = &#32;&LT;<BR>
Less-than mixed-case:&#32; &amp; Lt &#59; &#32; = &#32;&Lt;<BR>
Less-than mixed-rev :&#32;&#32; &amp; lT &#59; &#32; = &#32;&lT;<BR>
</TT></BODY></HTML>
```

2. The numeric codes for reproducing characters within HTML do not come from the ASCII collating sequence; they come from the ISO-Latin-1 character set codes, shown later in this chapter in Table 8-1.

Figure 8-1:
Using and misusing character entities.

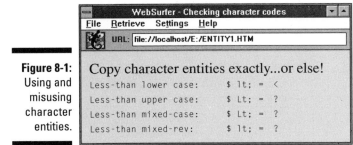

If you concentrate on reproducing characters exactly as they appear in Table 8-1, or copying the numbers that correspond to the ISO-Latin-1 scheme, you'll be able to produce exactly the right effects on your readers' screens.

Nothing Ancient about the ISO-Latin-1 HTML

The name of the character set that HTML uses is ISO-Latin-1. The "ISO" part means that it's taken from the International Standards Organization's body of official international standards — in fact, all ISO standards have corresponding numeric tags, so ISO-Latin-1 is also referred to as ISO8859-1. The "Latin" part means that it's derived from the Roman alphabet commonly used worldwide to represent text in many different languages. The number "1" refers to the version number for this standard (in other words, this is the first version of this character set definition).

ISO-Latin-1 distinguishes between two types of entities used to represent characters:

1. **Character entities** are strings of characters that represent other characters; for example, "<" and "&egrave" show a string of characters (lt and egrave) that stand for others (< and È).

2. **Numeric entities** are strings of numbers that represent characters. These are identified by a pound sign (#) that follows the ampersand. For example, "<" and "è" show a string of numbers (60 and 232) that stand for characters (< and È).

Table 8-1 illustrates that there are many more numeric entities than character entities. In fact, every character in the ISO-Latin-1 set has a corresponding numeric entity, but this is not true of the character entities.

Table 8-1: The ISO-Latin-1 character set

Character	Numeric Entity	Character Entity	Description
			Em space - not collapsed
			En space
			Non-breaking space
		&#00; - &#08;	Unused
				Horizontal tab

		
	Line feed or new line

		&#11; - &#31;	Unused

Character	Numeric Entity	Character Entity	Description
		&#32;	Space
!		&#33;	Exclamation mark
"	&quot;	&#34;	Quote
#		&#35;	Number sign
$		&#36;	Dollar sign
%		&#37;	Percent sign
&	&amp;	&#38;	Ampersand
"		&#39;	Apostrophe
(		&#40;	Left parenthesis
)		&#41;	Right parenthesis
*		&#42;	Asterisk
+		&#43;	Plus sign
,		&#44;	Comma
-		&#45;	Hyphen
.		&#46;	Period (fullstop)
/		&#47;	Solidus (slash)
0-9		0 - 9	Digits 0-9
:		&#58;	Colon
;		&#59;	Semicolon
<	&lt;	&#60;	Less than
=		&#61;	Equal sign
>	&gt;	&#62;	Greater than
?		&#63;	Question mark
@		&#64;	Commercial at
A-Z		A - Z	Letters A-Z (uppercase)
[		&#91;	Left square bracket
\		&#92;	Reverse solidus (backslash)
]		&#93;	Right square bracket
^		&#94;	Caret

Character	Numeric Entity	Character Entity	Description
_		&#95;	Underscore
`		&#96;	Grave accent
a-z		a - &#122	Letters a–z (lowercase)
{		&#123;	Left curly brace
|		|	Vertical bar
}		&#125;	Right curly brace
~		&#126;	Tilde
		&#127; -	Unused
¡		&#161;	Inverted exclamation
¢		&#162;	Cent sign
£		&#163;	Pound sterling
¤		&#164;	General currency sign
¥		&#165;	Yen sign
¦		&#16;6	Broken vertical bar
§		&#167;	Section sign
¨		&#168;	Umlaut (dieresis)
©		&#169;	Copyright
ª		&#170;	Feminine ordinal
<<		&#171;	Left angle quote, guillemotleft
¬		&#172;	Not sign
-		&#173;	Soft hyphen
®		&#174;	Registered trademark
¯		&#175;	Macron accent
°		&#176;	Degree sign
±		&#177;	Plus or minus
2		&#178;	Superscript two
3		&#179;	Superscript three
/		&#180;	Acute accent
µ		&#181;	Micro sign

Character	Numeric Entity	Character Entity	Description
¶		&#182;	Paragraph sign
·		&#183;	Middle dot
¸		&#184;	Cedilla
¹		&#185;	Superscript one
º		&#186;	Masculine ordinal
>>		&#187;	Right angle quote, guillemotright
¹/₄		&#188;	Fraction one-fourth
¹/₂		&#189;	Fraction one-half
³/₄		&#190;	Fraction three-fourths
¿		&#191;	Inverted question mark
À	&Agrave;	&#192;	Uppercase A, grave accent
Á	&Aacute;	&#193;	Uppercase A, acute accent
Â	&Acirc;	&#194;	Uppercase A, circumflex accent
Ã	&Atilde;	&#195;	Uppercase A, tilde
Ä	&Auml;	&#196;	Uppercase A, dieresis or umlaut mark
Å	&Aring;	&#197;	Uppercase A, ring
Æ	&AElig;	&#198;	Uppercase AE diphthong (ligature)
Ç	&Ccedil;	&#199;	Uppercase C, cedilla
È	&Egrave;	&#200;	Uppercase E, grave accent
É	&Eacute;	&#201;	Uppercase E, acute accent
Ê	&Ecirc;	&#202;	Uppercase E, circumflex accent
Ë	&Euml;	&#203;	Uppercase E, dieresis or umlaut mark
Ì	&Igrave;	&#204;	Uppercase I, grave accent
Í	&Iacute;	&#205;	Uppercase I, acute accent
Î	&Icirc;	&#206;	Uppercase I, circumflex accent
Ï	&Iuml;	&#207;	Uppercase I, dieresis or umlaut mark
Ñ	&Ntilde;	&#209;	Uppercase N, tilde

Character	Numeric Entity	Character Entity	Description
Ò	&Ograve;	&#210;	Uppercase O, grave accent
Ó	&Oacute;	&#211;	Uppercase O, acute accent
Ô	&Ocirc;	&#212;	Uppercase O, circumflex accent
Õ	&Otilde;	&#213;	Uppercase O, tilde
Ö	&Ouml;	&#214;	Uppercase O, dieresis or umlaut mark
×		&#215;	Multiply Sign
Ø	&Oslash;	&#216;	Uppercase O, slash
Ù	&Ugrave;	&#217;	Uppercase U, grave accent
Ú	&Uacute;	&#218;	Uppercase U, acute accent
Û	&Ucirc;	&#219;	Uppercase U, circumflex accent
Ü	&Uuml;	&#220;	Uppercase U, dieresis or umlaut mark
ß	&szlig;	&#223;	Lowercase sharp s, German (sz ligature)
à	&agrave;	&#224;	Lowercase a, grave accent
á	&aacute;	&#225;	Lowercase a, acute accent
â	&acirc;	&#226;	Lowercase a, circumflex accent
ã	&atilde;	&#227;	Lowercase a, tilde
ä	&auml;	&#228;	Lowercase a, dieresis or umlaut mark
å	&aring;	&#229;	Lowercase a, ring
æ	&aelig;	&#230;	Lowercase ae diphthong (ligature)
ç	&ccedil;	&#231;	Lowercase c, cedilla
è	&egrave;	&#232;	Lowercase e, grave accent
é	&eacute;	&#233;	Lowercase e, acute accent
ê	&ecirc;	&#234;	Lowercase e, circumflex accent
ë	&euml;	&#235;	Lowercase e, dieresis or umlaut mark
ì	&igrave;	&#236;	Lowercase i, grave accent
í	&iacute;	&#237;	Lowercase i, acute accent
î	&icirc;	&#238;	Lowercase i, circumflex accent

Character	Numeric Entity	Character Entity	Description
ï	&iuml;	&#239;	Lowercase i, dieresis or umlaut mark
ñ	&ntilde;	&#241;	Lowercase n, tilde
ò	&ograve;	&#242;	Lowercase o, grave accent
ó	&oacute;	&#243;	Lowercase o, acute accent
ô	&ocirc;	&#244;	Lowercase o, circumflex accent
õ	&otilde;	&#245;	Lowercase o, tilde
ö	&ouml;	&#246;	Lowercase o, dieresis or umlaut mark
÷		&#247;	Division sign
ø	&oslash;	&#248;	Lowercase o, slash
ù	&ugrave;	&#249;	Lowercase u, grave accent
ú	&uacute;	&#250;	Lowercase u, acute accent
û	&ucirc;	&#251;	Lowercase u, circumflex accent
ü	&uuml;	&#252;	Lowercase u, dieresis or umlaut mark
ÿ	&yuml;	&#255;	Lowercase y, dieresis or umlaut

One thing to note about using this information: if you frequently need to work with character or numeric entities in your documents, it'll be easier to use some kind of HTML editing tool to handle character replacements automatically.

Part VIII of this book (Chapters 24–28) covers HTML and related tools for a variety of platforms. If you're a serious Web developer, or often need to use character codes in your pages, please check out the tools available on your favorite platform. These can save you time and effort, and make you a happier, more productive WebMaster. ▪

Chapter 9

Building Basic HTML Documents

*B*uilding your first Web page is exciting if you keep this thought firmly in mind: You can change anything at any time. Good Web pages are always evolving. Nothing is cast in concrete — change is just a keystroke away.

Now that the pressure is off, you can start building your own simple but complete home page. Think of it as a prototype for future pages. Later you can add all sorts of bells and whistles to change it into any kind of page you want, be it for a business, an academic institution, or a government agency.

The layout, or the way the page looks to the user, creates the first impression of your whole Web site. If that first impression isn't pleasing, it may also be the last time the user visits your page. Not to worry, though: Your home page will be pleasing to the eye if you follow the "KISS" (Keep it Simple, Stupid) approach.

The Web itself is a confusing concept to many users. Everything you do to keep your page intuitively obvious will make your viewers happy and keep them coming back for more.

Chapter 5 presented the basic concepts of a good Web page, emphasizing the form and content over the HTML controls, as well as the elements of page layout and information flow. You might want to review it before continuing here.

Remember: Layout, content, first impression, KISS. OK, let's get on with it.

The Template's the Thing!

All well constructed Web pages contain the following four sections: Title, Heading, Body, and Footer.

If you look at a number of Web pages, you will undoubtedly see that most of them contain these sections in one form or another. You have also probably noticed, with some amount of frustration, that the pages that don't contain all of these elements either aren't pleasing to your eye or don't "work." That is, they aren't intuitive in their presentation and you can't easily find what you're looking for. We're not going to let that happen to your pages because you are going to use the following template for each HTML file:

```
<HTML>
<HEAD><TITLE>Your Title</TITLE>
</HEAD>
<BODY>
Your Heading Text
<P>
Your wonderful text and graphics.
<P>
<ADDRESS>
Your Name<BR>
Phone number<BR>
Standard Mail Address<BR>
E-Mail Address
</ADDRESS>
<P>
Copyright  &copy; 1995,  Your Name,  Revised — (Revision Date)
</BODY>
</HTML>
```

It's really that simple to get started on the correct path. This template actually works. Figure 9-1 shows what it looks like when viewed with Netscape.

✔ Use your browser to open your Web page HTML document file from your local hard disk.

✔ If you're using Netscape, remember to set the memory and disk caches to zero, so it will *Reload* each new version of your file from the disk, rather than loading the one in its cache. Other browsers cache pages, too, so make sure you're reading what you've just edited — not some older version! ▪

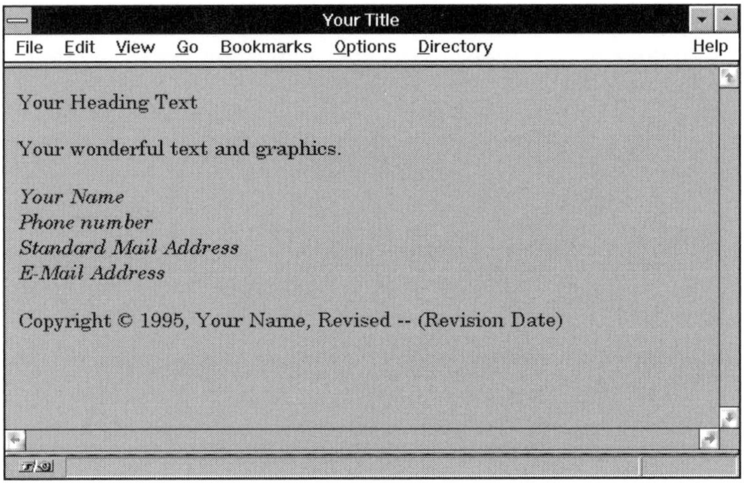

Figure 9-1:
The basic
Web page
template
viewed with
Netscape.

As you can see, your home page is currently plain and simple. That's not going to have folks flocking to see it, is it? You need to add your wonderful text and graphics to it. Since only a small but growing number of Internet surfers use GUI browsers, please follow our advice from Chapter 4 and put your energy into providing high-quality content and important links. Don't worry, in the next chapter you'll add some graphics, too. ▪

Page Layout: Top to Bottom

Now that you have a basic template, you can start changing it. To begin the fun, your first home page shouldn't occupy more than a single screen. This makes it much easier to edit and test. You can get more than enough information on a single screen, while helping your audience avoid unnecessary scrolling.

A single screen seems to be an easy concept to grasp, but is it? It is the amount of information a browser displays on the monitor without scrolling.

The amount of information displayed will vary depending upon the browser and monitor resolution. While you may not want to design for the lowest common denominator of browser and monitor, understand that if you assume the user will see your page the same as it looks in *your* browser, you are making a very bad assumption. Although there is no easy answer to this problem, testing your pages on a relatively low resolution monitor with several different browsers will help you to see your pages through your reader's eyes.

You will find it helpful to first sketch your design ideas on paper or use a drawing program to create a model of its layout and components. (Figure 9-2 shows an example.) This will show the spatial relationships on the page and the amounts and locations of the ever-important breathing room that page designers call "white space." While it is possible to have too much white space on a page, most designers err in the other direction, and wind up with far too little.

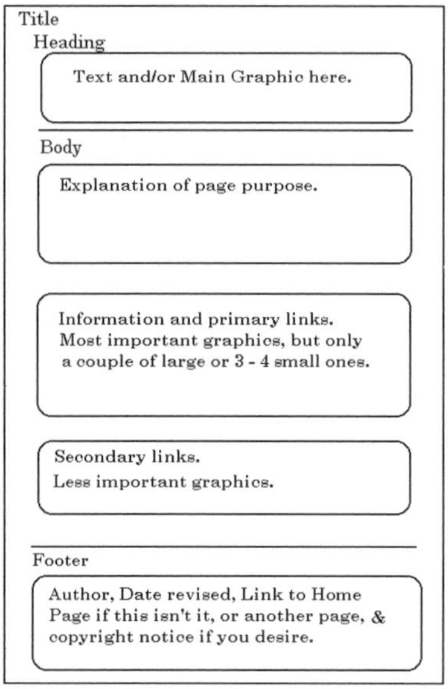

Figure 9-2:
Sketch of
Web page
layout.

It's essential to organize your page logically, and to make it easy for viewers to scan. Because everyone is always in a hurry, put the most important information near the top, in larger type, and with plenty of white space surrounding it. Place the remaining items below as you work your way through the content.

Remember, you're not trying to stuff as much as possible on a single page — you're trying to cover what's important for the topic at hand. If you have lots of material to cover, or more topics to deal with, you can easily make more pages and link them to this one. A good rule of thumb comes from professional presenters, who say that a single slide should try to convey no more than three to five pieces of related information.

What's in a Name? Thinking Up Good Titles and Headings

In HTML files, the title provides the most important basis for indexing a document. That's because titles are more readily available to casual surfers than the contents inside a page.

On the other hand, a document's headings provide an important visual contrast within any page. This happens because the user's browser settings determine the font and page size, and also control the line length. If you use appropriate heading content and layout, you can make your home page both attractive and readable, without making everybody read the fine print word for word.

Titles

The title of your page is important because it is used by many Web spiders and crawlers — the software robots that relentlessly cruise the Web, looking for information — to create index records for your pages in their databases. The title is also used for the name field in the bookmark or hot list sections of most browsers, meaning that they'll use your title to figure out what's on your page.

Since you want people to find and read your pages, you need to make titles as descriptive as possible. Try to limit the length of a title, so that it fits on a single line. Think of the title as the key words that describe the contents of your page. Understanding how titles get used should help you build titles that work — we hope you get the idea!

One way to arrive at a truly descriptive title is to type a list of the key words that best describe your page. Then, use them in a sentence. Next, delete the conjunctions, adverbs, and unnecessary adjectives. With a little rearranging, what's left should be a pretty good title.

Welcome to my parlor...

The vastness of the Web has spawned the development of lots of search tools to find and catalog what's out there. These tools are basically programs that traverse the Web, simply to look at everything they encounter, as they follow every link they can find and see where it takes them. That's why these software robots are called Web crawlers or Web spiders. They live on the Web, picking up all the tasty tidbits they can find. For more information on such exotic, but helpful, beasts, please consult Chapter 16.

Here's an example:

- ✔ **Words:** George, classical guitar player, bicycle racing.
- ✔ **Sentence:** George is a classical guitarist who races bicycles.
- ✔ **Title:** George's classical guitar and bike racing page.

This title should fit on one line when viewed by most browsers. Test it with your favorite browser to see how it looks.

Headings

Discussing headings can get somewhat confusing because each Web page should have a heading after the title followed by various headings in the body of the text. In the print world, for example in this book, headings are the emphasized text placed before paragraphs.

Headings may be the most important text in your Web page. They are the first text the viewer scans. If the headings aren't attractive and instantly informative, the viewer will be off to another page with a single click. If they can hook your audience, and make them want to learn more, then you've written good headings.

You are primarily concerned with the content of your headings and the consistency of their meaning and usage throughout your Web pages. Your headings should arise somewhat naturally after you analyze your text. They should paraphrase an important concept that you are about to present. If you remove all of the text from your document except the headings, you should be left with a very good outline or detailed table of contents.

If the situation permits, headings may even be humorous. Headings could contain a common theme to help catch the viewer's eye and interest. When it comes to headings, the best approach is to use your imagination with your audience in mind. This approach has been used with the headings in this book, and is a hallmark of the whole ...*For Dummies* series.

As a quick example, Table 9-1 shows some of the headings from this book in their "plain" and "humorous/theme" forms:

Table 9-1: Headings: plain vs. extra-spicy

Plain	*More Interesting*
Building Better Documents	Building Better Document Bodies
Building Good Paragraphs	Good Bones: Building Strong Paragraphs
Logos and Icons	Eye-Catchers: Logos, Icons, and Other Gems

In your Web page, you will have only a few headings per screen or page. Make the most of them. Keep the size of like headings consistent throughout your pages to help the viewer understand the level of importance of the information.

Although most browsers recognize at least four levels of headings, and the HTML DTD goes as deep as six levels, it is difficult for viewers to distinguish beyond the fourth level. Most well-constructed Web pages use no more than three levels of headings, even for very long documents.

Your home page will probably be more like the one in Figure 9-3 at this stage. It has one large heading line at the top and a medium-sized heading line toward the bottom. All graphics have been removed from this page to show you that you can still achieve a pleasing layout by using only a few well-worded headings and a few text links on an entire Web page.

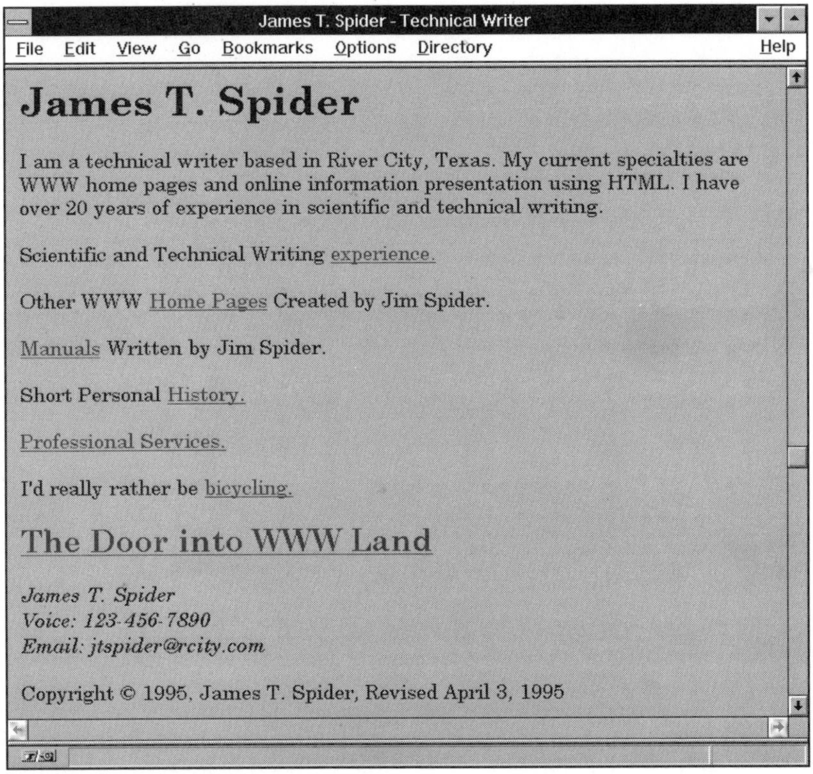

Figure 9-3: HTML document with headings and links viewed with Netscape.

The Web page shown in Figure 9-3 was created from the following HTML file, which your HTML files should resemble by the end of the next chapter.

The larger type font of the header line was produced by the <H1> ... </H1> tags, the largest heading. The heading "The Door Into WWW Land" is tagged with <H2> ... </H2>, the second level heading size. The standard heading tags <H1> through <H4> should be used for paragraph headings, hyperlinks, and other places where the text is to be on a line by itself with white space above and below.

```
<HTML>
<HEAD>
<TITLE>James T. Spider - Technical Writer</TITLE>
</HEAD>
<BODY>
<H1> James T. Spider </H1>
<P>
I am a technical writer based in River City, Texas. My current
specialties are WWW home pages and online information presentation
using HTML. I have over 20 years of experience in scientific and
technical writing.
<P>
Scientific and Technical Writing <A HREF="writ-gen.html"> experience.</A>
<P>
Other WWW <A HREF="hps.html">Home Pages</A> Created by Jim Spider.
<P>
<A HREF="manuals.html">Manuals</A> Written by Jim Spider.
<P>
Short Personal <A HREF="history.html">History.</A>
<P>
<A HREF="proservs.html"> Professional Services.</A>
<P>
I'd really rather be <A HREF="history.html#Bicycle">bicycling.</A>
<A HREF="amaze.html"><H2>The Door into WWW Land</H2></A>
<ADDRESS>James T. Spider<BR>
Voice: 123-456-7890<BR>
E-mail: jtspider@rcity.com
</ADDRESS>
<P>
Copyright  &copy; 1995, James T. Spider, Revised April 3, 1995
</BODY>
</HTML>
```

Two schools of thought exist regarding the use of heading sizes. The information school says heading tags should be used in increments or decrements of one and always start with <H1>. This approach definitely provides for an ordered, standardized structure to your content. It also makes it easy for Web crawlers to pick out the headings for their indexes.

The design school screams, "BORING!" when the incremental approach is mentioned. Use headings to draw attention to content. Putting an <H1> next to an <H3> or an <H4> creates more visual interest. As with most HTML design decisions, the choice is yours.

Experiment with heading tags to see what you think looks best. Remember, too much emphasized text diminishes the overall effect. Use it sparingly — emphasis works better when it remains exceptional. If you're a fan of fairy tales, it's kind of like crying "Wolf!"

Building Better Document Bodies

The body of your Web document lies at the heart of your page, between the header and the footer. Body content depends on the type and amount of information you want to put online, and what kind of audience(s) you're trying to reach.

Personal Web pages are generally quite different from business, academic, and government ones in the content and form of their bodies, although the layout for each type may be strikingly similar. The bodies of personal home pages (perhaps more accurately called "Welcome" pages, but who are we to quibble) tend to contain a brief textual introduction followed by numerous links to local pages and to pages at other Web sites. The primary differences in the layout and content of well-designed Web page bodies occur when the information they contain also differs significantly.

The bodies of most personal Web pages contain text for, or pointers to, the following elements:

- Résumé — mostly dense text with a picture.
- Personal History — mostly plain text.
- Favorite Sports or Hobbies — text with an occasional picture and links to sports or hobby sites.
- Favorite Web Sites — lists of links to Web sites.

The body of a commercial artist's Web pages might contain:

- Pictures, Pictures, Pictures — Usually small "thumbnail" size pictures that are links to the much larger versions.
- A page containing a résumé, or a list of shows and exhibits, awards, and other professional activities.
- Links to online samples of their work on other pages around the Net.

The bodies of many government agency pages contain large amounts of boring text (No! I don't believe it...) that should be revised into hypertext pages using HTML. In the meantime, many are friendly enough to provide a brief description of the text and an FTP hyperlink so you can easily download these monster file(s).

So, how much text is enough but not too much in the body of a Web page? The answer lies in the minds of your viewers. May we suggest, however, that large amounts of scrolling will almost always incline them to think "Enough already!"

Textual sound bites — NOT!

When Web surfers want to read pages and pages of dense text, they buy the book or download the file and print it. For online reading, large amounts of text isn't much fun and is viewed as a waste of bandwidth by many users (especially those who dial in with slower connections).

This doesn't necessarily imply that your Web pages should be the textual equivalent of 30-second sound bites on TV. It simply indicates that at the current level of WWW development, most users are looking for fast ways to find the information they want. They aren't going to dig very deeply into a sea of text to find it. It's up to you to make it easily available to them, by using an appropriate page layout and providing good indexes with hypermedia links within the body of your pages.

Balanced composition

The body on personal Web pages should contain three to five short, well written paragraphs. If these paragraphs are interspersed with moderately sized headings, and enough white space and small graphics to add visual interest, they'll probably be scanned in their entirety.

Good use of separators and numerous links to additional pages is also very much in vogue. Using these techniques should result in a page that's between one and three screens long. Avoid making pages longer than three full screens.

Controlling long pages

Pages composed of over five screens of text or screens full of URL link lists should be split into multiple pages. If you insist on serving long pages to your users, you can greatly increase their readability by linking a table of contents (TOC) to each section and providing a return link back to the top. This has an effect similar to splitting the page into multiple page files but still allows the user to capture the entire page as a single file. It also makes it easier for you to edit the HTML file. You'll want to balance this convenience against the penalty that moving a single large chunk of data can exact, just to make sure that you aren't overdoing things.

Speaking of chunks, a concept in writing exists called, "chunking." It deals with how to separate a long document. The basic chunking rule of thumb is: chunk the document at the idea or concept level. Large chunks take time to render, scroll, and search. Little-bitty chunks can make a concept fuzzy because the reader's concentration is interrupted too often while each separate page downloads. This is a good time for you to take the middle ground and chunk only as much as your users can easily catch.

It looks like we've drifted out of the content stream into the control stream. The two tend to blur together when the layout of long Web page bodies is discussed. Nevertheless, content should still remain your most important concern. It's just that when there's a lot of it, effective use of controls helps to make the content more approachable.

The bottom line on bodies

The basic rules for creating great Web page bodies are:

- ✔ Keep the layout consistent between pages to provide continuity for the reader.
- ✔ Provide plenty of white space and headings for easy visual scanning.
- ✔ Write short paragraphs and use them sparingly.
- ✔ Make liberal use of hypertext links to additional pages, rather than making your audience scroll, scroll, scroll.
- ✔ Vary the placement of the hyperlink words to provide more visual contrast to the page.
- ✔ Choose meaningful hyperlink words, NOT "click here."

Good Bones: Building Strong Paragraphs

"Omit needless words!" cried William Strunk, Jr. He also propounds Rule 17 in *The Elements of Style* (co-written with E.B. White), which states:

> *"Vigorous writing is concise. A sentence should contain no unnecessary words, a paragraph no unnecessary sentences, for the same reason that a drawing should have no unnecessary lines and a machine no unnecessary parts. This requires not that the writer make all his sentences short, or that he avoid all detail and treat his objects only in outline, but that every word tell."*

If we combine Rule 17 with Rule 13 from the same work, which reads: "Make the paragraph the unit of composition," these two principles inform the essence of writing clear, accurate prose.

WWW users demand the clearest and most concise text you can muster. But alas, not everyone on the Web is an English professor. Many have never heard of, much less read, Strunk and White. Nevertheless, all WWW surfers are readers of some language so clarity, no matter what the language, will promote accurate communication in your writing.

Remember, communicating with others is the reason you are creating Web pages in the first place. Therefore, write to communicate your information as clearly as possible. To this end, follow these steps to writing better paragraphs:

1. Create an outline for your information.

2. Write one paragraph for each significant point, keeping the sentences short, direct, and to the point.

3. Edit your text mercilessly, omitting all needless words and sentences.

4. Proofread and spellcheck.

5. Ask a few volunteers to evaluate your work.

6. Revise your text and edit it again as you revise it.

7. Solicit comments when you publish online.

Listward Ho: Choosing List Structures

You were exposed to the different types of HTML lists in Chapters 6 and 7. Now you will learn when, why, and how to use each type. ▣

Generally speaking, lists are used to distinguish lines of text from paragraphs via special formatting, usually some form of indentation. Some list types precede each line with a bullet or number.

The unordered list

The unordered or bulleted list is handy for emphasizing several short lines of information. This is HTML markup for an unordered list (displayed by Netscape in Figure 9-4):

```
<UL>
<LI> This is noticed.
<LI> So is this.
<LI> And so is this.
</UL>
```

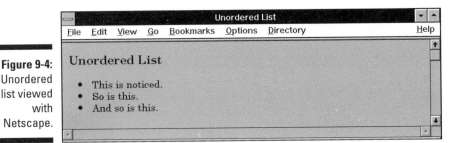

Figure 9-4:
Unordered
list viewed
with
Netscape.

The ordered list

The ordered or numbered list is used when the listed items have an obvious sequence. Here's the HTML markup for an ordered list (displayed by Netscape in Figure 9-5):

```
<OL>
<LI> First do A.
<LI> Then do B.
<LI> Lastly do C.
</OL>
```

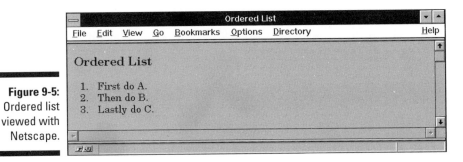

Figure 9-5:
Ordered list
viewed with
Netscape.

The definition list

The definition or glossary list combines items in pairs. The first is the term and the second is the definition. Here's the markup and the display is shown in Figure 9-6:

```
<DL>
<DT> Term A
<DD> Definition of Term A.
<DT> Term B
<DD> Definition of Term B.
</DL>
```

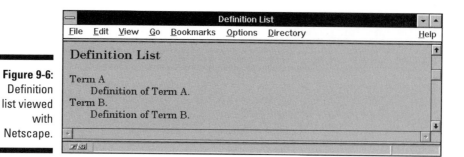

Figure 9-6:
Definition
list viewed
with
Netscape.

Le menu

The menu list is simply an indented group of lines. Some browsers currently recognize the menu list. Since HTML 3.0 may not include this type of list, it's a good idea to use one of the first three types instead. But here's how to write a menu list:

```
<MENU>
<LI>Item 1
<LI>Item 2
<LI>Item 3
</MENU>
```

which may produce the following result in some browsers; however, in Netscape it displays as an unordered list:

```
Item 1
Item 2
Item 3
```

The short list

The short or directory list is intended for use with very short items. It was originally used for lists of directories in UNIX with multiple columns across the page. Most browsers format the short list like the menu list, not in multiple columns. As with the menu list, you may want to use one of the first three list types instead, for better compatibility with future HTML releases. Here's the markup for a short list:

```
<DIR>
<LI>UNIX/
<LI>program/
<LI>generic/
</DIR>
```

which may produce the following result in some browsers; again Netscape displays it as an unordered list:

```
UNIX/
program/
generic/
```

Although you should keep your page layout simple, there are times when lists and even nested lists (to produce outline formatting as explained in Chapter 11) may be necessary to optimally display your specific type of information. However, use them intelligently and sparingly. ■

The following HTML document following shows the tags for an unordered list in the Web page body. The list is used to emphasize and separate the text lines:

```
<HTML>
<HEAD>
<TITLE>James T. Spider - Technical Writer / Web Weaver</TITLE>
</HEAD>
<BODY>
<H1> James T. Spider </H1>
<P>
I am a technical writer based in River City, Texas. My current
specialties are WWW home pages and online information presentation
using HTML. I have over 20 years of experience in scientific and
technical writing.
<P>
<UL>
<LI>Scientific and Technical Writing <A HREF="writ-gen.html"> Experience.</A>
<LI>Other WWW <A HREF="hps.html">Home Pages</A> Created by Jim Spider.
<LI><A HREF="manuals.html">Manuals</A> Written by Jim Spider.
<LI>Short Personal <A HREF="history.html">History.</A>
<LI><A HREF="proservs.html"> Professional Services.</A>
<LI>I'd really rather be <A HREF="history.html#Bicycle"> bicycling.</A>
</UL>
<A HREF="amaze.html"><H2>The Door into WWW Land</H2></A>
<ADDRESS>James T. Spider<BR>
Voice: 123-456-7890<BR>
E-mail: jtspider@rcity.com
</ADDRESS>
<P>
Copyright  &copy; 1995, James T. Spider, Revised April 9, 1995
</BODY>
</HTML>
```

Figure 9-7 shows how this displays in Netscape. The bulleted list definitely emphasizes the body lines and adds to the visual richness of the page.

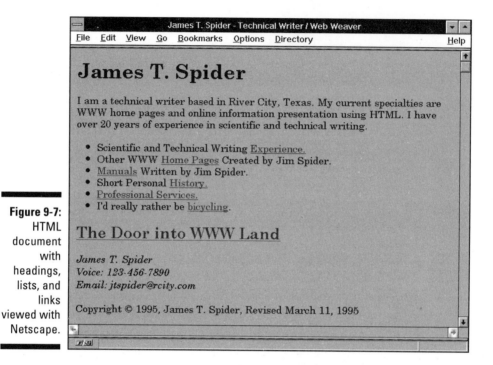

Figure 9-7:
HTML document with headings, lists, and links viewed with Netscape.

Hooking Up: Linking Your Pages

Hypermedia links within the body of your pages bring out the power of the Web. To many users, surfing the Web is the ultimate video game. Following links just to see where they go can be interesting and informative.

As a Web page designer and Web weaver, you obviously want your users to like your pages well enough to tell others, who will tell others, and so on. Therefore, it's up to you to provide good links both within your own Web pages and to other Internet resources.

Links to pages within your Web are relative

As you have seen in previous chapters, links come in two flavors, relative or full. A relative link, such as this one from the James T. Spider HTML document, <A HREF="manuals.html">Manuals</A> can only be used within your own Web since the URL referenced is relative to the directory of the page from which it is called. In this case, it is actually a file (manuals.html) in the same directory as the current HTML file (the current URL). It is relative to the server's document root plus the path in the file system where the current URL is stored.

When you create links to HTML documents, always use the ".html" extension. If the page resides on a DOS server, the fourth letter "l" will be ignored. Make sure you change the extensions of the .htm files you upload from a DOS or Windows computer to a UNIX server to .html. This is for the sake of the UNIX server which will require all four characters in the file extension since you used the .html extension in your Web document link. ▪

A bit of advice regarding overuse of links. Use them only when they convey needed information and then use each specific link only once per page. Users can get very irritable when you make a link out of each occurrence of a commonly used word or phrase on a single page.

All of the links you see in Figure 9-7 are relative links. This is the simplest form of a relative reference, and is the easiest kind for you to use in your home page and its related page-mates.

Links to the world outside of your Web are physical

A physical or full link, such as:

```
<A HREF="http://www.nps.gov/nbs/"> National Biological Service</A>
```

gives the entire http URL address. You may use physical URLs for all of your links without any noticeable difference in speed, even on your local server. However, relative links are much shorter to type in your HTML file, and may improve your overall productivity.

When including physical URLs for links, we strongly recommend that you link to the resource first, and capture the URL using your browser. Then, you can paste this URL right into your HTML file with little or no chance of introducing an error. ▪

Whether it is better to use relative or physical links is a debate for the newsgroups or your local UNIX user's group. You are primarily concerned with the content of the links within your Web, their relationships to each other, and their contribution to your overall Web. Chapter 11 contains more advanced information on using Web links. ▪

Choose your hyperlinks with care

Your home page may have links similar to those in the home page in Figure 9-7. Notice which words in the list have been included in the hyperlink text (highlighted and/or underlined). These are the words you must click on to open the link.

Choose your link text and images very carefully. Keep the text short and the graphics small. And never, never, never use the phrase "click here" as link text. Why, you ask? Because some users don't have mice or pointing devices. More important, it may appear to readers that you didn't care enough to write an appropriate sentence with a meaningful word or phrase for the link.

Well-chosen hyperlinks let your users quickly scan hyperlink text and choose links without reading surrounding non-highlighted text. The remainder of the text is usually included only to provide readers with clarification of the link text anyway.

In Figure 9-7, the word, "Experience" might be unambiguous enough to stand alone, but "History" and "Manuals" are not. Adding a few carefully chosen modifiers to your hyperlink text will usually clear up any ambiguities.

The entire heading, "The Door into WWW Land" is included in the link because the graphic of a door has been removed. In the next chapter this graphic will be put back into the HTML document to show the emphasis a small picture can add to a link.

Remember, users are in a hurry to scan your page and quickly pick out the important links by their unique wording or graphics. Make it easy for them by using meaningful hyperlinks.

The next chapter goes beyond the Web-building that has been introduced in this chapter. Let's move "onward, through the fog," to put the finishing touches on your first fantastic home page!

Chapter 10

Beyond Basics: Adding Flair and Impact to Your Pages

• •

In This Chapter

▶ Adding logos, icons, and other little gems

▶ Building high-impact graphic pages

▶ Putting your best footer forward

▶ Copyrighting your copy

▶ Including version information

▶ Pointing to the author

▶ Using comments in HTML documents

• •

*W*hen you see a Web page with a layout that you especially like, view its source to see the formatting. You can use your browser's Save As feature to save the HTML source to your own hard disk for later study, or you can print it.

At the same time, you can add the page to your bookmark file so you can find it again to look at its images. Some browsers also let you save the images associated with a page to files on your hard disk. However, before you publish somebody else's work on your pages, be aware of copyright laws (if you're in doubt whether it's OK to reuse something, the safest course of action is: "Don't do it!").

Borrowing Can Lead to Sorrow

Imitation may be the sincerest form of flattery, but stealing other authors' work and including it on your Web pages as if it were your own, is against the law in most countries. However, learning new techniques from the work of others is the way most Web weavers expand their horizons.

Use the techniques you learn to build your Web pages, with your information, in your own unique manner. You can always e-mail another Web author and request permission to use something of theirs in your page. Most Web authors will be happy to help you since they too have been helped by others in their quest for new Web tools and techniques.

Eye-Catchers: Logos, Icons, and Other Little Gems

Graphics add impact and interest to your Web pages for users with GUI browsers. Unless the primary focus of your Web pages is computer graphics, you should use small graphics and only where they add extra value to your pages. Again, keep in mind that the only acceptable speed for computer users is instantaneous. The larger the graphic, the slower it loads.

Speaking of small, fast-loading graphics, it's time for you to add some sparkle to your "plain Jane" home page. So far, it has nice-looking headings and a few bullets next to the list lines (Figure 9-7). Since the basic layout of the page is well established, all you need are a few splashes of color in appropriate locations to really spice things up.

Adding an image to your HTML document is as simple as inserting a line using the <IMG> tag:

```
<IMG SRC="ballred.gif">
```

This line contains the mandatory source reference (URL) to a GIF file named ballred. It is a relative reference to the file that the WWW server program expects to find in the same directory as the current page (i.e., the page from which the link is called). For example, if the URL that calls for the red ball image is:

```
"http://www.mysite.net/~jtspider/index.html"
```

using the relative URL shown above for the red ball would cause the server to look for:

```
"http://www.mysite.net/~jtspider/ballred.gif"
```

Alternatively, you may use the following image tag with the full URL for the red ball:

```
<IMG SRC="http://www.mysite.net/~jtspider/ballred.gif">
```

If you want to link to an image file of a red ball (redball.gif) located in some other Web site, you must use a full URL in the <IMG> tag like this:

```
<IMG SRC="http://www.someothersite.net/icons/redball.gif">
```

Using a full URL as a link means that each time the user's browser loads the icon, it actually links to the remote location. This increases the time it takes for the browser to load the file. If the remote location is not online, the image won't be loaded. Therefore, it usually works better to have your graphic files on your own WWW server.

An exception to this occurs when you want to include an image from another location that changes over time (weather map, clock, etc.) or an extremely large image. In the first case, the other site maintains the changing image and your users see it directly from their site but included in your page. In the second case, you save your server's disk space by pointing to the remote location for the 10 megabyte picture.

The rest of this section discusses several small graphic elements as they are used in the following HTML document and displayed in Figure 10-1. Only six different small graphic elements were used a total of eleven times. They range in size from 153 bytes for dotblue.gif to 1177 bytes for opendoor.gif.

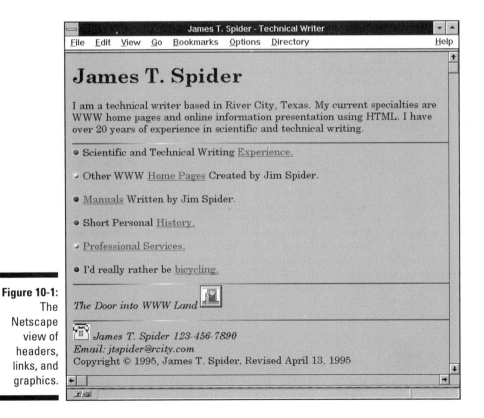

Figure 10-1: The Netscape view of headers, links, and graphics.

Reusing the same graphic on a single Web page adds no time or disk storage use when caching is activated in the user's browser. Therefore, using the rainbow line three times and each colored dot twice helps keep the load and display times for the images to a minimum. Recycling images makes as much sense for Web pages as it does for the environment!

```
<HTML>
<HEAD><TITLE>James T. Spider - Technical Writer </TITLE></HEAD>
<BODY>
<H1> James T. Spider </H1>
<P> I am a technical writer based in River City, Texas. My current special
ties are WWW home pages and online information presentation using HTML. I
have over 20 years of experience in scientific and technical writing.

<IMG SRC="rainbolg.gif">   <!— Rainbow line graphic —>

<IMG SRC="ballred.gif"> Scientific and Technical Writing
<A HREF="writ-gen.html"> Experience.</A>
<P>
<IMG SRC="ballwhit.gif"> Other WWW <A HREF="hps.html">Home Pages</A>
Created by Jim Spider.
<P>
<IMG SRC="ballblue.gif"> <A HREF="manuals.html">Manuals</A> Written
by Jim Spider.
<P>
<IMG SRC="ballred.gif"> Short Personal
<A HREF="history.html">History.</A>
<P>
<IMG SRC="ballwhit.gif"> <A HREF="proservs.html"> Professional
Services.</A>
<P>
<IMG SRC="ballblue.gif"> I'd really rather be
<A HREF="history.html#Bicycle">bicycling.</A>

<IMG SRC="rainbolg.gif">   <!— Rainbow line graphic —>

<EM> The Door into WWW Land</EM> <A HREF="amaze.html">
<IMG SRC="opendoor.gif" ALT=" WWW Land"></A>
<BR>
<IMG SRC="rainbolg.gif">   <!— Rainbow line graphic —>

<ADDRESS><IMG SRC="phone.gif"> James T. Spider  123-456-7890<BR>
E-mail: jtspider@rcity.com
</ADDRESS>
Copyright &copy; 1995, James T. Spider, Revised April 3, 1995
</BODY>
</HTML>
```

Horizontal rules — but rainbow lines bring smiles

Separating the text section from the large heading of Mr. Spider's name and occupation with the rainbow line graphic adds the first touch of color to our page. This separation could be accomplished with a simple HTML horizontal rule tag <HR>.

However, since <HR>'s only display is as a 3-D line (gray, black, and white to give the 3-D effect), you don't get the same impact as the rainbow line. This colorful baby changes from blue on both ends through reds and oranges, to yellow in the middle, for a much nicer look.

Using the rainbow line to bracket the door into WWW land and its graphic just above the footer information, sets them apart from the surrounding text, thereby drawing the user's attention. This is especially noticeable since "The Door into WWW Land" text is no longer the highlighted hyperlink.

Colored ruler lines are perfect for segmenting your pages into eye-pleasing information blocks. You can make them with most "paint" programs in any length, thickness, and color combination imaginable. You can also find many on public access graphic Web sites where they are available for your use, generally with no strings attached.

A few sources to get you started include:

```
http://www.cs.cmu.edu:8001/afs/cs/usr/mwm/www/tutorial/images.html
http://www.bsdi.com/icons
http://www.netspace.org/~dwb/www-authoring.html
http://www.di.unipi.it/iconbrowser/icons.html
http://www.uncg.edu/~rdralph/icons
http://www.cs.yale.edu/HTML/YALE/CS/HyPlans/loosemore-sandra/clipart.html
```

Just a couple of thoughts regarding using colored line images in place of <HR>. It may be quicker and easier to click the button on your HTML editor that inserts the <HR> into your document than to type the link to the colored line image, especially if you have more than a few of them over many pages. Also, future Web searching spiders or agents may use the <HR> to distinguish breaks in text for their indexes. They won't necessarily recognize the colored line image as being a replacement for the <HR> tag.

Colored balls beat list dots

The unordered list structure, used in the previous version of the page to provide black dots (bullets) to the left of the link lines, has been replaced by red, white, and blue ball graphics. These are not just colored dots. They contain highlights and shadows which make them look like three dimensional balls. Alternating them in red, white, and blue order increases their eye-catching effect, and differentiates each line from the lines above and below.

A word of caution about replacing lists with colored balls: the HTML 2.0 standard included the unordered or bulleted list for a reason. That was to list items in a nonsequential order and set them off by preceding each with a symbol. Each browser renders these bullets in a standard fashion. Some browsers even display 3-D colored balls instead of black dots. This can't be said about individual images of little colored balls.

As mentioned regarding colored lines, an active spider or agent looking at the page could deduce that an object following an <LI> tag is part of the list it just entered and could organize this information accordingly. They cannot be expected to recognize an imitation list with colored balls. If you're presenting a true list of items, you may want to use the actual HTML list tags. If you want to add some life to your page with colored balls next to some lines, go for it.

Colored balls are like ornaments on a Christmas tree: They can really add sparkle to a page when used sparingly. You can make colored balls with your paint program or download them from the WWW sites mentioned on the previous page. Do your users a favor, too, and please don't make them blink.

Using colored balls and other small icons within lines of text is as simple as inserting the tagged URL in the text at the point you want it displayed. In the line below, the blue ball is created by <IMG SRC="ballblue.gif"> and displayed before "I'd." Notice the space between the ">" and the "I." While browsers generally ignore spaces, Netscape, Mosaic, and others may recognize a single space before or after text to help you format sentences properly and keep images from crowding text.

```
<IMG SRC="ballblue.gif"> I'd really rather be <A
HREF="history.htm#Bicycle">bicycling.</A>
```

Also notice that there is a space after "be" but there is no space before "bicycling." This properly formats the line, "I'd rather be bicycling." You may be able to visualize this better if you think of the reference tag <A HREF= "history.htm#Bicycle"> as simply being inserted into the properly formatted sentence but taking up no actual space in the final browser display.

You need to be careful where you place the space, though. It should be outside the anchor text (i.e., not between the <A and </A> tags). If you include a space between the ">" and "bicycling," it will be considered part of the link and will be underlined by most browsers. This is poor HTML style and looks sloppy.

Icons

The term "icon" is used here to describe any small graphic image that can be substituted for a unit of text. A few well designed and carefully located icons will help your users quickly find their way around your Web pages.

Icons stored as GIF files are usually small and will load quickly. In most instances, an icon is simply added as a standard image-tagged URL in the position you want it to be displayed.

Most icons are so small that there is no need to align the text next to them, but for larger images, alignment is discussed later in this chapter. The default for most browsers is to align the text with the bottom of the image.

The telephone icon is used in Mr. Spider's home page to draw the user's eye to his telephone number, which he hopes many potential clients will be calling. This icon was added to the HTML document in the line shown below:

```
<ADDRESS><IMG SRC="phone.gif"> James T. Spider  123-456-7890
```

Graphics as hyperlinks

The open door icon used in Mr. Spider's home page illustrates the use of a graphic as the hyperlink. Netscape displays a colored border around the icon to indicate that it's a link. In the following line from the HTML document, the image icon tag is nested within the link reference tags to make the icon act as a hyperlink:

```
<H2> The Door into WWW Land </H2><A HREF="amaze.html">
<IMG SRC="opendoor.gif" ALT=" WWW Land"></A>
```

Notice also the use of the alternate text attribute, ALT="WWW Land", in the image tag. Text-only browsers will display "WWW Land" as the hyperlink instead of the open door icon. Some graphic browsers display an image holder icon and the alternate text when their image display function is turned off.

The creative use of the open door icon as the hyperlink to a page of WWW links adds visual interest to the home page. It also stimulates the user's interest in exploring what lies beyond the open door through which you see an inviting, pleasant mountain view. If you use a few well-selected icons in this manner, your Web pages will stand out and be remembered.

Logos

Logos are special-use graphics. They vary from icon size to much larger, sometimes too large. Remember KISS? Complex logos that take too long to load are nugatory on any Web page.

Use logos to identify your business or institution in a pleasing, eye-catching manner. Don't use them to overpower the page, or to irritate the users. A moderately-sized logo at the top of the home page is generally acceptable. Using icon-sized logos in the footer of each Web page is equally acceptable. Remember that text-only browsers and GUI browsers with image loading turned off (for faster page loading) won't display your fantastic logos anyway.

Figures 10-2 and 10-3 illustrate the use of a moderately-sized logo at the top of a page. The logo file is only 4,386 bytes long, so it loads in only a few seconds. It is 473 pixels wide and 116 pixels high, therefore it will easily fit on display screens with resolution as low as 640 X 480 pixels. These figures also illustrate the view with the image loading turned off in Netscape.

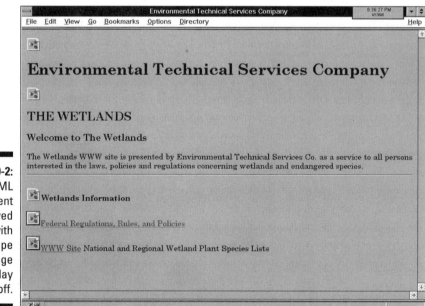

Figure 10-2:
HTML
document
logo viewed
with
Netscape
and image
display
turned off.

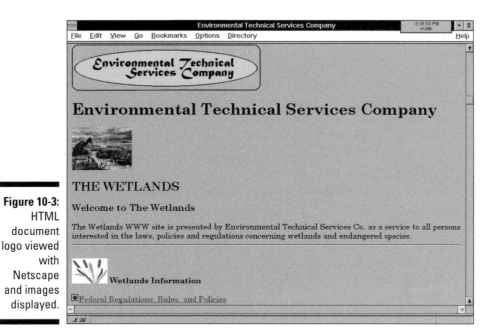

Figure 10-3:
HTML
document
logo viewed
with
Netscape
and images
displayed.

Here's the HTML code that produced these two views:

```
<IMG SRC="etslogo2.gif"><H1> Environmental Technical Services Company</H1>
<P>
<IMG src="jnc-lin.gif"><H2>    THE WETLANDS</H2>

<H3>Welcome to The Wetlands</H3>
The Wetlands WWW site is presented by Environmental Technical
Services Co. as a service to all persons interested in the laws,
policies, and regulations concerning wetlands and endangered species.
<BR>
<HR>

<P>
<IMG ALIGN=BOTTOM SRC="cattail.gif"><B>    Wetlands Information</B>
<P>
<A HREF="fedwetrg.htm"><IMG SRC="dotblue.gif">Federal Regulations,
Rules, and Policies</A>
<P>
<A HREF="http://www.nwi.fws.gov/Ecology.html">
<IMG S
RC="dotgreen.gif">WWW Site</A>
National and Regional Wetland Plant Species Lists
<P>
```

Building Graphic Page Layouts

As you now thoroughly understand, the graphic layout of the Web pages you see in this chapter did not occur by accident. The page layouts were drawn with the best locations for graphics noted. The graphics were carefully chosen and sized to fit the page layout and purpose of the page.

As you can see in Figure 10-1, the graphics were added sparingly to brighten and enhance the visual contrast within the page. Upon first viewing the page, the user sees the large name. This is good since the primary purpose of the page is to focus on the person and his accomplishments.

As the user scans down the page, the red, white, and blue balls and highlighted hyperlinks focus the attention on links to Mr. Spider's accomplishments. Finally, the phone and open door icons focus attention on the concluding key parts of the page. The overall layout is somewhat conservative yet interesting, which is what Mr. Spider thinks will catch clients in his Web.

The top portion of the business home page, shown in Figures 10-2 and 10-3, illustrates the additional thought that must go into the design and layout of pages that use larger graphics. The company wanted a page that worked well for non-GUI browsers yet showed their tasteful logo and some pertinent graphics on GUI browsers. The page designer drew the layout with and without the graphics and used the appropriate HTML features to accomplish the company's goals. If you experiment with the various formatting tags available in HTML, and follow the suggestions in this book, you can do the same for your Web pages.

Working with graphics files

You must work with graphics on two distinct levels to arrive at a good page layout and optimum functionality. You must be concerned not only with their size and complexity, but you must also be aware of the size of the image files and how long it takes to download them.

The original file for the wetland scene in Figure 10-3 was a one megabyte file that covered the entire screen. Careful cropping, resizing, and resampling using fewer pixels per inch resulted in the current file size of only 6,923 bytes. This change results in a dramatic improvement in load time — it's not unusual for a megabyte of data to require minutes to load over a slow link, but a 6,923-byte file moves in seconds even over slow telephone lines.

You don't have to become an expert at using graphics manipulation programs such as Paint Shop Pro, Photo Styler, Graphics WorkShop, or Lview Pro to produce high quality images for your Web pages. However, if you are going to do a lot of work with images, you probably should become fairly adept at one of these shareware programs or a similar commercial equivalent.

GIF and JPEG file formats

Although you can use many different types of graphic files on the Web, most browsers have internal display capabilities for only GIF and JPEG. Browsers use external helper applications to display the other file types. Also, compressed GIF and JPEG files are the smallest, and therefore the fastest to load of all the commonly-used file types.

Most good shareware image manipulation programs, such as those mentioned above, will load and save both GIF and JPEG format files. These programs also support the GIF87 and interlaced GIF89 formats. If you're using a Macintosh, the program to use for interlaced GIFs is GifConverter.

Seeing through the graphic to the background

The GIF89 format also introduced the "transparent background" feature. This allows you to set the color of the background of an image to match that of the browser's background color. The user then sees your image seeming to float on the browser's background rather than having a square of another color around the image.

Programs such as giftrans for UNIX and DOS, and Transparency for the Macintosh create images with transparent backgrounds for browsers that support the GIF89 format. This capability really adds to the impact and drama on a Web page.

Slice up your graphics for better response time!

What is an "interlaced GIF," you ask? It is a method of storing the GIF file so that the browser can load a low resolution image on the first of four passes, then fill in to the normal resolution on the subsequent passes. This gives the image a "Venetian blind" look as it is drawn.

The total load time for a given image remains the same but some browsers, such as Netscape, load the text of the page with the first pass of the images. This lets the user begin scrolling and reading while the other three image passes are completed. This gets the user to your information much faster, which generally results in a happier user.

Making it legal: GIF vs. JPEG

Although the GIF format is the most prevalent, legal problems with its usage may turn the Web community toward the JPEG format in the future. It would be a good idea for you to check this out yourself through the Web and with your legal adviser if you are going to use a large number of images in your Web system.

A new pic's resolution...

One last technical aspect of dealing with images is the number of bits per pixel stored in the file. Although this reduces the resolution and therefore the quality of the image as seen by the browser, if you really need to show a large image as quickly as possible, storing it with 7 or even 5 bits per pixel may help you. Check your graphics program for more information on this technique.

Rule for graphical thumbs

Keep these rules of thumb firmly in mind while you design your Web pages:

- Sketch your layout with and without the graphics.
- Focus on overall page look and content.
- KISS your images....small and simple.
- Use compressed interlaced GIFs or JPEGs.
- Link a thumbnail version of an image to the larger file instead of dumping the megabyte file on the unsuspecting user.
- Include the size of the image file in the text describing large images.
- Use graphics sparingly for maximum effect.
- Images or graphics should enhance the text information. ▧

Footers Complete Your Page

The *Yale C/AIM WWW Style Manual: Interface Design* provides a wonderful rationale for using footers on your Web pages as a matter of course:

> *State the title, the author, the date, and provide at least one link to a local home page in every WWW page in your system, and you will have gone 90% of the way toward providing your readers with an understandable WWW interface. (http://info.med.yale.edu/caim/StyleManual_Top.HTML)*

All of the elements mentioned, except the title, are contained in the footer of each Web page. Unlike the HTML header and body, the footer is not a marked element of an HTML document. By convention, it is the bottom portion of the page body.

Footers contribute greatly to your Web pages by providing the authorship, contact information, legal status, version/revision information, and a link to your home page. The footer should contain some or all of the elements listed in Table 10-1.

Table 10-1: Footer elements

Author's name

Author's institution or company

Author's phone number

Author's e-mail address

Author's postal mailing address

Page owner's name

Page owner's phone number

Page owner's e-mail address

Page owner's postal mailing address

Legal disclaimer or language designating the page as the official communication of the company or institution

Date of page's last revision

Official company or institutional seal, logo, or other graphic mark

Copyright notice

URL of the page

Hypertext link(s) to home page or to other pages

Hypertext link(s) to other sections of this page

Your basic home page HTML document already contains the minimum suggested footer information for a home page:

```
<ADDRESS>
Your Name<BR>
Phone number<BR>
Standard Mail Address<BR>
E-Mail Address
</ADDRESS>
<P>
Copyright  &copy; 1995,  Your Name,  Revised — (Revision Date)
```

Since it is a home page, it doesn't contain a link to itself. However, all of the other local pages in your Web should contain a link in the footer with your full home page URL similar to Mr. Spider's:

```
<A HREF="http://www.rcity.net/~jtspider/homepage.html">Spider's Home Page</A>
```

or an equivalent link to your home page:

```
<A HREF="/~jtspider/homepage.html">Spider's Home Page</A>
```

The name of your home page file will depend upon your WWW server's requirements. Some servers require a specific name and extension, such as index.html with the type being all four letters of "html." It's a UNIX thing. Don't worry though; it's easy to do. On an NCSA WWW server with a default configuration, the default HTML page is "index.html", therefore, these URLs are equivalent:

```
<A HREF="http://www.foo.net/goo">   <!— least desirable —>
<A HREF="http://www.foo.net/goo/">  <!— better —>
<A HREF="http://www.foo.net/goo/index.html"> <!— most desirable —> ■
```

Businesses and institutions may have special requirements regarding credits, addresses, logos, and other footer information. Frequently the author or person in charge of maintaining the page may not be the owner of the page. The owner may be a business and the author an employee. Depending on the purposes of the page, contact information for both may be required in the footer.

Government agencies and other public institutions frequently want to put what seems like their entire staff directory and departmental history in their footers. At least they're at the bottom of the page. However, if you are going to have a long footer, place a link back to the home page above it so the user doesn't have to scroll as far to find it.

Figure 10-4 illustrates a well balanced footer from an educational institution. It contains all of the important footer elements in a visually pleasing layout. Notice the use of graphic icons as hyperlinks for moving within the page and jumping back to the home page. This works well for GUI browsers but would frustrate users of text-only browsers had Mr. Lynch not added the ALT attribute.

Taking the time to do this is a nice gesture you should incorporate into your Web pages. It is as simple as placing the ALT="Text" after the image source file as shown below:

```
<A HREF="Man1Top.html"><IMG SRC="PrevPage.GIF" ALT="Prev Page"></A>
<A HREF="M1.html"><IMG SRC="NextPage.GIF" ALT="Next Page"></A>
<A HREF="Man1Top.html"><IMG SRC="Man1Top.GIF" ALT="Manual Top"></A>
<A HREF="HOME.html"><IMG SRC="HomePage.GIF" ALT="Home Page"></A>
```

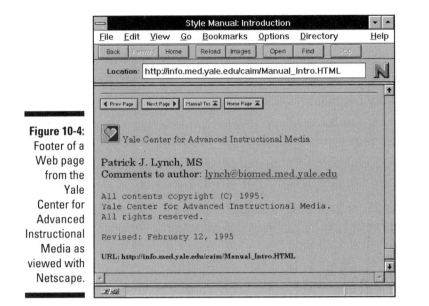

Figure 10-4:
Footer of a
Web page
from the
Yale
Center for
Advanced
Instructional
Media as
viewed with
Netscape.

Use a URL line as part of your page

Notice that the URL is visible in the footer. It's a good idea to put the URL for each page in the footer in small type. This helps viewers who print your page, but don't add it to their browser's hot list, to find it again on the WWW. Doing this is a nice finishing touch: It shows your viewers that you care about them.

Instead of placing all of the footer information directly in each page, you may want to put some of it in a page of its own and include a link to that information in the footer. This works especially well if your information requires a long legal disclaimer or other complex language. Please check with your legal representative concerning the fine points of using disclaimers on the Web. ▓

Copyright

Copyright law hasn't quite caught up with the explosion in electronic publishing on the Web. However, it won't hurt you or your organization to put your copyright notice at the bottom of any Web page that you don't want freely copied, without being attributed to you.

The copyright notice shown in Figure 10-4 is simply standard text with the copyright symbol simulated as (C). Most browsers will display the actual copyright symbol © if you use the character entity © in the file.

Counting coup: versions, dates, and times

Keeping track of changes in their programs has been a trying chore for programmers the world over. Recent advances in version control systems have greatly reduced the "wrong version" syndrome by automatically placing time and date stamps on each program routine. The bad news is that no automatic version control systems are available for your Web pages. You will have to keep track and make your users aware of changes in your pages that could affect them.

Why should you even bother to note when you change your pages? One of the greatest values of publishing on the Web is your ability to change your pages quickly after your information changes. Your users need to know when this occurs. You need to know which version you are providing so you can be certain you change it when the newer version is ready.

Version numbering

If it is appropriate to your information, you may want to use version numbers in addition to a revision date. This allows you to refer to a particular page as version 12B, for example, rather than the second revision of December.

Revision date

Placing the revision date in the footer of each page keeps track of its chronology. The format for the date should be March 12, 1995 to avoid confusion. In the USA, this date would be abbreviated 3/12/95. In Europe, this abbreviation would be read as the 3rd of December, 1995.

If for some reason you don't want to show the revision date on the page, you will be much happier in the long run if you use the HTML comment tags and hide the revision date inside them. The use of HTML comments is discussed later in this chapter.

Time stamp

The time may be added to the date for very sensitive information. Since users from all over the world can view your information at any time, 24 hour, GMT (Greenwich Mean Time) is the most appropriate format. Make sure you note the time as GMT (i.e., 18:30 GMT for 6:30 PM).

New

If some of the information on your pages changes frequently but at irregular intervals, you can alert your users with a small graphic or *** NEW *** notice followed by the revision date for the information. This marker should be removed after the information is no longer considered new. New notices that hang around for months are worthless and clutter your page.

Pointers to the Author or Owner

You can choose between using an e-mail link or a form as your method of obtaining feedback. Your choice may depend upon which of these options your Web service provider makes available to you. Of the two, e-mail is the simplest and most generally used for personal home pages. Businesses tend to use the custom form approach in an attempt to learn more specific information about their users.

The e-mail link for feedback

The "mailto:" link is a special link that starts an e-mail program on some servers that lets the user send e-mail to the page owner. Every well constructed home page has some way for the user to give feedback to the developer or owner of the page. The most general is providing your e-mail address in text inside <ADDRESS> ... </ADDRESS>. Although it is not supported by all Web server software or even all browsers, the e-mail link is a frequently seen method. If you want to use it in view of the above-mentioned limitations, here's how:

```
<A HREF="mailto:jtspider@rcity.com">E-mail</A> to Jim.
```

In this example, the hyperlink is "E-mail" and the "to Jim" has been added to make it more friendly. You can customize the wording to your heart's content, outside the actual address portion <A HREF="mailto:jtspider@rcity.com">. You can also put text in front of it:

```
Jim is waiting for your <A HREF="mailto:jtspider@rcity.com">E-mail.</A>
```

Notice that "E-mail" is still the hyperlink because it is the action word you want users to see quickly. The e-mail lines shown above are displayed in Figure 10-5.

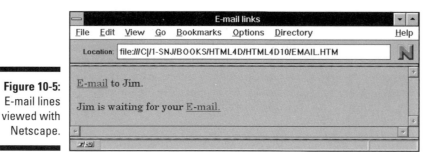

Figure 10-5:
E-mail lines
viewed with
Netscape.

Forms for feedback

Instead of using e-mail, some home page authors set up a form that generally requests the user's name, address, and other information and gives the user space to type a message to the page owner. Forms are an advanced HTML feature that provide an area on the screen for direct user input. They rely upon underlying UNIX based CGI (Common Gateway Interface) scripts on the Web server. Creating forms for feedback and other uses is discussed in more detail in Chapter 12. ■

Comment Your HTML Documents for Posterity

Do yourself a big favor and annotate your HTML documents liberally with comments. You will thank yourself many times over in the future if you add comments that explain links or lists more fully, or state when information needs to be updated.

Comment lines are formatted similar to this line:

```
<!- comment text ->
```

The comment line starts with <!— and ends with —>. Comments inside the HTML document are ignored by most newer browsers. As a general rule, place comments on a line separate from other HTML text. This won't interrupt your HTML text since browsers also ignore white space between HTML tags. Don't use any special characters (<, >, &, !) within comments.

If you have made it this far, congratulations, you are no longer a complete HTML ignoramus. You've already learned enough to design and create well-balanced, attractive, user-friendly Web pages. You're on a roll, so keep right on going to learn even more fun things to add to your Web pages.

Part IV
Advanced HTML

In This Part...

Once you've mastered the basics of HTML markup, you'll really begin to appreciate the wonderful things your documents can do for the Web. In this part of the book, you'll tackle the composition of complex pages, plus you'll learn how to use HTML's advanced features to solicit user input and to use graphics for navigation.

Along the way, we hope you start to develop an appreciation for readable page styles and begin to apply some of the ideas, tools, and techniques we provide along the way. This is your first real exposure to all of the capabilities that make Web pages beautiful and exciting, so we hope you'll take advantage of what you learn.

On the other hand, none of these bells and whistles should diminish your fixation on content. Users may wander by your pages and be sucked in by sexy graphics or compelling layouts, but what will keep them in your thrall is the quality and readability of your content. So don't let all the wonderful forms you'll be learning about in this part of the book get in the way — the idea is to enhance your content, not obliterate it!

Chapter 11

Going High-Rise:
Building Complex Pages

. . . .

In This Chapter

▶ Expanding your home page into a Web

▶ Moving around inside your documents and local Web

▶ Jumping to remote sites

▶ Sampling and analyzing sophisticated Web pages

. . . .

*Y*ou're probably not satisfied with your nice, simple, single-screen home page. Because of all the wonderful stuff you've seen out there, you really want to make a Web of pages with all sorts of great material in them, right? That's pretty natural and it doesn't compromise the KISS principle either.

If you recall, we suggested that you'd want to make more pages as you expanded your Web. But the more pages you add, the more difficulty your users will have in finding their way around. While you're growing your own Web your most important job is to make your users' journey through it as enjoyable as possible. In fact you've already learned the necessary methods and techniques in previous chapters. Now it's time to put them to use.

This chapter covers a few of the most important aspects of creating complex Webs. After this discussion you will see some examples of more advanced Web pages, with comments about their elements and layout.

There's No Place Like Home

Home isn't only your home page; it's your own Web, the local constellation of planets orbiting your home page. It's your local turf in cyberspace, where Web surfers can find the information you think is important. But even if your site is fantastic and beautiful, users will be put off if they have trouble navigating your Web. That's why you need a clear mental picture of its fully developed organization before you start expanding things.

Organization

If you listen closely to your content, it will tell you the structure it needs — or rather, demands. Hierarchical, linear, and randomly interlinked combinations of the two styles — which we'll call "Web structure" — are the standard organizational structures used in most Webs. These structures are illustrated in Figures 11-1, 11-2, and 11-3.

NOTE: it's straightforward to "Web-ify" a linear document but the converse is not true; organizing a random collection of ideas and concepts into a linear document is very difficult, if not impossible. When designing and using links within or among Web documents, you need to be clear about the organization and interconnectedness of their content.

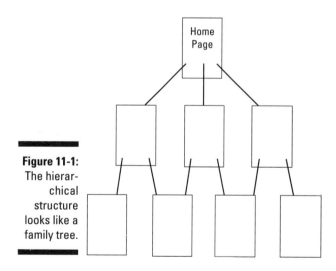

Figure 11-1:
The hierarchical structure looks like a family tree.

The hierarchical or tree structure is used most often in Web designs. It is logical and has an extremely familiar look to most computer users (hints: hard disk file tree and GUI help systems). This system is easy for users to navigate, especially when you include a link back to the home page at the top and bottom of each page.

When using a hierarchy, your information should progress from the most general level or table of contents on your home page, to the most detailed content in the outermost leaves. Your content will dictate the divisions in this tree, but you can also include interesting links between seemingly unrelated branches to better inform your users. You can also include multiple links to individual pages. In this way the structure includes aspects of the index of a book.

Keep in mind that readers can enter your Web space from somewhere other than your home page, so make sure that you give navigational clues to these "jumped-in readers" to your home page and any other relevant pages. It's frustrating to land on a page because you were sent its URL via e-mail by a cohort who said "Check out this page" and then be forced to blunder around from that point on, because you don't know where home is!

 Also, remember that your readers experience the "lost in hyperspace" problem quite often. That's one excellent reason why you should provide navigational clues at the top and bottom of each and every Web page you create. For an example of great style, check out this URL:

```
http://www.hal.com/products/sw/olias/Build-html01994-
          10-17/CGQL0ZBEfmg24aK.html
```

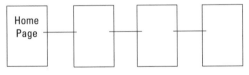

Figure 11-2: Linear structure.

"Simple," "book-like," but also "rigid and confining" are common descriptions of the linear structure. If your information presents a series of steps or follows a process from start to finish, linear structure is a fitting choice for document organization. It keeps users on-track and out of trouble. Here you can make good use of links to the "next page," "previous page," and "top or start page" in a linear structure.

Make sure you put a link to your home page or the starting point on each page in a linear structure. Without them, users trapped in the middle of your document will have only the browser's controls to get out. If you trap them in this way, they will talk about you and your Web on the Net and it won't be very flattering talk, either!

Of itself, the WWW is a Web structure. It's a great example of the fantastic freedom of movement and free-flowing design implicit in this kind of loosely linked environment. Web structure can also quickly demonstrate how easy it is to get lost.

Being lost on the Web isn't quite the same as being lost in a big city. The user can always use the browser's controls to go back to the previous URL or go to another URL. If you want users to get the most out of your Web, you need to provide obvious hyperlinks from each of your pages to other appropriate pages within your Web or to other locations on the WWW.

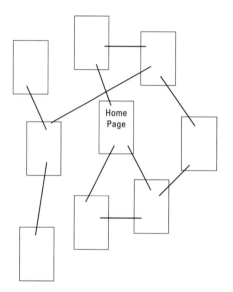

 Providing structure without constraining freedom to explore your space should be the goal of any well-designed Web structure. If your information on related subjects is extensive, put hyperlinks within the text to specific paragraphs in other pages where the user can see more detailed information about the content. Be careful how you do this, though — as we mentioned in Chapter 9, too much linkage can be just as detrimental as not enough! ▪

Hypertext linking is the most time consuming part of HTML programming. Do it well and your users will love you forever. This is discussed in more detail later in this chapter.

When you build a complex Web structure, always, always, always put a link to your home page on each page. It's also a great idea to reproduce the URL for each page in its footer in small type. Using this information, users can return to any specific page in your Web by using that URL, even if they didn't add it in their bookmark list.

It's story (board) time, boys and girls

Remember the sketch of your home page in Chapter 9? It's time for you to find your pencil and paper again. This time you'll be drawing your Web structure. For a personal Web, pencil and paper will probably do nicely.

First things first: list 'em out

Make a list of the major pieces of information you want to include in your Web. These will probably be the links on your home page. These are the major points on Mr. Spider's home page:

Experience
Home Pages created by Jim Spider
Manuals written by Jim Spider
History of Jim Spider
Professional Services
Bicycling
WWW Land

Sketch the Web

In this example, there are no other topics to consider so a simple hierarchical structure looks appropriate. The simple sketch of this structure (shown in Figure 11-4) looks familiar.

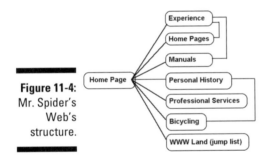

Figure 11-4:
Mr. Spider's
Web's
structure.

Using this sketch to analyze Mr. Spider's home page, you can see some links that weren't readily apparent from looking at the HTML document. These links exist between the "Experience page" and between both the "Home" and "Manuals" pages.

The link between the "bicycling" line of the home page and the "Personal History" page was actually stated in the HTML tag:

```
<A HREF="history.html#Bicycle">
```

The anchor for the reference is the NAME="Bicycle" attribute in the history.html file:

```
<A NAME="Bicycle"><H5>Bicycling</H5></A>
```

We'll discuss NAME anchors more fully a little later in this chapter.

Board the whole story

This simple sketch does not provide enough information for you to fully realize Mr. Spider's Web. What you really need to do now is prepare a storyboard for these pages — that is, unless you can mentally picture the elements and links on each of the seven separate pages of Mr. Spider's Web. Every movie, TV show, and comic book gets storyboarded before any production takes place. Producing a set of Web pages is a lot like making a TV show, especially if you think of each Web page as a separate scene. Over time, though, an entire collection of Web documents and associated materials will evolve from your work, making it resemble a whole season's worth of TV episodes rather than a single show.

To prepare a storyboard, simply prepare a sketch of the layout of each Web page with the URLs for links written on each one. For small Webs some Web authors use a white marker board with colored pens. The colors are handy for showing different types of links, forms, or other HTML elements.

For more complex Webs, many authors use a sheet of paper for each Web page, some string, some push pins, and a large bulletin board (cork type, not BBS). This allows very complex arrangements that are easily changed. When you are creating a Web of more than a handful of pages, create a storyboard. It will save you much more time than it will take you to do it.

You will find it invaluable for identifying potential hypertext links if you attach the text of each Web page to its layout sheet. That's how Mr. Spider decided to place the bicycling link in his home page using a NAME anchor to the bicycling section in his personal history page's file. This method kept him from having to create a separate page for his bicycling information.

Preparing a storyboard for a Web of only five pages or so may seem like overkill. But after you're finished, you'll appreciate its value.

Anchors Away: Jumping Around Your Documents

We did say it wasn't too terrible to create Web pages spanning up to three screens, if your information demands the extra room. You may even expand your home page to more than one screen, if you carefully drop your anchors and don't go overboard on the images.

You will use two different anchor tag attributes for movement within your pages. To provide viewers with links to specific parts within a Web page (called intra-document linking), use the NAME="text" anchor to provide the destination of an HREF="#label" tag. Use the standard HREF="URL" (called inter-document linking) to let users jump from page to page. Or to jump to a specific location within another page, you can combine both approaches and use HREF="URL#label".

There's an important distinction to understand when it comes to following links inside a browser program. With inter-document linking, most browsers will land the reader at the first line of the target document. On the other hand, intra-document linking takes you to a place other than the default "top of the page" unless there is a named anchor at the top of the page and the URL calls this anchor out.

Here's another interesting quirk about browsers—namely, their behavior with named anchors that occur near the bottom of a document. If an anchor appears near the bottom, most browsers do NOT bring the named anchor to the first line on the screen. This is because the browser usually renders a full screen of text; thus, if the anchor is near the bottom of a document, that's where the link will take you.

Linking to text in another page

Mr. Spider's home page provides a good example of how you should use the NAME="text" attribute in an anchor tag. The HTML line in the home page document:

```
<IMG SRC="ballblue.gif"> I'd really rather be
<A HREF="history.html#Bicycle"> bicycling.</A>
```

specifies a hypertext relationship between the word "bicycling" in the current document with the named anchor "Bicycle" in the target document which is in the "history.html" file. The pound sign (#) indicates that the browser should position the reader not at the top of the page, but at the named anchor in the target document. If the anchor is not found, you'd get the default instead, which is the top of the document.

The browser displays the information at that location in the file, starting with the heading, "Bicycling." This may seem unduly abstract but you'll catch on if you remember this: The anchor with the NAME="text" attribute is the destination for some link. As the author you have control over how your information is displayed. If you think applications or other pages will find a nugget of information within a specific page relevant and important, then give it a name with the NAME attribute and create a link to it.

Linking to text within a page: Table of Contents links

You use the NAME="text" attribute to create a really jumping table of contents (TOC) for long text documents. Providing a linked TOC takes a little more time but it's a great way to impress your users. Remember to provide a link back to the TOC after each block of text in the destination document.

The following HTML code illustrates how to use the TOC links within a large document:

```
<!- Make this an anchor for return jumps.->
<A NAME="TOC">Table of Contents</A>
<P>
<!- This is the link to the section 1. below.->
<A HREF="#SEC1">Section 1.</A><BR>
<A HREF="#SEC2">Section 2.</A><BR>
<A HREF="#SEC3">Section 3.</A><BR>

<!- This is a named anchor called "SEC1".->
<A NAME="SEC1"><H2> CFR Section 1.</H2></A>
<P> Text of section 1 is here.
<BR>
<!- This is a link back to the TOC at the top of the page->
<A HREF="#TOC">(TOC)</A>
<P>
<A NAME="SEC2"><H2> CFR Section 2.</H2></A>
<P> Text of section 2 is here.
<BR>
<A HREF="TOC">(TOC)</A>
<P>
<A NAME="SEC3"><H2> CFR Section 3.</H2></A>
<P> Text of section 3 is here.
<BR>
<A HREF="TOC">(TOC)</A>
<P>
```

Figure 11-5 shows the above HTML code when viewed with Netscape.

Seeing the (TOC) after each text section may seem strange at first but your users will quickly become accustomed to having the link available. We'd recommend using this approach for longer, more complex documents or for a collection of related documents, but not for shorter pieces. An omnipresent TOC in a short document might seem obtrusive to your readers.

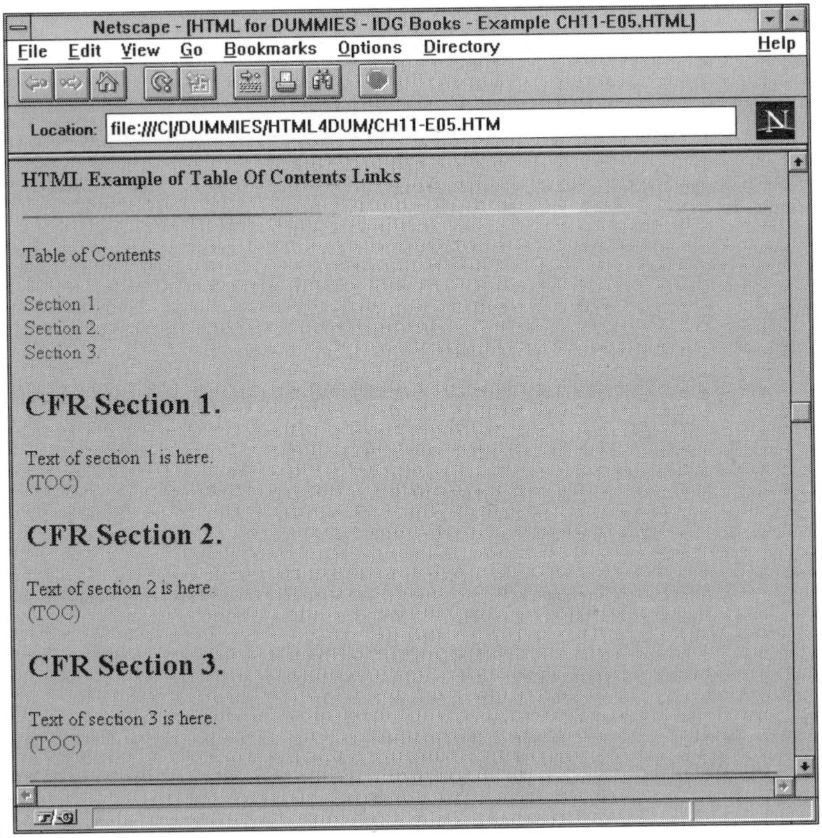

Netscape - [HTML for DUMMIES - IDG Books - Example CH11-E05.HTML]

File   Edit   View   Go   Bookmarks   Options   Directory   Help

Location: file:///C|/DUMMIES/HTML4DUM/CH11-E05.HTM

HTML Example of Table Of Contents Links

Table of Contents

Section 1.
Section 2.
Section 3.

CFR Section 1.

Text of section 1 is here.
(TOC)

CFR Section 2.

Text of section 2 is here.
(TOC)

CFR Section 3.

Text of section 3 is here.
(TOC)

Figure 11-5:
Table of
Contents
and text
links viewed
through
Netscape.

You can use this same general method for links to anything within a single HTML document. It may look strange in the HTML document but this is the way you create hypertext links within a text paragraph. Only use the "Text" in each NAME="Text" once per document though, to keep the browser from becoming terminally confused. Otherwise, you never know where your users might wind up!

Named anchors should be named with text starting with a character from the set {a-z, A-Z}. They should never be exclusively numeric, like <A NAME="12">blah</A>. Anchors should also be uniquely named within the same document. These names are case sensitive so that NAME="foo" and NAME="FOO" are different. So are these: NAME="Three Stooges" is not the same as NAME="ThreeStooges" is not the same as NAME="THREESTOOGES". We hope you get the idea... ■

Jumping to Remote Pages

Hypermedia links from text in your pages directly to other Web sites will
amaze and amuse your users. Although you can't create NAME="text"
anchors in the text at remote sites, you may be able to use anchors already in
place at the site. If you find a linked TOC at another site, you can reference
the same links as the TOC at the other site. Remember, if you can link to it
using your browser, you can copy the link into the text of your Web pages.
Just make sure you include the full URL in the HREF="URL".

Hypertext links to outside resources

Links to Web sites outside of your own Web require a fully qualified URL,
such as:

```
<A HREF="http://www.nps.gov/nbs/"> National Biological Service</A>.
```

This link connects to the National Biological Service home page at the
National Park Service server. The hypertext link in the HTML document is
"National Biological Service." This could appear for example, in the middle of
the following sentence:

```
If you are interested in finding out details of the wild goose migrations
across the United States, the <A HREF=" http://www.nps.gov/nbs/">National
Biological Service</A> is the place to look first.
```

This makes for difficult reading unless viewed through a browser, as shown
in Figure 11-6. Through the browser, the hypertext words are shown in a different color, underlined, or both, depending on its actual implementation.

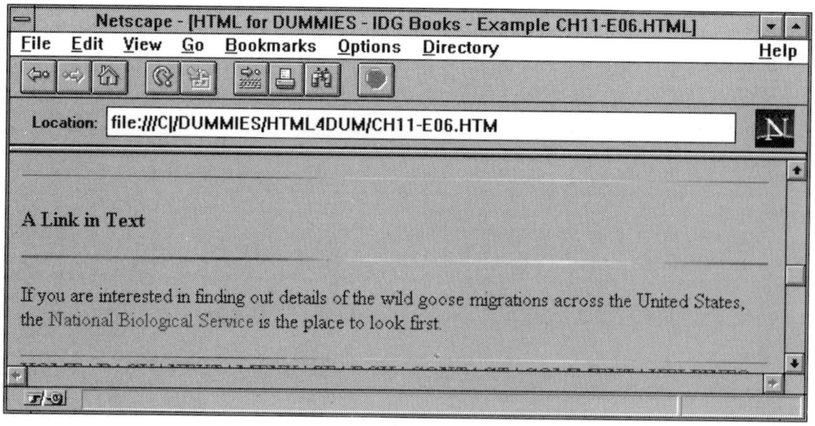

Figure 11-6:
A link in text
as viewed
through
Netscape.

Jump pages

The term "jump page" refers to a Web page that contains a list of URLs to other Web pages, usually remote sites. You will find the HTML list tags invaluable for quickly creating visually pleasing and easily understood lists of links. Jump pages differ from basic Web pages only because the viewer sees primarily highlighted hyperlinks. This is appropriate for quick scanning.

You can use icon images and spacer lines to visually separate sections of your list. You should carefully choose the words you use for each hyperlink, keeping in mind the main point of the information to which the link refers. Figure 11-7 illustrates a portion of a well-done jump page.

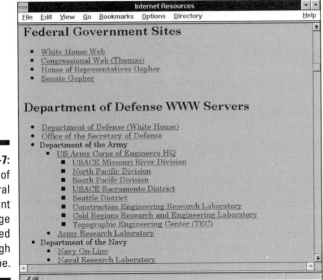

Figure 11-7:
Portion of
Federal
Government
jump page
as viewed
through
Netscape.

When typing URLs for links, we strongly recommend that you first link to the destination and capture the URL using your browser. Then paste the URL directly into your HTML file to cut down on syntax errors. ▪

A special <LINK>

The <LINK> tag provides information that links the current Web page to other Web pages or to other URL resources. When you want to be sure that your Web pages tell browsers and other WWW software about themselves, put a <LINK> in the <HEAD>...</HEAD> section. Chapter 7 shows several attributes you may use in the <LINK> tag. If you start using one of the advanced HTML-generating programs, it may insert several <LINK> tags of various types within the head section of each page, which it uses to keep track of the pages themselves.

Perhaps the most commonly used is NAME="text" to provide an anchor from other locations. This named anchor is used for reference access from other locations or documents. Your HTML code should look similar to the following:

```
<HTML>
<HEAD>
<TITLE> The Title of Your Page </TITLE>
<LINK NAME="Web Weaver's Home Page">
</HEAD>
<BODY>
<H1> The Heading of Your Page That Users See </H1>
and so on...
</BODY></HTML>
```

The Nesting Instinct: Lists Within Lists

When you create longer Web pages, you'll want to keep the visual diversity high by using text formatting. However, since you are working with text, you have only headings, emphasized text (bold, strong, font size), and indented lists as tools. Lists within lists create the old familiar outline form when displayed by most browsers.

The browser display in Figure 11-7 was created by the following HTML code. In fact what's shown in that figure is just a fragment of the original, which goes on for pages and pages, so you won't see every level of list that opened with a <UL> get closed with a corresponding </UL>. As you look through this HTML markup, remember that you're seeing only a fragment, and not the whole thing:

```
<H2>Federal Government Sites</H2>
<UL>
<LI> <A HREF="http://www.whitehouse.gov">White House Web</A>
<LI> <A HREF="http://thomas.loc.gov">Congressional Web (Thomas)</A>
<LI> <A HREF="gopher://gopher.house.gov">House of Representatives Gopher</A>
<LI> <A HREF="gopher://gopher.senate.gov">Senate Gopher</A>
</UL>
<BR>
<H2>Department of Defense WWW Servers</H2>
<UL>
```

```
<LI> <A HREF="http://www.whitehouse.gov/White_House/Cabinet/html/
          Department_of_Defense.html"> Department of Defense
          (White House)</A>
<LI> <A HREF="http://enterprise.osd.mil/">Office of the Secretary of
          Defense</A>
<LI>Department of the Army
  <UL>
  <LI> <A HREF="http://bbsun.usace.army.mil/"> US Army Corps of
          Engineers HQ</A>
    <UL>
      <LI> <A HREF="http://www.mrd-wc.usace.army.mil"> USACE Missouri
          River Division</A>
      <LI> <A HREF="http://npd41.npd.usace.army.mil/"> North Pacific
          Division</A>
      <LI> <A HREF="http://www.usace.mil/cespd.html"> South Pacifc
          Division</A>
      <LI> <A HREF="http://www.usace.mil"> USACE Sacramento District</A>
      <LI> <A HREF="http://www.nps.usace.army.mil/"> Seattle District</A>
      <LI> <A HREF="http://www.cecer.army.mil/welcome.html">Construction
          Engineering Research Laboratory</A>
      <LI> <A HREF="http://bbsun.usace.army.mil/inside/crrel-w3/crrel-
          text/">Cold Regions Research and Engineering Laboratory</A>
      <LI> <A HREF="http://cat.tec.army.mil/tec_home.html">
          Topographic Engineering Center (TEC)</A>
    </UL>
```

Carefully track the list start (<UL>) and end (</UL>) tags. In the Federal Government Sites section you see a start and end pair. This indents and bullets the items between them that are marked with the <LI> tags. This is a normal unordered list.

The Department of Defense WWW Servers section shows three list start tags before the first list end tag. The text marked with <LI> tags after the first start tag are shown as normal bulleted list elements. The <LI> lines after the second start tag are indented farther and bulleted. The <LI> lines after the third start tag are indented even farther and are marked by a black rectangle (in Netscape). Some browsers keep track of the number of nests you use and change the bullets of each successive nesting to blocks or other symbols.

The list end tag </UL> shown at the end of the preceding HTML sample belongs to the third start tag. This pair of tags encloses the third level of list nesting. The end tags that match the second and first start tags appear farther on in the HTML document, but they're not shown because the sample would be 4 or 5 pages long. Thus, it may be easier to visualize nested lists without the <LI> lines:

```
<UL> Start level 1.
    <UL> Start level 2.
        <UL> Start level 3.
        </UL> End level 3.
    </UL> End level 2.
</UL> End level 1.
```

Nested lists are a good way to instruct a browser to indent certain lines of text without using the <PRE> ... </PRE> or <BLOCKQUOTE> ... </BLOCKQUOTE> tags. Along with the indentations, your readers will have to cope with either bullets or numbers, but that's fine for lists, as shown in the earlier example.

The browser developers are already working on giving browsers the ability to respond to HTML tag attributes for various types of symbols instead of bullets and blocks in lists. Who knows what they'll think of next?

Sampling Sophisticated Pages

Now it's time for a quick look at some more complex Web pages. We also encourage you to surf the Web for pages that strike your fancy. When you find one, view its source to see how the author accomplished the magic. It's one of the few places where you can easily look behind the curtain to see how the illusion is created, so be sure to take full advantage of this opportunity.

In the rest of this chapter, we'll show you several examples of complex Web pages. You will see the page screen (or two) as viewed through a browser followed by the HTML markup for those screens. After each figure and HTML example you will see our comments on the techniques and coding used. All of the following examples are from government locations. They are generally well-constructed Web pages. However, each has its questionable aspects, which we will gleefully point out. Hey, after all, they're the FEDS.

National Biological Service

The NBS home page displays well on the screen with or without the images. The view above has been scrolled down so that the Department of the Interior's logo is not visible. It takes space at the top and time to display. It is superfluous to the NBS page but since that's where the NBS gets its funding, they're obligated to put it somewhere. Placing it at the bottom would be better since it is not the focus of the page.

The tasteful image of the bird to the left of the NBS name coupled with the short nested lists and <HR> spacing give the page a clean look. The addition of the Comments, questions section on the WebMaster's page, and its feedback forms is a welcome touch. Finally, the inclusion of the page's URL and revision date complete the page in good form. We did, however, take the liberty of cleaning up the listing that follows this paragraph, so that we couldn't be accused of exposing you to "bad HTML"— even if it is somebody else's work!

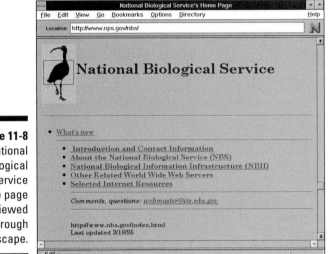

Figure 11-8
National Biological Service home page viewed through Netscape.

```
<HTML>
<HEAD>
<TITLE>National Biological Service's Home Page</TITLE>
</HEAD>
<BODY>
<A NAME="NBS0">

<H2>
<IMG ALIGN="middle" SRC="/nbs2/DOI.GIF"><A HREF="http://info.er.usgs.gov/
            doi/doi.html"> Department of the Interior</A><P>
</H2>
<H1>
<IMG ALIGN="middle" SRC="/graphics/nbs-logo.gif">National Biological
            Service</A>

</H1>
<HR>

<UL>
<LI><A HREF="/nbs/whatsnew.html">What's new</A>
<!- This is where we removed the extraneous end anchor ->
```

```
<HR>
<UL>
<LI><A HREF="/nbs2/nbshp1.html">Introduction and Contact Information</A>
<LI><A HREF="/nbs2/nbshp2.html">About the National Biological Service
            (NBS) </A>
<LI><A HREF="/nbii/">National Biological Information Infrastructure
            (NBII) </A>
<LI><A HREF="/nbs2/nbshp4.html">Other Related World Wide Web Servers</A>
<LI><A HREF="/nbs2/nbshp5.html">Selected Internet Resources</A>
<!- this is where the missing end unordered list tags go ->
</UL>
</UL>
<!- so we added them anyway ->

<HR>
<ADDRESS> Comments, questions: <A HREF="http://www.nbs.gov/Webmaster.html">
            Webmaster@its.nbs.gov</A>
</ADDRESS>
<HR>
<P>
<EM> http://www.nbs.gov/index.html<BR>
Last updated 3/16/95
</EM>



</BODY>
</HTML>
```

The HTML code for the NBS home page is well-constructed with all appropriate parts included. You can see that the nested lists did not originally end with </UL>, so we went ahead and fixed them. This wouldn't cause problems with most browsers but is not a good idea. Any <LI> tag after the second <UL> start tag would double indent the line to the position of the others above. If you intended the line to be indented only one position, you need the </UL> end marker to close the second level nest. There was also an extraneous </A> in the HTML markup. Can you find where we marked its removal? Luckily, it would be ignored by most browsers.

U.S. Geological Survey home page

The USGS home page is three screens long, if you don't open the images. It is reasonably well-designed but suffers from too many images at the start. Even with the default image replacement icons, the top of the page is cluttered. It is unclear what you should select and where your selections might take you. The use of (reference) as a hyperlink is confusing, to say the least.

Even with the images visible, navigation is difficult. Placing the Department of the Interior logo (with its indistinct, ambiguous clickable words: Network, Search, Help) at the top of the page is counter productive. The three large images are striking but not very informative, and the text doesn't align under the images very well either. These graphics would be much more effective as icon-sized images, vertically aligned, with the related text immediately to the right. Once again, we took the liberty of cleaning up the original HTML, so we wouldn't have to shock you with the vagaries it once displayed.

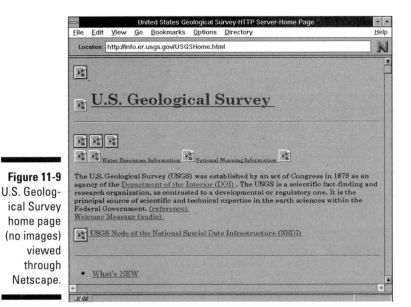

Figure 11-9
U.S. Geological Survey home page (no images) viewed through Netscape.

```
<TITLE>United States Geological Survey-HTTP Server-Home Page</TITLE>
<A HREF="http://www.usgs.gov/cgi-bin/imagemap/doi-bar"><IMG
          SRC="http://www.usgs.gov/icons/doi-bar.gif" ISMAP></A>
<H1>
<IMG ALIGN="middle" SRC="http://www.usgs.gov/images/usgs_t.gif">
<A HREF="http://www.usgs.gov/">  U.S. Geological Survey </A>
</H1>
<P>
<HR>
<H6>
<A HREF="http://www.usgs.gov/fact-sheets/earth/title.html">
<IMG SRC="http://www.usgs.gov/images/logo_page_s.gif"></A>

<A HREF="http://h2o.usgs.gov/">
<IMG SRC="http://www.usgs.gov/images/nawqamap_s.gif"></A>

<A HREF="http://www-nmd.usgs.gov/">
```

```
<IMG SRC="http://www.usgs.gov/images/grand-canyon_s.gif"></A>

<BR>
<IMG SRC="http://www.usgs.gov/images/place-75_s.gif">
<IMG SRC="http://www.usgs.gov/images/place-75_s.gif">
<A HREF="http://h2o.usgs.gov/"> Water Resources Information</A>
<IMG SRC="http://www.usgs.gov/images/place-75_s.gif">
<A HREF="http://www-nmd.usgs.gov/"> National Mapping Information</A>
<IMG SRC="http://www.usgs.gov/images/place-75_s.gif">
</H6>

<P>
<H5>

The U.S. Geological Survey (USGS) was established by an act of Congress
in 1879 as an agency of the <A HREF="http://www.usgs.gov/doi/doi.html">
Department of the Interior (DOI) </A>. The USGS is a scientific fact-
finding and research organization, as contrasted to a developmental
or regulatory one. It is the principal source of scientific and technical
expertise in the earth sciences within the Federal Government.
<A HREF="http://www.usgs.gov/reports/circulars/c1000//Introduction.html">
(reference) </A>
<BR>
<A HREF="http://www.usgs.gov/audio/intro.au"> Welcome Message (audio)</A>
</H5>
<P>
```

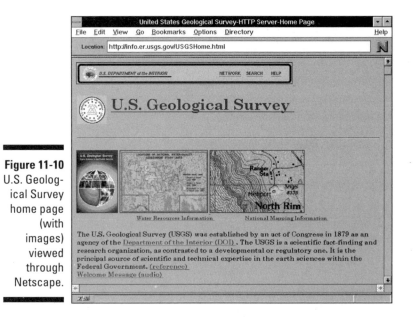

Figure 11-10
U.S. Geological Survey home page (with images) viewed through Netscape.

The HTML document for the USGS page omits the <HTML>, <HEAD>, and <BODY> tags which may cause it not to function properly with strict HTML browsers. It also appears that the author attempts to use a background colored image <IMG SRC="http://www.usgs.gov/images/place-75_s.gif"> to properly space the text under the three images. This technique doesn't work very well because it depends upon the type of font and the type size used by the browser. Remember KISS?

FedWorld Information Network home page

The layout of the FedWorld home page is visually adequate when no images are displayed. However, the first two hyperlinks are images with no text explaining them and no additional text hyperlink. The next hyperlink is also an image with a line of text somewhat explaining it; however, the text is not a hyperlink as it should be. The hypertext links in the paragraphs is fairly well integrated.

The FedWorld home page with images displayed is visually pleasing but the logo is completely overdone. It takes forever to load, with no warning about its large size. This page overpowers the first screen the user sees, making it necessary to scroll immediately to see any real content. Even the revision date is overly wordy — "Revised March 20, 1995" is all that is needed. Remember Strunk & White: "Omit needless words."

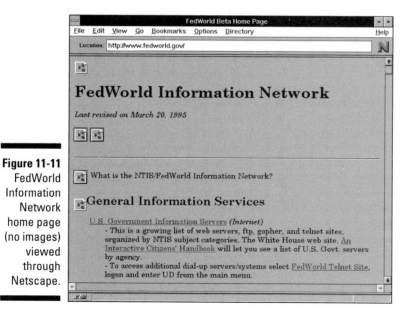

Figure 11-11
FedWorld
Information
Network
home page
(no images)
viewed
through
Netscape.

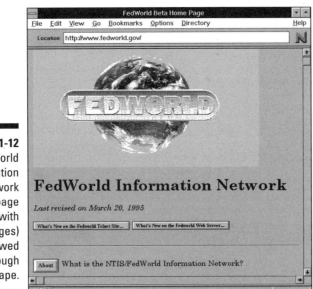

Figure 11-12
FedWorld
Information
Network
home page
(with
images)
viewed
through
Netscape.

The two hyperlink image buttons are perfect examples of how not to word buttons. The first five of the seven words on each are identical. This forces the user to carefully read both buttons to distinguish any difference.

Our advice is "Put the important words first." Since the page is FedWorld's, omit FedWorld. The buttons would be much more useful if they read, "Telnet News" and "Web Server News." An even better way would be to use a single phrase such as, "New additions to the FedWorld Telnet Site and Web Server" with Telnet Site and Web Server used as the hyperlinks.

```
<HTML>
<HEAD>
<TITLE>FedWorld Beta Home Page</TITLE>
</HEAD>
<BODY>
<A NAME="top"><IMG ALT="FedWorld" SRC="graphics/fwhome.gif"></A><P>

<H1> FedWorld Information Network</H1>
<P>
<I>Last revised on March 20, 1995</I><P>
<A HREF="wnewtel.html"><IMG ALT="What's New on the Telnet Site"
SRC="graphics/telntbtn.gif"></A>
<A HREF="wneWeb.html"><IMG ALT="What's New on the Web Site"
SRC="graphics/wbsvrbtn.gif"></A>
<P>
<HR>
<P>
<A HREF="about.html"><IMG ALT="About" ALIGN="MIDDLE"
```

```
SRC="icons/about.gif"></A>
What is the NTIS/FedWorld Information Network?
<P>
<DL>
<DT><H2><IMG ALT="*" ALIGN="MIDDLE" SRC="graphics/bullet.gif">General
            Information Services</H2><P>
<P>
<DL>
<DT><A HREF="#usgovt">U.S. Government Information Servers</A><I>
            (Internet)</I>
<DD>- This is a growing list of Web servers, ftp, gopher, and telnet
            sites, organized by NTIS subject categories. The White
            House Web site, <A HREF="http://www.whitehouse.gov">
An Interactive Citizens' Handbook</A> will let you see a list of U.S.
            Govt. servers by agency.

<DD>- To access additional dial-up servers/systems select
<A HREF="telnet://fedworld.gov">
FedWorld Telnet Site</A>, logon and enter UD from the main menu.
</DL>
```

The HTML document was originally written in questionable HTML form; even now, it's still pretty dicey. It didn't make consistent use of markup (it skipped a closing </A> tag on the fwhome.gif reference), and it mixed upper- and lowercase tags (which we think made it harder to read). That's why we cleaned all those things up, and added a missing </DL> tag at the very end. It's also why we feel compelled to point out another case where the closing structure tags: </HTML> and </BODY> are missing in action. On the plus side, the FedWorld document does use ALT="text" for images to assist text-only browsers.

A couple of screens further into the same page, which is a very long list of links, there's a category index with links to different sections of the list. This is a good touch, but it should appear closer to the first page, if not directly on it. The user must guess at too much on the FedWorld home page. It is a prime example of a pretty page with a less than optimal design. It's not easy to use.

There's a difference between sophisticated Web pages and complex ones. A Web page can be elegant and somewhat elaborate without being overly complicated to use. KISS and your users will love your Web. Whatever you do, don't slavishly imitate the last couple of documents we've looked at, unless you treat them as examples for things NOT to do!

Congratulations! You've now gone far enough into HTML to know where "home" is. Now that you really know your way around, you're ready to jump into the realm of HTML forms, where users get to talk back to their Web servers.

Chapter 12

Strictly Pro Forma:
Using Forms for Feedback

● ●

● ●

*W*hen all the pieces come together properly, it's easy to see how the Web brings people or organizations together. At first glance, the Web might look pretty much like a one-way street — that is, an environment where WebMasters communicate aplenty with Web users, with not much interaction between the two. But it doesn't have to be that way.

What HTML Forms Are For

The essence of serving up useful information is relevancy and immediacy. But the best judge of the quality of your information is your audience. Wouldn't it be wonderful if your readers could give you feedback on your Web pages? Then they could tell you what parts they like, what they don't like, and what other things they'd like to see included in your site.

This is where HTML forms come into the picture. Up to this point, you've learned all of the basics — and even a few advanced techniques — for communicating with your audience. In this chapter, you'll learn how to turn the tables and create HTML text that lets your audience communicate with you!

As it turns out, HTML supports a rich variety of input capabilities to let you solicit feedback. In the pages that follow, you'll learn about the tags to use, the controls and inputs they enable, along with some layout considerations for building forms. You'll also see some interesting example forms, to help you understand what HTML forms look like and how they behave.

Living Within Your Forms Limitations

Before you get too excited about HTML forms, we have to warn you that forms support is still a relative newcomer to the HTML world. As this chapter's being written, the last-minute wrangling that always precedes the adoption of a standard — in this case the HTML 2.0 DTD — is in full force.

This means that forms support in HTML, which you'll recall from Chapter 6 is a hallmark of HTML 2.0, still hasn't been finalized. In other words, the underlying HTML markup for forms could still change, and it still qualifies as "new and untried" rather than "old and familiar" for many Web users. ■

Beware of browser!

While most of the "hot" browsers — Mosaic and its variants, Netscape, Win-Web and MacWeb, etc. — already include forms support, other browsers may not. In fact, you won't know how well your favorite browser handles forms until you start testing your forms tags against it. If you follow our suggestions, and test your pages against multiple browsers, you'll immediately observe different levels of robustness and capability when it comes to forms implementations.

The bottom line is that not all browsers support forms equally, but that support is increasing every day. Perhaps by the time you read this, it will no longer be a problem — at least for users with current versions. But for older browsers, don't be surprised if forms don't work that well, or if they don't work at all.

Assuming the information your form solicits is important to you, consider adding an FTP URL to your page to let users download a file containing a text-only version of the form's content. Then, they can download the file, and complete it using any text editor. If you include an e-mail address inside the file, they can send it back to you and you'll get feedback, even from users who can't view your forms. That way nobody gets left out! ■

Sorry, servers...

Since the Web is a client/server environment, you should also be aware that just because your browser supports forms doesn't automatically imply that the server installed at your site can handle them. Unfortunately, keeping up with HTML advancements means that Web servers have to change right along with the clients. This means it's possible that your server doesn't support the input-handling programs necessary to process a form's input when it gets delivered.

However, there is a silver lining in this potentially dark cloud: the most common implementations of the HTTPD server come from NCSA and CERN and run in the UNIX environment. Both of these groups have standardized their forms-handling technology, and offer useful, robust forms-handling capability.

These implementations are so common, in fact, that we assume your Web server works the way that they do. This means you may have to alter some of the approaches to CGI scripting and other programming you might use to handle forms on your server. If you're not using UNIX and the NCSA or CERN implementations of HTTPD, you'll want to investigate the particulars that your server's implementation requires, and alter our instructions accordingly.

What's in a Form?

When adding forms support to a Web page, you'll be including special tags that let you solicit input from users. You'll surround these tags with text that prompts user responses. You'll also include tags that gather up the input and ship it off to your Web server, or to other servers that might offer services — like Gopher, or Archie — that your form knows how to query. Here's how the process works:

✔ On a particular Web page, you'll include tags to set up a form, and to solicit input from users. Some of your users will work their way through this material, and provide the information that you want. This essentially amounts to filling out the form that you've supplied.

✔ Once a form has been filled out, users can then direct their input to a program running on the Web server that delivered the form. In most cases, this amounts to selecting a particular control, called SUBMIT, that gathers up the information and sends it to the proper destination on your Web server.

✔ Assuming that the program is available for use (installing and running properly, that is), it will accept the input information. Then the program will decode and interpret the contents for further action.

✔ After the input is received and interpreted, the program can do pretty much anything it wants to. In practice, this boils down to recognizing key elements in a form's content, and custom-building an HTML document in response. Building a document isn't required, but it is a pretty commonplace capability within forms-handling programs.

✔ The custom-built document is then delivered to the user in response to the form's content. At this point, additional interaction can occur (if the "return page" includes another form), or requested information can be delivered (in response to requests on the form), etc.

The information collected from a form can be 1) written to a file; or 2) submitted to a database such as Informix or Oracle; or 3) e-mailed to someone in particular. Forms also allow a user to participate in building a Web document like the one Web site which allows users to dictate how a story is played out; in this case, the users collectively determine the outcome.

Thus, forms provide communication from users to servers, but also for ongoing interaction between users and servers. This is pretty powerful stuff, and adds a lot of value to your Web pages.

Forms involve two-way communication

The input-catching programs on your server rely on an interface between Web browsers and servers called the Common Gateway Interface (CGI). This interface codifies how browsers can send information back to servers. It sets up the formatting for the user-supplied input information, so that forms-handling programs know what to expect, and how to deal with what they receive.

The ACTION attribute in the <FORM> tag specifies a URL that indicates a specific CGI script or program which collects and munges the form data that a user entered.

Likewise, the METHOD tag describes the way in which input data will be delivered to a forms-handling program.

In this chapter, we'll concentrate on the input side of HTML forms — that is, you'll learn how to build forms. This will be a pure exercise in building the front end of a form — that is, the part the users see. You won't learn how to build the back end — that is, how to build CGI or equivalent programs so your server can deal with forms input — until Chapter 14. Not to worry, however — there's plenty of interesting front end material to master here! ▪

Tag! You're a form...

HTML includes several different classes of forms tags (for the details on syntax and usage, please consult Chapter 7). To begin with, all HTML forms occur within the <FORM> ... </FORM> tags. The <FORM> tag also includes attributes that specify where and how to deliver input to the appropriate Web server. ▩

Within the <FORM> ... </FORM> tags, all other forms-related tags and text must appear. These tags include methods for:

- ✔ specifying input (the <INPUT> tag and its many attributes).
- ✔ setting up text input areas (the <TEXTAREA> ... </TEXTAREA> tags).
- ✔ selecting values from a predefined set of possible inputs (the <SELECT> ... </SELECT> tags).
- ✔ managing the form's content (using the SUBMIT attribute for INPUT to deliver the content to the server, or the RESET attribute to clear its contents, and start over).

Forms input tags support multiple ways to interact with users, including:

- ✔ creating text input fields, where users can type in whatever they want to.
- ✔ generating pull-down menus, often called "pick lists" because they require making one or more selections from a set of predefined choices.
- ✔ creating labeled checkboxes or radio buttons on-screen, that users can select to indicate choices. Checkboxes allow multiple selections and radio buttons allow just one selection.

This may not sound like much, but when you combine it with the ability to prompt users for input with surrounding text, it provides a surprisingly powerful way to ask for information right on a Web page. Thus, the real answer to the question at the head of this section: "What's in a form?" has to be: "Almost anything you want to put there!"

The remainder of this chapter will step you through all the details of building a form, so you can use the capabilities we've just described.

Using Form Tags

To start out, you'll want to set up your <FORM> environment to build a form within a Web page. It's OK to add a form to an existing HTML file, or to build a separate one just to contain your form. We recommend that you add shorter forms (half a screen or less) to existing files but that you create new files for forms that are longer than half a screen.

Setting the <FORM> environment

The two key attributes within the <FORM> tag are METHOD and ACTION. Together, these attributes control how information is sent to the Web server and which input-handling program will receive the form's contents.

There's no rhythm to METHOD

The METHOD indicates how the information will be sent to the server when the form is submitted. METHOD can take one of two possible values: POST or GET.

Of these two methods, POST is preferred because it causes a form's contents to be parsed one element at a time. GET, on the other hand, concatenates all the field names and their associated values into one long string. Because UNIX (and most systems) have a limit on how long a single string can be (for UNIX it's 255 characters) it's not hard to imagine that some of the information might get lost when its contents gets truncated.

That's why you'll see us use POST as our only METHOD for submitting forms in this book. That's also why you should do the same, unless you're dead certain that the number of characters in a form will never, ever exceed 255.

Lights, camera...ACTION

ACTION supplies the URL for the CGI script or other input-handling program on the server that will receive a form's input. The URL can be a full specification, or simply a relative reference. Either way, you need to make sure it points at the right program, in the right location, to do the job that's expected. You also need to make sure that the CGI script or program is executable, and that it behaves properly. You'll hear a lot more about this in Chapter 17, which gets into the ins and outs of testing your HTML documents and their related CGI programs. ■

Let's make an assumption...

Because you won't have to worry about handling input until Chapter 14, we'll follow two conventions for all the syntax in this chapter:

1. In every <FORM> tag, METHOD="POST".

2. For every ACTION, URL="/cgi/*form-name*" where we replace the place-holder *form-name* with the actual name of the form under discussion (e.g., for the form named get-inf.html, URL="/cgi/get-inf").

This will make it easy to create sample HTML files to implement the forms in this chapter (you can also find these examples on the disk that comes with this book). ▪

Knowing what's (in)coming: the <INPUT> tags

The <INPUT> tag defines a basic form element. It takes at least two attributes — namely TYPE and NAME. TYPE indicates what kind of element should be displayed on the form. NAME assigns a name to go with the input field or value that corresponds to the <INPUT> tag.

NAME is used to identify the contents of a field in the form information that will ultimately be uploaded to the input-handling Web server. In fact, what the server receives is a series of name/value pairs. The name that identifies the value is the string supplied in the NAME="string" attribute, and the value is what the user enters or selects for that particular field. Read on — you'll see an example in the next section that should make all this clear!

TYPE-casting still works!

The TYPE attribute can take any of the following values:

- ✔ **CHECKBOX** — Produces an on-screen checkbox for users to make multiple selections.

- ✔ **HIDDEN** — Produces no visible input area; use this to pass data needed for other uses through the form. For instance, this might be an ongoing series of forms based on an earlier interaction during which the user identifies him- or herself — a HIDDEN field contains the name/value pair for that data, but doesn't show it on the current form (some browsers will display these fields but at the bottom of a form and each field will have no accompanying label, as with NetManage's WebSurfer browser).

- ✔ **IMAGE** — Lets you designate a graphic as a selectable item in a form. You can use this to include icons or other graphical symbols.

- ✔ **RADIO** — Creates a radio button for a range of selections, from which the user may select only one.

✔ **RESET** — Creates a button labeled "reset" in your form. Include this so that users can clear a form's contents and start over. Be sure to place it well away from other controls — you don't want them to clear the form by accident!

✔ **SUBMIT** — Creates a button labeled "submit" (by default, or whatever value you supply for the VALUE attribute for SUBMIT) in your form. The type SUBMIT tells the browser to bundle the form data and pass it all to the CGI script indicated by the ACTION attribute. In plain English (remember that??) SUBMIT is the button used to send in the filled-out form, so a form is useless without an <INPUT> field of type SUBMIT.

✔ **TEXT** — Provides a one-line area for text entry. Use this for short fields only (as in the example that follows). For longer text fields, use the <TEXTAREA> ... </TEXTAREA> tags instead.

This provides a wide range of input displays and data types for form input. As you look at HTML forms on the Web and in this book with a new (and more trained) eye, you'll see how effectively these types can be used.

Other <INPUT> attributes

Most of the remaining attributes exist to modify or qualify the <INPUT> attribute with TEXT type as the default. A quick review will remind you of what we covered in Chapter 7:

✔ **VALUE="value"** — Supply a default value for a TEXT or HIDDEN element, or to supply the corresponding value for a radio button or checkbox selection. This can be used to determine the label of a submit or a reset button, like VALUE="Submit to Admin" for a submit or VALUE="Clear Form" for a reset.

✔ **SRC="URL"** — Provide a pointer to the graphic for an IMAGE.

✔ **CHECKED** — This will make sure that a certain radio button or check-box is checked when the form is either visited for the first time or when it is reset. You can control default settings with the CHECKED attribute of <INPUT>.

✔ **SIZE="number"** — The number of characters that a TEXT element can display without scrolling.

✔ **MAXLENGTH="number"** — The maximum number of characters that a value in a TEXT element can contain.

✔ **ALIGN=(TOP | MIDDLE | BOTTOM)** — For IMAGE elements, how the graphic will be aligned on the form, vis-a-vis the accompanying text.

A TEXT-oriented <INPUT> example

That's it for the <INPUT> tag. Let's look at a relatively simple example of a survey form:

```
<HTML>
<HEAD>
<TITLE>Reader Contact Information</TITLE>
<!- the name of this form is usr-inf.html ->
</HEAD>
<BODY>
<H3>Reader Contact Information</H3>
<P>Please fill out this form, so we'll know how to get in
touch with you. Thanks!
<FORM METHOD="POST" ACTION="/cgi/usr-inf">
<P>Please enter your name:
<P>First name: <INPUT NAME="first" TYPE="TEXT" SIZE="12"
   MAXLENGTH="20">
MI: <INPUT NAME ="MI" TYPE="TEXT" SIZE="3" MAXLENGTH="3">
Surname: <INPUT NAME="surname" TYPE="TEXT" SIZE="15"
   MAXLENGTH="25">
<P>
<P>Please give us your mailing address:
<P>Address 1: <INPUT NAME="adr1" TYPE="TEXT" SIZE="30"
   MAXLENGTH="45">
<P>Address 2: <INPUT NAME="adr2" TYPE="TEXT" SIZE="30"
   MAXLENGTH="45">
<P>City: <INPUT NAME="city" TYPE="TEXT" SIZE="15"
   MAXLENGTH="30">
<P>State: <INPUT NAME="state" TYPE="TEXT" SIZE="15" MAXLENGTH="15">
   ZIP&#47;Postal Code: <INPUT NAME="zip" TYPE="TEXT" SIZE="10"
   MAXLENGTH="10">
<P>Country: <INPUT NAME="country" TYPE="TEXT" SIZE="15"
   MAXLENGTH="15">
<P>
<P>Thank you! <INPUT TYPE="SUBMIT"> <INPUT TYPE="RESET">
</FORM>
<ADDRESS>
Sample form for <I>HTML for Dummies</I> Version 2.1
3/23/95 http://www.noplace.com/HTML4D/usr-inf.html
</ADDRESS>
</BODY></HTML>
```

Figure 12-1 shows this HTML form on Netscape. Note the positions of the one-line text boxes immediately after the field names, and the ability to set these boxes on individual lines (as with Address1 and Address2) or together (as with First name, Middle initial (MI), and Last name (Surname)). This makes it easy to build simple, usable forms.

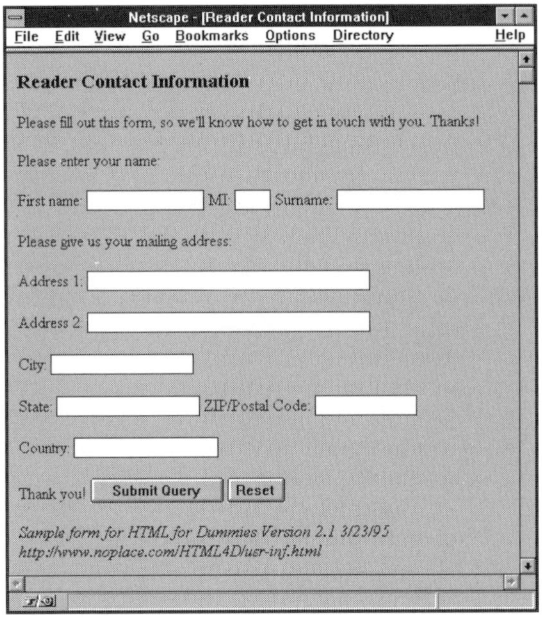

Figure 12-1:
The "User Informa-
tion" form
on-screen.

Being <SELECT>ive

The <SELECT> ... </SELECT> pair works much like a list style, except that it builds a pickable list of <OPTION> elements, instead of the <LI> list items. Within the <SELECT> tag, the following attributes can occur:

- ✔ **NAME="text"** — Provides the name that will be passed to the server as the identifying portion of the name/value pair for this element.

- ✔ **SIZE="number"** — Controls the number of elements that the pick list will display; while you can still define more than this many elements, it will keep the size of the list more manageable on-screen.

- ✔ **MULTIPLE** — Indicates that multiple selections from a list are possible; if it's not present, your users will only be allowed to select a single element from the pick list.

There's really not that much work involved in building a <SELECT> field for your form. In the following example, you'll see how easy it is to construct a list of spices from which a user can select and order:

```
<HTML>
<HEAD>
<TITLE>&lt;SELECT&gt; Spices</TITLE>
    <!- the name of this form is sel-spi.html ->
    </HEAD>
    <BODY>
    <H3>This Month's Spicey Selections!</H3>

<P>Spice up your life.  Order from this
    month's special selections.

<HR>
    <FORM METHOD="POST" ACTION="/cgi/sel-spi">

<P>Pepper Selections:
    <SELECT NAME="pepper" SIZE="4" MULTIPLE>
    <OPTION>Plain-black
    <OPTION>Malabar
    <OPTION>Telicherry
    <OPTION>Green-dried
    <OPTION>Green-pickled
    <OPTION>Red
    <OPTION>White
    </SELECT>
    <P>
    Please pick the button to indicate how the pepper<BR>
    should be delivered:<BR>
    Ground <INPUT TYPE="RADIO" NAME="grind" VALUE="ground"> <BR>
    Whole <INPUT TYPE="RADIO" NAME="grind" VALUE="whole"> <BR>
    <P>
    <HR>
    <P>Imported and Domestic Oregano:
    <SELECT NAME="oregano" SIZE="4" MULTIPLE>
    <OPTION> Italian-whole
    <OPTION> Italian-crumbled
    <OPTION> Greek-whole
    <OPTION> Indian
    <OPTION> Mexican
    <OPTION> Organic-California
    </SELECT>
    <P>
    <P>Thanks for your order! <INPUT TYPE="SUBMIT" VALUE="Send Order">
            <INPUT TYPE="RESET">
    </FORM>
    <ADDRESS>
    Sample form for <I>HTML for Dummies</I> Version 2.1
    3/23/95 http://www.noplace.com/HTML4D/usr-inf.html</ADDRESS>

</BODY></HTML>
```

Figure 12-2 shows what nice results you can get from using <SELECT> elements to provide options for your users to pick from. Notice also the radio buttons to specify whether they want whole or ground pepper. By giving both radio buttons the same NAME, we indicate that only one option can be chosen.

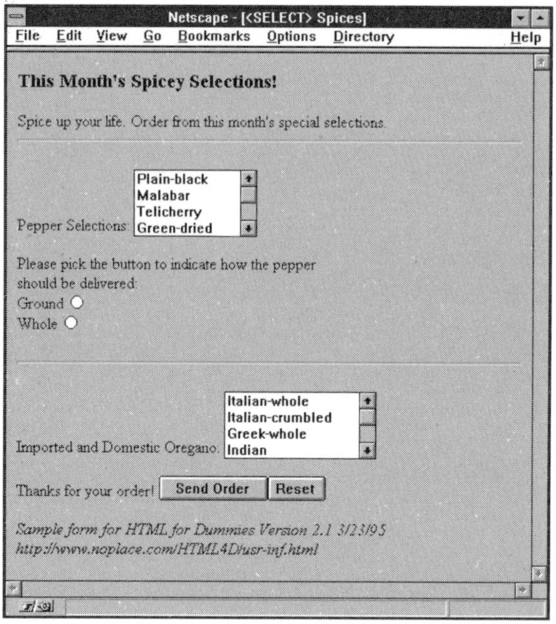

Figure 12-2:
The
<SELECT>
tag creates
scrolling
"pick lists"
of choices
for users to
select.

<TEXTAREA> lets users wax eloquent... or profane!

The <TEXTAREA> ... </TEXTAREA> tags let you create input elements of more or less arbitrary size on a form. Any text that appears between the opening and closing tags will be displayed within the text area on screen (and if left unaltered, supplies the default value delivered by the form).

<TEXTAREA> takes three important attributes:

- **NAME="text"** — Provides the identifier part of the all-important name/value pair delivered to the server.

- **ROWS="number"** — Specifies the number of lines of text the text area will contain.

- **COLS="number"** — Specifies the number of characters that can fit onto any one row of the text area; this value will also set the width of the text area on-screen.

The example that follows shows how a text area is used to provide space for free-form feedback or information as part of a survey-style form:

```
<HTML>
<HEAD>
<TITLE>&lt;TEXTAREA&gt; On Display</TITLE>
   <!- the name of this form is txt-ara.html ->
</HEAD>
   <BODY>
   <H3>The Widget Waffle Iron Survey</H3>
<P>Please fill out the following information so that we
   can register your new Widget Waffle Iron.
<HR>
   <FORM METHOD="POST" ACTION="/cgi/txt-ara">
<P>Model Number
   <SELECT NAME="mod-num" SIZE="3">
   <OPTION>102 (Single Belgian)
   <OPTION>103 (Double Belgian)
   <OPTION>104 (Single Heart-shaped)
   <OPTION>105 (Double Heart-shaped)
   <OPTION>204 (Restaurant Waffler)
   <OPTION>297 (Cone Waffler)
   </SELECT>
   <HR>
   <B>Please complete the following purchase information:</B><BR>
<P>Serial number: <INPUT NAME="snum" TYPE="TEXT" SIZE="10"
   MAXLENGTH="10">
   <P>Purchase Price: <INPUT NAME="price" TYPE="TEXT" SIZE="6"
   MAXLENGTH="10">
   <P>Location: <INPUT NAME="location" TYPE="TEXT" SIZE="15"
   MAXLENGTH="30">
   <HR>
   <B>Please tell us about yourself:</B>

<P>Male <INPUT NAME="sex" TYPE="CHECKBOX" VALUE="male">
   Female <INPUT NAME="sex" TYPE="CHECKBOX" VALUE="female">
   <P>Age:
   under 25 <INPUT NAME="age" TYPE="CHECKBOX" VALUE="lo">
   25-50 <INPUT NAME="age" TYPE="CHECKBOX" VALUE="med">
   over 50 <INPUT NAME="age" TYPE="CHECKBOX" VALUE="hi">
   <P>
   <HR>
   Please share your favorite waffle recipe with us. If we like
   it, we'll include it in our next Widget Waffler cookbook!
   Here's an example to inspire you.
   <P><TEXTAREA NAME="recipe" ROWS="10" COLS="65">
   Banana Waffles
   Ingredients:
```

```
          2 c. waffle batter (see Widget Waffler cookbook for recipe)
          2 ripe bananas, peeled, sliced 1/4" thick
          1 tsp. cinnamon
          Preparation:
          Mix ingredients together.
          Preheat Widget Waffler (wait 'til light goes off).
          Pour 1/2 c. batter in Waffler (wait 'til light goes off).
          Keep browned waffles warm in oven until ready to serve.
          </TEXTAREA>
    <P>Thank you! <INPUT TYPE="SUBMIT" VALUE="Register now">
     <INPUT TYPE="RESET">
      </FORM>
      <ADDRESS>
      Sample form for <I>HTML for Dummies</I> Version 2.1
      3/23/95 http://www.noplace.com/HTML4D/usr-inf.html</ADDRESS>

      </BODY></HTML>
```

The screen that results from this HTML document is shown in part in Figure 12-3. Notice the use of checkboxes for survey information, coupled with the text input area for recipes. Makes us wonder: "What time's breakfast?"

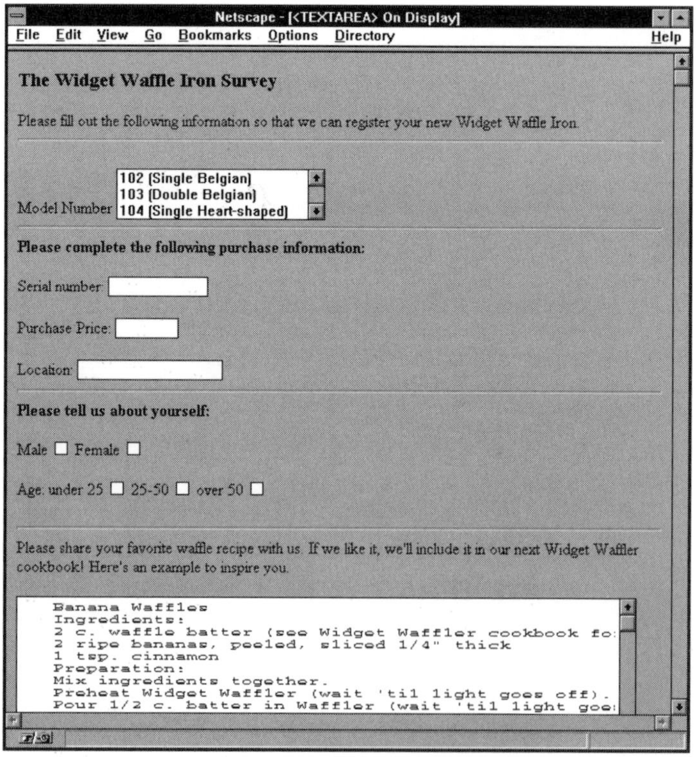

Figure 12-3:
Notice how you can supply example information for the text area in a form.

At this point, you've seen about all the nifty little tricks — we like to call them widgets — that work within forms, but you can't really appreciate what forms can do until you've browsed the Web to look at the many examples out there. Our examples barely scratch the surface, so there's a lot more to see!

Formulating Good Attitudes

Whenever you create an HTML form, it's especially important to test it against as many browsers as you possibly can. Don't forget to work with character-mode browsers, like Lynx, as well as more exciting graphical browsers. Remember also that although some browsers support some pretty keen extensions, the effort it takes to use them will be wasted on those readers who pass through in other browsers that don't support them.

Ultimately, the HTML rules regarding layout versus content apply to forms: if you can create a clear, readable layout and make the form interesting to your users, you'll probably be a lot happier with the information it returns than if you spend extra hours tuning and tweaking graphics elements and precise placement of type, widgets, and fields. Remember, too, that the form's just the front end for your user interaction or data collection. In Chapter 14, you'll pick up the back end of the forms business, as you tackle the demanding but rewarding task of building CGI scripts and other input-handling programs for your server. ▨

In the next chapter, you'll learn how to turn graphics into addressable on-screen selectors called clickable maps. These add zest to forms and other HTML documents, since they let users select links at different points within a graphic.

Chapter 13

The Map's the Thing!

*Y*ou've already learned how to insert graphics into your HTML documents, using the <IMG> tag. You've even seen examples of using graphics as hypertext links within anchor tags (<A HREF=...> <IMG SRC=...> </A>). In this chapter, you'll learn how to take the next logical step, and treat a graphic as a collection of selectable regions, each of which points to some kind of hypertext link or resource.

Where Are You? (Using Clickable Maps)

Geographically speaking, a map takes a land mass and divides it up along boundary lines into named regions: typically, these might be countries, counties, or other kinds of territories. When it comes to using graphics in this way on the Web, the boundaries are obvious in the graphic that's displayed, and users simply select the portion of the graphic that attracts their interest. Users familiar with graphical interfaces have no trouble interacting with on-screen buttons, icons, and other kinds of interface controls. Graphical maps add this kind of capability to a single image displayed on a Web page.

In Web-speak such graphical maps are usually called "image maps" or "clickable maps." We prefer the latter term, because it emphasizes the important aspects of this kind of graphical element:

1. It breaks a graphic into discrete regions that function as a map of individual hyperlinks.

2. Regions are selected by putting the cursor inside them, and clicking the mouse.

This should also cue you about the fundamental limitation inherent in a clickable map: it absolutely requires a graphical browser. The image that represents the map that drives the selection process doesn't appear in a character-mode browser, period. This means that alternate methods must always be implemented for users with text-only browsers.

An example of a clickable map should lend some reality to this concept. Figure 13-1 shows a button bar, where each button contains the name of a particular programming language. As part of a set of Web pages for a programming library, it acts as the gateway to a set of pages on each language mentioned.

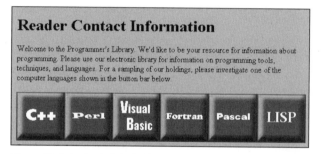

Figure 13-1: A nicely-labeled button bar that's just crying out for use as a clickable map.

In this chapter you'll learn how to set this kind of image up as a clickable map, and use it to drive page navigation. Just for grins we've shown the button bar included within our hypothetical Programmer's Library home page.

Cosmic Cartography: What It Takes to Present Maps on the Web

Building a clickable map requires three ingredients:

1. Creating (or selecting) a usable image — this could be an existing graphic or a custom-built one.

   Our button bar used a simple 3-D button to start with, duplicated six times in a straight line in a graphics program. Then, using the same program, we typed the names of our six chosen programs, choosing a variety of outline fonts in white to create the names of the programming languages laid down on top of each button.

2. Creating the "map file" — this requires a step-by-step investigation of the image file inside a graphics program that can give you the pixel addresses (coordinates) of each point on the boundary of the regions you want to create.

   Our button bar is really quite regular in shape, so working through this process is very easy: the image starts in the upper-left hand corner of the frame, and is consistently 94 pixels high. The individual buttons varied slightly in width, producing the following set of coordinates:

```
( 0, 0)----( 94, 0)---(188,  0)--(284,  0)--(380,  0)--(474,  0)--(570,  0)
|          |          |          |          |          |          |
|  button 1 | button 2 | button 3 | button 4 | button 5 |   button 6   |
|          |          |          |          |          |          |
( 0, 94)---( 94, 94)--(188, 94)--(284, 94)--(380, 94)--(474, 94)--(570, 94)
```

   Unfortunately, the only way to produce this collection of numbers is to view the graphic from within a graphics program (we used PaintShop Pro 3.0, a widely-available shareware program for Windows).

   In order to establish the coordinates, you must position the cursor on each boundary point and write down the corresponding x and y values. That's what our little diagram above represents: it's the map information for our button bar.

3. Establishing the right HTML information in your page to link the image, the map file, and a CGI script to handle decoding map coordinates and using that information to select the appropriate link to follow.

   Here, we'll take you through the generalities of making this work in your HTML document. Later on, we'll show you how to build a complete back-end CGI script to translate the pixel coordinates for a user's map selection into a corresponding HTML link. In this chapter, we'll only cover the techniques and generalities needed to construct the image map, and to create links between map regions and hypertext documents or resources.

By obtaining the information for steps 1 and 2, and establishing a convention to call the script that handles coordinate-to-link translation, we can tell most of what you need to know to set up a clickable map.

Just as we did in Chapter 12, we suggest you use the name of the image map as the name for its corresponding script file: thus if the image is named langbar.gif, the script would be called "langbar.exe," or simply "langbar." If your scripts are in a CGI directory one level down from your HTML files, the corresponding URL for this script would then be "/cgi/langbar."

Warning: different maps for different servers

Unfortunately, clickable maps are a topic where the two most popular *httpd* servers — NCSA and CERN — differ from one another. You will find format differences in defining image maps for one kind of server versus the other.

In order to get your clickable map to work, you'll have to work within the requirements of the server where the map resides. If you don't know what those requirements are, we strongly suggest that you contact your local WebMaster — or at least, the system administrator for your Web server.

He or she should be able to set you straight right away, and can probably help you find some useful information about how to build clickable maps for your system, above and beyond what we tell you here.

You can also consult Dr. Web at:

```
http://www.stars.com/Dr.Web/
```

Throughout the rest of this chapter, where there are differences between the CERN and NCSA requirements, we'll fill you in. If you're not using an *httpd* server of either variety, you'll want to investigate its requirements immediately, and adjust our examples and recommendations to meet those requirements right away!

Dealing with shapes in maps

There are various ways to identify boundaries when assembling coordinates to build a clickable map. Both CERN and NCSA image map definitions recognize the following kinds of regions:

- ✔ circle (specified by the coordinates for a point at the center, and the number of pixels for the radius). Use this to select a circular (or nearly circular) region within an image.

- ✔ rectangle (specified by the coordinates for the upper left and lower right corners). Use this to select any kind of square or rectangular region in your image (this is the one we'll be using in our map for the button bar).

- ✔ polygon (specified by the coordinates for the point at the vertex of each edge). Use this to outline the boundaries of regularly or irregularly shaped regions that aren't circular or rectangular. While it may take more effort, the more points you pick to define the outline, the more the region will behave as the user will expect it to when clicking.

> ✔ point (specified by its x and y coordinates). Use this only when a spe-
> cific point is easy for a user to select (this is usually too small a region
> on-screen, and requires exact control to select — we recommend sur-
> rounding a point with a small circle or square to give users a little room
> to be sloppy).

Selecting boundaries for map regions is what determines the selection of the
corresponding links. Even though users see a nicely shaped graphic to click
on, what really drives the selection process is the areas you've outlined on
top of that graphic.

The better the fit of the regions to the layout of the figure, the more the
map will behave like users will expect it to! The moral of the story is: take
your time and, when in doubt, pick more points to outline something,
rather than less! ▨

Building and Linking to CERN Map Files

Map files for CERN *httpd* servers take a general form that looks something like
this:

```
default URL
circle (x,y) r URL
rectangle (x1,y1) (x2,y2) URL
polygon (x1,y1) (x2, y2) (x3,y3) ... (xn,yn) URL
point (x,y) URL
```

The shapes are pretty much self-evident, except for the polygon, which represents an attempt to trace a region's outline by connecting a series of
points. If this sounds like "connect-the-dots" you've definitely gotten the
underlying concept! NOTE: don't forget to close your polygons; make sure
the last segment fills the gap between your last point and your first.

The other entry that might seem mysterious is the default, with its associated URL: this must be defined so that if a user clicks on a location that's
not defined in the map, a fail-safe connection can still be chosen. This might
be a script that sends a message back to the user that says "Click within the
lines!" or "You have selected an area of the image that is not defined. Please
try again."

The button bar map file

Thus, for our button bar example, the CERN map would be:

```
rectangle (0,0) (94,94) HTML4D/examples/cplus.html
rectangle (94,0) (188,94) HTML4D/examples/perl.html
rectangle (188,0) (284,94) HTML4D/examples/vb.html
rectangle (284,0) (380,94) HTML4D/examples/fortran.html
rectangle (380,0) (474,94) HTML4D/examples/pascal.html
rectangle (474,0) (570,94) HTML4D/examples/lisp.html
default HTML4D/examples/nolang.html
```

Because the button bar is a collection of rectangles, it's easy to fill in the coordinates (why do you think we picked this example?). Then, we provide a default link to the "nolang" page if somebody insists on staying outside the nice little boxes we gave them to play in! Notice, too, that we use URLs here that are relative to where the current document is in the file system of the server. Absolute URLs are easier to debug, and to relocate, but relative ones are less work to enter. You plays your keystrokes, and you takes your chances!

Creating and storing map files

The map file can be created using any plain text editor, but should be stored on the server in a special directory for your map definition files. For this example, we'll call the file "langbar.map" and store it in the /HTML4D/maps directory, along with all of our other maps.

With either CERN or NCSA servers, image maps need to be placed in a certain part of the file system. Contact your sys admin or your WebMaster to find out where this is and if you have write permissions.

Using map files

In order to use a map file with the CERN *httpd*, your system must already have a program that handles image maps. The name of this program, which is included with the CERN distribution *httpd* materials, is *htimage*. If it's not installed, you'll have to arrange for that to happen in order to use image maps on your system. Once it's available, you must also know how to invoke it on the server. For the purposes of this example we assume it lives on the directory path "/bin/cgi/."

Defining a clickable map in your HTML document

Once the map's defined and stored in the right location, it's time to bring all three elements together in your HTML file. Here's how you do it:

```
<A HREF="/bin/cgi/htimage/HTML4D/maps/langbar.map">
<IMG SRC="HTML4D/gifs/langbar.gif" ISMAP>
</A>
```

Here's what's going on in this series of statements:

1. The opening anchor tag combines the *htimage* location, which will handle the coordinate-to-URL translation, with the full specification for the map file. Even though there's no space between the name of the program (*htimage*) and the map file specification, the server still knows what to do.

2. The IMG tag points to the button bar graphic, but adds the ISMAP attribute to indicate that it's a clickable map.

3. The closing anchor tag </A> indicates that the graphic specified by IMG is the target for the map file specified in the opening anchor tag.

There you are! Once you've made sure all the right pieces are in place on your CERN server, you can try this, too.

Building and Linking to NCSA Map Files

Map files for NCSA httpd servers, look an awful lot like those for CERN servers, but there are some differences. They take a general form that looks something like this:

```
default URL
circle URL x,y r
rect URL x1,y1 x2,y2
poly URL x1,y1 x2,y2 x3,y3 ... xn,yn
point URL x,y
```

The shapes are the same as the CERN variety, and are defined by the same kinds of coordinates, but the names are shorter, and the URLs come first in the list of attributes, rather than last. Here again, defaults work the same way: to provide a handler for people who click outside the image frame.

The button bar map file

For our button bar example, the NCSA map would be:

```
rect HTML4D/examples/cplus.html (0,0) (94,94)
rect HTML4D/examples/perl.html (94,0) (188,94)
rect HTML4D/examples/vb.html (188,0) (284,94)
rect HTML4D/examples/fortran.html (284,0) (380,94)
rect HTML4D/examples/pascal.html (380,0) (474,94)
rect HTML4D/examples/lisp.html (474,0) (570,94)
default HTML4D/examples/nolang.html
```

Except for a slight change in the shape's name (rect instead of rectangle), and a reordering of the arguments (URL first, then coordinates), it's pretty much identical to the CERN variety.

Creating and storing map files

The NCSA map file can be created using any plain text editor, just like the CERN variant. It should also be stored on the server in a special directory for your map definition files. For this example, we'll use the same name: "langbar.map" and store it in the same /HTML4D/maps directory, along with all of our other maps.

Using map files

Like CERN, in order to use a map file with the NCSA *httpd*, your system must already have a program that handles image maps. The name of this program, which is included with the NCSA distribution *httpd* materials, is *imagemap*. If it's not installed, you'll have to arrange for that to happen in order to use image maps on your system. You'll also want to check that you have the latest version; check the information in:

```
http://hoohoo.ncsa.uiuc.edu/docs/setup/admin/imagemap.txt
```

against what's installed on your server. If the date is more recent at the NCSA server, download the file, rename it to "imagemap.c" and recompile it. Throw the old version away and use your new one instead.

Once *imagemap* is available, you must also know how to invoke it on the server. For the purposes of this example we assume it lives on the directory path "/bin/cgi/."

Defining a clickable map in your HTML document

Once the map's defined and stored in the right location, again it is time to bring all three elements together in your HTML file, this time the NCSA way. Here's how you do it:

```
<A HREF="/bin/cgi/imagemap/HTML4D/maps/langbar.map">
<IMG SRC="HTML4D/gifs/langbar.gif" ISMAP>
</A>
```

Here's what's going on in this series of statements:

1. The opening anchor tag combines the *imagemap* location, which will handle the coordinate-to-URL translation, with the full specification for the map file. Even though there's no space between the name of the program (*imagemap*) and the map file specification, the server still knows what to do.

2. The IMG tag points to the button bar graphic, but adds the ISMAP attribute to indicate that it's a clickable map.

3. The closing anchor tag </A> indicates that the graphic specified by IMG is the target for the map file specified in the opening anchor tag.

There you are! Once you've made sure all the right pieces are in place on your NCSA server, you can try this, too.

While the differences between the two flavors of *httpd* may seem trivial — and we think they are, too — they're still essential to creating clickable images that actually work. When it comes to computers in general, and the Web in particular, the devil is in the details. If you don't get your details straight, you get bedeviled instead!

"The Map Is Not the Territory"

Although Alfred Korzybski wasn't thinking of clickable images when he uttered the title of this section, it's still a point worth pondering. Because not all of your users can see an image map, you need to be prepared to give them the same set of selections that your graphically able users get in visual form. How might you go about doing this?

Since what you're providing in the image map is an array of choices, you could also add an equivalent set of text-based links right below the image. Here's what the HTML for this would look like:

```
<HTML>
<HEAD>
<TITLE>The Programmer's Library</TITLE>
<!- the name of this document is plb-home.html ->
</HEAD>
<BODY>
<H1>Reader Contact Information</H1>
Welcome to the Programmer's Library. We'd like to be your
resource for information about programming. Please use our
electronic library for information on programming tools,
techniques, and languages. For a sampling of our holdings,
please investigate one of the computer languages shown in
the button bar below:
<P>
<!- we're assuming a CERN httpd server is operating ->
<A HREF="bin/cgi/htimage/HTML4D/maps/langbar.map">
<IMG SRC="langbar.gif" ISMAP>
</A>
<P>
<A HREF="cplus.html>C++</A>|
<A HREF="perl.html">Perl</A>|
<A HREF="vb.html">Visual Basic</A>|
<A HREF="fortran.html">FORTRAN</A>|
<A HREF="pascal.html">Pascal</A>|
<A HREF="lisp.html">LISP</A>
<P>
<ADDRESS>
Programmer's Library example <BR>
<I>HTML for Dummies</I> Chapter 13-1 3/23/95<BR>
http://www.noplace.com/HTML4D/usr-inf.html
</ADDRESS>
</BODY></HTML>
```

As shown in Figure 12-3, this results in a text bar right underneath the graphic that offers the same choices that it does. Users with graphical browsers won't be discommoded by this redundancy, and character-mode browsers will see a reasonable facsimile of what their graphically advantaged brethren see in living color. This is what we call mastering the art of compromise!

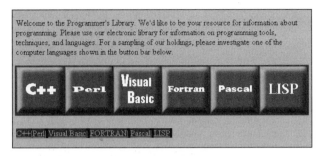

Figure 13-2: A text-based alternative combined with the button bar keeps everybody in the know.

Of Clickable Maps and URLs

Image links can sometimes play hob with relative URL specifications within HTML documents. One unforeseen side effect of following the links through a map-reading script — to the map and back to the target page — can be a complete mangling of the context within which URLs are addressed. In English, this means it's a really, really, really good idea to use full URLs, rather than relative references, in HTML documents that also include clickable maps.

Another solution is to include a <BASE> tag inside the <HEAD> ... </HEAD> tags, with the URL for the document in which it's included. This forces the server to treat the directory where the current document resides as the default context for relative references, even if clickable map references are used.

Either way, it's smart to be cagey when using relative URL references in documents with clickable maps. You should either avoid this practice, or make sure to use the <BASE> tag. Avoiding trouble is, in general, the best way to cure the URL "relative reference" blues!

Get ready for some real action in the next chapter, as you finally roll up your sleeves and get down and dirty on the back end side of the Web environment. Here, you'll get the lowdown on what happens with CGI scripts, input-handling programs for forms, search engines, and other tools that extend what the Web can do for your users. Better buckle up!

Chapter 14

Stick Out Your Neck!
HTML Extensions

- -

In This Chapter

▶ Understanding what's ineffective

▶ Adding on through the standards process

▶ Coming HTML attractions

▶ Going proprietary: the Netscape extensions

▶ Playing HTML by the rules...or not?

- -

*B*y now, you've probably seen or written enough HTML to know that it's easy to make the occasional mistake. In case you haven't noticed, most browsers are pretty forgiving about such things. Maybe you thought it was just a case of open-minded software, but it's really part of the way that HTML processing works: the specifications require that any HTML tags that can't be recognized should simply be ignored.

Of course many browsers take that even further. The newer ones are capable of making all kinds of assumptions regarding the fallibility of the all-too-human authors who write HTML documents. Among other things, this means some browsers will make educated guesses about where missing closing tags should have been placed — for instance, that the closing anchor tag </A> belongs at the end of the next word or line break after the opening <A...> anchor tag.

In fact, not all browsers are the same — some recognize markup tags that others don't. In some cases, this is because one browser may track recent additions to an HTML specification more closely than another. In other cases — as you'll learn more about later in this chapter — it means that one browser may recognize its own unique "enhancements" to HTML, in addition to standard markup.

If Your Browser Can't See It, Is It Really There?

When it comes to HTML markup, either your browser recognizes it and renders it on-screen, or it doesn't recognize it, and skips the tags altogether. This raises the interesting question at the head of this section. It also helps to explain why some browsers are more popular than others. The bottom line, though, remains the same. If your browser can't recognize the markup, it behaves as if it weren't there.

This behavior lets browsers render content in their own way rather than just skipping what's inside nonstandard tags. But it does cause some inconsistencies among browsers, so you never know what a page is going to look like until you see it drawn on the screen. These differences among browsers can sometimes be subtle — for example, Netscape puts more white space on pages than Mosaic. In case we haven't said it enough, test your Web pages with as many browsers as possible and always include a character-mode browser in your test.

The State of the HTML Art

HTML is governed by a standard specification for any given version: We've already discussed these in Chapter 6 as the Document Type Definitions (DTDs) for HTML versions 1.0, 2.0, and 3.0. At this point in the book, though, you need to understand how the standards-making process works, in order to understand why browsers may differ for perfectly good reasons, even though they claim to support the same HTML standard(s). ▪

A "simple explanation" for browser diversity

The simple explanation for browser differences is that they all track standards differently. If you care about such things, please read the sidebar, "Why are computer standards like seashells?". If you don't, skip ahead to "What's in Store for HTML?"

The upshot of working with evolving standards leads to the following assumptions, when it comes to computer programs like Web browsers:

- ✔ It's usually safe to assume that any new implementation will completely replace the current official (frozen) standard.

- ✔ Developers will adopt features and functions already present in developing standards. This is true for a variety of reasons, ranging from personal taste to a firm belief that certain features are more or less guaranteed to be in the "emerging standard" when it finally becomes official.

> ✔ Some developers will even add features and capabilities outside the
> standard. This can range from behaviors that modify parts of an exist-
> ing standard (like Netscape's addition of the "HEIGHT" and "WIDTH"
> attributes to the <IMG> tag) or that add new functionality or controls
> that were never part of any standard (like Netscape's <CENTER> ...
> </CENTER> tags).

This is a common pattern for software in many industries, including networking protocols like the TCP/IP that the Web uses for networking communications, to compiler implementations for standards-governed
programming languages like FORTRAN and C. It can get confusing, but it
reflects the living, breathing nature of the "state of the art" in any kind of
computer activity.

Vive la difference: adding value... or adding confusion?

There are even some cynics in the room who think that vendors add
"enhancements" to standards to try to shape the future direction that
standards will take. For their part, most vendors defend such things as
ways of "adding value" to a standard, to make their products more attractive to users. In English, this means they purposely make their browsers
different to create unique capabilites that people will pay extra to buy.

Why are computer standards like seashells?

Because they evolve continuously, standards
are very much like the chambered nautilus.
The nautilus is always adding onto its shell,
extending the walls of its current living quarters, while pulling out of and sealing off the
lower chambers that it is busily outgrowing.
In fact, standards don't really become standards until the chamber is sealed at the top
and bottom, this being the point at which it
can't change any more.

Standards also resemble the nautilus in that
there's always a current, official standard in
use at the same time that the next version is
under development. As standards go, HTML is
a little more ambitious than most, because it's
working on two chambers at a time. As the DTD
and specification for HTML 2.0 is nearing completion (as Dan Connolloy has moved from HaL
Software Systems to the W3 Organization to
finish the job), there's already significant work
underway on a 3.0 version (led by the
redoubtable Dave Ragget, of Hewlett-Packard
in the United Kingdom). This gives browser
developers lots of options to choose from, if
they decide to track and implement "emerging standards" before they get finalized.

It's tough to say whether difference is an attempt to anticipate new standards, or to deliberately try to appeal to users. We'd like to sidestep this burning issue and take this opportunity to warn you that standards are like Scripture or the Law — that is, they are subject to interpretation around a core of commonly held beliefs (or an "official standard") and tend to differ from one another, even though they all start with the same foundation.

What's in Store for HTML?

In general, what's in store for future versions of HTML is:

✔ the addition of new markup tags to support sophisticated layout and formatting capabilities

✔ the obsolescence of simpler, less useful markup

It's "any day now" for HTML 2.0

For HTML 2.0, this means adding forms support, and getting rid of formatting commands that were never used very much — such as "obsolete" tags like <XMP>, <PLAINTEXT>, and <LISTING>, all of which have now been superseded by the <PRE> tag. 2.0 also introduces the character highlighting elements — like <I> (italic), <B> bold, and <STRONG> — to replace the older HPx (highlighted phrase, type x) markup, which are already supported in most new browsers (even though the 2.0 specification is not yet "frozen").

HTML 3.0 is still developing...

HTML 3.0 is still fairly fluid, but appears sure to introduce all kinds of interesting capabilities. There's even some discussion about creating an interim standard, 2.1, to make sure that some features and functions proposed for HTML 3.0 arrive sooner, rather than later.

You might be wondering who decides the future of HTML. It's in the hands of the HTML working group, a group of researchers involved in discussing and developing HTML standards, including 2.0 and 3.0, through a mailing list at html-wg@oclc.org.

HTML 2.1, anyone?

In fact, a recent communication in the working group identifies the following enhancements as top priorities for an "interim release" that's being called 2.1:

✔ **Tables:** Today, the only way to supply tabular text in HTML is to preformat it with another tool and insert the formatted text into HTML with <PRE> ... </PRE> tags. One of HTML 3.0's most-mentioned enhancements will be support for defining tables, including row and colum headings, and adjustable column sizes.

✔ **FIG:** This is a way of referencing figures with captions in HTML 3.0; it adds to HTML's current ability to display graphics along with text. In 3.0 you can create figures with associated caption labels that are automatically linked to caption references within the text.

✔ **SUB and SUP:** These stand for subscript and superscript, used for mathematics and other kinds of formal notation. Their lack is currently keenly felt which is why they're being given precedence over other equation support such as multiline equations, complex matrix notation, and all kinds of mathematical symbols.

✔ **File upload in forms:** Today, users are limited to typing in data at their keyboards when providing input through HTML forms. The ability to upload files inside forms has a great deal of appeal, especially as a way of controlling how users can move files around on the Internet.

✔ **Unicode and other character sets:** Unicode is a 16-bit character encoding scheme that supports all kinds of non-Roman alphabets like Arabic, Mandarin, Korean, Japanese kanji, and many other ideographic alphabets. Many argue that making the Web truly "World Wide" means support for any human language. This is why Unicode support is so important in the international community.

These capabilities would add significantly to HTML's ability to present information to users and to support a truly global audience. It's not unreasonable to guess that most of these are already under development inside the locked doors of most browser developers' workshops. It's also a safe guess that these things will start showing up inside browsers before mid-1995.

The "real" HTML 3.0

Even though the features already mentioned appear to have priority in the development and standards communities, HTML 3.0 is like a RonCO product: "But wait, there's more..." Here are some of the other elements under consideration for HTML 3.0, many of which represent major increases in capability and functionality:

✔ Document divisions

✔ Style sheets

✔ Footnotes (and other embedded text elements)

✔ Text flow around graphics

✔ Object-oriented text and formatting variables

There's actually quite a bit more to the 3.0 DTD that's under development (and it'll probably still be in flux by the time you read this).

The only way to check out the state of HTML 2.0 and 3.0 (and possibly, even 2.1) is to go out and look at what's happening. You can start with the following URLs:

HTML 2 DTD and terminology

    http://www.w3.org/hypertext/WWW/MarkUp/html-spec/html.dtd.html
    http://www.hpl.hp.co.uk/people/dsr/html/terms.html

HTML 3 DTD working draft

    http://www.w3.org/hypertext/WWW/MarkUp/html3-dtd.html

If you start looking at the URLs mentioned in Chapter 11, you'll probably be able to find links to new specifications and other HTML works-in-progress there, too! ■

Some Nonstandard HTML Extensions

The folks at Netscape Communications are the developers of Netscape, a highly functional, graphically-oriented Web browser. Today, Netscape is widely regarded as the most popular browser in use on the Net. The systems administrator at Netscape has already logged over one million download attempts of the latest version of their browser, even though it's been available only two months at this point.

Today, Netscape is the only browser development company that we know of who has added capabilities to HTML outside the standards effort. While these extensions make for more attractive pages if you're using Netscape, they don't do anything for the other browsers. Can this possibly help to explain Netscape's burgeoning popularity? Well, we don't think HTML extensions are the only reason for Netscape's success, but it certainly means there are lots of browsers out there in daily use that can't understand and render these exotic features.

Netscape's changes to HTML markup

We'll tackle the changed and new markup introduced within Netscape in alphabetical order, just like we did for markup in Chapter 7. For a look at a "Web-ified" version of the Mozilla DTD (a cross between "Mosaic" and "Godzilla"—get it?) please consult the following URL:

    http://www.hal.com/~markg/docs/SGML/MOZILLA/DTD-HOME.html! ■

Where it's just a matter of enhancement of an existing HTML tag, we'll talk only about the enhanced or added attributes (see Chapter 7 for the same command for the already-defined attributes). For new commands, we'll provide definitions and suggested style information as well. We'll also label new tags with [New] in the Definition line. Here goes:

<BASEFONT> Change the basic font size

[New] Definition:

<BASEFONT> changes the size of the base (default) font that all relative font changes (for headings, etc.) are based on. This provides explicit control over font size within a page, anywhere such changes are desired.

Attributes:

SIZE="number"

> The default base font size in Netscape is 3, but can vary anywhere from 1 to 7. The default base font appears to be 12-point in most of the browsers we've seen; the range supported by this command appears to go from 7- or 8-point to 24-point or thereabouts. Note: this is a required attribute.

Context:

<BASEFONT>is legal within the following markup tags:

> <A> <ADDRESS> <B> <BLINK> <BLOCKQUOTE> <BODY> <CENTER> <CITE> <CODE> <DD> <DT> <EM> <FONT> <FORM> <H*> <I> <KBD> <LI> <NOBR> <P> <SAMP> <STRONG> <TT> <VAR>

No markup can be used within <BASEFONT> because it is a singleton tag.

Suggested style/usage:

To enlarge text for better readability; to compress text to put more information on a single screen; to get better control over page layout and appearance. You can use <BASEFONT> multiple times in a single document to change base font sizes, and it will apply just where you think it should: from right after the <BASEFONT> tag that picks a current size, to right up to the next <BASEFONT> tag that changes the base font.

*
 Line break*

Definition:

Forces a line break in running text.

Attributes:

CLEAR=(LEFT | RIGHT | ALL)

Without the CLEAR attribute, <BR> behaves as it always has. CLEAR breaks the line and moves vertically down until there is a clear left margin (="LEFT"), a clear right margin (="RIGHT"), or a clear margin on both sides of the page (="ALL").

Context:

 is legal within the following markup tags:

<A> <ADDRESS> <B> <BLINK> <BLOCKQUOTE> <BODY> <CENTER>
<CITE> <CODE> <DD> <DT> <EM> <FONT> <FORM> <H*> <I> <KBD>
<LI> <NOBR> <P> <PRE> <SAMP> <STRONG> <TT> <VAR>

Because <BR> is a singleton tag, no markup can be used within the tag.

Suggested style/usage:

To force line breaks in text, with optional control over where the next line appears vis-à-vis on-page graphics.

<CENTER>... </CENTER> Center text

[New] Definition:

Centers all text between the beginning and ending tags, over as many lines as are required to render the text information.

Attributes:

None.

Context:

<CENTER> ... </CENTER> is legal within the following markup tags:

<BLOCKQUOTE> <BODY> <CENTER> <DD> <FORM> <LI>

The following markup can be used within <CENTER> ... </CENTER>

<A> <ADDRESS> <B> <BASEFONT> <BLINK> <BLOCKQUOTE>
,
<CENTER> <CITE> <CODE> <DIR> <DL> <EM> <FONT> <FORM> <H*>
<I> <IMG> <ISINDEX> <KBD> <LI> <MENU> <NOBR> <OL> <P> <PRE>
<SAMP> <STRONG> <TT> <UL> <VAR> <WBR>

Suggested style/usage:

Wherever text or graphics need to be centered on the page. It's especially good for sidebars, headings, images, and address information.

<FONT> Adjust font size

[New] Definition:

Provides a mechanism to adjust the font size in running text. See attribute information for the details.

Attributes:

SIZE="number"

Valid ranges for the number are 1-7, as with BASEFONT. Unlike BASEFONT, you may also prefix the size by a plus or minus sign (e.g., SIZE="+2" or SIZE="-1") to adjust the size relative to the current <BASEFONT> setting. Note: this is a required attribute.

Context:

<FONT> is legal within the following markup tags:

<A> <ADDRESS> <B> <BLINK> <BLOCKQUOTE> <BODY> <CENTER> <CITE> <CODE> <DD> <DT> <EM> <FONT> <FORM> <H*> <I> <KBD> <LI> <NOBR> <P> <SAMP> <STRONG> <TT> <VAR>

Because <FONT> is a singleton tag, no markup can be used within the tag.

Suggested style/usage:

To adjust font size relative to current running text. Works well to size up for emphasis or readability, or to size down to fit more information on a page, or to reproduce the "fine print" in the spirit in which it was intended!

<HR> Horizontal rule

Definition:

Extends the ability to place a horizontal rule across a page beyond the default, which is a shaded engraved line extending from left to right margins. See Attributes information for the wide range of controls that Netscape has added.

Attributes:

ALIGN=(LEFT | RIGHT | CENTER)

Because horizontal rules may not fill the line completely, this control allows placement to be left- or right-justified, or centered on the line.

NOSHADE

If present, NOSHADE eliminates shading of the horizontal rule, to provide just a separator bar.

SIZE="number"

By supplying a number from 1 to 7, the width of the rule can be altered (1 is the default, 7 is a very thick bar).

WIDTH=(number | percent)

The default horizontal rule is as wide as the page, but with the WIDTH tag, the size can be specified in terms of the number of pixels, or the percentage of the line that the rule is to occupy.

Context:

<HR> is legal within the following markup tags:

    <BLOCKQUOTE> <BODY> <CENTER> <FORM> <PRE>

Because <HR> is a singleton tag, no markup can be used within it.

Suggested style/usage:

To separate logical divisions in a document, and to add visual effects to page endings, beginnings, or divisions (check the Netscape home page at http://www.mcom.com/ for some good examples of <HR> use).

<IMG> Image placement tag

Definition:

Supplies image source, placement, and behavior information. Used to place in-line graphics on a page.

Attributes:

ALIGN=(LEFT | RIGHT | TOP | TEXTTOP | MIDDLE | ABSMIDDLE |

    BASELINE | BOTTOM | ABSBOTTOM)

LEFT:

Floats graphic down and over to the left margin into the next available space.

RIGHT:

Floats graphic down and over to the right margin into the next available space.

TOP:

Aligns graphic with tallest item in the current line.

TEXTTOP:

Aligns graphic with the top of the tallest text in the line.

MIDDLE:

Aligns the baseline of the current text with the middle of the image.

ABSMIDDLE:

Aligns the middle of the current line with the middle of the image.

BASELINE:

Aligns the bottom of the image with the baseline of the current line. This is the default attribute.

BOTTOM:

Same as BASELINE.

ABSBOTTOM:

Aligns the bottom of the image with the bottom of the current line.

WIDTH="number" HEIGHT="number"

These values represent the outline boundaries of an image by number of pixels. When supplied, these values can speed graphics display because they prevent the browser from having to fully download an image to calculate how much display area it needs (and how to handle alignment).

BORDER="number"

Provides a control over the thickness of the border around an image, in number of pixels (default is typically 3). Tip: do not set border to zero because users may not be able to recognize an image as an anchor without the highlighted border to indicate it's a link.

VSPACE="number" HSPACE="number"

For floating images, this provides vertical and horizontal spacing to control how much white space is left around an image (to keep text from butting directly against images).

Context:

<IMG> is legal within the following markup tags:

   <A> <ADDRESS> <B> <BLINK> <BLOCKQUOTE> <BODY> <CENTER>
   <CITE> <CODE> <DD> <DT> <EM> <FONT> <FORM> <H*> <I> <KBD>
   <LI> <NOBR> <P> <SAMP> <STRONG> <TT> <VAR>

As a singleton tag, no markup can be used within <IMG>.

Suggested style/usage:

Keep images small and use them judiciously; graphics should add impact and interest to pages without adding too much bulk (or wait time).

<ISINDEX> Searchable index marker

Definition:

The ISINDEX element can occur within numerous tags to indicate that the document is searchable with an index.

Attributes:

PROMPT="message"

> This new attribute lets you supply a message to describe what is searchable. It replaces the standard HTML default message which reads: "This is a searchable index. Enter search keywords:". This message appears immediately before the text input field for the index.

Context:

<ISINDEX> is legal within the following markup tags:

> <BLOCKQUOTE> <BODY> <CENTER> <DD> <FORM> <HEAD> <LI>

As a singleton tag, no markup can be used within <ISINDEX>.

Suggested style/usage:

To mark a document as including a searchable index.

<LI> List item

Definition:

Defines an element within any of the HTML list types.

Attributes:

TYPE=(DISC I CIRCLE I SQUARE) or (A I a I I I i I 1)

> TYPE lets you set the type of display for list elements. If TYPE is one of the shapes, this makes the list item follow the extended <UL> definitions mentioned later; if TYPE is one of the character or number types, this makes the list item follow the extended <OL> definitions mentioned later.

VALUE="text"

> For ordered list types, this lets you manually control the value assigned to the list element.

Context:

<LI> is legal within the following markup tags:

   <DIR> <MENU> <OL> <UL>

As a singleton tag, no markup can be used inside <LI>.

Suggested style/usage:

Use to set off elements within lists.

<NOBR> ... </NOBR> No break

[New] Definition:

This tag pair specifies that all the text between the start and end tags cannot have line breaks inserted. <NOBR> is helpful for text sequences that cannot be broken, but it's important to note that long strings within <NOBR> ... </NOBR> can look strange when displayed.

Attributes:

None.

Context:

<NOBR> ... </NOBR> is legal within the following markup tags:

   <A> <ADDRESS> <B> <BLINK> <BLOCKQUOTE> <BODY> <CENTER>
   <CITE> <CODE> <DD> <DT> <EM> <FONT> <FORM> <H*> <I> <KBD>
   <LI> <P> <SAMP> <STRONG> <TT> <VAR>

The following markup can be used within <NOBR> ... </NOBR>:

   <A> <B> <BASEFONT> <BLINK>
 <CITE> <CODE> <EM> <FONT> <I>
   <IMG> <KBD> <SAMP> <STRONG> <TT> <VAR> <WBR>

Suggested style/usage:

To keep together short sequences of characters that should not be broken.

<OL>... </OL> Ordered list

Definition:

An ordered list of elements, enumerated with a variety of counters in this enhanced definition. See Attributes section for details.

Attributes:

TYPE = (A|a|I|i|1)

A:	Use uppercase alphabetic letters (letters double at position 27, unless overridden).
a:	Use lowercase alphabetic letters.
I:	Use uppercase Roman numerals.
i:	Use lowercase Roman numerals.
1:	Use arabic numerals.

Context:

<OL> ... </OL> is legal within the following markup tags:

<BLOCKQUOTE> <BODY> <CENTER> <DD> <FORM> <LI>

The only markup that can be used within <OL> ... </OL> is <LI>.

Suggested style/usage:

These enhancements support a wide range of enumerated lists, including classic outlining styles.

<UL>... </UL> Unordered list

Definition:

A bulleted list of unordered items.

Attributes:

TYPE = (DISC|CIRCLE|SQUARE)

TYPE gives you control over the shape of bullets in the list at the current level, which ordinarily varies according to the browser's default shape selection for the current list level (within nested lists). The shape names are self-documenting, so we don't explain them further (you can always experiment, if you're curious).

Context:

<UL> ... </UL> is legal within the following markup tags:

<BLOCKQUOTE> <BODY> <CENTER> <DD> <FORM> <LI>

The only markup that can be used within <UL> ... </UL> is <LI>.

Suggested style/usage:

To create attractively arranged bulleted lists, we suppose!

<WBR> Word break

[New] Definition:

Permits a possible line breakpoint to be marked within a <NOBR> ... </NOBR> text block.

Attributes:

None.

Context:

<WBR> is legal only within:

> <A> <ADDRESS> <B> <BLINK> <BLOCKQUOTE> <BODY> <CENTER> <CITE> <CODE> <DD> <DT> <EM> <FONT> <FORM> <H*> <I> <KBD> <LI> <NOBR> <P> <SAMP> <STRONG> <TT> <VAR>

As a singleton tag, no markup is legal within <WBR>.

Suggested style/usage:

To mark an optional breakpoint in <NOBR> text.

By the time you read about these Netscape extensions, this information may very well be out-of-date. For the latest news on the subject, please check the following URL:

```
http://home.mcom.com/home/services_docs/html-extensions.html
```

In the evanescent, ever-changing world of the Web, the only way to get the freshest information is to go out and pick it up yourself! For the latest version of the Netscape browser, please check the following URL:

```
http://home.mcom.com/home/ ▉
```

The Perils of (In)Compatibility

There are those who argue passionately that extensions to any standard, whether proprietary to one vendor or generally adopted, are a good thing. They give users a chance to try out new and hopefully interesting capabilities, and provide a platform for "informed consensus" about what really should be included in the next standard. "This helps make things better in the long run," runs the argument.

We view proprietary extensions as more of a mixed blessing: true, they can help advance the state of the art, but they also create "haves" and "have-nots" on the Web. That is, those who have the right browser can partake of this bounty, but others who do not have the right software cannot. Even though this division is as inevitable on the Web as it is anywhere else in the world, that doesn't mean we have to like it!

The only truly rational argument we can find against using these kinds of extensions is that it complicates page testing. Because some browsers will not be able to render what other browsers can, it becomes important to test your pages in both environments, to make sure they work equally well on both sides of the tracks. If properly approached, this means more work for you. But since you can do anything you want with HTML anyway, we'll let *you* decide!

This concludes our discussion of the innards of HTML. While the topic will never be far away from our minds, in the following chapters you'll move on to the back end, server side of the Web world. We think you'll agree that understanding both sides of the Web equation will help you build better pages, and to take full advantage of the services that the Web can offer. So please read on!

Part V
Beyond HTML?
CGI Programs and
"Real" Applications

In This Part...

One of the Web's most fascinating but least understood capabilities is its ability to manage interaction
between users running browsers and the programs and
protocols on Web servers that make things happen. This
capability stands behind the forms-handling and clickable
maps we discussed in Chapters 12 and 13. It also provides the capability for online search engines, query processing, and any other customized interaction you might
encounter on the Web.

The cornerstone holding up Web-based interaction is the
Common Gateway Interface (CGI), which specifies how
browsers can request services from properly-equipped
Web servers. In Chapter 15, you'll have a chance to get
acquainted with CGI, and with the kinds of programs and
services it supports. These truly open up the Web to all
kinds of interesting functionality by providing a way to
communicate information from just about any kind of
computer-based program and service to Web users.

Chapter 16 discusses interesting tools and technologies to
make your Web documents more usable, especially through
a variety of programs and services available with CGI programs. It also addresses some of the ways in which you can
deal with long or complex documents, and how to avoid the
pitfalls of perfectionism.

You should find this part of the book an eye-opening discussion of how to extend your Web pages to encompass whatever services you think your users need. We'll also try to
point you at important repositories for CGI programs and
other useful gizmos, so you won't have to reinvent the wheel!

Chapter 15

The Common Gateway Interface (CGI)

● ●

In This Chapter

▶ Getting acquainted: a quick CGI overview

▶ Specifying CGI

▶ Making smart programming choices

▶ Forming connections: handling forms data

▶ Sampling the capabilities

● ●

*B*uilding HTML forms and handling user interaction through Web pages requires action on both sides of the client-server connection. So far this book has concentrated mainly on the client side, except for the clickable image map files we described in Chapter 13.

In this chapter we'll move across the network connection from the client to the server side, and describe the Common Gateway Interface (CGI) that lets Web pages communicate with programs on the server to provide customized information, or to build interactive exchanges between clients and servers.

Along the way you'll learn about the history and foundations of CGI, and cover the basic details of its design and use. You'll also get acquainted with the issues surrounding your choice of a scripting or programming language for CGI, and have a chance to read through some interesting example programs. Since you're getting these programs — and the code to run them — as part of this book (the code's on the diskette), we hope you'll end up using them as part of your own Web pages!

The "Common Gateway" Is NOT a Revolving Door!

Gateway scripts or programs add the capability for true interaction between browsers and servers across the Web. This is a powerful capability that's limited only by your imagination and the tools at hand. Gateway scripts supply the underlying functions that let you perform searches on Web documents or databases, that provide the ability to accept and process forms data, and that deliver the intelligence necessary to customize Web pages based on user input.

If you build Web pages, you become responsible for managing this interaction across the Web: that is, you must build the front-end information that users see and interact with, as well as the back-end programming that accepts, interprets, and responds to user input and information. This does require some effort and some programming, but if you're willing to take the time to learn CGI, you'll be limited only by the amount of time and energy you have for programming your Web pages.

Describing CGI programs

It doesn't really matter whether you call your server-side work a program or a script — in fact, this distinction is often used to describe the tools you'd use to build one. That is, scripts get built with scripting tools or languages; programs get built with programming languages. For convenience, we'll simply refer to them as "CGI programs." You can call them whatever you want!

CGI is the method that UNIX-based CERN and NCSA Web servers use to mediate interaction between servers and programs. Because UNIX was the original Web platform, it sets the model yet again for how the Web behaves in this aspect. Although you might find other platforms that support Web servers — like Windows NT and the Macintosh — they too must follow the standard set for these two primary implementations of *httpd* to provide CGI capabilities, or provide a similar set of functions to match what CGI can do.

What's going on in a CGI program?

You can think of a CGI program as an extension to the core WWW server services. In fact, CGI programs are like worker bees that do the dirty work on behalf of the server. The server serves as an intermediary between the client and the CGI program. It's good to be the Queen Bee, and make all those workers do their things at your behest!

CGI programs are invoked by the server, based on information provided by the browser (as in the <FORM> tag, where the ACTION attribute supplies a URL for the particular program that services the form). This sets the stage for a series of information hand-offs and exchanges:

✔ The browser makes a request of a server for a URL, which actually contains a call to a CGI program.

✔ The server fields the URL request, figures out that it points to a CGI program (usually by parsing the filename and its extension or through the directory where the file resides), and fires off the CGI program.

✔ The CGI program performs whatever actions it's been built to supply, based on input from the browser. These actions could include obtaining the date and time from the server's underlying system, accumulating a counter for each visit to a Web page, searching a database, etc.

✔ The CGI program takes the results of its actions and returns the proper data back to the server; often the program will format these results as a Web page for delivery back to the server (if the Content-type is "text/html").

✔ The server accepts the results from the CGI program and passes them to the browser, which renders them for display to the user.

✔ If this exchange is part of an ongoing, interactive Web session, these results would include additional forms tags to accept further user input, along with a URL for this or another CGI program, thus beginning the cycle anew.

This is a kind of disjointed way to have a "conversation" over the Web, but it does allow information to move both ways. The real beauty of CGI programs is that you can extend a simple WWW server in every conceivable direction, making that server's services richer and more valuable.

What's in CGI Input?

A request for a CGI program is encoded in HTML in a basic form as shown in this example:

```
<A HREF="http://www.hal.com/hal-bin/silly_quote.pl">Silly Quote</A>
```

The URL declaration says to execute the *silly_quote.pl* CGI program on the *www.hal.com* WWW server from the *hal-bin* directory. This request has no additional input data to pass to the CGI program (the clue is that there is no "?" appended to the URL — the question mark argument is explained later in this chapter). The result of the CGI program is a Web page created on-the-fly and returned to the browser.

The information gathered by an HTML form or requested by a user with a search request or some other kind of information query, is passed to CGI programs in one of two ways:

1. As an appendage to a CGI program's URL (most commonly for WAIS requests or other short information searches). Uses the METHOD="GET" option.

2. As a stream of bytes through the UNIX default input device *stdin* in response to the ACTION setting for an HTML <FORM> tag. Best used with the METHOD="POST" option.

In this section, you'll learn how forms create special formats for information intended for use in CGI programs, and how that information can be delivered and used in those programs.

Short and sweet : the "extended URL" approach

Most search engines use what's called a document-based query to obtain information from users. This consists of nothing more than special characters appended to the end of the URL for the search engine itself. Document-based queries are intended to get search terms or keys from a browser and then deliver them to a CGI program that uses them to search a database or a collection of files. This is what makes document queries so good for soliciting small amounts of input from users and why you see them in so many Web pages.

Document-based queries depend on three ingredients for their successful operation:

1. The <ISINDEX> tag within the <HEAD> section of an HTML document enables searching of the document by the browser.

2. A special URL format is generated by adding the contents of a query to the URL, with the search terms added at the end and denoted by question marks.

3. Special arguments in your underlying CGI program.

Here's how this actually works:

1. The <ISINDEX> tag in the <HEAD> of the document causes the browser to supply a SEARCH widget that allows the user to enter keywords. These keywords are then bundled into an HTTP request and are passed to the corresponding CGI program. If the CGI program finds that no arguments are appended to the URL, it returns a default page which includes

the SEARCH widget to the browser. This sometimes happens the first time a search is requested because the complete search widget may not be included on every Web page.

2. The reader enters a string to search for at the prompt, and hits return or otherwise causes the string to be shipped to the CGI program for handling.

3. The browser calls the same URL as before, except it appends the search string following a question mark. So, if the search engine program's URL is:

```
http://www.HTML4d.com/cgi-bin/searchit
```

and the string to be searched for is "tether", the new URL then becomes:

```
http://www.HTML4d.com/cgi-bin/searchit?tether
```

4. The server receives the URL exactly as formatted and passes it to the searchit program, with the string after the question mark passed as an argument to searchit.

5. This time the program will perform an actual search and return the results as another HTML page, instead of the default prompt page that was sent the first time the program was invoked.

Every part of this operation depends on the others: the browser provides activation of the <ISINDEX> tag which allows the query to be requested and entered. The browser also appends the query string to the URL, which is then passed as an argument to the search program. This value is used as the focus of the search operation, after which the program returns the results to the browser, via another custom-built HTML document.

Long-winded and thorough: the input-stream approach

As you build an HTML form, some of the most important definitions involved are the assignments of names to variables or selections, and the definitions of the values associated with each one. When a user fills out a form, they're actually instructing the browser to build a list of associated name,value pairs for each selection made or for each field that's filled in.

Name,value pairs take the form:

```
name=value&
```

The equal sign (=) separates the name of the field from its associated value. The ampersand (&) separates the end of the value's string from the next item of text information in a completed form. For <SELECT> statements where MULTIPLE choices are allowed, this results in multiple name,value pairs where the name remains the same, but the value assignment changes for each value chosen for that named field.

Reading through forms information delivered to a CGI program's standard input (*stdin*) becomes a matter of checking certain key environment variables (covered in the next section), and then parsing the input data. This consists of separating name and value pairs, and of using the names to guide subsequent processing with the values supplied for them. The easiest way to do this, from a programming perspective, is to first parse and split out name,value pairs by looking for the ending ampersand (&), and then divide the pairs into the name and value parts by looking for the equal sign (=).

Here's some Perl code fragments you can use to parse your forms' input data (it assumes that METHOD="POST" is used, in keeping with our recommendation of that method):

```
# this reads the input stream from the Standard Input
# device (STD) into the buffer variable $buffer, using
# the environment variable CONTENT_LENGTH to know how
# much data to read
read(STDIN, $buffer, $ENV{'CONTENT_LENGTH'});

#Split the name,value pairs on '&'
@pairs = split (/&/, $buffer);

# Go through pairs and determine the name and value for
# each named form field
for each $pair (@pairs) {
# Split name from value on "="
  ($name, $value) = split(/=/,$pair);
# Translate URL syntax of + for blanks
  $value =~ tr/+/ /;
# Substitute hexadecimal characters with their normal equivalents
  $value =~ s/%([a-fA-F0-9][a-fA-F0-9])/pack("C",hex($1))/eg;
# Deposit the value in the FORMS array, associated to name
  $FORM($name) = $value; ■
```

Handling environment variables

As part of the CGI environment, the *httpd* server's software version and configuration is of interest as are the multiple variables associated with the server. The following shell program can be used to produce a complete listing of such information, and is a valuable testing tool when installing or modifying a Web server:

```sh
#!/bin/sh

echo Content-type: text/plain
echo

echo CGI/1.0 test script report:
echo

echo argc is $#. argv is "$*".
echo

echo SERVER_SOFTWARE = $SERVER_SOFTWARE
echo SERVER_NAME = $SERVER_NAME
echo GATEWAY_INTERFACE = $GATEWAY_INTERFACE
echo SERVER_PROTOCOL = $SERVER_PROTOCOL
echo SERVER_PORT = $SERVER_PORT
echo REQUEST_METHOD = $REQUEST_METHOD
echo HTTP_ACCEPT = $HTTP_ACCEPT

echo PATH_INFO = $PATH_INFO
echo PATH_TRANSLATED = $PATH_TRANSLATED
echo SCRIPT_NAME = $SCRIPT_NAME
echo QUERY_STRING = $QUERY_STRING
echo REMOTE_HOST = $REMOTE_HOST
echo REMOTE_ADDR = $REMOTE_ADDR
echo REMOTE_USER = $REMOTE_USER
echo CONTENT_TYPE = $CONTENT_TYPE
echo CONTENT_LENGTH = $CONTENT_LENGTH
```

This UNIX shell script is widely distributed around the Net. We found this version in the NCSA hoohoo collection, at:

```
http://hoohoo.ncsa.uiuc.edu/cgi-bin/test-cgi
```

Running this script on a Web server (in this case, the NCSA Web server hoohoo) produces the following output:

```
CGI/1.0 test script report:

argc is 0. argv is .

SERVER_SOFTWARE = NCSA/1.4b2
```

```
SERVER_NAME = hoohoo.ncsa.uiuc.edu
GATEWAY_INTERFACE = CGI/1.1
SERVER_PROTOCOL = HTTP/1.0
SERVER_PORT = 80
REQUEST_METHOD = GET
HTTP_ACCEPT = */*, image/gif, image/x-xbitmap, image/jpeg
PATH_INFO =
PATH_TRANSLATED =
SCRIPT_NAME = /cgi-bin/test-cgi
QUERY_STRING =
REMOTE_HOST = etittel.zilker.net
REMOTE_ADDR = 198.252.182.167
REMOTE_USER =
AUTH_TYPE =
CONTENT_TYPE =
CONTENT_LENGTH = ▓
```

All of the capitalized variable names on the left-hand side of the script and its associated output are environment variables set by CGI. These are always available for use in your programs.

There are two environment variables that are especially worthy of note:

✔ The QUERY_STRING variable is associated with the GET method of information-passing (as is common with search commands) and must be parsed for such queries or information requests.

✔ The CONTENT_LENGTH variable is associated with the POST method of information-passing (as is recommended for forms or other lengthier forms of input data). It is accumulated by the browser while assembling the forms data to deliver to the server, and tells the CGI program how much input data it has to read from the standard input device.

The environment variables also identify other items of potential interest, including the name of the remote host and its corresponding IP address, as well as the request method used, and the types of data that the server can accept. As you become more proficient in building CGI programs, you'll find further uses for many of these values.

Forming Up: Input-Handling Programs

When you create a form in HTML, each input field in the form has an associated unique NAME. Filling out the form usually associates one or more values with each name. As shipped from the browser to the Web server (and on to the CGI program targeted by the URL), the form data is a stream of bytes, consisting of name,value pairs separated by ampersand characters (&).

Each of these name,value pairs is URL-encoded, which means that spaces are changed into plus signs (+) and some characters are encoded into hexadecimal. This decoding is what caused the interesting translation contortions in our Perl code sample in the preceding section.

If you visit the NCSA CGI archive, you'll find links to a number of input-handling code libraries that can help you build forms. These include:

- **Bourne Shell:** The AA Archie Gateway, which contains calls to *sed* and *awk* to convert a GET form data string into separate environmental variables. (AA-1.2.tar.Z)

- **C:** The default scripts for NCSA *httpd*, including C routines and example programs for translating the query string into various structures. (ncsa-default.tar.Z)

- **Perl:** The Perl CGI-lib contains a group of useful PERL routines to decode and manage forms data. (cgi-lib.pl.Z)

- **TCL:** The TCL argument processor includes a set of TCL routines to retrieve forms data and insert it into associated TCL variables. (tcl-proc-args.tar.Z)

What this means to you, gentle reader, is that most of the work of reading in and organizing forms information is widely and publicly available in one form or fashion already. This simplifies your programming efforts because you can concentrate on writing the code that interprets the input and builds the appropriate HTML document that's returned to the user as a response.

Coding CGI

We'll conclude this chapter by examining three different CGI programs. We've also included that code and a great deal of associated information on the diskette that comes with this book. Each of these programs is available in three versions: AppleScript (for use on an Apple *httpd* server), Perl (for use on any system that supports a Perl interpreter/compiler), and C (for use on any system that supports a C compiler).

Ladies and gentlemen: Choose your weapons!

Before we launch you into these excellent examples — which we'd also like to encourage you to use in your own HTML documents and CGI programs (we're giving the license to this code away, so you can use it without restrictions) —

we'd like to conclude the discussion portion of this chapter with an investigation of why we chose to implement each of these programs in three forms, and how you might go about choosing a suitable language to write your CGI programs.

It's quite true that you can build your CGI programs with just about any programming or scripting language that your Web server supports. There's nothing stopping you from ignoring all of the options we've covered here and using something completely different.

Nevertheless, we think there are some good reasons why these options should be considered and some equally good reasons why some other options are better ignored. We'll cheerfully concede that there are probably as many opinions on this subject as there are CGI programmers, but we'd like you to consider carefully before deciding on a CGI language that you're likely to spend considerable time and effort learning and using.

For instance, we included the NCSA *test-cgi* script earlier in this chapter. It's written in the basic C shell, a command-language common on many UNIX systems that makes an adequate scripting language for many uses. Nevertheless, we don't think that any of the UNIX shells is suitable for heavy-duty CGI programming, because they mix UNIX system commands freely within their own syntax.

The problem with CGI programming in general under UNIX is that it depends on the standard input (*stdin*) and standard output (*stdout*) devices as the methods for moving data between Web servers and browsers. Each new UNIX process automatically creates its own *stdin* and *stdout*; sometimes the shell can get confused regarding where its input is coming from and its output is going. This can be the side effect of spawning tasks or running system commands, but whatever the cause, it can lose the input or output for CGI programs. That's the main reason why we don't recommend it for heavier-duty (e.g., forms-processing versus query-handling) applications.

On the plus side, Perl offers straightforward access to UNIX system calls and capabilities within a tightly structured environment. It includes the positive features of languages like C, Pascal, *awk*, *sed*, and even Basic, and offers powerful string-handling and output management functions. It's emerging as the favorite of many Web programmers (and is certainly our favorite CGI guru's language of choice). Best of all, Perl implementations are already available for UNIX, DOS, Macintosh OS, and the Amiga, with numerous other implementations underway. We've had excellent luck moving Perl from one platform to another, with only small changes necessary.

We include C because it's a powerful programming language and remains a tool of choice in the UNIX environment. What features and functions it doesn't offer as built-ins are readily available in the form of system APIs and code libraries of many different types and capabilities. C is also very portable (barring use of

system APIs); one version or another of C is available for just about every platform, with multiple implementations available for popular platforms and operating systems. We're especially fond of the Gnu C and the related Gnu Tools
from the Free Software Foundation pioneered by Richard Stallman.

When it comes to using the Macintosh as a Web server, AppleScript is pretty
much your only option. Even so, it's proven to be a worthwhile tool for building CGI programs and is widely used in the Macintosh Web community. Be
sure to consult Chapter 24 for some excellent pointers on Macintosh tools
and technologies for the Web, if you're a real Mac-o-phile!

Whatever language you choose for your CGI programs, be sure that it provides good string-handling capabilities, and that it offers reasonable output
controls. Since you'll be reading and interpreting byte stream input and creating HTML documents galore, these are important capabilities to look for.
Other than that, we'd also recommend picking one of the languages that have
been widely used in the Web community already, because you'll be likely to
find lots of useful modules, libraries, and code widgets available that may save
you programming time and make your job easier. But hey — it's your choice!

Example 1: What time is it?

This short Perl program accesses the system time on the server, and writes
an HTML page with the current time to the user's screen.

```perl
#!/usr/local/bin/perl
#
# time-cgi.pl
#
# CGI to return the time on the server
# v 1.0  —  2/14/95
# singe@outer.net <Sebastian Hassinger>
#
# called from simple anchor
# (i.e. <A HREF="http://www.outer.net/cgi-bin/time.pl">)
# the first line tells the UNIX shell that this script should be run #
#             using perl in the /usr/local/bin directory
#
#

$| = 1;        # output *not* buffered - this is a switch used by
               # perl internally. It tells perl not to buffer
               # the text the script sends back to the Web client.
               # All data will be output immediately to the client
               # thereby avoiding any data loss when the connection
               # to the client is broken
```

```perl
print "Content-Type: text/html\n\n\n";
                    # this is the first line the CGI
                    # must return to signal the web client that the data
                    # to follow should be interpreted as HTML.
                    # the line states the MIME type of the document to
                    # follow, and the carriage returns after the
                    # 'Content-Type:' line (\n) are required.

chop ( $time = `/bin/date '+%r'` );
                    # sets the $time variable to the current time
                    # using the UNIX 'date' command and the %r format
                    # built-in to that command to return the time in
                    # AM/PM 12 hour format. The ` ` (back-ticks) tell
                    # perl to use the text in between as input to the
                    # Bourne shell and to return the results. The 'chop'
                    # command wrapping variable assignment deletes the
                    # trailing carriage return from the shell output
                    # (i.e. the raw data returned to the variable will
                    # be '11:15:30 AM\n' and the chop command takes away
                    # the \n)

print "<HTML><HEAD><TITLE>Current Time on this Web Server</TITLE>",
    "</HEAD><BODY>\n";
                    # set up the top of the page for the client. From
                    # here on out, everything we output is going to be
                    # HTML-formatted — in essence, we are creating an
                    # HTML document on the fly.
                    # the print command can be broken up over several
                    # lines using comma-separated chunks of double-
                    # quoted text.

print "<H2>The time on the server is now:<BR><STRONG>$time</STRONG><BR></H2>";

                    # we just outputted our variable using HTML tags to
                    # pretty up our text. Note that \n carriage returns
                    # do not affect a carriage return on the client —
                    # only <BR> tags do.

print "<HR><ADDRESS>This page generated by time-cgi.pl<P>",
    "Contact: singe@outer.net</ADDRESS></BODY></HTML>";
                    # Finish off the page with contact info

# the script will now complete its execution, the shell opened by
# the httpd server to run the CGI script will close, and the
# connection between the server and the client will be broken.
```

Example 2: Counting page visits

This AppleScript program establishes a counter that tracks the number of times a page is visited. This kind of tool can provide useful statistics for individuals or organizations curious about how much traffic their pages actually receive.

```
— counter.acgi  (AppleScript CGI to return the number of times
          — the CGI has been accessed )
—
— singe@outer.net <Sebastian Hassinger>
— 2/15/95
— simple example of AppleScript CGI for running on a Mac
— equipped with MacHTTP 2.0.1

— first, set up variables as properties so that they will
— persist inside the object that is called when the client
— accesses the cgi. Regular variables in AppleScript
— don't need to be declared as properties before use, but
— they would lack the scope to be used inside event handling
— objects. Also, the counter and access_date properties will
— retain their values even if you quit and launch the script
— again, so long as it isn't edited.

property crlf : (ASCII character 13) & (ASCII character 10)
— set up a UNIX-style carriage return/line feed to make sure
— the lines break properly on the web client

property http_10_header : "HTTP/1.0 200 OK" & crlf & "Server: MacHTTP" &
          crlf & "MIME-Version: 1.0" & crlf & "Content-type: text/html"
          & crlf & crlf
— this is a standard http header, we're constructing it for
— use later in the script, to signal the client what type of
— data we're returning. MacHTTP is unlike the NCSA UNIX-based
— httpd server in that it does not supply any missing http
— headers for the CGI's output, so in addition to the usual
— 'Content-type:' header we used in the UNIX CGI's, we supply
— the HTTP version, the server name, MIME version and result
— code (200, in this case, signalling the client that we're
— returning a complete HTML document.)

property html_footer : "</BODY><HR><ADDRESS>This page generated
by counter.acgi.<P>" & "Example AppleScript CGI<P>Contact
singe@outer.net with questions." &
"</ADDRESS>"
```

```
— this is a boilerplate for the bottom of the page we'll
— return to the client

property access_time : current date
— create the variable used to return the current time to
— the client, initialize to date and time.
— properties persist from one running of the script to another,
— so this should tell us how long the script has been running,
— too.

property counter : 0
— initialize counter variable to zero

on event WWWsdoc
— this is the event trigger for the message MacHTTP will send
— to the CGI

    set counter to counter + 1
    — increment counter

    try —wrap the whole script in an error handler
        return http_10_header & "<TITLE>AppleScript Counter CGI</TITLE>" &
            "<H2>Counter CGI</H2><P>" &
            "<P>This script has been run " &
            counter & " times since " & access_time & html_footer
— spit back at the client our http document header, the body
— of the HTML document, our counter and access_time variables,
— and the HTML footer boilerplate

    on error msg number num
— report the error message and number to the WWW client
        return http_10_header & "Error " & num & ", " & msg
    end try
end event WWWsdoc
```

Example 3: Decoding clickable map coordinates

This C program can distinguish whether the right or left side of a graphic is selected (as well as defining a default to handle when the graphic isn't selected at all). It shows how a script handles the definitions inside an image map file.

```
/*
 * Copyright (c) 1995 Mike W. Erwin
 * mikee@outer.net
 * All rights reserved.
 *
 * Redistribution and use in source and binary forms, with or
 * without modification, are permitted provided that: (1) source
 * code distributions retain the above copyright notice and this
 * paragraph in its entirety, (2) distributions including binary
 * code include the above copyright notice and this paragraph in
 * its entirety in the documentation or other materials provided
 * with the distribution, and (3) all advertising materials
 * mentioning features or use of this software display the following
 * acknowledgement:
 * THIS SOFTWARE IS PROVIDED ``AS IS'' AND WITHOUT ANY EXPRESS OR
 * IMPLIED WARRANTIES, INCLUDING, WITHOUT LIMITATION, THE IMPLIED
 * WARRANTIES OF MERCHANTABILITY AND FITNESS FOR A PARTICULAR
 * PURPOSE.
 *
 * x and y coordinates are passed by the Web client on the command
 * line, and this program will store them in the argv variable.
 * the 'hot spots' will be read from the configuration file
 * '/www/conf/ismapper.conf,' which should be in the form:
 * <top left coordinates>,<bottom right coordinates> <url>
 * with one line for each rectangle, and one line in the form:
 * default <url> in case the click does not fall into any of the
 * hot spots. Note that there is no space between the comma and
 * the coordinates, and whitespace between the coordinates and the
 * URL.
 */


/*
 *    C CGI used to return a URL to hot spots being clicked on
 *    Version 1.0.0
 *    2/28/95
 */


/*
 *    To compile: "cc -o ismapper ismapper.c"
 */


/*
 *    Standard UNIX include files
 */
```

```c
#include <stdio.h>
#include <ctype.h>

/*
 *   Globals
 */

#define MAX_LINE_SIZE   255
#define true                    1
#define    false                0

char   *author = "mikee@outer.net";
char   *config_file = "/www/conf/ismapper.conf";

char   URL [ MAX_LINE_SIZE ];
char   default_URL [ MAX_LINE_SIZE ];
char   global_error [ MAX_LINE_SIZE ];


/**********************************************************************
 * main()
 *
 * This function takes the x and y mouse down as its arguments and
 * will return a pointer to the start of the URL in the file
 * that matches the boundaries of the rectangle specified in the
 * file.
 *
 * The format of the config file is:
 *
 * 6,6:73,144        http://www.outer.net/ismap.test/left.html
 *
 **********************************************************************/

char *read_config_file (int x, int y)

{
   FILE *config;
   char *line, new_line[MAX_LINE_SIZE];
   char *url = NULL;
   short found = false;

   if ((config = fopen(config_file, "r")) == NULL) {
      strcpy(global_error,"Configuration file not found");
      return (NULL);
   }

   do {
      int top, left, bottom, right;
```

```
        line = fgets(new_line, MAX_LINE_SIZE, config);

        sscanf(new_line,"default%*[\t ]%s", default_URL);
        sscanf(new_line,"%d,%d:%d,%d%*[\t ]%s",&top, &left,
                &bottom, &right, URL);

        if ((x >= top) && (x <= bottom) && (y >= left) &&
            (y <= right))
            found = true;
    }
        while (line && !found);

    if (found)
        url = URL;
    else
        url = default_URL;

    fclose(config);
    return(url);
}


/***********************************************************************
 * main()
 *
 * This is the official start of the C program.  It makes a single
 * call to our "get_time" function above then formats the output for
 * HTML on the standard output.
 *
 ***********************************************************************/

main (int argc, char **argv)
{
        int x_coordinate = 0 , y_coordinate = 0;
        char *destination_url;

        if (argc != 3) {
            printf("Content-Type: text/html\n\n\n");
            printf("<HTML><HEAD><TITLE>CGI Error</TITLE></HEAD><BODY>\n");
            printf("<H2>Invalid number of arguments</H2>");
            exit (1);
        }

        x_coordinate = (int) atoi(argv[1]);
        y_coordinate = (int) atoi(argv[2]);

        destination_url = read_config_file(x_coordinate, y_coordinate);
```

```
        if (destination_url != NULL) {
            printf("Location:\t%s\n",destination_url);
        }
        else {
            printf("Content-Type: text/html\n\n\n");
            printf("<HTML><HEAD><TITLE>Ismapper ERROR");
            printf("</TITLE></HEAD><BODY>\n");
            printf("<H1>No area matched and no default URL is defined.");
            printf("%s</H1>\n",global_error);
            printf("<HR>Contact %s for help.\n",author);
        }
        exit(1);
    }
```

As these examples illustrate, there are as many ways to skin the proverbial CGI program, as there are ideas and approaches about how to solve them. We sincerely hope you can use these paltry tools we've included with this chapter, and that you investigate the contents of the diskette that comes with the book, where you'll find C, Perl, and AppleScript versions for all three programs. In the next chapter, we'll extend our coverage of server-side Web activities, as we investigate search engines, Webcrawlers, and other interesting server-side services.

Chapter 16

Help Them Find Their Way: Aids to Web and Document Navigation

● ●

In This Chapter

▶ Searching for Web satisfaction

▶ Staying out of the maze

▶ Providing added document structure

▶ Doing things the database way

▶ Avoiding diminished returns

▶ Where's the search leading us?

● ●

*I*f you think forms are where the fun is in HTML, be prepared to enjoy yourself further here. In this chapter you'll learn about additional widgets and techniques you can use to make your documents searchable, so that users can find things by topic or key word search. This is probably overkill for basic home pages, but it's a wonderful thing for larger, more complex documents (in fact, without a searchable version of the HTML 2.0 DTD, we probably couldn't have written this book).

Webcrawlers and Search Engines

If you think of the Web as a vast gossamer skein of interconnected documents all over the world, you're pretty close to understanding the basic topology. But knowing how the strands of the Web are arranged is only half the picture. You've also got to understand what kind of denizens inhabit this mythical half-world of humans and computers.

Searching the Web for goodies...

In addition to the oodles and scads of users, happily browsing their way through the countless legions of documents on the Web, there are other kinds of inhabitants out there, too. Some of these inhabitants are computer programs sometimes called robots or spiders, that do nothing but follow links around the Web to see where they lead, and to catalog and categorize what they find along the way.

We've already mentioned their existence a time or two — like in Chapter 9 when we talked about the importance of using informative titles on your HTML documents. These tireless, automatic searchers use document titles to help them catalog and report on what they find. Then, humans use these catalogs when running a variety of Web search programs to help locate items. ■

The importance of these programs shouldn't be overlooked, which is why it's a good idea to follow our advice and use helpful, informative titles for your documents. Think of this technique as just another way for your Web pages to be "discovered," which they will be, if you can only bring them to the right people's attention.

Searching documents for details...

But these Web robots and crawlers don't really delve deeply into the content of the documents they find — in computer lingo, they search broadly (go everywhere) but not deeply (i.e., they don't catalog the contents fully, if at all). For serious researchers or to make large, complex documents easier to use, a different kind of search tool is needed.

The functionality that's required is something like the electronic equivalent of an index for a book: a list of key words, topics, or phrases that provide pointers to their locations within the document. Fortunately for users, this kind of technology is easy to employ because the documents are already in electronic formats, and merely require a bit of extra massaging and treatment to make themselves accommodate this kind of use.

As a budding Web author, you may be wondering what you have to do to add this kind of capability to your documents. If you think back to our discussion of CGI programs in Chapter 15, we can give you two different kinds of answers to this question:

1. In nontechnical terms, you have to create an index to your document and then figure out how to link that index to the actual content.

2. In technical terms, you must do the following:

   a. Add the <ISINDEX> tag to your document's <HEAD> ... </HEAD> section.

   b. Use a database or some similar program to build an index of key words and phrases for your document.

   c. Identify all the index words as anchors for hypertext links in your document (so the index can take you to those words and phrases).

   d. Establish the anchors in your document.

   e. Create a CGI program to handle user requests for key words or phrases, that builds a list of links for each instance in the document. ■

Basically, the way this sort of thing works is that you turn on the search capability in the user's browser (if available) by including the <ISINDEX> tag in your document's head section. Then, you provide a URL for the input-handling CGI program that will build search responses for users with specific requests. This program is built around an electronic equivalent of an index — a list of key words and phrases with pointers to their locations in the document's text — that you'll use to respond to queries. These responses will consist of HTML documents with links to the locations in your document where the requested key words or phrases reside.

As programming problems go, this one is not too difficult. You will have to locate or build an indexing tool to prepare the data files that you'll search in response to user queries. These data files usually consist of alphabetized (or ASCII-collated) lists of the key words and phrases that your index recognizes. If you build your program so that it returns information for unsuccessful searches ("string not found" is good; a list of near-matches is even better), you'll be able to field some of the weird nonsequiturs that bored users may sometimes be tempted to try on your indexing program.

Then you can use the CGI program that searches the list to build an HTML document that lists the "hits" in order of occurrence, with links to the various locations in your document where matches were found. This will create a hotlist of these locations that your users can select to find the information they're seeking.

We'd also suggest pulling some surrounding text from each part of the document where a hit occurs and writing that to your "return page" with your CGI program as well. This will let users understand some of the context in which a "hit" occurs, and help them to decide which links they really want to follow.

For an outstanding example of what a well-organized index can offer, please investigate the searchable version of the HTML 2.0 specification available at the following URL:

```
http://hopf.math.nwu.edu:80/html2.0/dosearch.html
```

This document is the work of the HTML working group, an Internet Engineering Task Force (IETF) group focused on making HTML into an Internet RFC-level specification. ■

The Bigger Things Get The Easier It Is to Get Lost!

If you're wondering why such indexing tools are worthwhile, it's because finding one's way around complex collections of information — like the HTML 2.0 specification and its related DTD — can get kind of hairy, without computer-aided assistance. A good rule of thumb for deciding whether indexing is a good idea is to print out all the pages in your Web creation: if the pile of pages gets more than one-quarter to one-half an inch thick, it's time to start thinking about indexing.

If you're worried about how much work is involved, don't be. If your question is "Do I have to get into heavy database programming, and implement all of the functionality mentioned in the preceding section, just to make my document searchable?" the answer is (fortunately) "No."

In fact, using the first type of search engine we mentioned at the beginning of this chapter — the kind that looks for documents based on titles — we were able to come up with a number of pointers to help you get started on this kind of effort for your own materials. Using the following search query (edited to remove control characters at the ellipsis) to Yahoo's search engine:

```
http://konishiki.stanford.edu/yahoo/bin/search?p=indexing...
```

we came up with a number of tools and locations that we can recommend for further investigation:

✔ Indexmaker is a Perl script whose function is to produce an index for a virtual document consisting of a number of HTML files in a single directory (this is the tool used to build our searchable HTML 2.0 Specification, in fact):

```
http://hopf.math.nwu.edu/docs/utility.html#indexmaker
```

✔ For inclusion in an online searchable index at the MIT Artificial Intelligence Laboratory, try either of these URLs:

> http://www.ai.mit.edu/tools/site-index.html
> http://www.cs.indiana.edu/item-index/intro.html

✔ For local indexing and related services, please consult:

> http://www.dlr.de/~greving/EN-ice.html

✔ Harvest is an integrated set of tools to gather, extract, organize, search, cache, and replicate relevant information on the Internet (this may be a bit too formal for documents not in need of wide distribution):

> http://rd.cs.colorado.edu/harvest/

✔ Finally, here's the URL for a whole page of information about indexing and related tools:

> http://union.ncsa.uiuc.edu/HyperNews/get/www/indexing.html ■

Rest assured that somewhere in the haystack of information we've just shared with you is the needle you may very well be looking for. Plus, it's no accident that the tool we admired most shows up first on the list!

Documentary Integuments: Indexes, Jump Tables, and Internal Links

You've already heard this in several chapters, but we feel compelled to remind you that as documents get bigger and more complicated, more structure is called for. That's one reason why we think indexes are a great idea. But it's also why you should make liberal and extensive use of internal links in your documents, to help readers navigate without having to keep scrolling all the time.

Usable structure is why starting off a long document with a hyperlinked table of contents is a good idea. It's why you always want to break longer chunks of text into regular screenfuls of information, coupled with navigation controls (which may only be "navigation bars" or may be full-blown clickable image maps with nice-looking 3-D buttons, or whatever). Explicit document navigation should never be more than one screenful of information away (even better if there's always a control at hand when it's needed).

Searchable indexes can greatly help readers in search of specific information, which is why they're a natural complement to our recommended frequency of navigation controls.

Doing Things the Database Way

For really long or complex documents, there's only one way to manage such information: through a database of some kind. Whether you decide to operate within the confines of a document management program, or use Paradox to build your own set of HTML document controls, when the number of files you have to manage exceeds 100, you'll appreciate getting some mechanical help and organization. Plus, the ability to search files on keywords or specific text will make finding things an awful lot easier (not to mention search and replace, automatic update propagation, and the other nice things a good database can do for you).

This added level of structure and control will cost you, to be sure, but it's worth considering because of the time and effort it can save you. If you don't believe us, try managing a huge, intertwined collection of files without computer assistance for awhile. You'll be singing a different tune after dealing with changes (and dealing with changes, and dealing ...).

Stay Away from Diminishing Returns

On the other hand it is possible to go overboard in organizing your materials. The temptation may be nearly overwhelming to break your documents into perfectly formatted single screens full of beautifully formatted information, for your user's delectation. Before you succumb to this impulse, remember the following "home truths" about the Web:

- ✔ All your beautiful graphics and on-screen controls won't do squat for character-mode browsers.

- ✔ What looks wonderful to you on your 21" monitor with the latest Gee-Whiz 3-D browser may be merely ho-hum to the guy down the hall running Cello or Mosaic.

- ✔ When aiming for perfection, the "last 10%" usually costs as much — and takes as much time to achieve — as the first 90%. Don't waste your time making the excellent sublime; you have better ways of filling your days (we hope)!

As thrilling as the quest for the perfect page may be, it's usually not worth the effort. And, if the people who pay the bills (and your salary), find out about your quest for the "holy grail" it may be far more trouble than it's worth. Remember the words of the mystic sage upon seeing the infinite majesty of the Universe: "Enough already!"

Where's the Search Leading Us?

As the Web becomes more commonplace and its publishing model better understood, you should expect to see more tools to help you add structure to your creations. Today it's considered good practice to index larger, more complex documents.

By the time you read this, you may also be able to create graphical road maps of your documents' overall structure and relationships. You may even be able to orient your users with animated tutorials and other amazing feats of technology. The trend is clear, though: more and better communications based on a shared model of what Web pages can deliver, along with shared toolsets to help realize those models.

With this metaphorical flight of fancy, however, we'll leave the tools and advanced capabilities of HTML and CGI behind, and dive back into the reality of Web publishing, as you move on to tackle the nitty-gritty details of testing your work!

Part VI

Call the Exterminator!
Debugging Web Pages

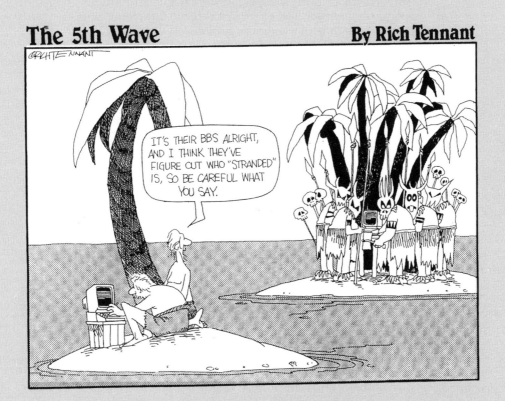

The 5th Wave   By Rich Tennant

IT'S THEIR BBS ALRIGHT,
AND I THINK THEY'VE
FIGURE OUT WHO "STRANDED"
IS, SO BE CAREFUL WHAT
YOU SAY.

In This Part...

We've tried repeatedly to stress the idea that once you think you've finished your HTML documents, only then does the real work begin. None of the subsequent effort is as important, demanding, and persnickety as the focus for this part of the book — namely, checking your work and testing your pages to make sure they behave the way you want them to.

Testing involves everything from spell-checking your content, to tracing each and every link on each individual page to make sure that all the pieces hook together properly. In Chapter 17, we'll take you through a semiformal approach to testing that should prepare you to thoroughly check your work.

In Chapter 18, the really crucial side of testing comes into play — that is, once you've checked your work to make sure it's mechanically correct and accurate, you need to make sure that your content is being properly communicated. This means interacting with prospective users, soliciting their feedback, and then acting on what they have to say. Then, because you need to recheck your work each time you make a change to one of your pages, you get to start all over again before you can proceed any further.

You may ask yourself "What's the point of testing, if it means more work and rework?" The answer, in a word, is quality: in this part of the book, in addition to explaining the mechanics and methods of testing and working with feedback, we'll also justify the effort involved by the results it produces. If you want quality Web pages that create a positive impression of you or your organization, testing is a crucial ingredient. By the time you work through the next chapters, we sincerely hope you'll agree!

Chapter 17

Testing, Testing, 1-2-3

- -

In This Chapter

▶ Learning why to test your Web pages

▶ Investigating what to test

▶ Surveying testing methods

▶ Finding the right testers

▶ Wondering when to quit testing

- -

Will they talk about you this way: "Did you see that mess of a home page Spacecadet put up yesterday?"

"Yeah. What a rookie. He forgot to close a heading tag and I got inch high text for a zillion screens."

"That was a bummer. Did you run into the missing links, too? I guess he's never heard of testing before publishing."

Of course you want to get your wonderful Web creations on the Net ASAP. But *** clichè warning *** — "You only get one chance to make a good first impression." Nobody has time to get it right the first time but they can always find the time to fix it later. So why not take that little bit of time while you're creating your Web pages and run them through a few tests to validate their HTML syntax and to judge their acceptance by your audience?

The who, what, when, where, why, and how of testing your Web pages are discussed briefly in the remainder of this chapter. Chapter 18 delves more deeply into testing and validation procedures along with how to obtain user feedback and what to do with it. ■

Web-Builder, Test Thyself

The two strongest reasons for testing your Web pages prior to making them available to the WWW community are:

1. Your Web pages may contain HTML tag errors or nonstandard tags which would cause them to display improperly on some browsers.

2. Your Web pages may not contain either required or optional HTML tags that will be important to Webcrawlers or spiders in the future. Without proper usage of the tags that crawlers search on, your pages will not be listed in future indexes and jump pages, therefore it won't be easy for users to find your Web.

Iteration, iteration, iteration

Creating your Web pages and assembling your Web is a repetitive "build-and-change" process. Once you have more than one page, changes on any single page may affect others. Unless you repeat the same tests each time you make a change, you'll find out the hard way from your users that errors have crept into your pages. Among the many things that "build-and-change" means — unless you have Data's perfect recall — is that you'll need to write down your testing procedures and keep track of things as you go.

Written test plan

You actually started the testing and validation of your Web pages when you sketched the layout of each page and your overall Web structure. These are the first documents in your test plan (see — you've already finished something, and you didn't even know you'd started yet).

For your personal Web, your test plan may consist of only a copy of these layout sketches with a checklist of testing steps you want to use on each page of your Web. This effort will take a bit of thinking and some of your valuable time, but the results will make you happy later. If you think the Maytag guy is unlucky, you should try things the other way around sometime!

Expect (and Test for) the Unexpected

"I should test for WHAT?" You should test for every possible, impossible, logical, illogical, expected, and unexpected occurrence. "But I want to publish my pages this century." OK, then make sure you plan for the somewhat unexpected.

In particular, you'll want to test in the following three areas:

1. Predicted ranges and values — are everything you intentionally put into your Web pages and expect users to access. This includes all links, images, ALT="wording", forms input sections and expected values, clickable map areas, and so on.

2. Boundaries — are the edges of the envelope of the expected. More problems occur at the edges than in the middle of most computer programs, which is what your HTML coded Web page strongly resembles. Many programs work perfectly with expected values and correctly ignore values outside their boundaries, but then fail on those values at the exact boundaries between the expected and the unexpected.

   For example, making the expected range from 1 to 100 and putting in an error-checking routine for values less than zero and more than 101 may work fine until someone puts in zero or 100. Make sure you try the boundary values, too!

3. Outside the boundaries — means everything not included in 1 or 2 above. Of course you can't click on every pixel on every page any more than you can enter every out-of-range value on every form. You can try a few out-of-bounds values and clicks to make sure you haven't missed the somewhat obvious. Many a mistake has been found in a program when the programmer sneezed, causing him to click his mouse button with the cursor on a place where, "no user in his right mind would click."

Don't lose sleep over testing absolutely everything. Do approach testing as something that will definitely benefit your Web pages if done logically, methodically, and repeatedly during your Web page development and maintenance.

In Vitro Vitrification: Alpha Testing Methodologies

Testing your Web pages is very much like testing any computer program. A certain amount of testing occurs while you are in the midst of creating the page since you have to look at it with a browser or your HTML editor's browser view. If you are using a completely WYSIWYG HTML authoring environment, most of the developmental HTML syntax testing will be done for you by the authoring program.

As you proceed with your development of a page, you tag and view, tag and view, and so on, until you decide that you like what you see. When you have coded all of the features you want into the page, it's ready for more stringent testing steps:

1. Run it through a spell checker. (Correct the spelling.)

2. Test the page by itself on your own computer with local files and relative URLs. (Fix the problems and test again.)

3. Test the page in the Web of other pages on your own computer. (Fix the problems and test again.)

4. Test the page by itself on the Web server in your private area with relative or full URLs. (Fix the problems and test again.)

5. Submit the page's URL to an online HTML validation form for syntax checking. (Fix the problems and resubmit until it is clean. Hey, nobody produces perfect code the first time.)

6. Test the page with the other pages in your private Web on the Web server. (Fix the problems and test again.)

7. Enlist a few work associates or close friends to critique the page. Keep it private otherwise and get them to keep quiet about it. (Fix the problems and test again.)

After iterations of comments and revisions until your alpha testers abandon you — or until they don't find anything else to nit-pick — your page(s) may be ready for honest-to-goodness beta testing. That's discussed a bit later in this chapter and in the next chapter as well.

The steps listed above generally guide you through what is called the alpha testing phase. This is accomplished by the developer and a few assistants only. Most of the big, ugly, and obvious problems should be removed by the end of this phase. If you're developing your own home page and personal Web, you should still go through the above steps because the reason you're developing a Web is to show it off to the WWW community.

If you're in a business or institutional environment, you will be more accustomed to formalized, structured development and testing, which will help your undoubtedly more complex Web accomplish its goals.

The following section presents a generic alpha test plan. Those of you who have a need to produce this type of document for your organization or anyone who really wants to proceed with testing your Web pages in an extremely orderly fashion may modify it to suit your specific needs. It wouldn't do the rest of you any harm to read over the plan, too. It might save you some time later on.

Web page alpha test plan

Introduction

Purpose

Provide a comprehensive plan for testing the accuracy and completeness of the Web page at stages during the development cycle or prior to the release of a new version.

Scope

The test plan will encompass testing the user level functionality of all features, the accuracy of the data generated, the agreement of the user guide information with the Web page operation, the agreement of the normative data from the manuals and errata sheets with the Web page data, and the compatibility of the Web page with various hardware and software configurations.

Test overview

- Test all functions of the Web page under expected usage conditions with appropriate hardware and software.
- Test all functions under abnormal usage conditions, such as inappropriate hardware or software, incorrect or extreme data conditions, and operator errors.
- Test the accuracy of any data by comparing Web-page generated values with known values.

Goals

- Determine the level of functionality and performance of the Web page.
- Document all operational abnormalities and Web page errors in an efficient and flexible test-tracking system.
- Verify Web page and user information correlation.

Schedule and resources

Testing will begin on (date) and will continue until the test plan is completed and there are no correctable errors found on the Web page. The Software

Testing and Quality Assurance Department staff (you and your friends) will provide full-time testing.

System configurations

Testing will be conducted using the following system configurations as representative of systems in the field:

- ✔ Browsers — List all browsers to be tested. If possible, try all browsers that you think your target audience will use.
- ✔ Computers — List all computer systems to be tested using the above browsers. Many of the browsers work on more than one system (i.e., PC with Windows, Macintosh, X-Windows, etc.)
- ✔ Web servers — List Web server software to be tested with CGI scripts and forms. You may be limited to your own Internet service provider or your business or institution's Web server, but test it thoroughly and completely.

Test method and evaluation

1. Testers will evaluate Web page functionality and performance primarily at the user level by performing operations using keyboard and mouse input and evaluating data generated by the Web page.

2. Testers will document Web page errors and operational abnormalities by recording the following information when a problem is encountered: feature/function affected, page version date/time, date problem found, tester's name, description of problem, method of recreation, and any other notes that may help the developer understand and resolve the problem. Priorities shall be assigned to the problems as they are received: priority 1 — system lockup or data corruption, priority 2 — cosmetics (spelling, wording, screens), priority 3 ± inconvenient operation.

3. The document containing Web page problems will be updated as often as possible and be made available to the developers for resolution of the problems.

Performance and functionality testing

Screen appearance

Inspect each screen looking for inaccuracies or omissions related to spelling, formatting, and layout.

Link operation and content

Verify that each link functions correctly and that each destination URL exists and presents the information named in the hyperlink text.

Forms operation

Verify that each form correctly receives, processes, and records the user's responses. Verify that the Web server properly stores the data and delivers it to the appropriate location in the desired format.

Clickable map operation

Verify that clicking on each portion of the map displays the appropriate image or page.

Limits and boundary checking

Test all limit and boundary conditions, such as high and low numerical values and text amounts in forms. Make sure you test the "edge," not just outside the expected limits.

Alpha, Beta, Gamma, Delta: Lining Up Your Testing Team

You're not alone in your quest for the perfect Web. Practically everyone on the WWW would like every single page they view to match their vision of perfection. In fact, millions of them will be more than happy to judge your Web. The key is to get a few of them to help you make it better.

Alpha

Perhaps programmers started using the Greek alphabet because calling it "A testing" wasn't as pleasing to the ear as "Alpha testing." Anyway, alpha testing comprises you and your good buddies trying to break your pages.

Keeping your pages tightly controlled and getting rapid problem reports ensures fast correction of problems. If you've designed your pages well, you don't need a lot of superfluous nit-picking of your style or layout at this point in the testing. You want to make sure the pages display properly and the links work.

Beta

During beta testing you enlist a larger but manageable group of WWW users to help you make your Web pages the best thing since coffee and candy bars. They will not only test the performance and functionality, they will generously advise you as to how stupid you were to put the image of the sparrow in with the finches, and so on. They will spot problems that you didn't even know were problems. What? Things that you looked at every day but ignored will bother enough of your beta testers that you will decide to change them, the problems, that is — not the beta testers!

A subset of your beta testers may be enlisted to perform as a focus group does in market research and advertising companies. That is, they actually critique your Web pages with their focus being the effects on your intended user group. They ask the questions: Do the pages present the material in the best manner to attract the intended user? Do the pages answer the intended user's questions quickly and obviously? Will the pages cause the users to do whatever they are attempting to get them to do (buy product, visit location, call on phone, etc.)?

Gamma?

While there is no actual gamma category of testing that is commonly discussed, you should consider all of the users who view your Web pages as testers and potential assistants in your ongoing page development. Of course you understand that the Web is alive, don't you? And your Web pages are a living part of the whole WWW. Therefore you'll be feeding and nurturing your Web to keep it up-to-date, otherwise it will lose its users and fade away into the cosmos. To prevent this you'll need to use good methods of requesting and encouraging user feedback right in your Web pages. Your e-mail address will suffice at a minimum but a nice form will do the job much better. You'll find more details on this in the next chapter.

Knowing When to Quit (Testing)

Now that you're completely catatonic with fear about opening up your precious Web to the prying eyes of the WWW masses, take solace in knowing that it's only a bunch of electrons running around in wires and silicon. You've nothing to fear from the WWW. No matter how carefully you plan, design, code, and test your Web pages, someone will find something that they don't like. This is a function of the differences in outlook and perspective of millions of people on the WWW.

*** clichè warning *** "You can't please everyone." You can try to please as many of your intended audience as possible within your time and energy limits. Unless you have a deadline imposed by your business or institution that will dictate when you open your Web to the Net, you are the sole judge of when it's ready for its grand opening. So open it up when you've tested it thoroughly but never quit testing.

Chapter 18

It Doesn't Matter
What YOU Think

In This Chapter

▶ Simulating the user's view

▶ Testing your own pages

▶ Keeping your sanity

▶ Promoting feedback

▶ Learning from your users

*O*f course you like your Web pages; you created them. They look great on your browser and your monitor and you're proud of them. So you can keep'm on your computer for only you to view, you can print'm, frame'm and hang'm on your wall, or you can publish'm on the WWW. The choice is always yours.

You decided to publish'm, did ya? You want to share them with the WWW community, and show them your creations. You want them to visit your Web frequently and applaud your work. Now the tables have turned. No matter how much you like your Web pages, your user's likes and dislikes will determine your Web's future.

The rest of this chapter assumes that, regardless of the content in your Web pages and regardless of your desired user audience, you want to provide Web pages that will keep your users pleased and coming back for more. The testing procedures discussed below are aimed at helping you make an enjoyable and informative site for your audience.

Rule number 1: Users Rule.

Rule number 2: When in doubt, refer to Rule number 1.

These rules do not mean that you must do everything every user requests. If your information is about earthquakes, you certainly don't want to include information on kite flying just because somebody requests it. However, if some of your users request a different arrangement of earthquake information so they can find it more easily, you would be well advised to accommodate their wishes. Change for the sake of change is upsetting to most folks but change for the better with valid reasons and advanced user education can be beneficial to everyone involved.

Simulation Is Better Than the Real Thing

How do you determine what needs changing? You test, test, test your Web pages. You perform the first level of testing while you're adding tags and typing your HTML files. You look at your work through a browser or via the WYSIWYG function of your HTML editor. By doing this, you are simulating the user's viewpoint. If you notice a misspelling or the incorrect use of a word, you correct it because you know your users would notice the error. By the way, this is the time to run a spell checker on your HTML file.

When you have developed a page that works to your satisfaction on your own computer, upload it to the appropriate subdirectory on your Web server. If you're using a DOS computer and uploading the page to a UNIX server, make sure you remember to change the file extension from *.htm* to *.html*. Once your page is on the server, you can become a user and browse it. If you haven't created your page on HoTMetaL or another strict HTML 2.0 syntax checking authoring system, submit it to one of the online HTML syntax validation programs available at any the following URLs:

Georgia Tech College of Computing HTML Validation Service at:

    http://www.cc.gatech.edu/grads/j/Kipp.Jones/HaLidation/validation-form.html

HaL HTML Validation Service at:

    http://www.hal.com/~markg/WebTechs/validation-form.html

Note: The HaL Validation Service validates HTML 2.0, 3.0, and the Mozilla DTD from Netscape (but the Mozilla DTD is not supported fully, because the Netscape developers are sometimes slow about sharing information on their proprietary extensions).

HTML Form-Testing Home Page at:

    http://www.research.digital.com/nsl/formtest/

Or you can download a stand-alone UNIX HTML syntax checker from:

```
http://uts.cc.utexas.edu/~churchh/htmlchek.html
http://www.hal.com/~markg/HaLSoft/html-check/
```

After you get the report from one of the syntax checkers, revise your Web page if necessary. Most of these syntax checkers adhere to the HTML 2.0 DTD so any tags you use that don't conform may be marked as errors (the HaL Validation Service also supports HTML 3.0 and the Mozilla DTDs). If you want to continue to use tags that are specific for certain browsers, do it knowing that your page will not look the way you expect on other browsers. Understand also that your pages may not be included properly in Webspider compiled indexes, depending on which extended tags you used.

Browsing Through Your Hard Work

Next, you need to know how your pages will look when viewed with other browsers and on different kinds of computers. Rectify this situation by downloading and installing all the browsers that will run on your own computer and test with them first. Make a deal with Web friends who have different types of computers. Have them test your pages in return for you testing their Web pages with your computer. Turnabout is still fair play, and it may give you (and them) exposure to ideas and materials that everyone can learn from!

Alpha testers

Make sure that you draft only people close to you who will keep the location of your pages to themselves. You don't need the aggravation of unwanted testers at this point in your page development. When you get these helpers, you'll need to give them some instructions on what type of feedback you want. At the simplest, you can just ask them to e-mail you with any problems or suggestions they may have. This will work if they are conscientious, organized people, which is the only type you want for your alpha test helpers.

It will really help them and you if you provide them with a simple text form to complete and e-mail to you with each problem. Request at least the following on your form:

- ✔ Tester's name and e-mail address
- ✔ Date problem was found
- ✔ Page title and URL
- ✔ Page version date/time

- ✔ Feature/function affected
- ✔ Formatting
- ✔ Text/data
- ✔ Link (URL)
- ✔ Image (URL)
- ✔ Form (URL)
- ✔ Description of problem
- ✔ How to duplicate problem
- ✔ Comments and suggestions for solutions

Suggest to your alpha testers that it would greatly help you if they would religiously fill in all of the information on a separate form for each different problem. When the forms start clogging up your e-mail in-box, you'll need a place to store them and a method of sorting them. Any reasonable method from printing each and visually sorting them to importing them into a database program will work. Use the easiest one that works for you. Keep in mind that you'll probably want to use it for the beta test feedback also so choose a method that will handle the number of messages you expect, then double the number to get ready for the unexpected.

Beta testers

So your trusty alpha testers are all giving the thumbs-up to your Web. It's time to enlist a larger group of people you don't necessarily know to help test your pages. Hopefully you can find beta testers who are directly interested in the content you are presenting. You need feedback on their likes and dislikes from that standpoint as well as their impressions of your Web's functionality. They are your primary audience, albeit a small portion of it, so treat them well.

Find them by posting an invitation to participate in relevant newsgroups. Simply ask for people who are interested in helping you test your new Web page. Filter them by asking them to e-mail their name, address, phone number, background in your area, and some reasons why they think they would be good beta testers. E-mail immediate thank-yous to everyone who replies with a noncommittal statement that you were overwhelmed by the response and will get back to everyone shortly.

If you decide not to use some respondents, which is unlikely, send each of them a very nice e-mail thanking him or her profusely and saying that you ran out of your allotted testing spaces before getting to their name, or something equally nice. *** cliché warning *** Do a good deed for someone and he will tell three friends about it. Do something that makes someone mad and he'll tell eleven people what a jerk you are. You may not be able to make everyone happy, but try your best not to irritate your users.

E-mail each of your beta testers announcements of each change cycle with a list of revisions and a copy of the beta test report form you would like them to complete and return. Thank each tester for each problem report. Make sure you notice the ones whose problem reports resulted in a revision. Take the time to make real friends out of your beta testers and you will benefit from it for a long, long time. Your beta testers are your users. Remember Rule Number 1?

Covering All the Bases

The simple list above is a good start on ensuring that each and every important part of your Web page is tested after every revision cycle. If you're creating a large Web site comprising tens to hundreds of pages, you'll need a checklist for each page that includes each of the page's major features.

You'll also need a checklist for your site as a whole that includes each page's title and URL, and possibly its links to other pages in your space. This should look familiar to you. It's your Web layout drawing. The larger your Web, the more important the layout drawing and checklists will be in ensuring that your testing is thoroughly performed in each revision cycle.

Making a List and Checking It Twice

No, a revision cycle isn't something you pedal backwards. It's a method of handling problems and changes in your pages in an orderly fashion. Simply stated, you don't fix problems in the order in which you receive them. Sure, you're anxious to clean up your pages but you must prioritize the problems you (or others) find or it will cost you more time in the long run.

From your testing report database, make and keep an ongoing list of problems. Prioritize them in your own order. Then decide which one or group to fix. Consider not only the time it will take to revise the HTML documents but the time needed to run the changed pages on the entire Web completely through your test checklists on all appropriate browsers and platforms. With this in mind, you'll probably wisely decide that daily changes aren't possible.

You'll find that for a large complex Web, a one-week revision cycle is probably the shortest time period possible, with a two-week cycle less anxiety-provoking.

This is especially true when your Web is being accessed by hundreds or thousands of users a week. They will appreciate seeing positive action at reasonable time periods with thorough documentation from you on what you changed, when, and why.

Staying Ahead of the Gremlins

Cycling your revisions will help you keep ahead of the insidious gremlins called "unexpected side effects." These occur when a seemingly small change is made in one page without enough thought put into its effects and without any testing of the entire Web afterward. An example would be changing an image that is linked to every page in your Web. Suppose you put it in the wrong directory. It wouldn't show up at all. That would be easy to detect. But suppose you change the e-mail address for feedback and make an error. You may not find out about it for quite a while, unless you use it to send yourself mail immediately upon installing it (now that we think about it, this is a good testing technique, too — why don't you try it?).

By batch-processing the prioritized problems you will be able to give everyone in your testing crew adequate time to thoroughly perform their validation. While they are testing your most recent set of revisions, you can be working on the next set. Be sure you note your fixes on each problem form as completely as the problem itself was noted. You should also be careful to change the version number and revision date/time on each page you change, and include this information on the problem fix section of the form or database.

There's Nothing Crazy about a Sanity Check!

By now you're saying to yourself, "What's all this about two week revision cycles, fancy forms, and testers all over the place? My pages aren't going to be as buggy as a stray dog." You're probably correct in that sentiment, but you have the idea now that without careful planning and cyclic testing, you may be the one who goes buggy.

To keep this from happening, take the following advice: Keep two separate copies of your Web on your own computer and on your Web server if the space is available. Perform all changes on the "working" copy while the "published" copy is in use. While you're testing, you can compare the performance and functionality of the working copy to the published copy and see the changes.

When you've completed a revision cycle, copy the working files over the published files — after making a backup of course. If you've used the relative URLs properly, you shouldn't need to change anything in the revised working files before copying them over the old published files. They'll be ready for users instantly.

Stick It to Me: The Importance of Feedback

Ahhhh, users. Funny how they keep popping up here, there, and everywhere. Funny how you feed them your Web pages and ask for feedback from them. User feedback is the lifeblood of your Web but if you're not careful it will be as useful as the feedback from an amplifier with a microphone in front of the speaker. It will make you sit up and take notice, but it won't give you enough useful information to solve the problem. If you like playing Sherlock Holmes, by all means just put a little message at the bottom of your home page requesting feedback to your e-mail address.

Change, change, change is what the World Wide Web is all about. The Web is definitely the message in this case and it's changing so rapidly that you'll need all the help from your beta (and ultimately your "gamma") testers that you can get. They are the folks who are using your Web. They are the only ones who really know what they need or want, and how they want to quickly obtain it.

However, they may not know exactly how to phrase their wants and needs so that you can instantly understand them. It's up to you to give them a hand with feedback forms, nicely worded requests, and a warm e-mail thank-you when they do respond, no matter what they say. You'll definitely get e-mail when things are broken or awry, and you'll learn to appreciate the occasional pat on the back that comes all too rarely from your users.

Getting the News You Need

If you don't ask for what you want, you may get it anyway — that is, a big fat nothing. You can ask users to send you feedback until your fingers are numb, and you may still receive nothing in return. This may mean you're doing a perfect job but nobody wants to tell you how great you are for fear of giving you a superiority complex. It probably means that you haven't asked them in the proper way or encouraged them enough.

If you really want information, ask about something specific. Tell them you're thinking of adding something or changing something and ask them to tell you what they think about your idea. Have a contest in which you give a prize to the person who submits the best or worst feature of your Web and why. Get your users involved in your Web and its design and you'll all benefit.

Building in a Report Card

A simple text form on a page of its own for users to copy, fill in, and e-mail back to you is better than nothing. A real form with questions and response boxes is much better. You learned about these in Chapter 12. Although it's important to be specific in your requests for information, a detailed checkbox form with no place for general comments will miss some valuable information. Give the users space to be creative after you've aroused their interest with your questions or checkboxes. ▩

One of the better ways of deciding what kind of feedback form to use is to look around the Web for forms you like. Check out their source to see how the author created them. If the author used a script that will work on your Web server, create one like it for yourself. The server WebMaster (or "God" to you) can probably help you in this area if you ask nicely.

Hocus-Pocus, Focus Groups

If you're seriously trying to accomplish a set of goals with your Web pages, you may want to use the Focus Group approach used so successfully by marketing and advertising companies. They get ten or so people who are highly knowledgeable about an industry together in a conference room for a couple of hours to review and comment on a proposed advertising or marketing campaign. Frequently they video the entire session so they can look at each participant's expressions and body language when they are presented with different ads. If your situation warrants this type of approach, you may want to try it. It is customary to pay these folks a small honorarium for their trouble, in a sealed envelope on their way out the door.

Alternatively, you may want to try an online focus group approach. This would be similar to beta testing but with a very select group. You would e-mail each of them a request to participate and provide them with a special URL to view the pages in question. To make this approach work well, you need to plan it carefully. This becomes more of a marketing exercise than

Web page testing, but it may be very important to you and your enterprise. You may want to involve your marketing department or advertising consultant in the planning process and in creating the appropriate questionnaires.

Making Friends with Movers and Shakers

Don't just lurk in the newsgroup, PARTICIPATE. Make online friends with the folks who are in-the-know in your industry's newsgroup. If you know the addresses of some of the important folks in your chosen field of interest, e-mail them an announcement of your Web's grand opening and invite them to drop in. Keep them informed of great new information on your site, but don't make a pest of yourself. Ask them if there is some type of information they would like to see on the Net but can't seem to find in your area. Then find it, provide it, and let them know about it while you thank them profusely for their suggestion.

Don't Just Listen, Do Something!

When your users lavish you with their feedback, thank them via e-mail, of course. But then use the feedback to better your Web. The best thanks you can give your users is to put their great ideas to use in a timely manner and let everyone know that you appreciate their support.

Be careful though in giving credit directly in your Web pages to folks whose feedback you use for a specific change. There may be a few people who don't like the change and will blame the feedback provider rather than you. You're the one who is trying to keep your audience happy so you're the one who has to take the abuse from the disgruntled users. It's usually better to thank users personally via e-mail and as a general group in your Web pages if you feel the need to do so publicly.

Making the Most of Your Audience

If you're into the WWW for other than altruistic reasons, you'll want to consider the overall effects of your Web pages on your target audience. Whether you're providing your space for a business, educational institution, government agency, non-profit organization, or as a private citizen, you may be interested in what your audience thinks about the fact that you have made your Web site public. How do they perceive your organization because of your Web presence? Do they view it as an advance in their relationship with you or your organization? If so, how? If not, why? Ask your users these questions and any others that may be of interest to you.

Provide a means of feedback that is anonymous if you feel your users will be more forthcoming with their responses, but be prepared for a few "crank calls." There are a few curmudgeons in every crowd who have an overwhelming need to be noticed, but can't think of anything constructive to say. Ignore them completely and they will go away. Concentrate your energy on making the most of your Web space and on keeping your rational, reasonable users as happy as possible.

Part VII

Going Public: Serving Up Your Web Pages

The 5th Wave — By Rich Tennant

Arthur inadvertently replaces his mouse pad with an Ouija board. For the rest of the day, he receives messages from the spectral world.

YOU WILL FORGET YOUR PASSWORD. YOUR HARD DISK WILL CRASH AAAHAHAHAHA

In This Part...

Having survived the rigors of testing and the eye-popping advantages of user feedback, you're finally ready to publish your Web pages and invite the world on in. In this part of the book you'll learn the brutal truth about getting your message out to the users who stop by to visit your site.

In fact, just because you've got some pages doesn't mean the world will beat a path to your door. You need to be prepared to deliver those pages on a Web server, and you'll want to decide whether that server should be yours or if you should join forces with a service provider to play host to your content. Chapter 19 will help uncover the costs and consequences of the "build versus buy" decision when it comes to Web servers.

When your pages are available for public access, you can then start worrying about how to publicize their availability. Chapter 20 takes you through the kind of public relations blitz you might want to undertake to drag the world to your Web site, hopefully without too much kicking and screaming. Along the way, you'll learn about acceptable use policies on the Internet and where to draw the line between "tasteful self-promotion" and "shameless hype." Maybe you can prevent a potential flame war, just by observing a few discreet rules of netiquette!

Once you've lived with your Web pages for awhile, you'll have to learn how to live with change. Your content will get stale and need updating, your links will grow cold, and you'll have to run to keep up with the relentless changes in your content and your users' interests. Chapter 21 helps to brace you for this activity. We hope you'll learn to think of maintenance as an adventure and a way of life, rather than as a total waste of time! Just remember, repeat visits to your pages require a regular refreshment of the value that they can provide.

All in all, you should be ready to deal with the public on its own terms by the time you've completed this part of the book. If you're ready for change, you'll be ready for anything!

Chapter 19

So You've Woven a Web: What Now?

· ·

In This Chapter

▶ Inviting the world to your door

▶ Staying focused

▶ Maintaining control

▶ Should you publish, or perish?

▶ Making arrangements with a service provider

▶ Doing it yourself

· ·

*O*K, so you've decided to go ahead and share your Web pages with God and everybody. Once you've made this decision, though, you'll have to grapple with some interesting issues and get ready to make your pages (and yourself) available to the world at large.

Inviting the World to Your Door

When you start thinking "It's time to publish these pages," you'll have to decide if they are really ready for prime time. You'll also have to be prepared to face scrutiny, the likes of which you may never have faced before. (Remember, there are estimates of 20+ million Internet users!) Then, there's the implication of asking for feedback — which we heartily recommend — which means adopting a regular routine of tweaking and fiddling to get (and keep) things current and correct.

Finally, there's the build versus buy decision when it comes to serving up Web pages — that is, should you hire a service provider to offer your pages on their server, or should you consider putting up your own server, and invite the world to your door?

In this chapter we'll tackle all these issues, and more, as we investigate how to publish your Web pages. By the time you've read the whole thing, you should be prepared to do some comparison shopping with your friendly neighborhood (and national) service providers. You should also be armed to make the decision whether to have a provider publish your pages, or to do it on your own.

Stay Focused on Your Purpose

Before you show your pages to the world, you need to ask yourself yet again: "What it is it that my Web pages are trying to communicate?" Write down your list of objectives and keep them handy.

Next, talk to your beta testers and selected members of your target audience about your pages. Let them look it over, and then ask THEM what they think you're hoping to communicate. Write this stuff down, too.

Compare your list of objectives to your informal survey of your audience. If you don't get at least a 50% overlap, it's time to figure out what's not working, and why. If you can follow up to get someone you know and trust to give you completely honest feedback, that's the best thing to try next. If you can't, you'll want to dig through your survey materials and try to figure out what's missing the mark, and adjust your content accordingly.

Until you get the overlap you're shooting for, you'll have to keep testing your pages on your target audience. There's simply no point in going public until you're pretty sure that what you think your pages communicate is what your audience thinks they communicate, too. This may seem incredibly obvious, but take our word for it — this is the most important quality control you can do.

Make Sure Your Users Know Who's in Charge!

The freewheeling nature of the Web poses a nearly irresistible temptation to turn your home page into the crossroads of the world, and make it a meeting place for all and sundry. Don't forget that the main purpose of your pages is to communicate the information that you so laboriously developed.

This means that the key factor in deciding what other links to include on your pages has to be "relevance." Here are some questions you should ask before including links to other people's URLs:

- ✔ Do these other sites have content related to yours?

- ✔ Do they appeal to the same audience, for more or less the same reasons?

- ✔ Do they complement your material, or detract from it?

- ✔ Can they handle more traffic or are they already overloaded with hits?

- ✔ Are those other sites willing to reciprocate, and include pointers to your pages on theirs, as well as the other way around? Don't expect this kind of treatment from CERN, or W3, or other large and important sites on the Web, but do expect it from your colleagues and fellows, and from organizations you're affiliated with.

The whole idea is to connect your pages with other resources that enhance the value of your content, and that complement your overall goals and objectives. Among other things, this means that if you're trying to sell widgets to your audience, you probably don't want to include links to your competitors' pages. On the other hand, you probably do want to include links to relevant widget standards, and to the Institute for Widget Research.

Publish, or Perish the Thought!

But hey, don't let these steps that we recommend for your Web page production process stop you from making your content available on the Internet. If you frequently communicate with your customers or colleagues using printed materials, the best way to view the Web is as an alternative to print.

It's good for business...

This is a useful way to think about the Web, if your interests are business-related. If that's the case, you're probably already familiar with the concept of "corporate communications" — that is, the deliberate design and delivery of messages, in whatever medium, to create an image and aid the purchase of products.

For you, the Web can be another way to disseminate your finely-crafted messages. Just be sure to observe the antihype leanings of the Internet crowd, and you'll do just fine. This means that upfront, high-pressure sales tactics aren't appreciated; it also means it's a VERY BAD idea to cross-post an announcement of your Web pages to every newsgroup known to man (this is called "spamming" in Internet-speak, and is universally reviled).

Another term for publishing a blurb about your company is "hanging your shingle on the Internet." This is a passive advertisement, not an in-your-face beer commercial between innings. Unless your blurb includes meaningful content, and you can appeal to the interests of a fickle, impatient group of netsurfers, hanging a shingle on the Internet can be a real ho-hum experience!

...and it's good for pleasure!

If yours is a personal page, or you're caught in the grip of what some people — not us! — would call a fond obsession, your reasons for Webbing up may be different from commercial enterprises. In this case, you still want to make sure that a target audience agrees that you're not sending mixed messages to the World Wide Web. But you can give yourself a lot more latitude in focus, goals, and objectives.

Back to the content

Be your focus crassly commercial or pristinely personal, it all comes back to the content. If your pages read well, include a modicum of easily accessible, interesting information, and are easy to navigate, you'll find yourself on the berm of the information superhighway, with lots of traffic whizzing by. If your pages don't scan, if they're completely idiosyncratic or totally boring, you'll find yourself in the electronic equivalent of the boondocks, far from the madding crowds with nary a traveler in sight.

How do you find out which path you're on? It's simple: ask your target audience! Most of the comments you get will be driven by the content, so that should tell you where to spend the bulk of your efforts.

Dealing & Wheeling: Making Arrangements with an Internet Service Provider

When you're ready to go public, one option to consider is: Simply transport your Web pages en masse to a provider who already offers a Web server.

This is a pretty straightforward process, but it does require some planning. It also requires checking some basic compatibility issues. Here are some questions you'll want to ask yourself, and any Internet service provider whose Web server you consider jumping onto:

- What kind of *httpd* server do they have? Does it conform to the CERN release, the NCSA release, or neither?

  Depending on the answer, you'll need to make some script adjustments. Web spaces are not completely portable so make sure you're calling the right kind of map-handling application, and that your image map files are in a compatible format. Be warned that adapting an existing set of Web documents from one environment to another can be time-consuming, hair-raising, and a downright pain in the you-know-what!

- What kind of dependencies do you have in your Web pages? Do you use <BASE> tags to set reference URLs?

  If so, you'll have to change the URLs to reflect their new location. While you're at it, check every link in every page to make sure all the proper changes get made. The only good link is a working link, and the only known working link is a tested link!

- How much data do you have in your pages? How likely is it that users will download all of your pages?

  Most service providers charge a per-megabyte transfer fee for Web access, in addition to a monthly account fee (and usually setup fees, as well). The more data you want to share with the world, the more likely it is that transfer costs will contribute to your build versus buy decision.

- How much demand is there likely to be for your pages?

  This is just another way of asking "How big is your audience?" If you already know the audience, you can probably guess at the answer. This will also help to guesstimate the amount of traffic you will generate.

If you decide to work with an Internet service provider, the amount of data transferred from your pages to your users in a month is likely to be a primary determinant of cost.

Most of the vendors we surveyed indicated monthly account fees of $50 to $150 for a commercial account with Web page services available. The same vendors assessed charges of two to ten cents per megabyte of data transfer per month. This might not sound like much, until you stop to figure that only 20 users a day at two megabytes apiece accounts for charges of $12.00 to $61.00 a month; 100 users a day raises those figures from $120 to $610 for the same period.

If your space become heavily visited — for instance, like the CBS Web site for the NCAA College Basketball Tournament in March, 1995 — it's possible they may be visited tens of thousands of times per day. At the rates listed above, your costs to an outside provider would go from $12,000 to $61,000 *per month* for such service.

Where to draw the line?

Somewhere between 100 and 1,000 users a day, and you cross the line between buy versus build. For charges of less than $500 per month, contracting for Web server access makes sense. Consider the analysis in Table 19-1.

Table 19-1: Calculating monthly charges for various usage profiles

Web Size (MB)	$Cost per MB xfer	Users per day (avg)	Monthly account	Monthly Costs
2	$0.10	50	$50	$354.16
5	$0.07	50	$100	$632.29
10	$0.05	100	$150	$1,670.83

Assumptions: average of 30.416 days per month used for calculations (30.416 = 365/12)

By the time you get to the second row in the table, it's time to start thinking about installing your own Web server. By the time you reach the third row, the numbers make your choice clear (just be sure to adjust these meaningless averages with your own researched numbers before making any rash decisions).

In fact, the closer your projections are to the high end of this scale, the more likely you will be to consider setting up your own Web server. Table 19-2 covers the flip side of this analysis — figuring the costs of doing it yourself — based on the assumptions covered immediately after the table.

Table 19-2: Average costs for Web do-it-yourselfers

Monthly costs Server	Phone Line	Provider Account	Staff	Monthly Total
$350.00[1]	$36.00[2]	$80.00[3]	$600.00[4]	$906.00
$350.00	$70.00[5]	$150.00[5]	$600.00	$1,170.00
$500.00[7]	$70.00	$150.00	$750.00[18]	$1,470.00
$500.00	$140.00[9]	$300.00[10]	$750.00	$1,690.00

Assumptions:

1. Pentium P90, 32 MB RAM, 1.2 GB HD, etc. (Total system cost: $4k, amortized over 36 months at 10% interest; based on equivalent system lease costs.)
2. Average monthly cost for dedicated 28.8 Kbps line to provider (telephone costs).
3. Average monthly cost for dedicated 28.8 Kbps line to Internet access provider.
4. One-fourth time for system administrator earning approximately $30K per year.
5. Average monthly cost for ISDN connection through phone company.
6. Average monthly cost for dedicated ISDN account with Internet access provider.
7. Pentium P90, 64 MB memory, 4 GB disk, etc. (Total system cost: $6k, amortized over 36 months at 10% interest; based on equivalent system lease costs.)
8. One-quarter time for system administrator/Web programmer at $36K per year.
9. Average monthly cost for two "B" channels' ISDN access from the telephone company.
10. Average monthly account cost for a dedicated 128 Kbps line from Internet access provider to support two "B" channels.

The quick-and-dirty restatement of Table 19-2 is: "If the bill from your Internet service provider runs more than $900 a month, it's time to consider putting up your own server." You'll still want to adjust costs (especially the salary for your Web administrator) to your own figures, but this is a reasonably good rule of thumb to follow.

What to work out with your provider

If your analysis puts you down on the "buy" side of the decision, you'll want to find an Internet service provider that can host your Web pages for you. In addition to the questions we mentioned earlier, you'll want to find out a few more things. It's also reasonable to expect your provider to have some questions for you.

What else you need to find out:

✔ Ask the provider for references from individuals and organizations that already have their Web pages on the provider's server.

Be sure to check with as many of these references as you can. Ask them questions about the provider's quality of service, their responsiveness to problems, the percentage of the system's overall uptime, and user complaints, if any.

You want to find out how good the provider is at providing Internet access, so ask anything else along these lines that you can think of. If the reference accounts use forms or other input-handling programs, ask them to explain how they managed to install and use these programs.

✔ Have the service provider explain their accounting system to you: how do they know how many users are visiting your pages each day, and how do they measure the data transfer they're charging you for?

✔ Find out how widely distributed this server's links are on the Web: use a search engine like Lycos or Yahoo to look for their URL in other pages, and see what turns up. More links is better, in this case!

✔ Ask how long they've been in this business and what their growth plan is — in other words, what's their plan to accommodate increased traffic?

✔ Find out how easy it is to run your own CGI scripts or other input-handling programs on their system. Ask for a free trial period, and see how things go. Ask about all the tools and other widgets you might need (i.e., how current is their Perl interpreter? Do they have the right version of the map-handling software?). Ask about consulting services, or what other kind of help is available to get your forms and other back-end services working properly.

The whole idea is to figure out what things your users need from your Web pages, and then to make sure that you've worked out all these details with your service provider.

What they're going to ask you:

From their side of the business, the service provider will probably have some questions for you. These will mostly concern how URLs are handled in your pages, and what services your users will expect the server to provide:

✔ They'll probably give you a new specification for your <BASE> URL definitions, and will ask you to change these accordingly. They'll also ask you what kind of URL references you use in your pages, and if the answer's anything other than "relative links for all local pages" they'll make you talk them through your references, and how they need to change.

✔ They should also ask you what kinds of input-handling scripts you need to install on their system, and what kinds of languages and services they require. This will range from questions about programming languages like C or C++, to scripting languages like AppleScript or the Bourne Shell (UNIX), to predefined functions like CERN's *htimage* or NCSA's *imagemap* for handling clickable image maps.

✔ Finally, they should ask you what kind of help you need in transferring your Web files (html documents, maps, graphics files, scripts and other programs, etc.) to their server. This could be something as simple as setting up special FTP access to a directory inside their Web environment, to outright hand-holding during the transfer process. The more hand-holding you get, though, the more this kind of service will cost!

The service provider's goals are simple: get your pages up and running on their server as quickly as possible, so they can start earning money for user access and data transfer. Their ideal customer scenario is someone like you, who's thoroughly researched and tested their pages, who just wants to get all the links and services working. They don't want to spend lots of time holding hands with you either.

Webbing It Yourself: What's That Mean?

It's not easy setting up and managing your own Web server, assuming you decide that's what you need to do. Besides the costs involved, there are other requirements that you'll want to ponder long and hard before hooking a server up to the Internet — especially that the server should be up and running 24 hrs/day.

Understand the tariffs

Just because we've given you some estimates of what it costs to mount your own server on the Internet doesn't mean that we've determined what your actual costs are going to be. You need to research the options available from your Internet service provider, and calculate your precise costs.

Some considerations vary from one location to another: For instance, you might not be able to get an ISDN link to your server, which might require using multiple, slower telephone lines, or leasing bandwidth directly from the telephone company (for a fractional or full T-1 connection). Either option could add to the cost, and change your decision to buy rather than build.

UNIX, or no UNIX?

We strongly recommend that you use a UNIX system for your Web server, since UNIX offers the greatest variety of *httpd* implementations, and the broadest range of Web-related editors and production tools. It also offers some of the best deals on programming languages and scripting tools, to provide back-end, input-handling services.

While UNIX will run nicely on Intel-based PCs, UNIX expertise is rare in the PC community, and you may have to import some fairly expensive talent to help deal with a UNIX system.

Try though you might, there's no escaping maintenance!

If you look carefully at the figures in Table 19-2, you'll see that the costs for personnel either equal or exceed all the other costs for a Web connection — that is, personnel costs are greater than or equal to the combined costs of hardware, communication, data transfer, and access. Don't try to skimp on this outlay, even if you're contracting most of your Web access.

Change is a sure and wearing constant on the Web. As your information ages, it becomes more and more likely to need patching or replacement. This takes time and costs money — you're best off if you recognize this right up front, and factor it into planning your Web presence. Keeping your space current takes time and effort.

Running a server of your own makes you liable to different forms of obsolescence. You'll have to keep tabs on the versions and patches for the following elements on your system, to stay current:

- ✔ the operating system you're running, be it DOS and Windows, any of the flavors of UNIX, or the Macintosh OS

- ✔ the *httpd* server software, and related elements on your server (like TCP/IP stacks and drivers, etc.) that make your Web server run

- ✔ the programming and scripting languages (like the various UNIX shells or scripting languages available for many types of servers) that make your input-handling and other services run

- ✔ the software and hardware that lets the server communicate with the Internet, be it a modem and an asynchronous communications package, or a dedicated router and a full-blown T-1 link to your service provider

Here again, these factors argue strongly for making the care and feeding of a Web server at least part of someone's official, paid job responsibilities, if not a full-time task. The level of involvement (and expense) will depend on how much business or traffic the Internet brings you, vis-à-vis how much it costs you. This balance will change over time, and we'd also argue that the scales are tipping in favor of more expenditure over time, not less.

For more information on what's required to roll your own Web server, we recommend some additional reading, and some online resources:

Cricket Liu, et al., *Managing Internet Information Resources*, O'Reilly & Associates, Sebastopol, CA, 1994. (List Price: $29.95) This is an excellent overview of providing all kinds of Internet services, and includes valuable chapters on all kinds of Web-related stuff. Excellent coverage of Web server management and Web-access CGI scripts and programs.

Susan Estrada, *Connecting to the Internet*, O'Reilly & Associates, Sebastopol, CA, 1993. (List Price: $15.95) Covers most aspects of selecting an Internet service provider, including contact information for most of the larger regional and all the major national service providers.

Peter Kaminski, "The Public Dialup Internet Access List (PDIAL)," a comprehensive online document posted regularly to USENET newsgroups:

```
alt.internet.access.wanted, alt.bbs.lists,
alt.online-service, ba.internet, news.answers
```

and via ftp from:

```
ftp.netcom.com:/pub/info-deli/public-access/pdial
```

or via -email: include the phrase "Send PDIAL" in the body of a message addressed to info-deli-server@netcom.com

For more help on installing your own Web server, look for the forthcoming *Setting Up Shop on the Internet for Dummies* by Jason and Ted Coombs.

For compiled, ready-to-run *httpd* resources, please check:

```
http://hoohoo.ncsa.uiuc.edu/docs/setup/PreCompiled.html
```

For uncompiled, *httpd* source code, please check:

```
ftp://ftp.ncsa.uiuc.edu/Web/httpd/Unix/ncsa_httpd/current/httpd_source.tar.Z
```

Are You Ready for Success?

Now let's assume that your Web site is up, either through a service provider, or by bringing your own server online. What happens if you've struck a collective nerve, and traffic swells to gargantuan levels?

Will you be ready to deal with the onslaught, or will it catch you by surprise? If so, will it frustrate your potential users, who would be only too happy to access your information, if only they could get the URL to come up?

Barring the element of real surprise, we'd like to suggest that you create some contingency plans to deal with the burden of popularity, should it strike your Web pages. You should be aware that national Internet service providers like PSI, Delphi, CompuServe, ComNet, ANS, and others can offer services that you probably wouldn't want to finance, let alone manage, on your own.

Even if you don't intend to take advantage of their services immediately, it's a good idea to contact them and start building a relationship for possible future business. That way, if your pages become notorious, you'll be able to shift them quickly to an environment that can handle thousands of accesses a day (or more). Even if you decide to bring that kind of capacity online to handle this load, you'll be able to handle your users in the interim, while you're getting the equipment and resources running. If you like, you can simply consider this another sub-case of the famous maxim: "Always leave yourself a way out!"

The Answer to the Ultimate Question

If you recall the central, burning issue of Douglas Adams' five-volume trilogy *The Hitchhiker's Guide to the Galaxy* this is the question about "… life, the Universe, and everything…" Well, hate to disappoint you, but if it isn't "42" we don't know the answer any better than you do!

But when it comes to situating your Web presence, we hope we've given you the ammunition you need to decide whether or not to run your own server. Remember, though, that no decision is final — you can always change your mind! In the meantime, we hope you're ready to decide what to do. If so, it's time to learn how to tell people that your pages are ready for browsing — onward to Chapter 20!

Chapter 20

If You Build It, Will They Come?

. . . .

In This Chapter

▶ Announcing new Web sites and services

▶ Getting the word out

▶ Staying on the right side of the law

▶ Giving value and getting value

▶ Making sure your Web stays on-target

. . . .

The big day has finally arrived: You've built your pages and tested them thoroughly. Your beta testers are ecstatic, and your survey of the testers shows that your Web site is ready for the world to see. Now, finally, it's time for you to go ahead and publish your stuff on the Web.

At this point, your pages will truly be up and running, ready for access. While you may expect the world to beat a path to your door, let us give you a few recommendations about how to let the world know where your door is, and what's behind it. If nobody knows what wonderful Webs you've woven, you can't be surprised if nobody comes to visit them. In other words, if you don't blow your own horn, nobody else will blow it for you!

In this chapter, you'll learn how to get the word out. Pretty soon, you should start to see links to your pages popping up here and there, and a trickle of users should begin to flow in. If they like what they see, links will start popping up everywhere, and the trickle could grow to a torrent. In this chapter, we'll give you some pointers to make sure your chances of success are as good as possible.

Announcing Your Web Site to the World

Once you're online and ready to provide your valuable information to the public, you'll want to spread the word about what you have to offer. In keeping with the Web's chaotic nature, there is no formal registration or announcement process, but there is a well-understood process for letting the world know that your site is ready for access.

Write a "semi-formal" announcement

To begin with, you'll want to write a one-page announcement. If you've ever written a press release, this is a similar kind of document. It should be brief to the point of terseness, and cover the following points:

✔ Indicate who owns the Web site, be it an organization, a person, or some other kind of legal entity. Be sure to include contact information and a contact name to call or e-mail.

✔ Indicate whether the pages are "ready for use" or still "under construction."

✔ Be sure to highlight your home page URL so that interested users can find it.

✔ Summarize the content your pages contain, emphasizing the value and interest in the materials.

Here's a sample announcement for a hypothetical cookie company:

World Wide Web Information Release

March 27, 1995

New York, NY. Terry's Cookie Company (TCC), a leading purveyor of chocolate chip and other delectable cookies, is pleased to announce the release of its comprehensive collection of cookie information to the World Wide Web. For immediate access, please point your browsers to the following URL:

http://www.tcc.com/

Here's what you can expect to find in our Web pages:

• a fascinating history of cookies, with references to recipes and cookies from pre-Christian times, to the present day.

• a comprehensive cookie recipe library, with over 2,000 tested cookie recipes.

• a discussion of cookie-baking tools and techniques, including discussion of ingredients, mixers, baking sheets, cookie guns, and other "cookie technology."

If your research has a cookie in it, we'd like you to be able to find the information you need in the TCC Web pages. Our pages are ready and waiting for you to peruse them!

Terry's Cookie Company also wants its Web pages to become the place for cookie fanciers to meet, so we're setting up a forms-based "Reader's Recipe Exchange." Anyone who browses our pages can submit as many cookie recipes as they'd like. These will be gathered together and published monthly via electronic mail. Individuals wishing to receive the monthly recipe exchange can sign up for the mailing list in the TCC pages, or send an e-mail message to "majordomo@tcc.com" with the following text in the body: "join exchange" (for information on the mailing service put "help info exchange" in the body instead).

While you're visiting our cookie archives, the recipe bank, and the tools and techniques library, be sure to check out our TCC Cookie Catalog. We make it easy for you to order any of our more than 50 varieties of fresh, delicious cookies, or to join our "Cookie of the Month" club. We're sure you'll find a cookie that suits your taste! And if you don't like our cookies, we'll give you your money back!

For more information about the TCC Web pages, or any of TCC's information offerings or products, please contact Gail Shayne at TCC. She can be reached by phone at 212-555-1177; by fax at 212-555-1188, or by e-mail at gshayne@tcc.com. Please visit our Web site soon!

This announcement follows the model we've proposed: it identifies itself clearly, highlights the URL, and stresses the content available in the Web pages. It manages to barely suggest some commercial aspirations toward the end of the announcement, after all the important information's already been stated.

Where to direct your announcement

There are lots of ways to get the word out about your new Web pages, but there are certain bases you'll want to be sure to tag:

✔ Send the announcement to this moderated newsgroup, which publicizes new Web offerings: **comp.infosystems.www.announce**

✔ Post the announcement to the following mailing lists for inclusion in various What's New information:

www-request@info.cern.ch — gets your announcement on CERN WWW servers list (for new servers only)

whats-new@ncsa.uiuc.edu — send your announcement in HTML format, written in the 3rd person (e.g., "Terry's Cookie Company announced their..."), to get included on the Mosaic "What's New"page

www-announce@W30.cern.ch — gets your announcement on the CERN mailing list for new Web servers (servers only)

✔ Other What's New listings worth pursuing include:

"What's New" at Netscape home page — download the electronic submission form at URL: http://home.mcom.com/escapes/submit_new.html for possible inclusion

The "Topics" list in the EINet Galaxy — for placement on the home pages from the makers of WinWeb and MacWeb, consult the "Galaxy Annotation Help" page at http://galaxy.einet.net/annotate-help.html

✔ Publications to notify:

Computer Life — a monthly publication with family-oriented circulation, the BUZZ section of this magazine often features interesting or off-beat Web locations. Send your announcement via e-mail to ceditors.notes@mail.zd.ziff.com or call 1-415-357-5355. Address: 135 Main Street, 14th Floor, San Francisco, CA, 94105.

Internet World — a monthly publication aimed specifically at Internet topics and technology, new Web announcements proliferate here. Send your announcement via e-mail to info@mecklermedia.com or call 1-603-924-7271. Address: 20 Ketchum Street, Westport, CT, 06880.

IWAY — a bimonthly publication aimed at the Internet, with coverage for beginning to intermediate users trying to master related tools and technologies. Send your announcement via e-mail to editors@iway.mv.com or call 1-603-924-9334. Address: 86 Elm Street,Peterborough, NH 03458.

NetGuide — An online services magazine, it covers all of the major online information services by category. Submit your announcement via e-mail to netmail@netguide.cmp.com or call 1-526-562-5000. Address: 600 Community Drive, Manhasset, NY, 11030.

Wired — This is the trendiest and most fashionable of the online coverage magazines. Chances are your announcement will only appear if it's something catchy or outrageous. Submit your announcement via e-mail to editor@wired.com or fax to 1-415-222-6249. Address: 520 Third Street, San Francisco, CA, 94107.

Your local newspaper (if applicable) — Fax or mail your announcement to the Business Section Editor or the Technology Editor, depending on their masthead positions. This will help with local publicity.

Your local computer magazine (if applicable) - Look for a local news section, or a column or reporter who regularly deals with Web issues. This can help get you more local publicity.

The idea here is to plaster your announcement over as many avenues for potential dissemination as possible. These particular recommendations can reach a large — but potentially distinterested — audience. They may provide some welcome initial exposure, but you'll want to target your publicity more closely to your audience as well. Read on for some more specific advice.

Trolling the USENET newsgroups

Beyond this basic list, there are sure to be ways to target your information for more precise delivery to your audience. For Terry's Cookie Company, the following additional USENET newsgroups look appealing:

- ✔ alt.creative-cook
- ✔ alt.creative-cooking
- ✔ alt.food.chocolate
- ✔ ny.forsale
- ✔ rec.food.cooking
- ✔ rec.food.historic
- ✔ rec.food.recipes

For your own Web pages, you'd want to peruse the list of newsgroups on USENET, and select those that appear interesting. Before posting anything on a USENET newsgroup, please locate and read the Frequently Asked Questions list (FAQ) for that newsgroup.

Some newsgroups frown on anything that's even the slightest bit commercial, so you'd want to edit your announcement to eliminate any sales-related information for such groups. Others are pretty free-wheeling and laissez faire. The only way to find out what's what is to read the FAQ, and spend a few days skimming the online traffic before posting anything.

If you try to fit into the mindset for the newsgroup, you'll be much less likely to provoke a mail-bombing session or a flamewar. It's far better to avoid breaking the rules of local netiquette out of ignorance. Think of these precautions as a way of learning how to communicate with yet another audience for your content!

Niche or industry publications

In addition to the general-purpose magazines we've already mentioned, if you're working in a particular marketplace, or have a specific subject area, chances are good that there will be one or more publications serving that niche.

Find out about these niche publications, and fax them your Web announcement. This can very often provide the best publicity you'll get, especially when the audience you're trying hardest to reach has already been targeted by a publication. If you're interested in the subject matter they cover, your announcement will probably come as welcome news, rather than just another Web announcement, as it might for some of the more broadly-focused publications.

Whatever happens with niche publications, it's nice to ride on somebody else's coattails for a change!

The old-fashioned kind of networking

Don't forget that your business and professional contacts form a network of people that you can draw on to get the word out. Local professional societies, informal groups, or other congregations of like-minded people can help broadcast your Web location for you, provided you can appeal to their interest.

Many of these contacts may also have Web sites or pages of their own. If your interests overlap sufficiently, why not ask them to include a link to your new site in their existing pages? You can even offer to return the favor, provided the relevance works both ways. Don't forget to let your colleagues and customers know about your pages, too — send your announcement to these individuals or organizations via e-mail or fax, and update your business card to include your home page URL.

You could even rent a billboard and include your company's name and WWW URL. It's a sure way to get someone from *WIRED* to come out and take a picture and include it in their magazine; it could be like a free form of advertising. Be ready to try the new and offbeat, and you'll get attention for your innovative approach, as well as your content!

Finally, don't forget to cultivate the gurus, consultants, and other experts in your niche. Many of them have personal Web pages that include links to other pages as well. Again, if there's a fit between what they specialize in, and the content on your Web pages, encourage them to check out your materials and ask for feedback.

Professional organizations are popping up on the Web. Often these groups will include a list of members and a link to their Welcome pages. So join a couple and spread your URL even further.

Unless you know these consultants and colleagues really well, it's probably not a good idea to boldly ask them to include a link to your pages. But if you encourage them to look at your content — perhaps by e-mailing them a copy of your announcement — it shouldn't be too surprising if you find your URLs showing up in links on some of their pages.

Staying on the Safe Side of Acceptable Use Policies

Starting in the late 1970s, but most clearly from the mid-1980s and onward, the issue of "acceptable use" of the Internet has been a difficult issue. On the one hand, it's always been a good idea to have a mix of government, research, academic, and business users on the Internet. On the other hand, certain parts of this network are heavily subsidized by us taxpayers.

In the earliest days, the only organizations using the Internet were those that had something to contribute to its development and deployment, or some kind of related effort. Admittedly, the interpretation of "related" was sometimes stretched, and the idea soon emerged that the exchange of information was acceptable on the Internet, but that outright commercial activities, like advertising, billing, or sales-related information, was not. This also helps to explain an anti-sales mentality that persists on the Internet to this day. Although this is changing dramatically, with the development of online transactions.

The charter of the NSFNET Backbone, which once acted as the primary coast-to-coast conduit for Internet information, helps to clarify matters somewhat. It clearly states that its role is to support educational and research activity, and to carry only traffic related to those things. While nobody is censoring each e-mail message or Web page to make sure that these guidelines are honored, the intent of this document is clear:

NSFNET Backbone Acceptable Use Policy

1. NSFNET backbone services are provided to support open research and education in and among US research and instructional institutions, plus research arms of for-profit firms when engaged in open scholarly communication and research. Use for other purposes is not acceptable.

Specifically Acceptable Uses:

2. Communication with foreign researchers and educators in connection with research or instruction, as long as any network that the foreign user employs for such communication provides reciprocal access to US researchers and educators.

3. Communication and exchange for professional development, to maintain currency, or to debate issues in a field or subfield of knowledge.

4. Use for disciplinary-society, university-association, government-advisory, or standards activities related to the user's research and instructional activities.

5. Use in applying for or administering grants or contracts for research or instruction, but not for other fund-raising or public-relations activities.

6. Any other administrative communications or activities in direct support of research and instruction.

7. Announcements of new products or services for use in research or instruction, but not advertising of any kind.

8. Any traffic originating from a network of another member agency of the Federal Networking Council if the traffic meets the acceptable use policy of that agency.

9. Communication incidental to otherwise acceptable use, except for illegal or specifically unacceptable uses.

Unacceptable Uses:

10. Use of for-profit activities (consulting for pay, sales or administration of campus stores, sales of tickets to sports events, and so on) or use by for-profit institutions unless covered by the General Principle or as specifically acceptable use.

11. Extensive use for private or personal business. This statement applies to use of the NSFNET backbone only. NSF expects that connecting networks will formulate their own use policies. The NSF Division of Networking and Communications Research and Infrastructure will resolve any questions about this Policy or its interpretation.

Here's the bottom line: if you're not sure whether or not what you're sending over the Internet will traverse public sector links, the safest course of action is to honor these guidelines, no matter what you're doing.

It's also wise to be wary of blatantly commercial activity of any kind on the Internet — particularly advertising. As you'll learn, sins of omission provoke far fewer firestorms than do the ones of commission! The best policy, therefore, is the one that minimizes commercial activity while sharing your content freely with all those who visit your Web pages.

Giving Value Means Getting Value

As we've said repeatedly throughout this book, the key to a successful Web presence is quality content. If you provide this to your users, and follow our publicity recommendations, your material will ultimately gain the attention it deserves.

As long as users feel like they're getting information, services, ideas, or anything else of genuine value from your Web pages, they'll not only use them regularly, they too will help spread the word to other users. This should bring considerable value back to you, whether it leads to new customers, new sources of information that's valuable to you, or new contacts who share similar pursuits and interests.

 Web's law of reciprocal value is: the more value you put into your Web pages, the more you'll get back from the user community in return, no matter how you measure that return value! ■

Making Sure Your Web Catches the Right Prey

Once your pages are published, and the word is out, it's time to relax and kick back, right? WRONG! After publication is when the real work begins: you should be encouraging your users to give you feedback at all times, especially about the value and usefulness of your content. Then you should actively work to incorporate their feedback on an ongoing basis. No matter how good your content is, it can always get better, especially if you're responding to user requests and suggestions.

Also, once your pages are published, the maintenance work begins. You'll need to stay on top of your own content and materials, to make sure you keep things up-to-date. Keep checking your links to other sites and sources — they can change without warning, rendering your potentially priceless link to the Widget Research Institute into the worthless error message "404 Unable to contact server www.wri.com," which indicates a stale link.

As time goes by, users' tastes in and needs for information will change, too. If you stay in close touch with your audience, you'll be able to anticipate these changes, and keep pace with them. Otherwise, your Web will get all dusty, bestrewn with the corpses of information that has long since been sucked dry. In the next chapter, we'll help you stay on top of the maintenance effort, with some tips for recognizing and coping with an ever-changing world.

Chapter 21

The More Things Change...

*N*ow you can bask in the afterglow of your grand Web achievements. You've published your pages, you've spread the word, and now your hard labor is beginning to bear fruit. Before you pack up your picnic basket and take the rest of the week off, we'd like to remind you that 95% of the life cycle for any information product is spent in maintenance mode.

In other words, what you think you've just finished is really just getting started. In fact, some people would argue that now is when the real fun begins in earnest. You've probably solved the technical problems you've encountered along the way without having to stress yourself too much, or stretch your mind too far from its normal configuration.

But now you will have to start dealing with the toughest problems of all: people problems and communication problems. It's almost guaranteed that some of your content won't make sense to some users, that others may disagree with your content (and even be offended by it), and that still others may delight in harping on what you consider to be trivial errors. Don't let negative feedback bring you down; use it instead as a reminder that your page can never be perfect and that there's always room for improvement.

In this chapter you'll learn about the kinds of problems and feedback you should expect to encounter, and how to deal with the day-to-day routine of keeping your Web pages and other resources in tip-top shape.

Quack! Quack! The Two-Dimensional Text Trap Redux

The temptation to add more content and (hopefully) more value will grow as you get feedback from users and learn more about the subject matter that drives the content. As pages grow, don't forget that users quickly get tired of scrolling around.

Keep a constant eye on the number of screens in any given page, especially when making changes. Even though you may be tempted to think of a sequence of screens as the same thing as a sequence of printed pages, the two are not the same.

We've all been strongly conditioned by a lifetime of linear printed text, so consider this a reminder that the H in HTML stands for Hypertext. This means that growing pages must be hyperlinked to remain readable, usable and to facilitate users who grow bored with one section of your document and want to jump to the next topic. If you don't make it easy for them to jump around, they'll jump ship.

Once the number of screens in an HTML document exceeds three, you should plan on adding internal hypertext links to your pages and break them up into chunks of no more than 20 lines of text. Judicious use of location anchors (<A NAME="spot">) and intradocument links (<A HREF="#spot">) will make it easy for your users to navigate as the spirit moves them.

Our final word on this topic is that as documents grow in length and complexity, the need for effective structure and navigation grows with them. Don't omit the introduction of these vital elements in some of your pages simply because they started small and grew from there.

Who Says This Stuff Is Stale? (The Mold's a Dead Giveaway...)

As we've suggested, the temptation to rest on one's laurels can be nearly irresistible after you've overcome the humps of writing, testing, soliciting user feedback, and finally, publicizing your pages. It's amazing how quickly after a "short rest" you can go back through your Web pages and exclaim: "Wow, did I really put those pages out there *last August*? Boy, this stuff is really out-of-date."

Like leftovers in the refrigerator that have turned to science experiments, stale Web pages can easily become an embarrassment to their owners. The only thing is, they can't alert you to their condition by turning funny colors or starting to smell. You have to keep checking them, just to see how they're holding up against the ravages of time.

Check in on your pages regularly, Doctor Web!

What we'd like to suggest is that you take on the job of maintaining your Web pages as if it were a real job, instead of something you do in your spare time when the phase of the moon is just right. In other words, make it a part of your scheduled activities to read over your content at least once a month, to see how well it's holding up. You'd be surprised how much quality control difference a little absence can make: We almost always find typos and minor gotchas in our pages whenever we revisit them after a while, and we bet you will, too.

Keep your content current!

But the real work comes from maintaining your content. If all the information on your "What's New" page is six months old, those pages won't be attracting too much notice anymore. If the stunning new advance in widgetry you spend half your pages on has been supplanted by an even more thrilling technological advancement, your coverage will seem like old hat. To pick up a newspaper metaphor and mangle it thoroughly: "Yesterday's pages are like yesterday's news; they're only good for lining the bottom of a virtual bird cage!"

Do your links point to nowhere?

In addition to keeping tabs on how current your information is, you'll want to make sure your links are all still current and correct, too. It only takes one change to make a link useless, but that might be the very link your users need most. It's probably a good idea to check links weekly or to locate a good webcrawling robot that can check them for you. Even if you point your users at a "no longer at this location" page with a <u>click here</u> (we *hate* that!) anchor to get them to the current location, you can still earn ill will from users for not getting them right where they want to be!

Another ARGH! is to follow a link to find an "Under construction icon" and that's all that's there. It's a wasted link and it can really perturb users. Don't fall into this trap: If a link is not ready yet, include the proposed link text but don't link it to anything. Indicate that this will soon be a link but it is currently under construction. This tells them what you want them to know, without making them follow a link to find out!

Is your HTML passè?

While you're examining your past efforts, check your HTML markup against the standard that browsers are supporting today. If you've set up tables in your pages using preformatted text and everybody else is using that newfangled, snazzy-looking HTML table markup, your stuff will look pretty lame by comparison. If some of those Netscape extensions ever get adopted in standard HTML, you may want to dress up your pages with some of their nice features, too.

The whole idea is to keep things on your pages fresh and interesting. If you consider regular checkups the moral equivalent of an open box of baking soda, your Web pages should retain their pristine quality and avoid ending up as the dread "science experiments" they could otherwise become!

If You Ask Them, They'll Tell You

Staying in touch with your users is a really good idea, especially when it comes to Web pages. Make sure you include a form or two in your pages, if only to capture more information about your visitors and to solicit feedback on what they liked or didn't like about your site. While you're at it, ask them what else they'd like to see there.

Always be sure to include an area on your feedback form for open-ended comments, remarks, criticisms, or whatever else your users feel compelled to share with you. As we mentioned in Chapter 18, the best feedback often comes from completely unexpected quarters and hits you in the least expected places. No matter how well you know a subject or a market, you'll always have a blind spot somewhere. Open-ended feedback can give you the opportunity to shed some light on that blind spot and may even broaden your horizons!

If you treat your pages as an open-ended communications tool with your users, they'll be more inclined to give you feedback. If you then respond to their feedback, you might even develop a relationship with some of your users that might otherwise never have happened. If so, these sources of quality feedback can become part of the group of movers, shakers, and influencers from whom you will always solicit feedback. You may even develop some of your best contacts through the Web.

Keeping Up with Changes

The thing about feedback is that it creates an impetus to change. Whether it's a dynamite suggestion about a better way to structure one of your pages, or a request for coverage of a topic that would complement your existing information perfectly, or something you saw on somebody's else page that you want to emulate, the net result is more work for you.

Since suggestions keep coming, and good ideas are never in short supply, it's easy to get overwhelmed by change. We suggest that planning for change, and handling it in bite-size chunks, will keep you from becoming a victim of change.

When dealing with suggestions, we recommend that you keep a list of the ideas sent by users and fellow Webheads. If a certain suggestion appears frequently, move this to a "Needed" list, which should be the focus of immediate attention. You can set the threshold to move a common response to "Needed" items to whatever seems appropriate. We've found that five repeats means the suggestion really belongs on the "Needed" list. We've also learned that our constituents are a fountain of good enhancement suggestions, so we also keep a "Cool Ideas" list for future whiz-bang enhancements to our Web site.

Let's assume that you decide to spend every other Tuesday working on your Web pages. During the interim from one of these Web-days to the next, you'd simply collect and prioritize incoming information. You'd also do your best to monitor changes and developments in your fields of interest, and keep another list of things to add to your "What's New" information, possibly culled from the newsgroups and trade magazines that you follow.

Come the next Web-day, you'd pull out your list, select the two or three elements you wanted to change, and formulate a plan of action to implement those changes. By incorporating change into your planned activities and building a process to accommodate it, you can avoid most of the frenzy that last-minute, ill-considered change can cause. If you know you need to update your "What's New" information every Web-day, and add whatever new information or page designs you think are appropriate, this can become just another part of your ongoing relationship with the Web. Remember, you need to run your involvement with the Web: don't let it run you!

Maintenance is an Attitude, and a Way of Life!

The whole idea is make your Web activities a part of your regular daily round. If working on your Web pages is something you do only when the opportunity presents itself, when crunch time comes, that opportunity will never arrive. If, on the other hand, you make working on your Web pages part of your routine, you'll know exactly what you have to deal with, when, and how long you'll be able to stay at it before you have to move on to something else. This approach treats your Web pages as a resource in need of regular maintenance, which is exactly the right attitude to take.

Among the many benefits that this kind of approach can confer, it will let you know when you need to adjust your schedule (or if that's not possible, when you need to think about hiring or acquiring some extra help). If your every other Tuesday isn't enough time, you may have to give up cleaning your wastebasket on Wednesday, and spend a little more time on your Web-related activities. If you just can't give up this essential task (or delegate it elsewhere, like maybe to the custodial staff), you may have to hire a helper or a part-time consultant to assist you with your Web work.

There's a wonderful Latin saying "Festina lente" which means "hurry slowly" that captures the essence of a good maintenance attitude. While you shouldn't overdo the time and energy you devote to any of your workaday tasks, it's important to recognize that regular attention to those tasks will produce the kinds of results you want. If you can't get to those tasks, you'll quickly learn to prioritize and focus on the ones most in need of attention. If that means hiring somebody else to handle your Web pages, so be it. Anything else invites the potential for stale and moldy pages!

When Things Change, They Also Break

While you're involved in maintenance and the gradual process of changing your Web pages, remember that change can introduce unforeseen side effects. In English, this means that every time you change (or add, or delete) information on your Web pages, you need to remember to test your pages as if they were brand-new.

You probably won't devote the same painstaking care to testing every little thing about your "old" pages that you did for them when they were still "new." But the sad truth is that you really should take that same care to check and recheck your work every time you introduce a change.

This means reading (and spell-checking) your content, just to make sure you haven't introduced another typo for your users to chuckle at. It also means checking and rechecking your links (especially the anchors within documents for link destinations) to make sure they still connect to the right places.

It's a good idea to make your changes on a set of copied (production) Web pages, rather than *in situ* on your server. That way, you'll be free to make as many changes (and mistakes) as you like. Nobody will be able to see your work until you want them to. We'd also suggest showing your new versions to a select audience and asking for feedback, before switching public access from an old version to the new one. Many a seemingly good idea has blanched in the face of a reality check; it's probably better to get one from somebody who knows how good you really are than from some user who's simply nonplused by your "strange pages."

We also keep a section on our server where we duplicate our entire Web space utilizing UNIX symbolic links to our entire real Web space. When we're changing a page or adding some others, we can test them thoroughly without disturbing the real Web space. If we're changing a file in our test Web, we delete the file's symbolic link. We then make a copy of the file into the test Web. We then do our edits and validations in the test Web. Once it's passed our visual inspection and survived the rigors of the HTML validator, we then copy the new file into the real Web space. We then delete the file from the test Web and replace it with a symbolic link to the real Web. Voila! A clean substitution, every time...

Keeping up with change is a real job, so why not treat it like one? If you do, you'll be rewarded with a steady sense of progress in the face of constant changes and course adjustment. As you face these vicissitudes, you may begin to wish for more help from your computer, though. In the next section of the book, we switch to an examination of the tools for building Web pages that make the mechanics of the job a bit easier. But there's nothing we can do — except prepare you — to buffer you from the unceasing pace of change on the Web.

Part VIII
It's Tool Time!
HTML Development
Tools and Environments

In This Part...

Here you've been slaving in a techno-wilderness, filled with arcane HTML tags and bizarre CGI programming rituals, and now you'll find out what kinds of tools there are that can help you with this work. Did we wait until near the end of this book-length adventure, only to tell you that you could have "automagically" reached Web nirvana just by buying or obtaining the right tools? Fortunately for us, the answer is "No." There are lots of useful and interesting tools available for many different development platforms, but nobody's built a completely automatic Web construction kit just yet.

We'll start this part of the book in Chapter 22 by explaining what kinds of HTML (and Web server) tools are available these days, to give you an idea of what the state of the art is. In the chapters that follow, you'll have a chance to inspect the offerings for UNIX machines, Macintosh desktops, and finally, the ubiquitous and ever-popular Microsoft Windows environment.

By the time you're through with this part of the book, you should have a good idea of what kinds of tools are available and where to start looking for them for your own favorite authoring environment. Finally, you should have a good feel for what kinds of Web server capabilities are available and how the various platforms can help to realize them.

Chapter 22

Picking the Right Web Platform

● ●

In This Chapter

▶ Choosing the right WWW platform

▶ Lining up your options

▶ Inspecting UNIX-based systems

▶ Biting into Apple systems

▶ Looking through Windows systems

▶ Scanning filters and file converters

▶ Looking over the Web servers

● ●

*T*hink of the platform as both the computer system you use to create your Web pages and the network server upon which your site resides. The platform you use for your Web authoring will undoubtedly be the computer you have in front of you — or somewhere around the desk, anyway. Ideally you would select the best HTML authoring software and then choose the computer that runs it best. Fortunately for you, there are now several good HTML authoring tools available for practically any computer platform.

Although you have several choices for your Web server, you will probably start by using the services of your current Internet provider, unless you have lots of information to serve up, and a budget to match. This is the most cost-effective method for individuals, but also for many companies. That's because maintaining your own Web server can be a time-consuming, expensive proposition.

This chapter will concentrate on helping you choose the best HTML authoring tools. It will also give you an idea of the Web server platforms used by most Internet service providers, with which you may become intimately familiar, if you decide to run your own Web server.

Ye Olde Authoring Toole Shoppe

Windows, DOS, Macintosh, UNIX, NextStep, X-Windows: where to shop for your HTML authoring software? This looks like another good opportunity to use the KISS approach. Our advice is: Don't get bogged down in the morass of choosing the perfect platform.

If you use a Mac, look at the Mac authoring tools. If you're a Windows wizard, look at the Windows tools. It's that simple to choose a platform for HTML authoring software — providing of course, that you actually enjoy the computer you're using. If you don't, maybe this is the excuse you need to jump ship!

If you want to buy a new computer for your HTML work, that's great. For personal use, either a PC running Windows or Windows for Workgroups, or a Mac (we recommend a Quadra 750 or better, or one of the PowerPC Macs, but almost any Mac will do the job) will be the most cost-effective solution.

Both Mac and Windows offer good HTML authoring tools, either free or as shareware. Commercial versions of some shareware programs are also available — generally for prices under $200. Just be sure to get the fastest computer you can afford with a high capacity hard disk (850 MB or more), and the highest resolution video card and CRT you can afford (1024 X 768 SVGA minimum). Of course any UNIX workstation will do quite nicely (if you have a spare $10,000 or so!).

A more important choice for you is which HTML authoring tool to use. They fall into the following categories:

- ✔ editors that can check HTML syntax for you, or editors that let you do things your own way
- ✔ standalone editors, or tools that add onto or into existing word processors
- ✔ "What you see is what you get" (WYSIWIG) editors, or editors that require you to launch a browser to display your HTML design work

An editor can have attributes from one or more of these categories, which we'll explain further in the sections that follow. Hang on, and be prepared to gape at the innards of the HTML tools available for the authoring trade!

Unchecked vs. checked editors

Unchecked HTML editors help you place your tags easily but do not check to see if the tags are correctly used. These editors are like using your word processing program with special toolbars for tags. They are adequate — if you remember what you have learned about HTML; if not, they won't give you much support.

Checked HTML editors use a set of HTML rules to make sure you put tags in their proper places, with all of the necessary attributes included in each tag. This approach helps beginners but can be highly confining after you become pretty good at coding HTML text. With this kind of tool, you are also at the mercy of a program that may not know the latest and greatest tags (or the Netscape extensions) and therefore, won't let you use them. Some of these tools do include forms and scripting features that are nice to have, though.

Stand-alone, word processor add-on, or document template

Stand-alone Editors are programs that can function on their own — they need no other programs or applications to function (except, of course, for the operating system that they run on).

Word Processor add-on HTML editors, if you can call them "editors," have just been introduced for Word for Windows and WordPerfect. They are actually programs that the main word processing program runs and integrates into itself, thereby giving it the ability to open, edit, and save HTML-tagged documents. Some even convert their standard formats into HTML-tagged documents automatically. But you must have a copy of the word processor software in order to use an add-on program.

Document Templates are similar to add-on editors but supply less functionality. They provide only a document template, along with a set of macros, to be used by an existing software package, like Microsoft Word. As with an add-on program, you need to run the word processor software to use the template and macros.

WYSIWYG or text-only HTML

WYSIWYG editors act as their own browsers, and can display your HTML document as it might appear to your users. Some WYSIWYG editors can even hide or display HTML tags at your command. Since these editors must recognize HTML, you may be constrained by their lack of knowledge about new tags in the future, unless you obtain an appropriately updated version. The same goes double for proprietary HTML extensions (like Netscape's).

Text-Only HTML editors display HTML documents as standard text with all tags visible along with the content. They're like plain-text editors on steroids, with some built-in HTML tag placement support.

Some HTML editors can't decide which way to go, so they display parts of HTML documents in browser view, and leave the rest in plain text. These are generally to be avoided since they are confusing to view or use.

Eeny, meeny, miny, moe...

Freeware or shareware versions of most types of HTML editors are available for most of the commonly-used computer platforms. If you feel like you have a pretty good grasp of HTML basics, download one or two of the stand-alone, unchecked, text-only editors and give them a try. Make sure you get one with graphical tool bars and online help. By following the instructions in previous chapters of this book, you can build any type of Web document with one of these tools.

For a more structured approach, download one of the stand-alone, checked editors and try it. You will have to learn more commands on this type of editor. You will also have to put up with the somewhat linear nature of the procedure that most of them require you to adopt. It won't take you long to make up your mind about this type of editor. You'll either love it or leave it!

If you're a word processing wizard, you may want to try one of the add-on editors. They are just coming out as this book is being prepared. These add-ons aren't a universal panacea for HTML authoring, but they can be good assistants for quickly converting existing word processor documents into usable HTML. Some will work on very long documents that stand-alone editors won't even load.

The document templates for word processors have been supplanted by the add-on editors in most cases. However, for some UNIX tools, they may still be your best bet. If you're really into UNIX, you'll probably be able to use a template for your UNIX editor (for example, emacs) with good results.

A quick tour of the tools

Now let's take a quick overview of the currently available HTML authoring tools. They're classified by their most prominent platform so you can easily read about only your type of computer. The three chapters following this one go into more detail about the most popular UNIX, Macintosh, and Windows tools. ▪

To go directly to an informative source of online information on all kinds of HTML editors, link to:

```
http://union.ncsa.uiuc.edu:80/HyperNews/get/www/html/editors.html ▪
```

So You'd Rather Fight than Switch from UNIX

UNIX-based HTML editors come in a wide variety of types and sizes. Try the free/shareware ones first to find one that suits your needs.

A.S.H.E.

A.S.H.E. is just what its acronym implies, A Simple HTML Editor. It can be downloaded from:

```
ftp.cs.rpi.edu/pub/puninj/ASHE/
```

Read the README file in the ASHE directory. You can FTP the README at:

```
ftp://ftp.cs.rpi.edu/pub/puninj/ASHE/README.html
```

Additional Information about ASHE is available at:

```
http://www.cs.rpi.edu/~puninj/TALK/head.html
```

Phoenix

Phoenix is an X-Windows WYSIWYG HTML editor with cut-and-paste features and is available at:

```
http://www.bsd.uchicago.edu/ftp/pub/phoenix/README.html
```

or via anonymous FTP on:

```
www.bsd.uchicago.edu/pub/phoenix/
```

Or send e-mail to L-Newberg@UChicago.EDU for more information.

TkWWW

TkWWW is a Tk/Tcl-based WWW browser that also supports editing and preparation of HTML documents. It is a semi-WYSIWYG editor. You can download various versions via FTP from:

```
ftp.aud.alcatel.com/tcl/extensions
```

as filename tkWWW-#.tar.z. The # is the number of the most recent version. It requires Tk/Tcl on your computer, which you can *ftp* from:

```
ftp.cs.berkeley.edu/ucb/tcl
```

at the University of California at Berkeley. This site has compressed *tar* files and documentation.

TkHTML

TkHTML is a semi-WYSIWYG HTML editor based on the Tk/Tcl language by Liem Bahneman (roland@cac.washington.edu). Download the source from:

```
ftp.u.washington.edu/public/roland/tkHTML
```

HoTMetaL

HoTMetaL for Sun/SPARC Motif is a free, stand-alone, error-checking editor from SoftQuad available by either Web or *ftp* from:

```
http://www.sq.com
ftp.NCSA.uiuc.edu/Web/html/hotmetal/SPARC-Motif
```

The commercial version is $195 from SoftQuad Inc., 56 Aberfoyle Crescent, Toronto, Ontario, Canada M8X 2W4. Phone: 1-416-239-4801; fax: 1-416-239-7105; e-mail: hotmetal@sq.com ▪

Miscellaneous tools

Emacs HTML mode (html-mode.el) supports Lucid Emacs menu bar and font-lock capabilities. It runs under GNU Emacs v18 and v19, Epoch, and Lucid Emacs.

psgml is a major mode for editing SGML documents. By using HTML DTDs, it may be used to edit HTML documents.

htmltext is an editor based on the Andrew Toolkit.

HTML Editor is an HTML editor for NextStep systems which contains support for building forms and inserting character entities and HTML tags. It will call a Web browser to display a WYSIWYG preview.

More information and links to the sources for these UNIX-based HTML authoring tools are readily available at the following CERN WWW site:

```
http://info.cern.ch/hypertext/WWW/Tools  ▣
```

Sweet Bites of Macintosh

Several HTML authoring tools are available for Macintosh users. Many can be downloaded from links to the CERN site at:

```
http://info.cern.ch/hypertext/WWW/Tools  ▣
```

The following is the list of the currently available programs from the CERN site. The program name is the hyperlink to its site or download location.

SHE stands for Simple HTML Editor for HyperCard. This freeware program is available by FTP from:

```
http://www..lib.ncsu.edu/staff/morgan/simple.html
ftp://ftp.lib.ncsu.edu/pub/software/mac/simple-html-editor.hqx
```

HTML.edit is a freeware editor available at:

```
http://nctn.oact.hq.nasa.gov/tools/HTMLedit/HTMLedit.html
```

BBEdit is a freeware Mac editor available from:

```
ftp://world.std.com/pub/bbedit
```

HTML Extensions, developed by The Web Project at Universitat Jaume I in Spain for BBEdit, is available from:

```
http://www.uji.es/bbedit-html-extensions.html
```

HTML Editor is a stand-alone WYSIWYG HTML editor you can download from:

```
http://dragon.acadiau.ca:1667/~giles/HTML_Editor/Documentation.html
http://dragon.acadiau.ca:1667/~giles/HTML_Editor/Documentation.html
```

HTML Grinder is a serious Mac editor with a powerful utility to assist you with intelligent link building. It is available at:

```
http://www.nets.com/site/matterform/grinder/htmlgrinder.html
```

HoTMetaL for Macintosh is a stand-alone, error-checking editor with strict rules for HTML 2.0. A freeware version and $195 HoTMetaL Pro version, with scripting and forms, is available from SoftQuad Inc., 56 Aberfoyle Crescent, Toronto, Ontario, Canada M8X 2W4. Phone: 1-416-239-4801; fax: 1-416-239-7105; e-mail: hotmetal@sq.com. ∎

Wide-open Windows

Since there are more Windows computers in use than all others combined, it is not surprising that there are also more Windows-based HTML editors available. Some template systems are even becoming obsolete with the appearance of the add-on editor extensions to Word for Windows and WordPerfect.

Stand-alone Windows HTML editors

HTMLed is a stand-alone, plain text editor with good toolbars and user interface. It is available from:

```
ftp://ftp.cica.indiana.edu/pub/pc/win3/util/htmed10.zip
```

HTML Assistant is a stand-alone, plain text editor for MS Windows which converts items in the Mosaic.ini file to an HTML file. It is available from:

```
http://cs.dal.ca/ftp/htmlasst/htmlafaq.html
```

HTML Writer is a stand-alone, plain text editor for MS Windows by Kris Nosack at:

```
http://lal.cs.byu.edu/people/nosack/
```

HoTMetaL for MS Windows from SoftQuad Corp. is a stand-alone, error-checking editor with strict rules for HTML 2.0. The freeware version and a $195 HoTMetaL Pro version, with scripting and forms are available at:

```
http://www.w3.org/hypertext/WWW/Tools/HoTMetal.html
http://www.sq.com
ftp.NCSA.uiuc.edu/Web/html/Windows
```

WEB Wizard: The Duke of URL is a stand-alone Windows home page creation application with versions for both 16 and 32-bit Windows. New in March 1995, it is available free from:

```
http://www.halcyon.com/webwizard ■
```

MS Word for Windows HTML add-ons, templates, and macros

The Microsoft Word Internet Assistant add-on HTML editor will save documents in HTML format and also uses Word as an Internet browser.

WebAuthor for Word for Windows 6.0 was recently released by Quarterdeck Corporation. This WYSIWYG HTML authoring tool converts documents between HTML and Word formats. Available as pre-release freeware or commercially:

```
http://www.qdeck.com
```

ANT_HTML.DOT is a WinWord 6.0 template. Jill Smith developed it to help her create HTML documents but won't say what "ANT" stands for. Download it from:

```
ftp://ftp.einet.net/einet/pc/ANT_HTML.ZIP
```

MS Word for Windows Macros, gt_html.zip, is a set of Macros that add HTML editing assistance to Word for Windows. This can be downloaded from Georgia Tech (GT):

```
http://www.gatech.edu/word_html/release.htm
```

CU_HTML.DOT is perhaps the best document template for Word for Windows 2.0 and 6.0. It can display inline GIFs inside the document, and let you insert hyperlinks and tags. Download it from Chinese University of Hong Kong (CU):

```
http://www.cuhk.hk/csc/cu_html/cu_html.htm ■
```

Weird and Wacky Miscellany

In addition to the HTML editing packages listed above, numerous filters or converters from one format to another are available for different platforms.

Filters and file converters

A wide variety of file converters and word processor file filters are available for HTML. A good place to start surfing for them is the CERN site:

```
http://info.cern.ch/hypertext/WWW/Tools/Filters.html
```

You can find other lists of converters and filters at:

```
http://www.oac.uci.edu/indiv/ehood/perlWWW
http://oneworld.wa.com/htmldev/devpage/dev-page.html
http://www.utirc.utoronto.ca/HTMLdocs/intro_tools.html
http://union.ncsa.uiuc.edu/HyperNews/get/www/html/converters.html
http://www.ncsa.uiuc.edu/SDG/Software/Mosaic/Docs/faq-software.html#editors
```

Image map editors

You can obtain information on the conversion utilities for bitmap and other graphics listed below at:

```
http://union.ncsa.uiuc.edu:80/HyperNews/get/www/html/editors.html
http://www.cis.ohio-state.edu/hypertext/faq/usenet/graphics/
fileformats-faq/faq.html
```

Mapedit is used to create new image maps and to edit your existing image maps.

Hypermap is a program for HyperCard on the Macintosh. Use it to create new image maps and to edit your existing image maps.

MapMaker is a UNIX-based tool for generating clickable image maps for use with HTML browsers. It requires TCL.

Web Server Primer

A brief look at the Web server software and where you can find more information. Again, the CERN site is the place to go to link directly with each of the following sites.

```
http://info.cern.ch/hypertext/WWW/Daemon/Overview.html
```

A W3 server is a program on the Web Server computer which responds to an incoming tcp connection and provides a service to the caller. There are many varieties of W3 server software to serve different forms of data.

CERN server is the W3 daemon program. It is full featured, with access authorization, research tools, and more on the way. This daemon is used as a basis for many other types of server and gateways. Platforms: UNIX, VMS.

NCSA server is a public domain server for files. It is written in C and has as many features as CERN's httpd. Platform: UNIX.

GoServe is a server for OS/2 supporting both HTTP and Gopher, from Mike Cowlishaw of IBM UK Laboratories.

Windows httpd 1.4 is a Windows server created by Robert Denny. Link to the home page for full details.

GN is a single server providing both HTTP and Gopher access to the same data. It is written in C and offered under a General Public License. It was designed to help servers transition from Gopher to WWW. Platform: UNIX.

Perl server from Marc VanHeyningen at Indiana University, is written in perl. Platform: UNIX.

Plexus is Tony Sander's server originally based on Marc VH's, but now incorporates additional features, including an Archie gateway. Platform: UNIX.

MacHTTP is "the" Server for the Macintosh. Link to its home page for information.

Netsite is a commercially supported server from Netscape Communications, Inc. Link to its home page for information.

VAX/VMS server uses DEC/Threads for speed.

REXX for VM is a server consisting of a small C program that passes control to a server written in REXX.

HTTP for VM By R. M. Troth has many sites using it.

SerWeb is a WWW server for the Windows 3.1 system.

CL-HTTP is a full-featured, object-oriented HTTP server written in Common LISP by John Mallery at the M.I.T. Artificial Intelligence Laboratory. It runs on Symbolics LISP Machines. Ports are underway to LISPs for the MAC and other platforms.

WebWorks Server from Quadralay Corp.

http://www.quadralay.com/products/WebWorks/Server/index.html ▨

If you're thoroughly confused, you're not alone. Your best bet will be to let your Internet provider handle the server. Then you can create your own fantastic Web site on their server, using one of the popular HTML authoring tools discussed in the next three chapters, without having to wrestle with all the ugly details.

Chapter 23

Using UNIX Uniformly

· ·

· ·

*W*onderful new HTML authoring tools for UNIX-based systems have sprung up in recent months. Many are still undergoing testing, but they all look quite promising to UNIX users tired of text-only systems. And for those of you who happen to like text-only, the old EMACS standby is alive and well, with a few added HTML modes to liven it up. To top it off, you can convert or filter almost any file type into or out of HTML using one of the myriad of HTML utility programs available for UNIX.

The UNIX mystique is one of sharing resources, so in that vein practically all of the UNIX-based HTML authoring systems are freeware. Even commercial UNIX packages typically offer a freeware version for downloading.

Because of their free status UNIX HTML authoring tools aren't supported in the same manner as commercial products. But then, they don't cost you anything, either. Thankfully, these tools are usually easy to learn because they either use familiar text editor metaphors, or they are add-ins to your own UNIX text editors. Either way, if you've ever used any kind of editor, you'll be able to easily learn one of these HTML tools.

Diving for Treasure in the UNIX HTML Tools Sea

The sections that follow describe several types of UNIX-based HTML authoring tools and give you important facts about each of them. These tools vary in their scope and functionality; however, all of them are designed to help you create HTML documents more easily.

Some of these tools are stand-alone UNIX programs that provide structure and error checking while they guide you through the creation of your Web pages. Some simply and elegantly provide you with quicker ways of inserting the requisite HTML tags into plain-text documents. Others comprise groups of macros for HTML editing to be used by existing UNIX text editors, such as EMACS. The file conversion tools take a different approach and change existing text files into HTML-tagged documents.

No matter which kind of tool you choose to try first, remember that the objective is to quickly create eye-catching, informative Web pages that will function on everybody's browser. If the tool you try doesn't help you meet this objective, try another tool. There's one out there that will do the job for you.

More information on UNIX authoring tools is readily available starting at the following CERN WWW site:

    http://info.cern.ch/hypertext/WWW/Tools/Overview.html ▪

Stand-alone HTML editors

The stand-alone plain-text HTML editors for UNIX, such as A.S.H.E (A Simple HTML Editor) simply give you a screen into which you type your text. They also provide buttons or menu options from which you select HTML tags, which you must then insert at the proper places in the text. The emphasis in A.S.H.E. is Simple.

Several other programs are semi-WYSIWYG in that they provide you with a somewhat standard text editing screen into which you type your text. The editor then helps you place the appropriate HTML tags in your text and keeps you from making errors in HTML syntax. These editors also help you with the creation of more complex HTML links and references. HoTMetaL is one example of this type of system.

Others, such as Phoenix, are complete WYSIWYG HTML authoring systems that let you type your text and format it the way it will be displayed by a browser. Then the system not only produces the appropriate HTML-formatted document, it lets you copy and paste from other HTML documents and carries the tags with the copied text. These systems also check your HTML syntax for proper usage. They are the most comprehensive of the HTML authoring systems available for UNIX.

EMACS modes and templates

The old tried and true UNIX EMACS editor has several add-in macro systems (modes) available to help you use it to create HTML documents. These modes vary in their features but generally are very basic in their approach. They save you from typing each tag in its entirety and show you a list from which to choose.

Filtering and converting your UNIX files

Since there are so many different file types used on UNIX systems, a long list of HTML filters and converters has accumulated over the past few years. These programs transform text, RTF, FrameMaker, or other file types into an HTML-tagged file based on the original file's formatting. Of course these converters are only as good as their HTML rule set and their authors' abilities to guess what you really want. Generally they give you a headstart on converting existing files to HTML documents.

Standing Alone Among the UNIX HTML Editors

A.S.H.E. (A Simple HTML Editor)

Type:

A.S.H.E. is a stand-alone, unchecked, plain-text HTML editor. (See Figure 23-1.)

A.S.H.E.'s claims to fame:

- ✔ Provides active hyperlinks.
- ✔ Supports multiple windows.
- ✔ Prints text or postscript.
- ✔ Offers automatic file backup.

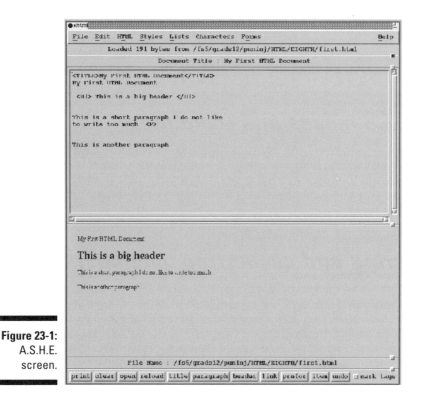

Figure 23-1:
A.S.H.E.
screen.

Pros:

✔ Menu Bar is well designed with: File, Edit, HTML, Styles, and Lists.

✔ Provides unique user Message Area.

✔ Displays HTML browser screen view.

✔ Has buttons with most frequently used commands.

Cons:

✔ Only works under Motif on SUN workstations.

✔ Requires the NCSA HTML Widget library.

Evaluation:

A.S.H.E was written using C language, Motif, and NCSA HTML Widgets. It provides very simple but adequate HTML assistance for users of Motif. If that sounds like it's up your alley, please give it a try!

Availability:

The A.S.H.E. beta version was created by John R. Punin, Dept. of Comp. Sci. RPI, Troy, NY 12180, E-mail: puninj@cs.rpi.edu. It can be downloaded from:

```
ftp://ftp.cs.rpi.edu/pub/puninj/ASHE
http://www.cs.rpi.edu/~puninj/TALK/head.html
```

Phoenix

Type:

Phoenix alpha release 0.1.7 is a stand-alone, error-checking, WYSIWYG HTML editor/browser for X-Windows systems.

Phoenix's claims to fame:

✔ Offers true WYSIWYG HTML creation with a built-in browser.

✔ Copies and pastes plain, heading, anchor, and/or styled text with the attributes retained.

✔ Provides for easy Anchor editing with no need to type the URL in most cases.

Pros:

✔ Supports character styles: B, CITE, CODE, DFN, EM, I, KBD, SAMP, STRONG, TT, U, and VAR.

✔ Copies and pastes text from other applications.

✔ Supports full forms-browsing.

✔ Copies and pastes images and ismaps from Web pages.

Cons:

✔ No significant negatives were apparent.

Evaluation:

You don't have to know what HTML is to use Phoenix, at least not for simple Web pages. Its cut-and-paste features are well-implemented. If you're an X-Windows user, give it a try. But remember that version 0.1.7 is still an alpha test version and has a few minor bugs that Lee is working diligently to eradicate.

Availability:

Phoenix, by Lee Newberg, Biological Sciences Division, office of Academic Computing, The University of Chicago, 924 E. 57th Street, Chicago, IL 60637-5415 is available at:

```
ftp://www.bsd.uchicago.edu/pub/phoenix/README.html
http://http.bsd.uchicago.edu/~l-newberg/ ■
```

tkWWW

Type:

tkWWW is a Tk/Tcl-based WWW browser with semi-WYSIWYG HTML editing capabilities.

tkWWW's claims to fame:

✔ Provides "Mosaic-like" browsing capabilities with minimal editing functions.

Pros:

✔ Places the editing features in the Generate Source button for easy access while browsing.

Cons:

✔ It's mostly a browser rather than an HTML editor.

✔ Does not contain an undo function.

✔ Requires Tk/Tcl to run.

✔ Requires Xli (X Image library, for viewing images).

Evaluation:

tkWWW is a browser with aspirations of being an HTML editor but it hasn't made it there yet.

Availability:

tkWWW is free from:

```
ftp://www0.cern.ch/pub/www/dev ■
```

TkHTML version 2.3

Type:

TkHTML is a semi-WYSIWYG HTML editor based on the Tk/Tcl language.

TkHTML's claims to fame:

- ✔ Provides WYSIWYG previewing.
- ✔ Uses tear-off menus.
- ✔ Supports Netscape's extensions to HTML.

Pros:

- ✔ Provides shortcut keys for easy formatting.
- ✔ Supports multiple platforms.
- ✔ Converts text documents to HTML format.

Cons:

- ✔ Requires wwwish, instead of standard wish interpreter.
- ✔ Requires Tcl 7.3 and Tk 3.6 installed on your system.

Evaluation:

TkHTML is a simple HTML editor based on the Tcl script language and the Tk toolkit for X11. It provides adequate functionality for creating HTML documents. It may serve you well if your system meets its requirements for running.

Availability:

TkHTML was written by Liem Bahneman. E-mail: roland@cac.washington.edu. Download the source from:

```
ftp://ftp.u.washington.edu:/public/roland/tkHTML
ftp://sunsite.unc.edu:/pub/packages/infosystems/WWW/tools/editing/unix/tkhtml
http://www.infosystems.com/tkHTML/tkHTML.html ▪
```

HoTMetaL

Type:

HoTMetaL is a stand-alone, error-checking, semi-WYSIWYG editor with strict rules for HTML 2.0 only. (See Figure 23-2.)

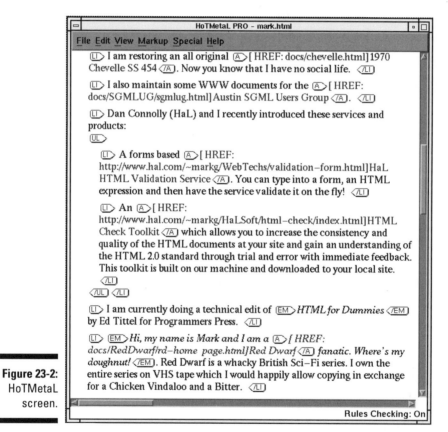

Figure 23-2:
HoTMetaL
screen.

HoTMetaL's claims to fame:

- ✔ Requires conformation to HTML 2.0 standards.

- ✔ Contains a comprehensive list of HTML 2.0 compliant tags for insertion.

- ✔ Semi-WYSIWYG display shows some formatting along with its own version of tags.

- ✔ The commercial version sets up HTML tables and includes a spell checker and a thesaurus.

Pros:

- ✔ Error checking is comprehensive.
- ✔ Provides highly-structured HTML authoring environment.
- ✔ It always creates valid HTML 2.0 documents.

Cons:

- ✔ Requires 6 meg of RAM to run.
- ✔ Uses HTML 2.0 conforming tags only.
- ✔ Fails to open some HTML files with tags not conforming to HTML 2.0 standards.
- ✔ Overly complex and may be difficult to learn.
- ✔ Semi-WYSIWYG display is confusing to many users.
- ✔ No online help.

Evaluation:

HoTMetaL does not use any extensions to HTML recognized by the newer browsers (Netscape, Mosaic, and others). It forces you to use its rigid structure and its minimalistic graphical interface reveals its UNIX origin. HoTMetaL may be just the tool you want to try for building extremely complex webs with hundreds of pages, but it may intimidate a beginner building a simple home page.

Availability:

The freeware version for Sun/SPARC Motif is available at:

http://www.sq.com ■

The commercial version is $195 from SoftQuad Inc., 56 Aberfoyle Crescent, Toronto, Ontario, Canada. M8X 2W4. Phone: +1 416 239 4801, fax: +1 416 239 7105. E-mail: hotmetal@sq.com

EMACS HTML Modes

EMACS users will understand this section and everyone else will wonder what it's all about. But then EMACS is a foreign language to most non-UNIX computer users.

Various EMACS macro packages are available for editing HTML documents. The first and oldest is Marc Andreesen's html-mode.el. It was written while he was at the University of Illinois. (Marc is the primary designer of Mosaic and Netscape.) Heiko Muenkel of the University of Hannover, Germany added pull-down menus (hm—html-menus.el) and template handling (tmpl-minor-mode.el).

Later, Nelson Minar of Reed College wrote html-helper-mode.el, which supports Lucid EMACS menu bar and font-lock capabilities and runs under GNU EMACS v18 and v19, Epoch, and Lucid EMACS.

Generally speaking, the various iterations of HTML mode display text and HTML tags alike in fixed-size fonts. By using the hilit.el package, tags and references can be colored differently than text. The HTML modes do not support inline display of graphics. The more recent versions of HTML mode can call a Mosaic process to display pages in browser view.

All of the HTML modes work primarily from direct keyboard commands which create paired begin/end HTML tags with an entry point available between the tags. It is possible to select a segment of text and the tags will be inserted around it. None of the modes check the validity of tags or suggest possible tag usage. However, html-helper-mode and tmpl-minor-mode provide templates for entering the multiple fields in link tags.

For EMACS users, these modes may be just the thing for creating HTML documents. Using them should make HTML tagging easier and less prone to errors than manually typing in the complete tags. You still must know what tags to use and where to use them.

You can download the entire html-helper-mode package from:

```
ftp://ftp.reed.edu/pub/src/html-helper-mode.tar.gz
```

UNIX-based HTML Filters and File Converters

Numerous conversion programs and filters that transform documents from Microsoft RTF, LaTeX, FrameMaker, etc. to HTML are available from several Web and FTP sites. Remember that the HTML definition is constantly changing, which means the filters and converters will need frequent upgrading to be useful.

More than you ever wanted to know about UNIX-based HTML filters and file converters is probably available at the following sites or via a link from one of them:

```
http://info.cern.ch/hypertext/WWW/Tools/Filters.html
http://www.oac.uci.edu/indiv/ehood/perlWWW
http://oneworld.wa.com/htmldev/devpage/dev-page.html
http://www.utirc.utoronto.ca/HTMLdocs/intro_tools.html
http://union.ncsa.uiuc.edu/HyperNews/get/www/html/converters.html
http://www.ncsa.uiuc.edu/SDG/Software/Mosaic/Docs/faq-software.html#editors
```

UNIX Web Server Search

A WWW server is a daemon program constantly running on an Internet-attached computer which responds to an incoming TCP connection and provides a service to the caller. The vast majority of WWW servers are probably running on UNIX platforms around the world. And as everyone knows, there are more flavors of UNIX than ice cream at Baskin Robbins. Concomitantly, there are also many different kinds of WWW servers on those UNIX platforms.

For the most recent information on UNIX-based WWW servers, check out the CERN site below and follow the links:

```
http://info.cern.ch/hypertext/WWW/Daemon/Overview.html
```

This chapter has provided you with a brief overview of the major UNIX-based HTML authoring systems as well as some of the ancillary packages. The Web itself is the best place to obtain the latest and greatest UNIX Web tools so "The Web's up. Let's go surfin' now."

Chapter 24

More Macintosh Madness

A plethora of excellent HTML authoring tools for the Macintosh are available for downloading from numerous online sites. All but a couple of these tools are freeware or shareware. Most of them are appropriate for beginning to advanced HTML authors.

Because of their low cost/no cost status, these tools don't offer the handholding support you might expect from commercial products. But then, they don't cost much, either. Most come with very good to pretty good documentation files and some have online or even balloon help. Thankfully, these tools are usually easy to learn because they use familiar Macintosh word processing or text editor models and the Macintosh menuing system.

Surveying the Orchard of Macintosh HTML Tools

In the subsections that follow, you'll encounter information on several types of Macintosh HTML authoring tools that are available to help you create Web pages. These tools vary in their scope and functionality but all of them can provide you with solid HTML help.

Macintosh HTML authoring tools are generally more advanced than either Windows or UNIX-based HTML tools. Many of them have the ability to internally display a WYSIWYG or semi-WYSIWYG view of your HTML document. Along with this comes a certain amount of error checking as their internal display mechanism simulates a browser and recognizes the HTML tags. The best tools let you see both WYSIWYG and tagged views of your document. All of the truly complete tools provide balloon help.

Several of the stand-alone WYSIWYG programs check your HTML code and keep you from making syntax or placement mistakes. Some of these tools add to the functionality of existing word processing and text editors, thereby giving them the ability to help you include HTML tags. Some go as far as converting existing text files from their normal formats to HTML, and vice versa.

If you already use BBEdit or BBEditLite, the quickest way for you to get into HTML authoring is via the add-in templates available for this fine editor. Microsoft and Novell will probably have MacWord and WordPerfect for the Macintosh add-in HTML packages available during 1995 also.

Other than using a familiar editor, the stand-alone editors such as SHE (Simple HTML Editor), HTML Editor, and HTML.edit may be the easiest to learn and use. On the other hand, although Arachnid is probably the most complete Macintosh HTML authoring system, it may be the easiest to use since it creates the HTML tags for you as you type into its WYSIWYG editor. You'll just have to try some of these or the other tools discussed below and see which one is easiest for you.

While you're trying out one or more of these tools, ask yourself, "Does this make writing HTML any easier?" If your answer is "No," try another tool. Regardless of the kind of tool you choose, you can reasonably expect it to make your HTML creation job easier, not harder.

You can find the most up-to-date information on Macintosh HTML tools at these sites:

```
http://atlantis.austin.apple.com/people.pages/carldec/carldec.html
http://www.txinfinet.com/wwwdev.html
http://www.uwtc.washington.edu/Computing/WWW/Macintosh.html
http://www2.excite.sfu.ca/tools/
http://werple.mira.net.au/%7Egabriel/web/html/editors/indexold.html ■
```

Stand-alone HTML tools

The stand-alone authoring tools for the Macintosh range in complexity from the Simple HTML Editor (SHE) to the complete Web creation environment of

Arachnid. The simple, generally plain-text HTML editors like HTML Editor, HTML.edit, and Simple HTML Editor (SHE) are the easiest to learn. They basically let you type your text and give you buttons or menu options to select tags at appropriate insertion points.

For example, to create a title for your Web page, you select the line of title text and then click the TITLE button. The editor places the opening <TITLE> tag at the start of the selection and places the closing </TITLE> at the end. Most of the stand-alone Macintosh HTML tools help you with creating links to images and URLs also.

Text editor extensions and templates

Editor or word processing add-in functions are templates and programs that are installed into your existing editor or word processing program. These extensions appear in the editor's menus as HTML functions which insert tags, create forms, and the like. Some extensions give the program the ability to open and save HTML-tagged documents.

The HTML add-ins for BBEdit and BBEditLite are quite extensive and provide a well-rounded HTML authoring system. Tools of this kind can cause the editor to open a standard text file and save it with HTML tags automatically. To use these add-ins you must first have the editor or word processing software on your computer to which the add-in installs.

HTML document templates

Document templates are similar to add-in extensions but supply less functionality. They provide only a template and some accompanying macros to be used by an existing editor or word processing software package. ANT_HTML, for example, is a template package for MacWord. As with the add-in extensions, you must have the appropriate editor or word processing software to use its template package.

Biting into Stand-alone HTML Editors for Macintosh

Virtually all of the stand-alone HTML editors on the Macintosh provide complete editing and tag insertion assistance. Many even contain their own WYSI-WYG pseudo-browser to show you how your Web screens may look online. Others will start a browser of your choice to display your HTML document.

Several stand-alone editors have been available for quite awhile and a few have popped out recently like cactus flowers after a thunderstorm. All of the stand-alone HTML authoring packages reviewed below are highly functional and will provide assistance to you in your Web page creation, if you follow their instructions and understand their limitations.

At the time this book was written, most of the software below could be obtained from:

    ftp://ftp.uwtc.washington.edu/pub/Mac/Network/WWW ■

HTML Editor

Type:

HTML Editor is a stand-alone, error-checking, semi-WYSIWYG editor. (See Figure 24-1.)

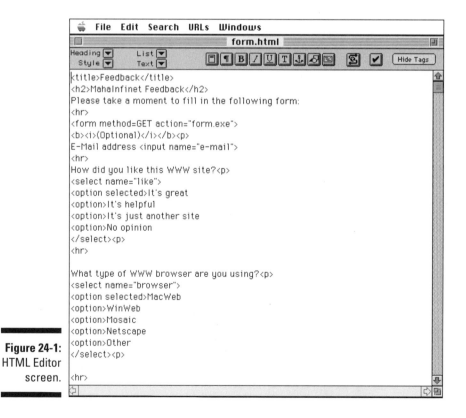

Figure 24-1:
HTML Editor
screen.

HTML Editor's claims to fame:

- ✔ Combines a plain text editor with a WYSIWYG viewer.
- ✔ Tags appear in light gray on color screens.
- ✔ Text is shown in the proper format for the tag being used.
- ✔ View text without the tags using the Hide Tags button.

Pros:

- ✔ Opens any size file.
- ✔ Contains editable palette of user tags.
- ✔ Opens existing HTML files and recognizes most tags when in "auto style" mode.
- ✔ Unrecognized tags are shown as text but do not cause problems.
- ✔ Converts UNIX and DOS text files to Macintosh text.
- ✔ Contains online documentation.

Cons:

- ✔ Does not allow printing (supposed to be added in later version).
- ✔ No built-in tags for <HTML>, <HEAD>, or <BODY>.

Evaluation:

HTML Editor by Rick Giles is written in Prograph. It is a very well designed package. It's a good choice to start with.

Availability:

 Shareware. Pay $25 registration fee to Rick Giles, Box 207, Acadia University, Wolfville, N. S., B0P 1X0, CANADA. Contact him at: rick.giles@acadiau.ca or Phone (902)542-2201 x 1269. Available online from:

```
http://dragon.acadiau.ca /~giles/HTML_Editor/Documentation.html ▓
```

HTML.edit version 1.5 (beta 1)

Type:

HTML.edit is a stand-alone, checked, semi-WYSIWYG editor.

HTML.edit's claims to fame:

✔ Performs substantial HTML structural error checking.

✔ The Add All Structural Tags command adds all structural elements and checks for duplicates and correct placement.

✔ Remembers the full path name to an exported document, so you can update the entire contents of your server with a single command from the Index card.

✔ Index HTML command returns a list of instances of a specific HTML tag within your document.

Pros:

✔ You can also set the target location by using a document label associated with specific project folder.

✔ The Editor Window is now sizable up to 640 by 824 pixels.

✔ Supports both WWW browser Preview and HTML source viewing (set your browser's "View Source" editor to HTML.edit).

✔ The Index card has been substantially improved with a cleaner interface and new document management features including sorting and labeling.

Cons:

✔ No serious negatives in version 1.5.

Evaluation:

HTML.edit v1.5 is a very well constructed HTML editing system. Murray has greatly improved this version. Definitely download it and see if you like it.

Availability:

HTML.edit is a freeware application by Murray M. Altheim of Equinox Development. It is written in HyperCard but does not require HyperCard to run. Contact Murray at: murray.altheim@hq.nasa.gov. Download the program from:

`http://nctn.oact.hq.nasa.gov/tools/HTMLedit/HTMLedit.html` ▪

HTML Grinder

Type:

HTML Grinder is a stand-alone, unchecked, text-only editor and Web page handler.

HTML Grinder's claims to fame:

✔ HTML Grinder does batch processing of HTML text files.

✔ It has functions that find and replace chunks of text in several files simultaneously.

Pros:

✔ Expandable with plug-ins called wheels. (Cost of wheels varies.)

✔ Creates index lists.

✔ Makes expandable lists.

✔ Creates sequential links in files.

Cons:

✔ Must add commercial "wheels" for full functionality.

Evaluation:

HTML Grinder is free with the fully functioning Find and Replace wheel and several demo wheels. Other wheels must be purchased from Matterform Media for varying costs. Michael Herrick of MatterForm Media created it and continues to improve it. Try the free version if you need to move your Web from one site to another.

Availability:

Free version from MatterForm Media, 1270 Calle de Comercio # 3, Santa Fe, NM 87505-3108 Phone 505-438-0505. Commercial version is $65. Download from:

```
http://www.matterform.com/mf/grinder/htmlgrinder.html ▪
```

Arachnid

Type:

Arachnid is a stand-alone, checked, WYSIWYG HTML environment. (See Figure 24-2.)

Figure 24-2:
Arachnid tool palette screen.

The entire Arachnid Tool palette

Arachnid's Claims to fame:

- ✔ Page layout includes in-line GIFs and rulers.
- ✔ Offers a full suite of drawing tools for creating the interactive objects.
- ✔ Automatically links multipage Webs.
- ✔ Drag and drop linking to pages, URLs, or multimedia.
- ✔ An Arachnid project consists of an unlimited number of pages.
- ✔ Any number of pages can be open at once for editing. Multiple projects can even be open at the same time.
- ✔ Any number of objects on a particular page can be selected and copied to any other page, including pages in other projects.

Pros:

- ✔ Forms support includes eight tools for drawing interactive objects directly on the screen.
- ✔ URLs are added to a database with each labeled with a name that you provide.

Cons:

- ✔ No apparent negatives. (Seems too good to be free.)

Evaluation:

Arachnid is the first Macintosh application that offers a true graphical layout environment for building Internet home pages. No "Post Export" text editing is necessary on the contents of the HTML files. No Helper applications are needed to test the behavior of the interactive links within the pages. Since Arachnid was just released (March 1995), its future is uncertain but it appears to be the rising star of Mac HTML authoring tools. Download it and see for yourself.

Availability:

Arachnid is free from the Second Look group at the University of Iowa. Second Look Computing, Weeg Computing Center, University of Iowa, Iowa City, Iowa, 52242. Download it from:

```
http://sec-look.uiowa.edu/
```

HoTMetaL

Type:

HoTMetaL is a stand-alone, error-checking, semi-WYSIWYG editor with strict rules for HTML 2.0 only.

HoTMetaL's claims to fame:

- Requires you to conform to HTML 2.0 standards.
- Contains a comprehensive list of HTML 2.0 compliant tags for insertion.
- Semi-WYSIWYG display shows some formatting along with its own version of tags.
- The commercial version sets up HTML tables and includes a spell checker and a thesaurus.

Pros:

- Comprehensive and correct to the max.
- Highly-structured HTML editing environment.
- Complete list of character entities for easy insertion.
- It always creates valid HTML 2.0 documents.

Cons:

- Requires 6 meg of RAM to run.
- Uses HTML 2.0 conforming tags only.

✔ Fails to open some HTML files with tags not conforming to HTML 2.0 standards.

✔ Allows little or no flexibility in tag placement.

✔ Difficult to learn.

✔ Semi-WYSIWYG display is confusing to many users.

✔ No online help.

Evaluation:

HoTMetaL does not use any extensions to HTML recognized by the newer browsers (Netscape, Mosaic, and others). It forces you to use its rigid structure. It's an obvious port from its UNIX origin and doesn't have a standard Mac interface. It may be just the tool you want to try for building extremely complex webs with hundreds of pages, but it may be daunting to a neophyte building a simple home page.

Availability:

The freeware version of HoTMetaL is available at:

```
http://www.sq.com ▦
```

The commercial version is $195 from SoftQuad Inc., 56 Aberfoyle Crescent, Toronto, Ontario, Canada. M8X 2W4. Phone 1 (416) 239-4801, fax 1 (416) 239-7105. E-mail: hotmetal@sq.com.

HTML Pro 1.06

Type:

HTML Pro is a stand-alone, semi-WYSIWYG/plain text, checked editor.

HTML Pro's claims to fame:

✔ Combines WYSIWYG HTML display with a separate view of the actual HTML tagged text.

Pros:

✔ It is small and fast.

✔ Provides easy selection of tags for insertion.

Cons:

🗸 Doesn't show inline images.

🗸 Only opens one document at a time.

🗸 Has a 32K file size limit.

Evaluation:

HTML Pro is a pretty good HTML editor. It still needs some work before it arrives at the final release level.

Availability:

Freeware from Niklas Frykholm, Rothoffsv. 37 A, S-903 42 UmeÂ, Sweden. Phone: +46 (0)90-13 50 13. E-mail: nisfrm95@student.umu.se. Download from:

```
http://www.ts.umu.se/~r2d2/
ftp://ftp.uwtc.washington.edu/pub/Mac/Network/WWW/HTML+1.0b1.sit.bin
```

HTML Web Weaver version 2.5 (used to be HTML SuperText)

Type:

HTML Web Weaver is a stand-alone, plain text, unchecked editor.

HTML Web Weaver's claims to fame:

It makes interesting use of color and fonts to show the effect of various codes.

Pros:

🗸 Easily customized.

🗸 Provides an easy method of previewing your document.

🗸 Provides extensive online help.

🗸 Includes a large library of HTML features and options.

Cons:

No known serious drawbacks.

Evaluation:

HTML Web Weaver provides you with a simple yet flexible interface. It is designed to be very modular, allowing easy addition of new functions (specifically HTML tags) using a simple "plug-in and play" interface. It's worth downloading for a tryout.

Availability:

Freeware from Robert C. Best III, 118 Leroy St. Apt. N2, Potsdam, NY 13676. Phone (315) 265-0930. E-mail: Robert.Best@potsdam.edu. The latest version is available from:

```
http://www.potsdam.edu/Web.Weaver/About.html
```

Simple HTML Editor (SHE) version 2.9

Type:

Simple HTML Editor is a HyperCard stack-based plain-text, unchecked editor.

Simple HTML Editor's claims to fame:

- ✔ Has simple user interface.
- ✔ Provides intelligent forms creation.
- ✔ Supports most Netscape-enhanced HTML tags.
- ✔ Offers point-and-click insertion of special characters.
- ✔ Uses the S H E droplet, an AppleScript droplet facilitating the opening of text files with S H E via drag and drop. (requires AppleScript extensions)
- ✔ Includes a graphical description of the palette options.

Pros:

- ✔ Offers preview and open URL capabilities. (requires the MacWeb browser)
- ✔ Supports headers and footers.

✔ Contains user palette for often used commands.

✔ Has many command key options.

✔ Provides Find, Find Again, and Find/Change functions.

✔ Uses default HTML template upon the creation of a new document.

✔ Offers extensive Balloon Help™.

Cons:

✔ Has 30K file size limit.

✔ Truncates imported files at 30K with no warning.

✔ Requires HyperCard or HyperCard Player.

Evaluation:

The author continues to update SHE with new features while keeping it as simple to use as possible. For a HyperCard stack, it's a good HTML editor but not a complete authoring tool.

Availability:

Freeware by Eric Morgan, Systems Librarian, NCSU Libraries, Box 7111, Room 2316-b, Raleigh, NC 27695-7111. Phone (919) 515-6182. E-mail: eric_morgan@ncsu.edu. Download from:

```
ftp://ftp.lib.ncsu.edu/pub/software/mac/simple-html-editor.hqx
ftp://dewey.lib.ncsu.edu/pub/software/mac/simple-http-editor.hqx
http://www.lib.ncsu.edu/staff/morgan/simple.html ■
```

Tackling Text Editor Extensions and Templates

If you use BBEdit, two excellent sets of add-ins for HTML editing are available. They are BBEdit HTML Extensions by Carles Bellver and BBEdit HTML Tools by Lindsay Davies. They will be discussed together here since they are so similar in form and function.

Using either of these add-ins with BBEdit or BBEditLite will give you access to most, if not all of the HTML authoring functions you will probably need for most Web pages. Since you may already use BBEdit or BBEditLite, you will be able to get going very quickly with these add-ins. It won't take you much time to try one of these and see if you like it.

BBEditLite

BBEditLite, the shareware version of BBEdit, is available at:

```
ftp://ftp.uwtc.washington.edu/pub/Mac/Text/   ■
```

BBEdit HTML Extensions and BBEdit HTML Tools

Type:

The BBEdit HTML Extensions and BBEdit HTML Tools are both add-ins for either BBEdit or BBEditLite. (See Figure 25-3.)

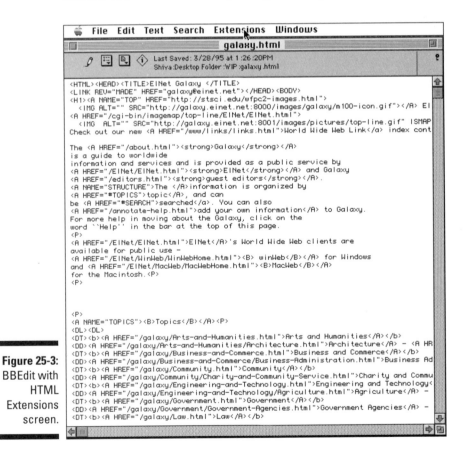

Figure 25-3:
BBEdit with
HTML
Extensions
screen.

BBEdit HTML Extensions and BBEdit HTML Tools claims to fame:

- ✔ User interface is familiar.
- ✔ Provides fast HTML document production to BBEdit users.

Pros:

- ✔ Provides menus of HTML tags and entities for selection.

Cons:

- ✔ Must have BBEdit or BBEditLite to function.

Evaluation:

Both packages are well designed and function well. The authors are continually striving to update their packages. If you already use BBEdit, download one and try it. If it doesn't have features you need, try the other. The Davies' extensions include balloon help.

Availability:

Freeware. BBEdit HTML Extensions by Carles Bellver bellverc@si.uji.es Universitat Jaume I, Spain. Available from:

```
http://www.uji.es/bbedit-html-extensions.html
```

Freeware. BBEdit HTML Tools by Lindsay Davies. E-mail: LD11@unix.york.ac.uk. Available from:

```
http://ctipsych.york.ac.uk/WWW/BBEditTools.html
```

ANT_HTML

ANT_HTML is Jill Swift's Word for the Macintosh template that converts Word documents into HTML documents in a WYSIWYG environment. Also available is the ANT_PLUS utility, which converts HTML files to WYSIWYG, ASCII, RTF, or any other format possible in Word. ANT_HTML has been available for Windows for years and was scheduled for release on the Macintosh in early 1995. Contact jswift@freenet.fsu.edu for more information.

Magnificent Miscellaneous Mac Tools

Numerous tools for assisting you to create maps, forms, cgi applications, and more are readily available for your Macintosh. An extensive list of these tools is provided at the following site:

http://www.uwtc.washington.edu/Computing/WWW/Macintosh.html ▪

Web Server Primer

Here's a brief look at the Macintosh Web server software and where you can find more information. Again, the CERN site is the place to start:

http://info.cern.ch/hypertext/WWW/Daemon/Overview.html ▪

A W3 server is a daemon program constantly running a computer that responds to an incoming TCP connection and provides a service to the caller. There are many varieties of W3 server software to serve different forms of data.

MacHTTP Web server

MacHTTP by Chuck Shotton of BIAP Systems, is a fast, full-featured HTTP server. It runs on the Macintosh OS without requiring UNIX. Available from:

http://www.biap.com/ or E-mail: cshotton@oac.hsc.uth.tmc.edu

MacHTTP 3.0 will be marketed by StarNine Technologies as the products WebSTAR and WebSTAR Pro (see WebSTAR below):

http://www.starnine.com/webstar.html ▪

WebSTAR

WebSTAR along with WebSTAR Pro and a multiserver package named OmniSTAR are newly announced products from StarNine Technologies. Web-STAR and WebSTAR Pro are new versions of MacHTTP 3.0. The Pro version adds secure transactions (using SSL) and support for online purchases using First Virtual. For more information, link to:

http://www.starnine.com/ ▪

Netwings

NetWings is a full-featured HTTP server for Macintosh built on the 4D database system. It is scheduled for release in early 1995 by NetWings Corp.

httpd4Mac

httpd4Mac is a free, minimal functionality, http server by Bill Melotti (E-mail: bill.melotti@rl.ac.uk). The server runs as a background application and has been tested under System 7.1. Download it from:

```
ftp://ftp.uwtc.washington.edu/pub/Mac/Network/WWW/httpd4Mac1.2a.sit.bin
```

Isn't your head about to explode with all of this information? Congratulations, you must be *really* stuck on the Web. Grab one of these editors and get cracking on your own super Web, or dive into a server, and see what it can do.

Chapter 25

Webbing Up Windows

· ·

· ·

*N*umerous HTML authoring tools for Windows are available for downloading from numerous sites. Most of these tools are freeware or shareware but even so they are generally useful for beginning to advanced HTML authors.

Because of their low cost/no cost status, these tools aren't supported as well as commercial products would be. But then, they don't cost you much, either. Thankfully, these tools are usually easy to learn because they use familiar word processing or text editor models, and behave like software tools most of us are already used to.

Surveying the Field of HTML Software Tools

In the subsections that follow, you'll encounter the various kinds of software tools that are available to help you create Web pages. These tools vary in their scope and ability but all of them can provide you with some "automagic" HTML help.

Some of these tools are stand-alone programs that understand HTML editing quite well and can even stop you from making syntax or placement mistakes. Some of these tools extend the functionality of existing word processors, giving them the intelligence to help you build HTML outright, or to convert documents between their normal formats and HTML. Still others provide predefined page layouts, called templates, that you can simply fill in to build HTML documents of your own.

Whatever kind of tools you choose to investigate, however, it's reasonable to expect a tool to make your job easier, not harder. It's also reasonable to expect a tool dedicated to creating HTML documents to provide online help and complex tag insertion that you might otherwise have to do by hand. While you're investigating these tools, you might want to ask yourself the question: "Does this make writing HTML any easier, or not?" If not, our advice is: Keep moving, and leave that tool behind!

 You can find the most up-to-date information on Windows HTML tools at Gabriel's HTML Editors List:

    http://werple.mira.net.au/%7Egabriel/web/html/editors/indexold.html ■

Stand-alone HTML tools

The stand-alone plain-text HTML editors like HTMLed, HTML Assistant, and HTML Writer are the quickest to learn and the easiest to use. They simply let you type your text and give you buttons or menu options to select tags at appropriate insertion points.

For example, if you select a line of text, and then click the H1 button, the opening <H1> tag is placed at the start of the selection and the closing </H1> is placed at the end. Some of these tools even have ways to help you with your links — hyperlinks, that is — you're still on your own at golf or sausage.

Word processor add-ons

Word Processor Add-On editors, if you can call them "editors," have recently been introduced for Word for Windows and WordPerfect. These add-ons are actually programs that the main word processing program runs, thereby giving it the ability to open, edit, and save HTML-tagged documents.

Some tools of this kind can even convert word processing documents into their HTML-tagged (near)-equivalents automatically. But in order to use one of these add-ons, you must first have a copy of the word processing software to which the add-on program adds on!

HTML document templates

Document Templates are similar to add-on editors but supply less functionality. They provide only a template and some accompanying macros to be used by an existing software package like Microsoft Word. As with the add-on editors, you need to have a copy of the word processing software to use the templates and macros that depend on its presence.

Looking at Stand-alone HTML Editors for Windows

Stand-alone editors provide complete editing and tag insertion assistance. Some even contain their own WYSIWYG pseudo-browser to show you how your Web screens should look.

As we're writing this chapter, new stand-alone editors are popping up almost daily. It seems like everyone is trying to produce a better mousetrap for Windows-based HTML authoring tools. Some of them appear to be well-constructed and low on bugs, but we've decided to cover the cheesy, buggy ones instead (just kidding!) — we've included only the best ones that we could find in our discussions.

HTMLed version 1.2

Type:

HTMLed is a stand-alone, plain-text, unchecked editor. (See Figure 25-1.)

HTMLed's claims to fame:

- ✔ Uses floating toolbars for commonly used tags, extended characters, and your own custom tags.

- ✔ The intelligent tag insert function inserts tags in or around lines containing a specified text string

- ✔ Saves documents as DOS HTML, UNIX HTML, or plain text without HTML tags.

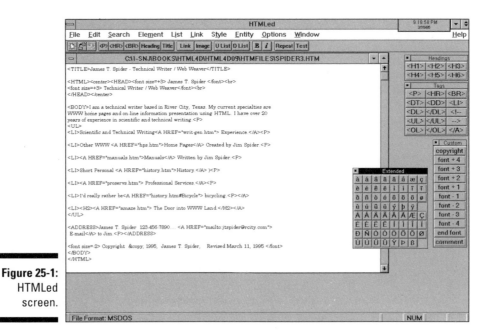

Figure 25-1:
HTMLed
screen.

Pros:

✔ HTMLed is small, runs fast, and includes well designed toolbars and buttons.

✔ Provides automatic list markup of selected text.

✔ Includes good link creation assistance.

✔ Can save files as reusable templates.

✔ Opens multiple files in cascaded windows with cut and paste capability between windows.

✔ Launches your favorite browser to test HTML documents.

Cons:

✔ No online help.

✔ No manual and only a small readme file.

✔ No forms creation support.

✔ Limited to 30K maximum file size.

Evaluation:

HTMLed is a capable plain-text HTML editor. Use it to create small Web pages with file sizes of less than 30K, sans forms, and it will serve you well. Compare it to HTML Assistant and HTML Writer.

Availability:

Shareware. Send registration fee of $39 to Internet Software Technologies, P.O. Box 756, Sackville, N.B., Canada, E0A 3C0. Phone (506) 364-8088. E-mail to: inettc@nbnet.nb.ca. Download from:

```
ftp:pringle.mta.ca/pub/HTMLed ■
```

HTML Assistant version 1.4

Type:

HTML Assistant is a stand-alone, plain-text, unchecked editor. (See Figure 25-2.)

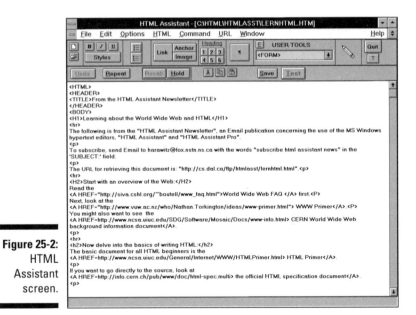

Figure 25-2: HTML Assistant screen.

HTML Assistant's claims to fame:

- ✔ Converts menu items from the MOSAIC.INI file to an HTML file (jump page).
- ✔ Uses a well-designed toolbar with a configurable pull-down menu for additional tags.
- ✔ Contains functions available to replace hard carriage returns with either breaks or paragraph tags.

Pros:

- ✔ File loading, scrolling, and general program operation are very fast.
- ✔ Link, anchor, and image builder functions via dialog boxes include options for alternate text and image alignment.
- ✔ Provides for automatic list markups.
- ✔ Very good online help system includes an introduction to HTML creation.

Cons:

- ✔ Not possible to add compound tags to the custom menu.
- ✔ Will not import or create files larger than 32K.
- ✔ No forms support.
- ✔ Toolbar is text based instead of GUI-based.
- ✔ Must purchase commercial version to get UNIX file format support.

Evaluation:

HTML Assistant is another capable plain-text HTML editor. Use it to create small Web pages with file size less than 32K and no forms and it will serve you well. Compared to HTMLed and HTML Writer, it isn't quite as full-featured unless you buy the Pro version.

Availability:

Freeware from Brooklyn North Software Works, Bedford, Nova Scotia, Canada. Author is H. Harawitz. E-mail to harawitz@fox.nstn.ns.ca or phone (902) 835-2600. Download from:

```
ftp:\\ftp.cs.dal.ca/htmlasst/  ▪
```

HTML Assistant Pro version 1.5

The Pro version contains the same features as the freeware version plus these:

- ✔ Function to strip HTML tags and save file as DOS or UNIX text only.
- ✔ Function to extract all URLs and their linked text to create lists of URLs for other Web pages.
- ✔ Saves files in UNIX format.

Evaluation:

Well-constructed and full-featured for a stand-alone, plain-text HTML editor. Unique for its URL extraction and listing capabilities, but not significantly different from HTMLed or HTML Writer in functionality.

Availability:

HTML Assistant Pro costs $99.95 from Brooklyn North Software Works, Bedford, Nova Scotia, Canada. Author is H. Harawitz. E-mail to harawitz@fox.nstn.ns.ca or phone (902) 835-2600.

HTML Writer version 0.9 beta 4a

Type:

HTML Writer is a stand-alone, plain-text, unchecked editor. (See Figure 25-3.)

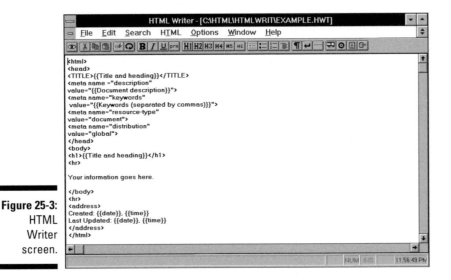

Figure 25-3:
HTML
Writer
screen.

HTML Writer's claims to fame:

- The icon-laden toolbar uses Windows' new "description function" when you move the cursor onto any button (this is a good reminder for what all those buttons are for).
- The display features a status line at the bottom that shows an example of the tag or the function when the cursor is on a particular button.
- Forms creation is elegantly supported.
- Has a remove code feature by selected block or entire document.
- Imports and creates files larger than 32K.

Pros:

- Very well designed and easy to use.
- The URL builder steps you smoothly through creating a URL to images or hyperlinks.
- Test your HTTP documents via Netscape, Cello, or Mosaic.
- Good online help.

Cons:

- Limited toolbar with no option to add new tags.

Evaluation:

This well-designed plain-text editor may be a good choice for first-time users, if you can't really remember which tags are used where. It's definitely worth a try to see if you like it better than HTMLed or HTML Assistant.

Availability:

Shareware. $10 donation suggested but not required by Kris Nosack, 376 North Main Street, Orem, Utah, U.S.A. 84057. E-mail to: html-writer@byu.edu. Download from:

```
http://lal.cs.byu.edu/people/nosack/ ∎
```

HoTMetaL

Type:

HoTMetaL is a stand-alone, error-checking, semi-WYSIWYG editor with strict rules for HTML 2.0 only. (See Figure 25-4.)

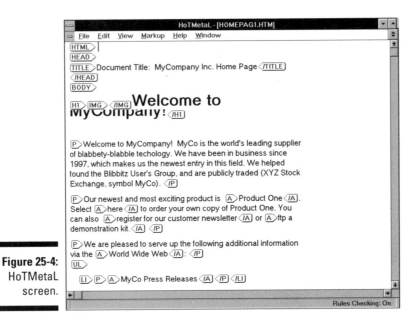

Figure 25-4:
HoTMetaL
screen.

HoTMetaL's claims to fame:

- ✔ Requires you to conform to HTML 2.0 standards.

- ✔ Contains a comprehensive list of HTML 2.0 compliant tags for insertion.

- ✔ Semi-WYSIWYG display shows some formatting along with its own version of tags.

- ✔ The commercial version sets up HTML tables and includes a spell checker and a thesaurus.

Pros:

- ✔ Comprehensive and correct to the max.

- ✔ Highly-structured HTML editing environment.

- ✔ Complete list of character entities for easy insertion.

- ✔ It always creates valid HTML 2.0 documents.

Cons:

- ✔ Requires 6 meg of RAM to run.

- ✔ Uses HTML 2.0 conforming tags only.

- ✔ No toolbar.

✔ Fails to open some HTML files with tags not conforming to HTML 2.0 standards.

✔ Allows little or no flexibility in tag placement.

✔ Difficult to learn.

✔ Semi-WYSIWYG display is confusing to many users.

✔ No online help.

Evaluation:

HoTMetaL does not use any extensions to HTML recognized by the newer browsers (Netscape, Mosaic, and others). It forces you to use its rigid structure. It may be just the tool you want to try for building extremely complex webs with hundreds of pages, but it may be daunting to a neophyte building a simple home page.

Availability:

Freeware version is available at:

```
http://www.sq.com
ftp.NCSA.uiuc.edu/Web/html/hotmetal/Windows
```

The commercial version is $195 from SoftQuad Inc., 56 Aberfoyle Crescent, Toronto, Ontario, Canada. M8X 2W4. Phone: +1 (416) 239-4801, fax: +1 (416) 239-7105. E-mail: hotmetal@sq.com.

Web Wizard: The Duke of URL

Type:

Web Wizard is a stand-alone Windows home page creation application with versions for both 16 and 32-bit Windows. Version 1.0 was released in March 1995. (See Figure 25-5.)

Web Wizard's claims to fame:

✔ Fast and easy completion of simple pages.

✔ Produce a home page without knowing what HTML stands for.

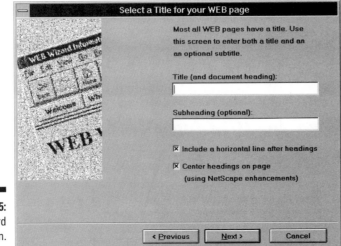

Most all WEB pages have a title. Use
this screen to enter both a title and an
an optional subtitle.

Title (and document heading):

Subheading (optional):

☒ Include a horizontal line after headings

☒ Center headings on page
(using NetScape enhancements)

Figure 25-5:
Web Wizard
screen.

Pros:

✔ Step-by-step dialog boxes lead you through the process.

✔ No muss, No fuss, No tags.

✔ Will include a single image and two links in the page.

Cons:

✔ Makes only one, very simple page.

✔ Only two choices for formatting: exclude or include two ruler lines.

✔ Version 1.0 didn't save the file in the expected place.

✔ Version 1.0 tried to copy an image file onto itself and created a 0 byte
file, erasing the original.

Evaluation:

More of a toy than a tool at this time. Don't bother with it unless it's been
significantly improved and debugged by the time you read this.

Availability:

Free from David P. Geller, ARTA Software Group, 15520 Mill Creek Blvd., Suite H201, Mill Creek, WA 98012. fax (206) 337-2756 E-mail: davidg@halcyon.com. Download from:

```
http://www.halcyon.com/webwizard/welcome.html
```

MS Word for Windows HTML add-on editors

We're making a distinction between Microsoft's own Internet Assistant and the template/macro packages for Word for Windows. Perhaps it's an artificial distinction, but it should help you tell things apart!

The Internet Assistant is a set of library files (.dll) and some template files (.dot) that install into the WinWord screens and menus. Some of the template/ macro packages work in a similar fashion but are not typically as well-integrated into Word. Perhaps that should be future tense, since the beta version of Word IA currently available needs more work before it is ready for prime time.

Microsoft Word Internet Assistant

Type:

Word Internet Assistant is an add-on set of .dlls and templates for Microsoft Word for Windows 6.0a and up. It lets WinWord users create HTML directly in a WYSIWYG, unchecked environment. You can also browse the Web with it, if you don't have any other browsers. (See Figure 25-6.)

Word IA's claims to fame:

- ✔ Familiar WinWord menu and toolbar contains new choices to create HTML tags.
- ✔ Saves document as an HTML file or a WinWord document.

Pros:

- ✔ Saves any size WinWord document with complete set of standard HTML tags.

Figure 25-6:
Word for
Windows
Internet
Assistant
screen.

Cons:

✔ Not possible to view the document and modify the tags directly.

✔ No good direct tag insertion features.

✔ Very slow to load and operate, even on a 486-66 with 16 meg RAM.

✔ WYSIWYG view shows tabs that aren't converted to HTML tags since they aren't available in HTML 2.0.

✔ Browser view recognizes only standard HTML 2.0 tags and shows others as <<Unknown HTML Tag>>.

✔ Still has a few operational idiosyncrasies (bugs) in the beta version.

Evaluation:

If you're a WinWord 6.0a user (or use a newer version of the package), download Word IA, install it, and have fun converting your text files directly to HTML with the SAVE AS command.

But then, after you save a file in the HTML format, close it immediately thereafter. If you then open it as a Text Only formatted document, you can edit all of the HTML tags yourself. It beats trying to use the Word IA formatting method, whatever that is (honest, we tried to figure it out, but we just couldn't make sense of it).

Today, Word IA is not suitable for creating complex HTML documents. No doubt Microsoft will get it right by the final version, but who knows when that will be? Hopefully, the answer — if you're a Word for Windows users — is "before you read this!" Check the Web reference below to find out.

Availability:

Free to owners of Word for Windows 6.0a and up since it only runs on this platform. Currently in unsupported beta version from Microsoft Corporation, One Microsoft Way, Redmond, WA 98052. Support phone: (206) 462-WORD. Or look online:

`http://www.microsoft.com/pages/deskapps/word/ia/default.htm` ■

Templates and macros

These products are generally sets of library files, macros, and template files that install into the WinWord screens and menus. Some are more tightly integrated into WinWord than others. Most have been created by frustrated WinWord users who wanted an easier way to create HTML documents. Some, such as the CU_HTML.DOT, have been around awhile and are quite good.

ANT_HTML.DOT is a WinWord 6.0 template. Jill Smith created it to help her create HTML documents but won't say what "ANT" stands for. Download it from:

`ftp://ftp.einet.net/einet/pc/ANT_HTML.ZIP`

MS Word for Windows Macros, gt_html.zip, is a set of macros that add HTML editing assistance to Word for Windows. This can be downloaded from Georgia Tech (GT):

`http://www.gatech.edu/word_html/release.htm` ■

CU_HTML.DOT is perhaps the best document template for Word for Windows 2.0 and 6.0. It can display inline GIFs inside the document, and let you insert hyperlinks and tags. Download it from Chinese University of Hong Kong (CU):

`http://www.cuhk.hk/csc/cu_html/cu_html.htm` ■

Filters and file converters

Automatically converting existing text documents into HTML is supported by several of the stand-alone and add-on editors. If you use Word for Windows with the Word IA add-on, simply save the file in HTML format via the Save As command and it's converted. Most of the text formatting that really counts, including headings, is converted but tabs are lost since HTML 2.0 doesn't recognize a tag for tabbing.

The soon-to-be-released WordPerfect HTML add-on reportedly has a similar feature. The stand-alone editors will import text files and save them as HTML files but some only support relatively small ASCII text files.

There are many converters available for other text formats. You should be able to find one that suits your needs at one of these sites:

```
http://info.cern.ch/hypertext/WWW/Tools/Filters.html
http://oneworld.wa.com/htmldev/devpage/dev-page.html
http://www.utirc.utoronto.ca/HTMLdocs/intro_tools.html
http://union.ncsa.uiuc.edu/HyperNews/get/www/html/converters.html
http://www.ncsa.uiuc.edu/SDG/Software/Mosaic/Docs/
faq-software.html#editors ▨
```

KISS: plain text editors

No doubt we will all be using WYSIWYG editors in the relatively near future. But for the time being, you'll need to fire up your trusty browser to get a true user's eye view. Especially while you're learning HTML, use a plain text editor so you can work directly with the HTML tags. HTML Assistant, HTMLed, and HTML Writer do this very well. Take a little time and try them all. They're free for the downloading.

Web Server Primer

A brief look at the Web server software and where you can find more information. A W3 server is a program on the Web Server computer that responds to an incoming TCP connection and provides a service to the caller. There are many varieties of W3 server software to serve different forms of data.

The CERN site at the following URL is the place to look first:

```
http://info.cern.ch/hypertext/WWW/Daemon/Overview.html ▨
```

Windows Web servers

If you are determined to setup your own Web server, here are a few suggestions on possible Windows based servers:

✔ Windows httpd 1.4 — a Windows server by Robert Denny.

✔ HTTPS for Windows/NT — httpd service for NT; configurable using control panel.

Netsite — Commercially supported Windows NT servers from Netscape Communications Corp., 501 East Middlefield Rd., Mountain View, CA 94043 Administrative Contact: William Foss (415) 528-2604 E-mail to: bill@NETSCAPE.COM or visit:

```
http://home.netscape.com/MCOM/products_docs/server.html
```

SerWeb — SerWeb is a WWW server for the Windows 3.1 system.

WebWorks Server from Quadralay Corporation, 8920 Business Park Drive, Austin, Texas 78759. Phone: (512) 346-9199 or Fax: (512) 346-8990. E-mail: info@quadralay.com. Obtain information from:

```
FTP Server: ftp.quadralay.com
WWW Server: http://www.quadralay.com/products/WebWorks/Server/index.html
```

You sure are a glutton for information if you've read this far! Congratulations, you must be *really* stuck on the Web. Grab one of these editors and get cracking on your own super Web or pick up a server and see what it can do.

Part IX
The Part of Tens

The 5th Wave   By Rich Tennant

PORTRAIT OF A CYBERHOLIC

SO, HOW'S DAD?

CYBERHOLICS DON'T WRITE LETTERS. IF YOU DON'T HAVE A MODEM THEY DON'T WANT TO TALK TO YOU.

In This Part...

Here are some *lists of ten* designed to add to your
HTML experience. The chapters that follow will
explore some important do's and don'ts for HTML. We'll
also remind you of the most important considerations for
good page design, for testing your work, and for making
the sometimes difficult "build-versus-buy" decision when it
comes to choosing a Web server.

We'd like you to think of these final chapters as a way of
reviewing what you've already learned, and a way of
reminding you of what's really important. Along the way,
expect to find our tongues firmly planted in your cheeks —
if you can't get a laugh out of what we hope by now is
familiar territory, maybe you can get a laugh out of the
incongruous juxtaposition of strange and wonderful ideas!

Chapter 26

The Top Ten HTML Do's and Don'ts

*B*y itself, HTML is neither excessively complex nor overwhelmingly diffi-cult. As better wags than we have put it: "This ain't rocket science!" Nevertheless, it's good to have a set of guidelines to help you make the most out of HTML, without stepping away from your need to communicate effectively with your users.

This chapter will attempt to underscore some of the fundamental points we've made throughout this book regarding proper and improper use of HTML. Hopefully, you'll adhere to the prescriptions and avoid the maledic-tions. But hey, they're your pages and you can do what you want with them. The users will decide the ultimate outcome! (Just don't make us say, "We *told* you so!")

Remember Your Content!

Darrell Royal, the legendary coach of the University of Texas Longhorn football team in the 60s and 70s is rumored to have said to his players: "Dance with who brung ya." In normal English, we think this means that you should stick to the people who've supported you all along and give your loyalty to those who've given it to you.

We're not sure what this means for football, but for Web pages it means keeping the content paramount. If you don't have strong, solid, informative content, the users will quickly realize that your Web pages are relatively content-free. Then they'll be off elsewhere on the Web looking for the content your pages may have lacked.

The short statement of this principle for HTML is "Tags are important, but what's between and around the tags — the content — is what really counts." Make your content the very best it can possibly be!

Structuring Your Documents

Providing users with a clear roadmap and guiding them through your content is as important for a home page as it is for an online encyclopedia. But the longer or more complex the document, the more important a road map becomes.

We're strong advocates of top-down page design. You should start the construction of any HTML document or collection of documents with a paper and pencil (or whatever modeling tool you like best). Sketch out the relationships within the content and the relationships among your pages. Don't start writing content or placing tags until you understand what you want to say and how you want to organize your materials.

Good content flows from good organization. It will help you stay on track during page design, testing, delivery, and maintenance. It will help your users find their way through your site. Need we say more?

Keeping Track of Tags

While you're building documents, it's often easy to forget to use closing tags where they're required (for example, the </A> that closes the opening anchor tag <A>). Even when you're testing your pages, some browsers can be so forgiving that they'll compensate for your lack of correctness, leading you into possible problems from other browsers that aren't quite so understanding (or lax, as the case might be).

There are lots of things to say on this subject, so we'll try to stick to the ones that count:

✔ Keep track yourself while you're writing or editing HTML. If you open an anchor, or text area, or whatever, go back through and find the closing tag for each opening one.

✔ Use a syntax-checker to validate your work as part of the testing process. These are mindless, automatic tools that will find missing tags for you and also find other ways to drive you crazy along the way!

Here's a URL that's a jump page for HTML validation tools:

```
http://www.charm.net/~web/Vlib/Providers/Validation.html
```

✔ Try to obtain and use as many browsers as you possibly can when testing your pages. This will not only alert you to the "missing tag" problem; it will also point out potential design flaws and remind you of the importance of providing ALTernate text for users with nongraphical browsers.

✔ Always follow the rules of HTML document syntax and layout. Just because most browsers don't require the use of structure tags like <HTML>, <HEAD>, and <BODY> doesn't mean it's OK to leave them out; it just means they don't care if you break the rules. Your users may and we certainly don't want you writing any improperly-structured HTML, either! ▪

Although HTML isn't exactly a programming language, it still makes sense to treat it like one. Therefore, following formats and syntax will help avoid trouble, and careful testing and rechecking of your work will ensure a high degree of quality and standards compliance.

Making the Most from the Least

More is not always better, especially when it comes to Web pages. Try to design and build your pages using the least amount of ornament and structure that you can, rather than overloading pages with lots of graphics, as many levels of headings as you can fit, and links of every possible description.

Remember that structure exists to highlight the content. The more the structure dominates, the more it takes away from content. Therefore, use structure sparingly, wisely, and as carefully as possible. Anything more will become an obstacle to delivering your content.

Building Attractive Pages

Working within a consistent framework lets users learn how to view and navigate your pages. Making them easy to navigate only adds to their appeal. If you're in need of inspiration, cruise the Web and look for layouts and graphics that work for you. If you take the time to analyze what you like about them, you can work from other people's design principles without having to steal the details of their layout and look.

When designing your Web documents, start with a fundamental layout for your pages. Pick a small but interesting set of graphical symbols or icons and adopt a consistent navigation style. Use graphics sparingly and tune them to be as small as possible (by reducing size, number of colors, shading, etc.), while still retaining their "eye-candy" appeal. It's possible to make your pages both appealing and informative, if you're willing to invest the time and effort to create the right look and feel.

Avoiding Browser Dependencies

When building Web pages, the temptation to view the Web in terms of your favorite browser can prove nearly irresistible. That's why you should always remember that users view the Web in general and your pages in particular, from many different perspectives, through many different browsers.

During the design and writing phase, it's common to ping-pong between the HTML text and a browser's eye-view of that text. At this early point in the process, we recommend switching among a group of browsers, including at least one character-mode browser. This will help balance your viewpoint on your pages and usually helps to maintain a focus on the content as well.

During testing and maintenance it's even more important to browse your pages through as many different viewports as you can. Make sure to work from multiple platforms and to try both graphical and character-mode browsers on each one. This takes time but will repay itself with pages that are easy for everyone to read and follow.

Evolution, Not Revolution

Over time Web pages will change and grow. Keep looking at your work with a fresh eye or keep recruiting fresh eyes from the ranks of those who haven't seen your pages before, to avoid the process of what we call "organic acceptance."

This is best explained by the analogy of your face and the mirror: you see it every day, you know it intimately, so you might not be as sensitive to the impact of change over time as someone else. Then you see yourself on video-tape, or a photograph, or through the eyes of an old friend. At that point, changes obvious to the entire world become obvious to you: "my hairline's really receded," or "I've gone completely gray," or "my spare tire could mount on a semi!"

Just as with the rest of life, changes to your Web pages are evolutionary, not revolutionary. That is, they usually proceed by small daily steps, not big radical ones. Nevertheless, you need to remain sensitive to the supporting infrastructure and readability of your content as things evolve on your pages. Maybe the lack of on-screen links to each section of the Product Catalog didn't matter when you only had three products to deal with; now that you have 25, it's a different story. Over time, structure needs to adapt to follow the content.

This is where user feedback is absolutely crucial. If you don't get feedback through forms and other means of communication, you should go out and aggressively solicit some from your users. "If you don't ask them," the common wisdom goes, "you can't tell how you're doing!"

Navigating Your Wild and Woolly Web

A key ingredient for building quality Web pages is the inclusion of navigational aids. In Chapter 11 we introduced the concept of a "navigation bar" that provides users with a method to avoid or minimize scrolling. By judicious use of intratext links and careful observation of what constitutes a "screenful" of information, use of text anchors makes it easy to move to the "previous" or "next" screens, as well as the "top," "index," and "bottom" of a document.

We don't believe that navigation bars are required or that the names of the controls should always be the same. We do believe that the more control you give users over their reading, the better they'll like it (and the more traffic your Web pages will get). The longer any particular document, the more important such controls become. We find they work best if they occur about every twenty lines in longer documents.

Beating the Two-Dimensional Text Trap

Conditioned by centuries of printed material, and the linear nature of books, our mindsets about hypertext can always use some adjustment. When building your documents, remember that hypermedia should add interest, expand on the content, or make a serious impact on the user. Within these constraints, this kind of material can vastly improve any user's experience of your site.

If you can avoid old-fashioned linear thinking, you may not only succeed in improving your users' experience, you may even make your information more readily available to your audience. That's why we encourage careful consideration of document indexes, cross-references, links to related documents, and other tools to help users navigate within your site. Keep thinking about the impact of links and looking at other people's materials, and you may yet shake free of the linear trap imposed by Gutenberg's great legacy (the printing press)!

Overcoming Inertia Takes Constant Vigilance

Finally, when dealing with your Web materials post-publication, remember that your tendency will be to come to rest regarding future efforts. Maintenance is nowhere near as heroic, inspiring, or remarkable as creation, yet it represents the bulk of activity needed to keep a living document alive and well.

Make maintenance a positive term and look for ways to improve its perception. If you start with something valuable and keep adding value, your materials will appreciate over time. If you start with something valuable and leave it alone, your materials will become stale and lose value. Keeping up with constant change is a hallmark of the Web; ignore this trend with your materials and they'll quickly be ignored.

Chapter 27
Ten Design Desiderata

*W*hen building a Web site, it's always essential to know what it is you're trying to communicate. The content should always remain king. Nevertheless, we'd like to suggest a bevy of design desiderata to consider when assembling the frames and devices for your pages.

Creating Page Layouts

The first thing to decide is a common layout (template) for your Web pages. This means deciding whether to use text links or graphical controls, and it also means setting a style for page headings and footers.

Headings may incorporate text navigation bars or other information you want to make consistent for your users. Footers should include contact information and the original URL for reference, possibly preceded by a horizontal rule.

Some organizations have gone so far as to lay down a border for each page, with the area above the frame used as the header, and the area below as the footer. Whatever layout you choose, make it as attractive as you can (without making it distracting), and use it consistently. This helps to create a welcome feeling of familiarity across your pages that will help users find their way around your site.

Building a Graphical Vocabulary

If you decide to use graphics as navigation links, keep the icons or buttons as small and simple as possible. This reduces transfer time and makes them faster for browsers to render.

Building a small, consistent set of graphical symbols (what we've called a "vocabulary") also improves browser efficiency: Most browsers cache graphics, so that they don't have to be downloaded after the first time they appear. It's much faster to reuse an existing graphic than to reference a new one. That's why we advocate a fairly limited graphics vocabulary as well.

Remember to supply ALT text definitions for these elements when they're referenced. This will keep users with character-mode browsers from being left in the lurch. These graphical elements should be simple enough that a single word, or short phrase, can substitute for them, and still deliver the same meaning and impact.

Using White Space

While content may be king in Web pages, it's still possible to have too much of a good thing. Don't try to limit the amount of scrolling by eliminating headings and paragraph breaks.

White space is the term used by page designers to describe the space on a page that's unoccupied by other things like graphics and type. A certain amount of white space is critical for the human eye. In general, the more complex or convoluted the images or content, the more positive the effect of white space on a page.

Be sure to give your content and images room to breathe by leaving at least 20% of any screen unoccupied. You can build white space into your documents with extra paragraph tags, or by regularly using headings to separate regions of text and graphics. Whatever method you use, be sure to give readers enough room to follow your lead through your pages!

Formatting for Impact

HTML includes a variety of descriptive (<EM>, <STRONG>, <CITE>, etc.) and physical (<I>, <B>, <TT>, etc.) character tags. It also employs larger fonts and text styles to set headings off from ordinary text. Remember when you're using these tools that emphasis and impact are relative terms: In fact, the less often such tags are used, the more impact they have.

Overuse of character-handling, whether descriptive or physical, can blunt the impact of your entire document. Be sure to use such controls judiciously, only where impact is critical.

When trying to decide whether to use a descriptive or physical character tag, be aware that certain browsers may provide wider latitudes in rendering descriptive tags. Physical tags will usually be associated with certain fonts (e.g., a monospaced Courier font is typical for the typewriter tag <TT>). Descriptive tags can be associated with the same characteristics, but they can also be represented through other fonts or text colors, especially for graphical browsers. Thus, it's important to consider whether the rendering or the emphasis is important: if it's the rendering, use a physical style; if it's the emphasis, use a logical one.

Enhancing Content

If a picture is worth a thousand words, are a thousand words worth a picture? When combining text and graphics in Web pages, be sure to emphasize the relationship between the two in the content. Graphics can be especially useful in diagramming complex ideas, in representing physical objects or other tangible phenomena, and in compressing large amounts of content into a small space.

Yet the surrounding text also needs to take cognizance of the graphics, to use it as a point of reference, and to refer back to key elements or components as they're being discussed. This makes labels, captions, and other methods of identifying particular elements on a graphic almost as important as the graphic itself. Careful integration of text and graphics enhances the content of a page.

The same is true for other hypermedia within Web pages. Beyond the novelty of including sounds or music, animation, or video, the content of these other media needs to be integrated with the text to have the greatest impact.

Rather than explaining a leitmotif only in words, it becomes possible to define and then discuss a leitmotif around a musical phrase from a symphony or string quartet. Likewise, discussion of film editing techniques, like dissolves, can be amplified with examples taken from the work of classic directors.

Whatever materials appear in or through your Web pages, they need to be solidly integrated, and to share a common rhetorical focus. This applies as strongly to hypermedia as it does to text, but the possibilities of enhancing content in this way should never be overlooked.

Making Effective Use of Hypermedia

Strong integration of hypermedia with the other content on a page is the most important ingredient for effective use. It's also necessary to understand the potential bottlenecks that some users face.

Effective use of hypermedia, therefore, implies asking your users for "informed consent" before inflicting such materials on them. For graphics, this means preparing thumbnails of larger images, labeling them with size information, and using them as clickable maps to let users request a download of the full-sized image. In other words, the user who decides to pull down a full-color image of "The Last Supper" cannot be dismayed when he or she already knows that it's a 1.2 Mbyte file that may take several minutes to download. By the same token, including such an image right on a Web page may irritate people who were merely looking for information about the picture.

This principle applies equally to sounds, video, and other kinds of hypermedia. Remember to ask for informed consent from your users, and you can be sure that only those individuals who are willing to wait will be subjected to delays in delivery.

Aiding Navigation

By including outlines, tables of contents, indexes, or search engines within your Web documents, you can make it much easier for users to find their way around your materials. So why not do it?

Forming Good Opinions

We think that no Web site is complete without an interactive HTML form to ask users for their feedback. Not only does this give you a chance to see your work from somebody else's perspective, it can be a valuable source of input and ideas for enhancing and improving your content. Just remember: "If you don't ask them, they won't tell you!"

Knowing When to Split

As pages get larger and larger, or as your content shows itself to be more complex than you originally thought, you'll come to a point where a single long document could function better as a collection of smaller ones.

How can you decide when it's time to split things up? By trading off convenience against impatience. A single long document will take longer to download and read than any individual smaller one, but each time an individual document is requested, it may have to be downloaded on the spot. The question then becomes: one long wait, or several short ones?

The answer lies in the content. If your document is something that's touched quickly and then exited immediately, delivering information in small chunks makes sense. The only people who have to pay a delay penalty are those who choose to read through many pages; in-and-outers don't have to pay much at all. If your document is something that's downloaded and then perused in detail, it may make sense to keep large amounts of information within a single document.

By using the materials frequently yourself (make sure to use them over a slow link as well as a fast one), and by asking users for feedback, you should be able to strike the happy medium between these extremes, as soon as one wanders by!

Adding Value for Value

Obtaining feedback from users is incredibly valuable, and makes HTML forms all the more worthwhile. But responding to that feedback in a visible, obvious way can make it as good for them as it should be for you.

It's a good idea to publicly acknowledge feedback that causes change, whether for reasons good or ill. The "What's New" page that links to many home pages (and maybe should on yours, too) is a good place to cover this kind of thing. We also believe in acknowledging strong opinions by e-mail or letter, to let the user know you've heard what they've said, and to thank them for their input.

If you can develop your users as allies and confederates, they'll help you improve and enhance your content. This could lead to improved business, or maybe just improved communications. Either way, by giving and acknowledging values, you've added to the sum total of what the Web delivers to the world!

Chapter 28

Decimating Web Bugs

● ●

In This Chapter

▶ Making a list and checking it twice

▶ Mastering the mechanics of text

▶ Lacking live links leaves loathsome legacies

▶ Looking for trouble in all the right places

▶ Covering all the bases

▶ Tools of the testing trade

▶ Fostering feedback

▶ Making the most of your audience

● ●

*W*hen you've put the finishing touches on a set of pages, it's time to put them through their paces. Testing is a key ingredient for controlling the quality of your content. It should include a thorough content review, a complete check of your HTML syntax and semantics, investigations of every possible link, and a series of sanity checks to make doubly and triply sure that what you've wound up with is what you really wanted to build. Read on for some gems of testing wisdom for ridding your Web pages of bugs, errors, and other undesirable elements.

Making a List and Checking It Twice

Your document design should include a roadmap that specified all of the individual HTML documents in your Web, and the relationships among them. If you're smart, you'll have kept this map up-to-date as you moved from design into implementation (and in our experience, things always change when you go down this path). If you're not smart, don't berate yourself — just go out and update this map now. Be sure to include all intradocument links as well as interdocument ones.

This roadmap can serve as the foundation for a testing plan, wherein you systematically investigate and check every page and every link. You just want to make sure that everything works like you think it does and that what you've built has some relationship, however surprising, to what you designed. This roadmap becomes your list of things to check, and as you go through the testing process, you'll be checking it (at least) twice.

Mastering the Mechanics of Text

By the time any collection of Web pages comes together, you're typically looking at thousands of words, if not significantly more. Yet the number of Web pages that are published without even a cursory spelling check is astonishing. That's why we suggest — no, demand — that you include a spelling check as a step in testing and checking your materials.

You can use your favorite word processor to spell-check your pages. As you check them, you'll be able to add all of the HTML markup to your custom dictionary, and pretty soon, the program will only puke on the URLs and other strange strings that occur from time to time in HTML files. Nevertheless, you should persist and root out all the real typos and misspellings. Your users may not thank you, but they will have a higher opinion of your pages if they don't find them full of errors!

Lacking Live Links Leaves Loathsome Legacies

Nothing is more irritating to users that to see a link to some Web resource on a page that they're just dying to follow, only to get the dread "404 Server not found" error instead. Our admittedly unscientific and random sampling of Web-heads shows us unequivocally that users' impressions of a set of pages is strongly proportional to the number of working links they contain.

The moral of this survey is: Always check your links. This is as true after you've published your pages as it is before they've been subjected to the limelight of public scrutiny. Checking links is as important for page maintenance as it is for testing initial pages for release.

Another hint: Just because a URL has a pointer in it to where the real content is located doesn't mean it's OK to leave the original link alone. If your link-checking shows something like this, do yourself and your users a favor and update the URL to its current location. You'll save them time and lower the number of bogus packets on the Internet, too.

Looking for Trouble in All the Right Places

When it comes time for beta-testing your pages, you want to bring in as rowdy and refractory a crowd to bang on them as you possibly can. If you have customers or colleagues who are picky, opinionated, pushy, or argumentative, be comforted to know that such people make ideal beta testers.

They'll use your pages in ways you never imagined possible. They'll interpret your content to mean things you never intended, in a million years. They'll drive you crazy, and crawl all over your most cherished beliefs and principles.

They'll also find gotchas, big and small, that you never knew were there. They'll catch the typos that the word processors couldn't. They'll tell you things you left out, and things you should have omitted. They'll give you a whole new perspective on your Web pages, and they'll help you to see them from all kinds of extreme points of view.

The results of all this suffering, believe it or not, will be positive. Your pages will emerge clearer, more direct, and more correct than they would have if you'd tried to do all the testing yourself. If you don't believe us, try skipping this step, and see what happens when the real users start banging on your materials!

Covering All the Bases

If you're an individual user with a simple home page, or a collection of facts and figures on your private obsession, this step may not apply. But go ahead and read along anyway — you just might learn something.

If your pages represent the views and content of an organization of some kind, chances are 100% that you'll want to subject your content to some kind of peer and management review before publishing them to the world. In fact, we'd recommend that you build reviews into each step along the way toward building your pages — starting with overall design, to writing copy for each page, to reviewing the final assembly of pages — to avoid hitting any potential stumbling blocks.

It may even be a good idea to build some kind of sign-off process into reviews, so that you can later prove that the materials were reviewed and approved by responsible parties. We hope you don't have to be that formal about publishing your Web pages, but it's far, far better to be safe than sorry. Is this covering the bases, or covering something else? You decide...and take appropriate action.

Tools of the Testing Trade

When you're grinding through your Web pages, checking your links and your HTML, remember that there is automated help available. If you check the validation tools in Chapter 17, you'll be well on your way to finding some computerized assistance in making sure your HTML is as clean and standards-compliant as the freshly-driven snow (do we know how to mix a metaphor, or what?). ▪

Likewise, it's a good idea to investigate the Web spiders covered in Chapter 16, and use them regularly to check the links in your pages. They'll be able to get back to you if something isn't current, so you'll know where to start looking for the real links you need. Remember to make this a regular part of your maintenance routine, while you're at it.

Fostering Feedback

You might not think of user feedback as a form (or consequence) of testing, but it represents some of the best reality checks your Web pages are ever likely to get. That's why it's a good idea to do everything you can — including prizes or other tangible inducements — to get users to fill out HTML forms on your Web site.

That's also why it's an even better idea to read the feedback you do get, and to go out and solicit as much as you can handle (or more). And finally, the best idea of all is to carefully consider the feedback you get, and implement the things that will improve your Web offerings.

Making the Most of Your Audience

Asking for feedback is an important step toward developing a relationship with your users. Even the most finicky and picky of your users can be an incredible asset: who better to pick over your newest pages, and to point out all the small, subtle errors or flaws that they revel in discovering? Working with your users can mean that, over time, some will become more involved in your work and in helping guide the content of your Web pages (if not the rest of your professional or obsessional life). Who could ask for better than that?

Chapter 29

Ten Ways to Decide to "Build or Buy" Your Web Services

- -

- -

*W*hen the time comes to publish your Web pages, you'll have to make one of the toughest and most important decisions there is about where they should live. Should you set up your own server, and handle this yourself? Or should you find a friendly national, regional, or local Internet service provider and let them do it for you?

These are good questions, indeed. Answering them will tell you whether you want to buy, or build, or perhaps buy now and build later (or even build now and buy later). Stick with us as we take you through the numbers and the reasons why you might choose to roll your own, or to get underneath somebody else's Web umbrella.

Understanding Objectives

The most important thing to understand is your overall objectives. If your organization is planning on making a major move onto the Internet, and views the Web as a key ingredient to its future success and well-being, building your own server might be a natural extension of other plans.

If your organization simply views the Web as yet another way to disseminate news and information, along with existing media and techniques, your own Web server might have no strategic value to add. At that point, you could perform some simple analyses and figure out whether building or buying makes more sense.

Point 1: If the Web is a paramount method for communicating with your audience, having your own server will help to establish your organization as a legitimate, full-time Web presence.

Counting Your Pennies

For a detailed analysis of the costs and considerations, please refer back to Chapter 19. The quick and dirty formula is: If Web-related costs from a provider will average $1,000 a month or more, it's worthwhile considering a server of your very own. If average costs are less than $1,000 a month, it's probably not worthwhile, unless there are other compelling factors to consider. For instance, an Internet service provider may not use its Web server as heavily as its clients might, yet they'd look kind of lame if they didn't have one! ■

When calculating costs, figure that at least one-fourth of a system administrator's time will be required to run a Web server. Remember also that costs include monthly communications fees, Internet access charges, and maintenance-related expenditures, in addition to amortizing the hardware and software costs to set the system up in the first place. It's not at all unusual for the after-purchase costs to add up to ten or more times the initial costs over the life of a system.

Point 2: At $1,000 a month or more for Web services, it's reasonable to start thinking about building, rather than buying a Web server.

Projecting and Monitoring Traffic

One of the key elements in determining Web services costs is download fees usually assessed by service providers. Normally, such costs run from two to ten cents per megabyte of data that's downloaded. This might not sound like much, but let's stop to crunch some numbers: if your pages are 2 Mbytes in size, and you average 30 users per day, that translates into $36.50 to $182.50 for an average month. Raise the amount of data to 5 Mbytes, and the costs go from $91.25 to $456.25 for an average month.

None of these costs is prohibitive, though, nor would they add up to enough, including telephone or access line costs, and monthly account fees, to exceed our $1,000 monthly ceiling. Things really get expensive, though, when hundreds to thousands of users a day start downloading your data. At that point, multiplying costs three- to thirty-fold really can get prohibitive. That's why some initial testing, and an audience survey, will be important in making such projections.

Point 3: If you're expecting (or even hoping for) lots and lots of traffic, you're better off building your own server, rather than buying space on somebody else's.

How Much is Too Much?

The principle of parsimony argues that you'd better try to limit the amount of data you publish on your Web pages, especially if you're paying by the megabyte of data transferred from your provider's server. It's important to keep an eye on the amount and kind of data that your Web server offers.

If you've got numerous large files or images that some, but not all, users find interesting, you might consider making them available through other means. This could include finding an anonymous ftp site on the Internet and directing users to pick up these large files there, or it might mean setting up an e-mail based file delivery system like that provided by listserv or majordomo.

Point 4: Keep an eye on the data that users download, and try to make large, infrequently-accessed files or documents available by other means.

Managing Volatility

The Web is an ever-changing galaxy of information. Keeping up with change means regular effort, and a fair amount of volatility in your Web page offerings. Many providers charge extra when you change your materials but even if they don't, the effort of making and testing changes has an associated cost.

We recommend that you manage and schedule changes on your server. Plan on regular updates and stick to the plan. Gather up incremental and incidental changes in the meantime, and apply them when the schedule or external factors say it's the right time. While you're at it, keep tabs on your materials' freshness, and regularly check your off-server links to other pages and locations for currency and correctness.

If you have loads of content that changes frequently, then you might want the extra control over the server that you get with building your own. Convenience and access to your data has value, too, and may influence you to build your own server even if your costs appear to hover below the $1,000 monthly cut-off.

Point 5: Constant, unceasing change is much more expensive than planned change. Whether you build or buy your Web server, you'll still have to manage change, or it will manage you! Where change is frequent and regular, the convenience of access to your own server can have significant value.

Communicating Corporately

If your organization has a well-planned communications strategy, effective use of the Web will complement other channels of communication already in use — like the trade press, the news media, and the industry analysts and pundits who follow your industry. In this kind of environment, Web documents will usually reflect and coordinate with documents of many other kinds, including advertisements, collateral, and a full range of other corporate publications.

In environments where tight controls over corporate or organizational communications must be maintained, it's pretty normal to find Web servers under the purview of a public relations or corporate communications department. Likewise, in environments where internal and external communications are formal and carefully managed, you might even find one set of servers for internal materials (not available to the public), and another set of servers for external materials.

Point 6: In tightly-managed organizations, especially those with carefully-orchestrated communications, control over the Web server may be an absolute requirement, irrespective of other considerations.

Reaching Your Audience

If you decide to build your own server, and connect up to the Internet via a 28.8 Kbps modem through a provider, you've limited the number of users who'll be able to access your Web pages at any given time (probably to 1 to 3 users for each such connection). If, on the other hand, you attach a full 1.44 Mbps T-1 link to your server, you've increased the size (and the cost) of your pipe significantly, but you'll still be limited to under 100 simultaneous users.

Projecting traffic, as it turns out, is not only important to understanding costs, it's also important to matching the size of the Web server pipe against the number of potential users. It's wasteful to use a large pipe for low-traffic situations, but it can be catastrophic to provide a small to medium pipe when a tsunami of interest is heading your way. Frustrate your users long enough, and they may decide to meet their interests elsewhere.

Monitoring usage and demand is the only way to cope with this phenomenon, but you'll be far better off if you start out with extra, unused capacity, than if your pipes are clogged from the word "Go!" Because operating your own server gives you the flexibility of negotiating the right sized pipe to the Internet with a telecommunications company and a service provider, many large-volume operations prefer to do it themselves. Even though these costs can be quite high, they're generally lower than if you paid someone else to provide them. Just don't expect to be able to add or expand pipes at a moment's notice, and you'll be able to avoid getting too, too frustrated when it's time to add more capacity.

Point 7: Make it easy for the audience to browse your materials, and they'll do just that. Make it difficult or impossible, and they'll go away...forever!

"Web-ifying" Commerce

Companies of many commercial stripes are hungrily eyeing the "millions" of Internet users as another customer base, ripe for electronic commerce. Today, there are several ways to conduct commercial transactions over the Internet, ranging from so-called "digital cash" to a variety of secure credit-card handling operations.

We don't want to take on the responsibility of recommending a particular approach (even though several of the principals at First Virtual Holdings, Inc. are friends of ours). We'll just say that electronic commerce via the Web is a trendy phenomenon whose potential still vastly outweighs its current use.

But if your company is thinking seriously about adding electronic commerce on the Web to its existing sales channels, you'll probably want to carefully consider building your own Web server. Issues of control, of access to customer information, and of managing the details of financial transactions all argue that the best hands for your Web server to be in are your own!

Point 8: If you're thinking about doing business via the Web, you'll probably want to control your own server, for a variety of good business reasons.

Understanding Your Options

Whether you're building or buying your Web services, you must clearly understand how those pages operate. This is especially true for forms-handling, or other Common Gateway Interface-related programs that run on the server to handle user information requests or submissions.

It's imperative that the server your pages run on is compatible with the services it's supposed to provide, and the programs it will attempt to run on your users' behalf. This means specifying the kind of *httpd* implementation you need, and it also means understanding the names and versions of surrounding standard services that CGI programs may call on (like the differing clickable image map implementations on the NCSA and CERN implementations of *httpd*, for instance).

Point 9: When selecting the server for your Web pages, compatibility with CGI programs and related libraries and other collections of widgets and data is an absolute must. Don't build or buy the wrong kind of server!

Overcoming Success

Finally, you may have to cope with what many people would consider an enviable problem: what happens if your Web pages become the latest rage, and your server gets completely inundated by users trying to avail themselves of your magnificent content?

If that happens, you'll want to make arrangements for fallback services. In this extreme case of demand, working with a national Internet service provider — like ANS, PSI, Delphi, CompuServe, etc. — will be an absolute must. If you can afford what these companies can offer, you'll be able to buy as much capacity from them as you can stand to pay for.

Point 10: If you're smitten with boundless success, be prepared to suffer (especially in the checkbook) for your fame, but make alternative arrangements with a national provider to avoid the perils of Point 7.

Glossary

absolute. When used to modify pathnames or URLs, it means a full and complete specification (as opposed to a relative one).

acceptable use. A doctrine originally formulated by the National Science Foundation restricting the Internet to research and academic, but not commercial, use.

alpha test. The testing on software performed by the developers, usually during the development process; also, the first of several stages in the software testing process (*see* beta test).

anchor. In HTML, an anchor is a tagged text or graphic element that acts as a link to another location inside or outside a given document, or it may be a location in a document that acts as the destination for an incoming link. The latter definition is most commonly how we use it in this book.

animation. A computerized process of creating moving images by rapidly advancing from one still image to the next.

anonymous ftp. A type of Internet file access that relies on the File Transfer Protocol service, where any user can typically access a file collection by logging in as *anonymous*, and supplying his or her username as a password.

AppleScript. The scripting language for the Macintosh operating system, used to build CGI programs for Macintosh-based Web servers.

Archie. An Internet-based archival search facility, based on databases of file and directory names taken from anonymous ftp servers around the Internet.

ARPA (Advanced Research Projects Administration; *see* DARPA)

attribute. In HTML tags, an attribute is a named characteristic of an associated tag. Some attributes are required, while others are optional. Some attributes may also take values (if so the syntax is ATTRIBUTE="value") or not, depending on the tag and the attribute (*see* Chapter 7 for tag details in alphabetical order)

AUP (Acceptable Use Policy; *see* acceptable use)

authoring software. In the context of HTML, authoring software refers to programs that understand HTML tags and their placement. Some such programs can even enforce HTML syntax; others can convert from word processing or document formatting programs to HTML formats.

awk. A powerful scripting language included with most implementations of UNIX, *awk* supplements the file-processing capabilities of the UNIX shells, including pattern-matching of fields and C-like structured programming constructs.

back end. The server-side of client/server is called the back end because it is usually handled by programs running in obscurity on the server, out of sight (and mind) for most users.

bandwidth. Technically, bandwidth is the range of electrical frequencies a device can handle; more often, it's used as a measure of a communications technology's carrying capacity.

Basic (Beginner's All-purpose Symbolic Instruction Code). A programming language, Basic (also called BASIC) is easy to learn and use. The most popular implementation is Microsoft's QuickBasic.

beta test. The phase of software testing where a program or system is turned over to a select group of users outside the development organization for use in more or less real-life situations.

body. The body is one of the main identifiable structures of any HTML document. It is usually trapped between the head information and the footer information.

bookmark. Most Web browsers include a facility for building a list of URLs that users wish to keep for future reference. Netscape calls such references bookmarks in its browser.

browser. A Web access program that can request HTML documents from Web servers, and render such documents on a user's display device. (*see also* client)

BSD (Berkeley Software Distribution). A flavor of UNIX that was particularly important in the late 1970s and 1980s when most of the enhancements and add-ons to UNIX appeared first in the BSD version (like TCP/IP).

BTW. Acronym for "By The Way"; commonly used in e-mail messages.

bugs. Small verminous creatures that sometimes show up in software in the form of major or minor errors, mistakes, and gotchas. Bugs got their name from insects found in antiquated tube-based computers of the late 50s and early 60s which were attracted to the glow of the filament in a tube.

C. A programming language developed at AT&T Bell Laboratories, C remains the implementation language for UNIX and the UNIX programmer's language of choice.

case sensitive. Means that the way computer input is typed is significant; for instance HTML tags can be typed in any mixture of upper- and lowercase, but because HTML character entities are case sensitive, they must be typed exactly as reproduced in this book.

CD-ROM (Compact Disk-Read-Only Memory). A computer-readable version of the audio CD, CD-ROMs can contain up to 650 MB of data, making them the distribution media of choice for many of today's large (some would even say bloated) programs and systems.

CERN (Centre European Researche Nucleare). The Center for High-Energy Physics in Geneva, Switzerland; the birthplace of the World Wide Web.

character entity. A way of reproducing strange and wonderful characters within HTML, character entities take the form &string; where the ampersand (&) and semicolon are mandatory metacharacters, and string names the character to be reproduced in the browser. Because character entities are case sensitive, the string between the ampersand and the semicolon must be reproduced exactly as written in Chapter 8 of this book.

character mode. When referring to Web browsers, character mode (also called text mode) means that such browsers can reproduce text data only. They cannot produce graphics directly, without the assistance of a helper application.

clickable map. A graphic in an HTML file that has had a pixel coordinate map file created for it, to allow regions of the graphic to point to specific URLs for graphically oriented Web navigation.

client. The end-user side of the client/ server arrangement, the term "client" typically refers to a consumer of network services of one kind or another. A Web browser is therefore a client program that talks to Web servers.

client/server. A model for computing that divides computing into two separate roles, usually connected by a network: the client works on the end-user's side of the connection, and manages user interaction and display (input and output, and related processing), while the server works elsewhere on the network and manages data-intensive or shared processing activities, like serving up the collections of documents and programs that a Web server typically manages.

common controls. When designing HTML documents, most experts recommend that you build a set of consistent navigation controls and use them throughout a document (or collection of documents), providing a set of common controls for document navigation.

Common Gateway Interface (CGI). The specification governing how Web browsers can communicate with and request services from Web servers; also the format and syntax for passing information from browsers to servers via forms or document-based queries in HTML.

computing platform. A way of referring to the kind of computer someone is using, this term encompasses both hardware (the type of machine, processor, etc.) and software (the operating system and applications) in use.

content. For HTML, content is its raison d'etre; although form is important, content is why users access Web documents and why they keep coming back for more.

convention. An agreed-upon set of rules and approaches that allows systems to communicate with one another and work together.

DARPA (Defense Advanced Research Projects Administration). A U.S. Department of Defense funding agency that supplied the cash and some of the expertise that led to the development of the Internet, among many other interesting things.

dedicated line. A telephone line dedicated to the purpose of computerized telecommunications; a dedicated line may be operated continuously (24 hours a day) by its owner. In this book, such lines usually provide a link to an Internet service provider.

default. In general computer-speak, a default is a selection that's made automatically in a program, instruction, or whatever when no selections are made explicitly. For HTML the default is the value assigned to an attribute when none is supplied.

desktop (aka desktop machine). The computer a user typically has on his or her desktop; a synonym for "end-user computer" or "computer."

dial-up. A connection to the Internet (or some other remote computer or network), made by dialing up an access telephone number.

directory path. The device and directory names needed to locate a particular file in any given file system; for HTML, UNIX-style directory paths usually apply.

DNS (Domain Name Server; *see* domain names)

document. The basic unit of HTML information, a document refers to the entire contents of any single HTML file. Since this doesn't always correspond to normal notions of a document, we refer to what could formally be called "HTML documents" more or less interchangeably with "Web pages" which is how such documents are rendered by browsers for display.

document headings. The class of HTML tags that we generically refer to as <H*>, document headings allow authors to insert headings of various sizes and weights (from 1 to 6) to add structure to their documents' contents. As structural elements, headings should identify the beginning of a new concept or idea within a document.

document structure. For HTML, this refers to the methods used to organize and navigate within HTML documents or related collections of documents.

document-based queries. One of two methods of passing information from a browser to a Web server, document-based queries are designed to pass short strings of information to the server, using the METHOD="GET" HTTP method of delivery. This method is typically used for search requests or other short lookup operations.

DoD (Department of Defense). The folks who paid the bills for and operated the earliest versions of the Internet.

domain names. The names used on the Internet as part of a distributed database system for translating computer names into physical addresses and vice versa.

DOS (Disk Operating System; *see also* operating system). The underlying control program used to make most Intel-based PCs run. Microsoft's MS-DOS is the most widely used implementation of DOS, and provides the scaffolding atop which its equally widely used MS-Windows software runs.

DTD (Document Type Definition). A formal SGML specification for a document, a DTD lays out the structural elements and markup definitions that can then be used to create instances of documents.

dumb terminal. A display device with attached keyboard that relies on the intelligence of another computer to drive its display and interpret its keyboard inputs. Such devices were the norm in the heyday of the mainframe and mini-computer and are still widely used for reservation systems, point of sale, and other specialized-use applications.

e-mail. An abbreviation for electronic mail, e-mail is the preferred method for exchanging information between users on the Internet (and other networked systems).

electronic commerce. The exchange of money for goods or services via an electronic medium; many companies expect electronic commerce to do away with mail order and telephone order shopping by the end of the century.

encoded information. A way of wrapping computer data in a special envelope to ship it across a network, encoded information refers to data-manipulation techniques that change data formats and layouts to make them less sensitive to the rigors of electronic transit. Encoded information must usually be decoded by its recipient before it can be used.

error message. Information delivered by a program to a user, usually to inform him or her that things haven't worked properly, if at all. Error messages are an ill-appreciated artform and contain some of the funniest and most opaque language we've ever seen (also, the most tragic for its unfortunate recipients).

Ethernet. The most commonly used local-area networking technology in use today, Ethernet was developed at about the same time (and by many of the same people and institutions) the Internet.

FAQ (Frequently Asked Questions). Usenet newsgroups, mailing list groups, and other affiliations of like-minded individuals on the Internet will usually designate a more senior member of their band to assemble and publish a list of frequently asked questions, in an often futile effort to keep from answering them quite as frequently.

file extension. In DOS, this refers to the 3-letter part of a filename after the period; for UNIX, Macintosh, and other file systems, this refers to the string after the right-most period in a filename. File extensions are used to label files as to type, origin, and possible use.

flame. Used as a verb ("he got flamed") it means to be the recipient of a particularly hostile or nasty e-mail message; as a noun

("that was a real flame") it refers to such a message.

flamewar. What happens when two or more individuals start exchanging hostile or nasty e-mail messages; this is viewed by some as an art form, and is best observed on USENET or other newsgroups (where the *alt.flame...* or *alt.bitch* newsgroups would be good places to browse for examples).

footer. The concluding part of an HTML document, the footer should contain contact, version, date, and attribution information to help identify a document and its authors.

forms. In HTML forms are built on special markup that lets browsers solicit data from users and then deliver that data to specially designated input-handling programs on a Web server. Briefly, forms provide a mechanism to let users interact with servers on the Web.

front end. In the client/server model, the front end part refers to the client side; it's where the user views and interacts with information from a server; for the Web, browsers provide the front end that communicates with Web servers on the back end.

FTP (sometimes ftp; File Transfer Protocol). An Internet file transfer service based on the TCP/IP protocols, FTP provides a way to copy files to and from FTP servers elsewhere on a network.

gateway. A type of computer program that knows how to connect to two or more different kinds of networks, and to translate information from one side's format to the other's, and vice versa. Common types of gateways include e-mail, database, and communications.

GIF. An abbreviation for Graphics Information File, *gif* is one of a set of commonly used graphics formats within Web documents, because of its compressed format and compact nature.

Gopher. A program/protocol developed at the University of Minnesota, Gopher provides for unified, menu-driven presentation of a variety of Internet services, including WAIS, Telnet, and FTP.

graphics. In HTML documents, graphics are files that belong to one of a restricted family of types (usually GIF or JPEG) that are referenced via URLs for in-line display on Web pages.

grep. An abbreviation for "general regular expression parser" *grep* is a standard UNIX program that looks for patterns found in files and reports on their occurrences. *grep* handles a wide range of patterns, including so-called "regular expressions" which can use all kinds of substitutions and wildcards to provide powerful search-and-replace operations within files.

GUI (Graphical User Interface). (pronounced "gooey") GUIs are what make graphical Web browsers possible; they create a visually-oriented interface that makes it easy for users to interact with computerized information of all kinds.

heading. For HTML a heading is a markup tag used to add document structure. The term will sometimes be used to refer to the initial portion of an HTML document between the <HEAD> ... </HEAD> tags, where titles and context definitions are commonly supplied.

helper applications. Today, browsers can display multiple graphics files (and sometimes other kinds of data); sometimes, browsers must pass particular files — for

instance, motion picture or sound files — over to other applications that know how to render the data they contain. Such programs are called helper applications, because they help the browser deliver Web information to users.

hierarchical structure. A way of organizing Web pages using links that make some pages subordinate to others (*see* tree-structured for another description of this kind of organization).

history list. Each time a user accesses the Web, his or her browser will normally keep a list of all the URLs visited during that session; this is called a history list, and provides a handy way to jump back to any page that's already been visited while online. History lists normally disappear when the browser program is exited, though.

hotlist. A Web page that consists of a series of links to other pages, usually annotated with information about what's available on that link. Hotlists act like switchboards to content information, and are usually organized around a particular topic or area of interest.

HTML (HyperText Markup Language). The SGML-derived markup language used to create Web pages. Not quite a programming language, HTML nevertheless provides a rich lexicon and syntax for designing and creating useful hypertext documents for the Web.

http or **HTTP** (hypertext teleprocessing protocol aka hypertext transfer protocol). The Internet protocol used to manage communication between Web clients (browsers) and servers.

httpd (http daemon). The name of the collection of programs that runs on a Web server to provide Web services. In

UNIX-speak, a daemon is a program that runs all the time listening for service requests of a particular type; thus, an httpd is a program that runs all the time on a Web server, ready to field and handle Web service requests.

hyperlink. A shorthand term for hypertext link, which is defined below.

hypermedia. Any of a variety of computer media — including text, graphics, video, sound, etc. — available through hypertext links on the Web.

hypertext. A method of organizing text, graphics, and other kinds of data for computer use that lets individual data elements point to one another; a nonlinear method of organizing information, especially text.

hypertext link. In HTML, a hypertext link is defined by special markup that creates a user-selectable document element that can be selected to change the user's focus from one document (or part of a document) to another.

image map. A synonym for clickable image, this refers to an overlaid collection of pixel coordinates for a graphic that can be used to locate a user's selection of a region on a graphic, in turn used to select a related hypertext link for further Web navigation.

IMHO. Acronym for "In My Humble Opinion" mostly used in e-mail messages.

Infobahn. A psuedo-Teutonic synonym for Information Superhighway (taken from Autobahn, the German highway system), commonly used because it's shorter and "cooler" than Information Superhighway.

Information Superhighway. The near-mythical agglomeration of the Internet, communications companies, telephone systems, and other communications media that politicians seem to believe will be the "next big thing" in business, academia, and industry. Many people believe that this highway is already here, and that it's called "the Internet."

input-handling program. For Web services, a program that runs on a Web server designated by the ACTION attribute of an HTML <FORM> tag, whose job it is to field, interpret, and respond to user input from a browser, typically by custom-building an HTML document in response to some user request.

Internaut. Someone who travels using the Internet (like "Astronaut" or "Argonaut").

Internet. A worldwide collection of networks that began with technology and equipment funded by the U.S. Department of Defense in the 1970s that today links users in nearly every known country, speaking nearly every known language.

IP (Internet Protocol; *see* TCP/IP). IP is the specific networking protocol of the same name used to tie computers together over the Internet; IP is also used as a synonym for the whole TCP/IP protocol suite.

ISDN (Integrated Services Digital Network). An emerging digital technology for telecommunications that offers higher bandwidth and better signal quality than old-fashioned analog telephone lines. Not yet available in many parts of the U.S. or in the rest of the world.

ISO (International Standards Organization). The granddaddy of standards organizations worldwide, the ISO is a body made of standards bodies from countries all over the place. Most important communications and computing standards — like the telecommunications and character code standards mentioned in this book — are the subject of ISO standards.

JPEG or **JPG**. JPEG stands for Joint Photographic Experts' Group, an industry association that has defined a particularly compressible format for image storage designed for dealing with complex color still images (like photographs). Files stored in this format usually take the extension .JPEG (except DOS or Windows machines, which are limited to the three-character .JPG equivalent). Today, JPEG is emerging as the graphics format standard of choice for use on W3.

Kbps (Kilobits per second). A measure of communications speeds, in units of 210 bits per second (2^{10} = 10^{24} which is just about 1,000 and explains the quasimetric "K" notation).

KISS (Keep It Simple, Stupid!). A self-descriptive philosophy that's supposed to remind us to "eschew obfuscation" except it's easier to understand!

LAN (Local Area Network). Typically, one of a variety of communications technologies used to link computers together in a single building, business, or campus environment.

layout element. In an HTML document a layout element is a paragraph, list, graphic, horizontal rule, heading, or some other document component whose placement on a page contributes to its overall look and feel.

linear text. Shorthand for old-fashioned documents that work like this book does: by placing one page after the other, ad infinitum in a straight line. Even though such books have indexes, pointers, cross-references, and other attempts to add linkages, they must be applied manually (rather than by clicking your mouse).

link. For HTML, a link is a pointer in one part of a document that can transport users to another part of the same document or to another document entirely. This capability puts the "hyper" into hypertext. In other words, a link is a one-to-one relationship/association between two concepts or ideas, similiar to "cognition" (the brain has triggers such as smell, sight, sound that cause a link to be followed to a similar concept or reaction).

list element. An item in an HTML list structure tagged with <LI> (list item) tag.

list tags. HTML tags for a variety of list styles, including ordered lists <OL>, unordered lists <UL>, menus <MENU>, glossary lists <DL>, or directory lists <DIR>.

listserv. An Internet e-mail handling program, typically UNIX-based, that provides mechanisms to let users manage, contribute and subscribe to, and exit from named mailing lists that distribute messages to all subscribed members daily. A common mechanism for delivering information to interested parties on the Internet, this is how the HTML working group communicates amongst its members, for instance.

logical markup. Refers to any of a number of HTML character handling tags that exist to provide emphasis or to indicate a particular kind of device or action is involved (*see* Chapter 6 for a discussion of HTML tags by category that includes the details on descriptive versus physical markup).

Lynx. A widely used UNIX-based character-mode Web browser.

MacWeb. A Macintosh-based graphical-mode Web browser implemented by MCC. (*see also* MCC)

maintenance. The process of regularly inspecting, testing, and updating the contents of Web pages; also, an attitude that such activities are both inevitable and advisable.

majordomo. A set of Perl programs that automate the operation of multiple mailing lists, including moderated and unmoderated mailing lists, and routine handling of subscribe/unsubscribe operations.

map file. A set of pixel coordinates on a graphic image that correspond to the boundaries of regions that users might select when using the graphic for Web navigation. This file must be created by using a graphics program to determine regions and their boundaries, and then stored on the Web server that provides the coordinate translation and URL selection services.

markup. A way of embedding special characters (metacharacters) within a text file to instruct a computer program how to handle the contents of the file itself.

markup language. A formal set of special characters and related capabilities used to define a specific method for handling the display of files that include markup; HTML is a markup language that is an application of SGML that is used to design and create Web pages.

Mbps (Megabits per second). A measure of communications speeds, in units of 2^{20} bits per second (2^{20} = 1,048,576 which is just about 1,000,000 and explains the quasi-metric "M" notation).

MCC (Microelectronics and Computing Corporation). A computing industry consortium based in Austin, Texas, that developed the WinWeb and MacWeb browser programs.

metacharacter. A specific character within a text file that signals the need for special handling; in HTML the angle brackets (< >), ampersand (&),pound sign (#), and semicolon (;) can all function as metacharacters.

MIME (Multipurpose Internet Mail Extensions). http communications of Web information over the Internet rely on a special variant of MIME formats to convey Web documents and related files between servers and users, and vice versa.

modem. An acronym for **mo**dulator/**dem**odulator, a modem is a piece of hardware that converts between the analog forms for voice and data used in the telephone system and the digital forms for data used in computers. In other words, a modem lets your computer communicate using the telephone system.

Mosaic. A powerful graphical Web browser originally developed at NCSA, now widely licensed and used for a variety of commercial browser implementations.

MPEG or **MPG**. An acronym for Motion Picture Experts' Group, MPEG is a highly compressed format designed for use in moving pictures or other multi-frame-per-second media (like video). MPEG can not only provide tremendous compression (up to 200 to 1), it also updates only elements that have changed on-screen from one frame to the next, making it extraordinarily efficient as well — .MPEG is the common file extension to denote files using this format and .MPG is the three-letter equivalent on DOS and Windows systems (which can't handle four-letter file extensions).

MPPP (Multilink Point-to-Point Protocol). An Internet protocol that allows simultaneous use of multiple physical connections between one computer and another, to aggregate their combined bandwidth and create a "larger" virtual link between the two machines.

multimedia. A method of combining text, sound, graphics, and full-motion or animated video within a single compound computer document.

MVS (Multiple Virtual Storage). A file system used on IBM mainframes and clones.

navigation. In the context of the Web, navigation refers to the use of hyperlinks to move within or between HTML documents and other Web-accessible resources.

navigation bar. A way of arranging a series of hypertext links on a single line of a Web page to provide a set of navigation controls for an HTML document or a set of HTML documents.

NCSA (National Center for Supercomputing Applications). A research unit of the University of Illinois at Urbana, where the original Mosaic implementation was built, and where the NCSA *httpd* Web server code is maintained and distributed.

nesting. In computer terms, one structure that occurs within another is said to be nested; in HTML, nesting happens most commonly with list structures which may be freely nested within one another, regardless of type.

netiquette. A networking takeoff on the term "etiquette," netiquette refers to the written and unwritten rules of behavior on the Internet. When in doubt if an activity is permitted or not, ask first, and then act only if no one objects (check the FAQ for a given area, too — it will often explicitly state the local rules of netiquette for a newsgroup, mailing list, etc.).

network link. The tie that binds a computer to a network; for dial-in Internet users, this will usually be a telephone link; for directly attached users, it will be whatever kind of technology (Ethernet, token-ring, FDDI, etc.) is in local use.

numeric entity. A special markup element that reproduces a particular character from the ISO-Latin-1 character set, a numeric entity takes the form &#nnn; where nnn is the 1, 2, or 3-digit numeric code that corresponds to a particular character (Chapter 8 contains a complete list of these codes).

on-demand connection. A dial-up link to a service provider that's available whenever it's needed (on demand, get it?).

online. A term that indicates that information, activity, or communications are located on, or taking place in, an electronic, networked computing environment (like the Internet). The opposite of online is offline, which is what your computer is as soon as you disconnect from the Internet.

OS (Operating System). The underlying control program on a computer that makes the hardware run and supports the execution of one or more applications. DOS, UNIX, and OS/2 are all examples of operating systems.

packet. A basic unit (or package) of data used to describe individual elements of online communications; in other words, data moves across networks like the Internet in packets.

pages. The generic term for the HTML documents that Web users view on their browsers.

paragraphs. The basic elements of text within an HTML document, <P> is the markup tag used to indicate a paragraph break in text (the closing </P> tag is currently optional in HTML).

path, pathname (*see* directory path)

PC (personal computer). Today PC is used as a generic term to refer to just about any kind of desktop computer; its original definition was as a product name for IBM's 8086-based personal computer, the IBM PC.

Perl. A powerful, compact programming language that draws from the capabilities of languages like C, Pascal, *sed*, *awk*, and BASIC, Perl is emerging as the language of choice for CGI programs, partly owing to its portability and the many platforms on which it is currently supported, and partly owing to its ability to exploit system services in UNIX quickly and easily.

physical markup. Any of a series of HTML markup tags that specifically control character styles (bold (<B>) and italic (<I>)) or typeface (<TT>, for typewriter font).

pick list. Generally, a list of elements displayed for user selection of one or more choices; in HTML, the result of the <SELECT> and <OPTION> tags to construct such a list for use in a form.

pipe. As used in this book, pipe generally refers to the bandwidth of the connection in use between a user's workstation and the Internet (or the server on the other end of the connection, actually).

plain text. Usually refers to vanilla ASCII text, as created or viewed in a simple text-editing program.

platform. Synonym for computer.

port address. TCP/IP-based applications use the concept of a port address to know which program to talk to on the receiving end of a network connection. Since there may be many programs running on a computer at one time — including multiple copies of the same program — the port address provides a mechanism to uniquely identify exactly which process the data should be delivered to.

POTS (Plain Old Telephone System). The normal analog telephone system, just like the one you probably have at home.

PPP (Point-to-Point Protocol). A modern, low-overhead serial communications protocol, typically used to interconnect two computers via modem. Most Web browsers require either a PPP or SLIP connection in order to work.

protocol. A formal, rigidly-defined set of rules and formats that computers use to communicate with one another.

provider (*see* service provider)

RAM (Random Access Memory). The memory used in most computers to store the results of ongoing work, and that provides space to store the operating system and applications that are actually running at any given moment.

relative. When applied to URLs, relative means that in the absence of the <BASE> tag, the link is relative to the current page's URL in which the link is defined. This makes for shorter, more compact

URLs and explains why most local URLs are relative, not absolute.

resource. Any HTML document or other item or service available via the Web. Resources are what URLs point to.

return (short for "carriage return"). In text files a return is what causes the words on a line to end and makes the display pick up at the leftmost location on the display. As used in this book, it means don't hit the Enter or Return key on your keyboard in the middle of a line of HTML markup or a URL specification.

robot. A special Web-traveling program that wanders all over the place, following and recording URLs and related titles for future reference (like in search engines).

ROM (Read Only Memory). A form of computer memory that allows values to be stored only once; after the data is initially recorded, the computer can only read the contents. ROMs are used to supply constant code elements like bootstrap loaders, network addresses, and other more or less unvarying programs or instructions.

router. A special-purpose piece of internetworking gear that makes it possible to connect networks together, a router is capable of reading the destination address of any network packet. It can forward the packet to a local recipient if its address resides on any network that the router can reach, or on to another router if the packet is destined for delivery to a network that the current router cannot access.

screen. The glowing part on the front of your computer monitor where you see the Web do its thing (and anything else your computer might like to show you).

search engine. A special Web program that can search the contents of a database of available Web pages and other resources to provide information that relates to specific topics or keywords supplied by a user.

search tools. Any of a number of programs (*see* Chapter 16) that can permit HTML documents to become searchable, using the <ISINDEX> tag to inform the browser of the need for a search window, and behind-the-scenes indexing and anchoring schemes to let users locate particular sections of or items within a document.

sed. A powerful UNIX-based text-editing program that makes it easy to locate and manipulate text elements within any of a number of files.

server. A computer on a network whose job is to listen for particular service requests and to respond to those that it knows how to satisfy.

service provider. An organization that provides individuals or other organizations with access to the Internet. Service providers usually offer a variety of communications options for their customers, ranging from analog telephone lines, to a variety of higher-bandwidth leased lines, to ISDN and other digital communications services.

setup. When negotiating a network connection, the phase at the beginning of the communications process is called the "setup." At this point, protocol details, communication rates, and error-handling approaches will be worked out, allowing the connection to proceed correctly and reliably thenceforth.

SGML (Standard Generalized Markup Language). An ISO standard document definition, specification, and creation mechanism that makes platform and display differences across multiple computers irrelevant to the delivery and rendering of documents.

shell (*see* UNIX shell)

SLIP (Serial Line Interface Protocol). A relatively old-fashioned TCP/IP protocol used to manage telecommunications between a client and a server that treats the phone line as a "slow extension" to a network.

SMTP (Simple Mail Transfer Protocol). The underlying protocol and service for Internet-based electronic mail.

spider (aka Web spider, Webcrawler). A Web-traversing program that tirelessly investigates Web pages and their links, while storing information about its travels for inclusion in the databases typically used by search engines.

stdin (UNIX standard input device). The default source for input in the UNIX environment, *stdin* is the input source for CGI programs as well.

stdout (UNIX standard output device). The default recipient for output in the UNIX environment, *stdout* is the output source for Web browsers and servers as well (including CGI programs).

superstructure. In HTML documents, we refer to superstructure as the layout and navigational elements used to create a consistent look and feel for Web pages belonging to a document set.

(**syntax**) Literally, the formal rules for how to speak, we use syntax in this book to describe the rules that govern how HTML markup looks and behaves within HTML documents. The real syntax definition for

HTML comes from the SGML Document Type Definition (DTD).

syntax checker. A program that checks a particular HTML document's markup against the rules that govern its use; a recommended part of the testing regimen for all HTML documents.

tag. The formal name for an element of HTML markup, usually enclosed in angle brackets (< >).

TCP (Transmission Control Protocol; *see* also TCP/IP). The transport layer protocol for the TCP/IP suite, TCP is a reliable, connection-oriented protocol that usually guarantees delivery across a network.

TCP/IP (Transmission Control Protocol/Internet Protocol). The name for the suite of protocols and services used to manage network communications and applications over the Internet.

teardown. When a network communication session is ending, the two computers agree to stop talking and then systematically break the connection, and recover the port addresses and other resources used for the session. This process is called teardown.

technophobe. Literally, someone who's afraid of technology, this term is more commonly applied to those who don't want to understand technology, simply to use it!

Telnet. The Internet protocol and service that lets you take a smart computer (your own, probably) and make it emulate a dumb terminal over the network. Briefly, Telnet is a way of running programs and using capabilities on other computers across the Internet.

template. Literally, a model to imitate, we use the term template in this book to describe the skeleton of a Web page, including the HTML for its heading and footer, and any consistent layout and navigation elements for a page or set of pages.

terminal emulation. The process of making a full-fledged, stand-alone computer act like a terminal attached to another computer, terminal emulation is the service that Telnet provides across the Internet.

test plan. The series of steps and elements to be followed in conducting a formal test of software or other computerized systems; we strongly recommend that you write — and use —a test plan as a part of your Web publication process.

text controls. Any of a number of HTML tags, including both physical and logical markup, text controls provide a method of managing the way that text appears within an HTML document.

text-mode. A method of browser operation that displays characters only. Text-mode browsers cannot display graphics without the assistance of helper applications.

throughput. Another measure of communications capability, this term refers to the amount of data that can be "put through" a connection in a given period of time. It differs from bandwidth in being a measure of actual performance, rather than a theoretical maximum for the medium involved.

thumbnail. A miniature rendering of a graphical image, used as a link to the full-sized version.

title. The text supplied between <TITLE> ... </TITLE> defines the text that will show up on that page's title bar when displayed, and is also used as data in many Web search engines.

token ring. The second most common type of local-area networking technology in use, token ring is always and forever associated with IBM, since they helped to develop and perfect this type of network. It takes its name from passing around special "permits to transmit" called "tokens," in a ring-shaped pattern around the network, to give all attached devices a fair chance to broadcast information whenever they need to.

transparent GIF. A specially rendered GIF image that will take on the background color selected in a browser capable of handling such GIFs. This makes the graphic blend into the existing color scheme and provides a more professional-looking page.

tree structure(d) (*see* hierarchical structure). Computer scientists like to think of hierarchies in graphical terms, which makes them look like upside-down trees (a single root at the top, multiple branches below). File systems and genealogies are examples of tree structured organizations that we're all familiar with, but they abound in the computer world. This type of structure also works well for certain Web document sets, especially longer, more complex ones.

UNIX. The operating system of choice for the Internet community at large and the Web community, too, UNIX offers the broadest range of tools, utilities, and programming libraries for Web server use.

UNIX shell. The name of the command-line program used to manage user-computer interaction, the shell can also be used to write CGI scripts and other kinds of useful programs for UNIX.

URI (Uniform Resource Identifier). Any of a class of objects that identify resources available to the Web; both URLs and URNs are instances of URIs.

URL (Uniform Resource Locator). The primary naming scheme used to identify Web resources, URLs define the protocols to be used, the domain name of the Web server where a resource resides, the port address to be used for communication, and the directory path to access a named Web file or resource.

URL-encoded text. A method for passing information requests and URL specification to Web servers from browsers, URL encoding replaces spaces with plus signs (+) and substitutes special hex codes for a range of otherwise unreproduceable characters. This method is used to pass document queries from browsers to servers (for the details, please consult Chapter 15).

URN (Uniform Resource Name). A permanent, unchanging name for a Web resource, URNs are seldom used in today's Web environment. They do, however, present a method guaranteed to obtain access to a resource, as soon as the URN can be fully resolved (it sometimes consists of human or organizational contact information, rather than resource location data).

Usenet. An Internet protocol and service that provides access to a vast array of named newsgroups, where users congregate to exchange information and materials related to specific topics or concerns.

V.32. CCITT standard for a 9.6 Kbps two-wire full duplex modem operating on a regular dial-up or 2-wire leased lines.

V.32bis. Newer higher-speed CCITT standard for full-duplex transmission on two-wire leased and dial-up lines at rates from 4.8 to 14.4 Kbps.

V.34. The newest high-speed CCITT standard for full-duplex transmission on two-wire leased and dial-up lines at rates from 4.8 to 28.8 Kbps.

V.42. CCITT error correction standard that can be used with V.32, V.32bis, and V.34.

V.42bis. CCITT data compression standard, capable of compressing files "on the fly" at an average rate of 3.5:1. It can yield speeds of up to 38.4 Kbps on a 9.6 Kbps modem, and up to 115.2 Kbps on a 28.8 modem. If your modem can do this, try to find an Internet service provider that also supports V.42bis. This feature can pay for itself very quickly.

VAX/VMS. The VAX is a Digital Equipment Corporation computer in wide use; VMS (Virtual Memory System) is the name of the proprietary operating system that many of these machines run. Today, many VAXes run UNIX instead of VMS.

Veronica. A search tool for navigating the global collection of Gopher servers, collectively referred to as *Gopherspace*.

WAIS (Wide-Area Information Service). A collection of programs that implement a specific protocol for information retrieval, able to index large-scale collections of data around the Internet. WAIS provides content-oriented query services to WAIS clients, and is one of the more powerful Internet search tools available.

Web. Shorthand for the World Wide Web (or W3), we also use Web in this book to refer to a related, interlinked set of HTML documents.

Web pages. Synonym for HTML documents, we use Web pages in this book to refer to sets of related, interlinked HTML documents, usually produced by a single author or organization.

Web server. A computer, usually on the Internet, that plays host to *httpd* and related Web-service software.

Web site. An addressed location, usually on the Internet, that provides access to the set of Web pages that correspond to the URL for a given site; thus a Web site consists of a Web server and a named collection of Web documents, both accessible through a single URL.

white space. The "breathing room" on a page, this refers to the parts of a document or display that aren't occupied by text or other visual elements. A certain amount of white space is essential to make documents attractive and readable.

Windows (aka MS-Windows). Microsoft's astonishingly popular (and sometimes frustrating) GUI environment for PCs, Windows is the GUI of choice for most desktop computer users.

WinWeb. The Windows version of a popular Web browser developed at MCC.

World Wide Web (aka **WWW** or **W3**). The complete collection of all Web servers available on the Internet, which comes as close to containing the "sum of human knowledge" as anything we've ever seen.

WYSIWYG (What You See Is What You Get). A term used to describe text editors or other layout tools (like HTML authoring tools) that attempt to show their users on-screen what final, finished documents will look like.

X Windows. The GUI of choice for UNIX systems, X Windows offers a graphical window, icon, and mouse metaphor similar to (but much more robust and powerful than) Microsoft Windows.

Index

IDG Books Worldwide License Agreement

· ·

4. **Limited Warranty.** IDG Warrants that the Software and disk(s) are free from defects in materials and workmanship for a period of sixty (60) days from the date of purchase of this Book. If IDG receives notification within the warranty period of defects in material or workmanship, IDG will replace the defective disk(s). IDG's entire liability and your exclusive remedy shall be limited to replacement of the Software, which is returned to IDG with a copy of your receipt. This Limited Warranty is void if failure of the Software has resulted from accident, abuse, or misapplication. Any replacement Software will be warranted for the remainder of the original warranty period or thirty (30) days, whichever is longer.

5. **No Other Warranties.** To the maximum extent permitted by applicable law, IDG and the author disclaim all other warranties, express or implied, including but not limited to implied warranties of merchantability and fitness for a particular purpose, with respect to the Software, the programs, the source code contained therein and/or the techniques described in this Book. This limited warranty gives you specific legal rights. You may have others which vary from state/jurisdiction to state/jurisdiction.

6. **No Liability For Consequential Damages.** To the extent permitted by applicable law, in no event shall IDG or the author be liable for any damages whatsoever (including without limitation, damages for loss of business profits, business interruption, loss of business information, or any other pecuniary loss) arising out of the use of or inability to use the Book or the Software, even if IDG has been advised of the possibility of such damages. Because some states/jurisdictions do not allow the exclusion or limitation of liability for consequential or incidental damages, the above limitation may not apply to you.

7. **U.S.Government Restricted Rights.** Use, duplication, or disclosure of the Software by the U.S. Government is subject to restrictions stated in paragraph (c) (1) (ii) of the Rights in Technical Data and Computer Software clause of DFARS 252.227-7013, and in subparagraphs (a) through (d) of the Commercial Computer—Restricted Rights clause at FAR 52.227-19, and in similar clauses in the NASA FAR supplement, when applicable.

Alternate Disk Format Available.

The enclosed disk is in a 3 1/2" 1.44MB, high-density format. If you have a different size drive, or a low-density drive, and you cannot arrange to transfer the data to the disk size you need, you can obtain the programs on a 5 1/4" 1.2 MB high-density disk or a 3 1/2" 720K low-density disk by writing to the following address: IDG Books Disk Fulfillment Department, Attn: HTML For Dummies, IDG Books Worldwide, 7260 Shadeland Station, Indianapolis, IN 46256, or call 800-762-2974. Please specify the size of disk you need, and please allow 3 to 4 weeks for delivery.

5/8/95

IDG BOOKS

Professional Technical Reference

For Dummies

who want to

program...

dBase 5 For Windows Programming For Dummies™
by Ted Coombs & Jason Coombs

ISBN: 1-56884-215-5
$19.99 USA/$26.99 Canada

PowerBuilder4 Programming for Dummies™
by Jason Coombs & Ted Coombs

ISBN: 1-56884-5-9
$19.95 USA/$26.95 Canada

C++ For Dummies™
by S. Randy Davis

ISBN: 1-56884-163-9
$19.95 USA/$26.95 Canada

Borland C++ For Dummies™
by Michael Hyman

ISBN: 1-56884-162-0
$19.95 USA/$26.95 Canada

Visual Basic 3 For Dummies™
by Wallace Wang

ISBN: 1-56884-076-4
$19.95 USA/$26.95 Canada

Covers version 3.

QBasic Programming For Dummies™
by Douglas Hergert

ISBN: 1-56884-093-4
$19.95 USA/$26.95 Canada

Mac Programming For Dummies™
by Dan Parks Sydow

ISBN: 1-56884-173-6
$19.95 USA/$26.95 Canada

Access Programming For Dummies™
by Rob Krumm

ISBN: 1-56884-091-8
$19.95 USA/$26.95 Canada

Delphi Programming for Dummies™
by Neil Rubenking

ISBN: 1-56884-00-7
$19.95 USA/$26.95 Canada

The Internet Direct Connect Kit
by Peter John Harrison

ISBN: 1-56884-135-3
$29.95 USA/$39.95 Canada

software included.

Type & Learn Windows Programming USING WinScope™
by Tom Swan

ISBN: 1-56884-071-3
$34.95 USA/$44.95 Canada

Software included.

Type & Learn C™
by Tom Swan

ISBN: 1-56884-073-X
$34.95 USA/$44.95 Canada

Software included.

Heavy Metal™ Visual C++ Programming
by Steve Holzner

ISBN: 1-56884-196-5
$39.95 USA/$54.95 Canada

Software included.

Heavy Metal™ OLE 2.0 Programming
by Steve Holzner

ISBN: 1-56884-301-1
$39.95 USA/$54.95 Canada

Software included.

The Type & Learn Programming Series is the complete starter kit for first-time programmers.

The Type & Learn Programming Series features books bundled with bestselling special edition products from leading companies like Borland International and The Periscope Company. New programmers get a cutting edge book, a proven, effective teaching method, *and* the critical software needed in order to start programming right away.

Bend the rules to your advantage with the Heavy Metal Series and take your programs from professional to legendary!

The Heavy Metal Series is the programmer's vehicle to learning precision programming techniques. These books, geared especially for the intermediate to advanced programmer, teach how to delve deep into programs to reclaim the power lost when they stick to conventional programming techniques.

Detour: The Truth About the Information Superhighway
by Michael Sullivan-Trainor

ISBN: 1-56884-307-0
$22.99 USA/$32.99 Canada

Lotus Notes Application Development Handbook
by Erica Kerwien

ISBN: 1-56884-308-9
$39.99 USA/$54.99 Canada

Covers versions 3.01 and 3.1.
Software included.

The UNIX-Haters Handbook
by Simson Garfinkel, Daniel Weise & Steven Strassmann

ISBN: 1-56884-203-1
$16.95 USA/$22.95 Canada

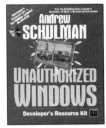

Macworld Ultimate Mac Programming: How to Write High-Performance Code
by Dave Mark

ISBN: 1-56884-195-7
$39.95 USA/$54.95 Canada

Software included.

Unauthorized Windows 95: A Developer's Guide to Exploring the Foundations of Windows 95
by Andrew Schulman

ISBN: 1-56884-169-8
$29.99 USA/$39.99 Canada

Unauthorized Windows 95: Developer's Resource Kit
by Andrew Schulman

ISBN: 1-56884-305-4
$39.99 USA/$54.99 Canada

Includes Software.

Order Center: **(800) 762-2974** *(8 a.m.–6 p.m., EST, weekdays)*

5/8/95

Quantity	ISBN	Title	Price	Total

Shipping & Handling Charges

	Description	First book	Each additional book	Total
Domestic	Normal	$4.50	$1.50	$
	Two Day Air	$8.50	$2.50	$
	Overnight	$18.00	$3.00	$
International	Surface	$8.00	$8.00	$
	Airmail	$16.00	$16.00	$
	DHL Air	$17.00	$17.00	$

*For large quantities call for shipping & handling charges.
**Prices are subject to change without notice.

Ship to:

Name _____

Company _____

Address _____

City/State/Zip _____

Daytime Phone _____

Payment: □ Check to IDG Books (US Funds Only)

□ VISA   □ MasterCard   □ American Express

Card # _____ Expires _____

Signature _____

Subtotal _____

CA residents add
applicable sales tax _____

IN, MA, and MD
residents add
5% sales tax _____

IL residents add
6.25% sales tax _____

RI residents add
7% sales tax _____

TX residents add
8.25% sales tax _____

Shipping _____

Total _____

Please send this order form to:

IDG Books Worldwide
7260 Shadeland Station, Suite 100
Indianapolis, IN 46256

Allow up to 3 weeks for delivery.
Thank you!